International HRM

CW00595149

This book provides a challenging and up-to-date approach to critical debates in international HRM, drawing on empirical and conceptual research from a wide range of countries.

This collection of edited papers from European experts in the field covers all aspects of international human resource management. The articles, following a detailed introduction, range from issues surrounding the strategic role of HRM in staffing, reward management and performance management, to discussions of the dynamics of culture and gender in international management. In doing so, contributors from Europe address key questions of crucial importance to our understanding of IHRM, such as: How do we decide on appropriate international HRM policies and practices? Can we continue to operate the same policies and practices that we have used in the domestic context? How applicable is the US model of HRM to European organisations? What are the key debates and issues surrounding international HRM in the context of Europe?

This book constitutes a valuable resource for researchers, teachers and students in the field of international human resource management.

Professor Chris Brewster is Director of the Centre for European HRM at Cranfield School of Management. He is also co-editor of *Human Resource Management in Northern Europe*, Blackwell (forthcoming), and *Policy and Practice in European Human Resource Management* (1994), Routledge. **Dr Hilary Harris** is a Lecturer in Organizational Behaviour at Cranfield School of Management. Her Ph.D. explores the issue of women in international management and she has written articles and consulted with many multinationals in the field of HRM.

International HRM

Contemporary issues in Europe

Edited by
Chris Brewster and Hilary Harris

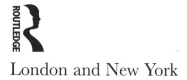

London and New York

First published 1999 by Routledge
11 New Fetter Lane, London EC4P 4EE

Simultaneously published in the USA and Canada
by Routledge
29 West 35th Street, New York, NY 10001

Typeset in Baskerville by Keystroke, Jacaranda Lodge, Wolverhampton
Printed and bound in Great Britain by TJ International, Padstow, Cornwall

British Library Cataloguing in Publication Data
A catalogue record for this book is available from the British Library

Library of Congress Cataloguing in Publication Data
International HRM: contemporary issues in Europe / edited by Chris
  Brewster and Hilary Harris.
      p.   cm.
  Includes bibliographical references and index.
  1. Personnel management–Europe. I. Brewster, Chris.
  II. Harris, Hilary, 1954– .
  HF5549.2.E9I58   1999
  658.3'0094–dc21   98–18992
                  CIP

ISBN 0–415–19489–X (hbk)
ISBN 0–415–19490–3 (pbk)

Contents

Figures

Tables

Contributors

Ingmar Björkman is a Professor of Management and Organization at the Swedish School of Economics in Helsinki, Finland. During 1998–9 he will be a visiting professor at INSEAD, France.

Jaime Bonache is Professor of Human Resource Management at the Universidad Carlos III, Madrid, Spain.

Paola Bradley was formerly a Research Fellow at City University Business School and is now a consultant with Hewitt Associates, London.

Chris Brewster is Professor of European Human Resource Management at Cranfield School of Management, UK.

Christopher Burke is a graduate of the Bachelor of Business Studies (Personnel Management) degree at the University of Limerick, Ireland.

Dr Dirk Buyens is Professor at the De Vlerick School voor Management, University of Ghent, Belgium, where he is Head of the Human Resource Department and Director of the Executive MBA programme.

Zulima Fernández is Professor of Strategic Management at the Universidad Carlos III, Madrid, Spain.

Geraldine Finn is a graduate of the National University of Ireland and the University of Limerick. She is currently pursuing a postgraduate degree by research at the University of Limerick, Ireland.

Professor John Hailey is Director of Research at Oxford Brookes University, Oxford.

Dr Hilary Harris is a Lecturer in Organizational Behaviour at Cranfield School of Management, UK.

Dr Anne-Wil Harzing works at University of Bradford, Management Centre, UK.

Chris Hendry is Centenary Professor in Organizational Behaviour at City University Business School, London.

Niklas Lindholm is a doctoral candidate at the Swedish School of Economics and Business Administration, Helsinki, Finland.

Christine Mattl is a University Assistant at the Interdisciplinary Department for Organizational Behaviour and Management, Vienna University of Economics and Business Administration, Vienna, Austria.

Michael Morley is Lecturer in Personnel Management and Industrial Relations at the Department of Personnel and Employment Relations, College of Business, University of Limerick, Ireland.

Tuomo Peltonen is at the Department of Management, Helsinki School of Economics and Business, Finland.

Stephen J. Perkins is Founder–Director of the Strategic Remuneration Research Centre and a Visiting Fellow at City University Business School, London.

Dr Hugh Scullion is a Reader in International HRM at the School of Management and Finance, Nottingham University.

Paul R. Sparrow is Professor of International HRM at Sheffield University Management School and Editor of the *Journal of Occupational and Organizational Psychology*.

Dr Vesa Suutari is Associate Professor in Management and Organization at the University of Vaasa, Finland.

Dr Marja Tahvanainen is Assistant Professor at the Helsinki School of Economics and Business Administration where she teaches Strategic International HRM.

Ans de Vos co-ordinates the Executive MBA programme at the De Vlerick School of Management in Ghent, Belgium.

1 International human resource management

The European contribution

Hilary Harris and Chris Brewster

Introduction

International human resource management

One of the few certainties in this uncertain world is the growing influence of internationalization on organizations, both large and small. There are increasing numbers of internationally operating organizations and internationally operating employees. The subject of international human resource management (IHRM) is becoming ever more critical for more and more organizations.

However, despite growing interest in IHRM, there is still much room for better understanding of successful HRM practices in an international context, as many researchers have argued (see, for example, Pucik 1984; Dowling 1986; Laurent 1986; Evans *et al.* 1989; Hossain and Davis 1989; Nedd *et al.* 1989; Shaw *et al.* 1990; Mendenhall and Oddou 1991; Weber and Festing 1991; Dowling *et al.* 1994; Boxall 1995; Scherm 1995). The world of international business may, of course, not involve IHRM: it is not relevant in, for example, the spread of franchising operations and the growth of conglomerates which have no strategic objective of maximizing their international operations. But for most enterprises, increasing internationalization equates with an increasingly important role for IHRM. While it is recognized that the international HRM issues which have been researched are of practical importance to human resource managers, this work has been criticized by Kochan *et al.* (1992) as focusing too narrowly on functional activities and as lacking appropriate theoretical structures. Summarizing the essence of their critique, it is that the current literature in international HRM defines the field too narrowly; is influenced by a discussion of concepts and issues with little backing in systematic research; and they argue that a new field of IHRM studies should be built round a broader set of questions.

The nature of IHRM

There is no consensus about what the term IHRM covers. How are we to conceptualize it? What areas and activities does it include and how does it relate to international business strategy? The majority of studies in the area have traditionally focused on expatriation: cross-border assignments of employees that last for a significant period of time (see e.g. Brewster 1991; Black *et al.* 1993; Dowling *et al.* 1994). Indeed, for many organizations and many commentators, IHRM and expatriate management are virtually synonymous. This is understandable. Expatriates are among the most expensive human resources in any internationally operating organization and they are almost invariably in crucial positions. They have, and their management involves, isssues and problems which go beyond those of most other employees. Yet our understanding of expatriates and their management is noteably less than that of other employees; and expatriates are often far from being the best managed employees.

IHRM, however, covers a far broader spectrum than the management of expatriates. It involves the worldwide management of people. Several researchers have proposed detailed models of how IHRM fits into the overall globalization strategy of organizations. Adler and Ghadar (1990) suggest that organizations will need to follow very different IHRM policies and practices according to the relevant stage of international corporate evolution, which they identify as: domestic, international, multinational and global. Linking this with the attitudes and values of top management at headquarters (classified by Perlmutter and Heenan (1979) as ethnocentric, polycentric and geocentric) they outline how organizations could adapt their HRM approaches and practices to fit the external environment in which the firm operates, and its strategic intent.

Evans and Lorange (1989) asked the question: 'How can a corporation operating in different product markets and diverse socio-cultural environments effectively establish human resource policies?' As a result, they developed two logics for shaping HRM policy; *product-market logic* and *social-cultural logic*. Under the product-market logic, different types of managers are seen to be needed for the various phases of the product life cycle. Categories of managers are also split into 'corporate', 'divisional' and 'business unit' levels, with different duties attributed to each category. Under the social-cultural logic, Evans and Lorange take Perlmutter's categories and propose two strategies for dealing with cultural and social diversity. The first strategy is labelled the *global* approach and relates to Perlmutter's ethnocentrism or geocentrism. In this, the company's own specific culture predominates and human resource management is relatively centralized and standardized. Under the second strategy, the *polycentric* approach, responsibility for human resource management is decentralized and devolved to the subsidiaries.

Evans and Doz (1992) discuss the concept of the dualities that are at the core of complex organization and apply this to building an international competence. They argue that HRM is a critically important tool for building dualistic properties into the firm. In terms of HRM, the key mechanism through which this can happen is layering. Layering involves building new capabilities and qualities into the organization's culture while reinforcing its past cultural stengths. They argue that layering leads to a richer structure of shared meanings, mindsets, relationships and networks. Management development is seen to be a key facet of layering. In the context of international organizations, it should be used to build an 'and–and' mentality in relation to international integration and local responsiveness. It can also be used to balance the focus of managers on key strategic competences and to manage strategic development such as in the case of Marks & Spencer where they are striving to build a balance between the traditional culture of merchandising experimentation with new needs for analytical marketing skills. It is noted that such an approach entails the use of subtle management processes which tend to be relatively slow to embed. Rapid switches between initiatives will destroy the value of such an approach which reflects a fundamental duality within organizations, that of mobility and continuity. Of equal importance is the fact that organizations which are deeply layered are far from simple to study. The method of operating is often more informal than can be seen from an examination of rules, hierarchies or management processes. Layering often occurs through managed long-term development of key managers and professionals who are recruited for careers rather than short-term jobs and therefore the HRM functions of recruitment and selection, development, retention and reward management are vital regulators of this process. Effort is also needed to ensure new blood and to minimize politicization of the decision-making processes.

Taking the concept of strategic human resource management (SHRM) into the international sphere, Schuler *et al.* (1993) offer an integrative framework for the study and understanding of strategic international human resource management (SIHRM) which goes beyond theories of strategic human resource management based in the domestic context and incorporates features unique to the international context (Adler and Bartholomew 1992; Sundaram and Black 1992). SIHRM is defined as: 'human resource management issues, functions and policies and practices that result from the strategic activities of multinational enterprises and that impact on the international concerns and goals of those enterprises' (Schuler *et al.* 1993: 720).

The breadth of issues is illustrated by the framework, which links SIHRM orientations and activities to the strategic components of multinational enterprises (MNEs)[1] comprising interunit linkages and internal operations. These authors argue that the key determinant of effectiveness for MNEs is the extent to which their various operating units across the world are to be differentiated and at the same time, integrated, controlled and co-ordinated (Galbraith 1987; Ghoshal 1987; Punnett and Ricks 1992). Evidence of different solutions adopted by MNEs to the tension between differentiation and integration, otherwise termed the 'global vs. local' dilemma, are seen to result from the influence of a wide variety of exogenous and endogenous factors. Exogenous factors include industry characteristics such as type of business and technology available, the nature of competitors and the extent of change and country–regional characteristics such as political, economic and socio-cultural conditions and legal requirements. Endogenous factors include the structure of international operations, the international orientation of the organization's headquarters, the competitive strategy being used, and the MNE's experience in managing international operations.

This discussion of SIHRM demonstrates the complexity of HR decisions in the international sphere and the broad scope of its remit; going far beyond the issue of expatriation, to an overall concern for managing people effectively on a global scale. By attempting to adopt an SIHRM perspective, HR practitioners in MNEs would be engaging in every aspect of international business strategy and adopting HR policies and practices aimed at the most effective use of the human resource in the firm. A key aspect of the framework is the acknowledgement of the many factors which influence the choice of 'global vs. local' HR practices and policies. The issue which has received most attention from researchers to date, namely the implications of culture, is but one aspect of IHRM. Although sensitivity to which aspects of business practices in any particular country are emic (i.e. culture-specific aspects of concepts or behaviour) and etic (i.e. culture common aspects) is regarded as essential to a strategic choice of HR levers, the influence of institutional factors such as economic, structural and political forms are also critical in shaping SIHRM choices. The framework therefore presents a valuable 'map' of the territory of SIHRM. It does not, however, consider SIHRM issues for small to medium-sized organizations, or for organizations operating in the public sector (the international governmental organizations, for example) or in the not-for-profit sector (international charities, churches, etc.). Guidance as to appropriate research design to test the linkages remains problematic.

Rosenzweig and Nohria (1994) explore the tension between the pressures for internal consistency and local isomorphism. They argue that of all functions HRM tends most closely to adhere to local practices as they are often mandated by local regulation and shaped by strong local conventions. Within HRM, they see the order in which six key practices will most closely resemble local practices as:

- time off;
- benefits;
- gender composition;
- training;
- executive bonus;
- participation.

This order is predicated on the assumption that HRM practices for which there are well-defined local norms and which affect the rank and file of the affiliate organization are likely to conform most to practices of local competitors. Practices for which there are diffuse and poorly defined local norms, or which are seen as being critical to maintaining internal consistency, are less likely to conform to local norms.

Three other factors are identified as being important in determining the extent of internal consistency or local isomorphism. The first is the degree to which an affiliate is embedded in the local environment. This refers to its method of founding and its age, as well as its size, its dependence on local inputs and the degree of influence exerted on it from local institutions. The second is the strength of the flow of resources such as capital, information and people between the parent and the affiliate. The third relates to characteristics of the parent, such as the culture of the home country, with a high degree of distance between cultures being predicated to lead to more internal consistency (i.e. an ethnocentric approach). Two final characteristics relate to the parent organization's orientation to control and the nature of the industry, with greater local isomorphism in a multi-domestic industry as opposed to a global industry (Porter 1986; Prahalad and Doz 1987).

Kobrin (1994) uses an empirical survey to operationalize and test relationships between a geocentric managerial mindset, geographic scope and the structural and strategic characteristics of firms and industries. The Perlmutter (1969) definition of a geocentric mindset is contrasted with multinational strategy, defined as a continuum between firms whose strategy is multidomestic or nationally responsive, and at the other by firms which are integrated transnationally. Kobrin argues that a geocentric mindset is not necessarily always linked to a transnationally integrated strategy and/or a global organizational structure. Kobrin puts forward a tentative hypothesis that the need to transmit knowledge and information through the global network may lead, through increased interpersonal interaction, to organizational geocentrism in terms of attitudes and IHRM policies.

Taylor *et al.* 1996 build on previous work on IHRM by drawing on concepts from the resource-based view of the firm and resource dependence to develop a theoretical model of the determinants of SIHRM systems in MNCs. Resource-based theory adds to prior models of SIHRM the fundamental notion that in order to provide value to the business, the SIHRM system of global firms should be constructed around specific organizational competences that are critical for securing competitive advantage in a global environment (Pucik 1992). The resource dependence framework helps identify those situations in which MNCs will exercise control over the SIHRM system of their affiliates. The authors define SIHRM as: 'human resource management issues, functions and policies and practices that result from the strategic activities of multinational enterprises and that impact the international concerns and goals of those enterprises' (Taylor *et al.* 1996: 961).

They quote Lado and Wilson's (1994: 699) definition of the resource-based view of HRM: 'The resource-based view suggests that human resource systems can contribute to sustained competitive advantage through facilitating the development of competencies that are firm specific, produce complex social relationships, are embedded in a firm's history and culture, and generate tacit organisational knowledge.'

Taylor *et al.* see the following main implications from their model. First it acknowledges the critical role that the HRM competence of the parent firm, as perceived by top management, plays in the transfer of HRM policies to affiliates and how this can contribute to competitive advantage. A second implication is the recognition of the pivotal role of top management in SIHRM. The authors see a key research area in an analysis of the factors that influence the ability of top management to perceive an MNC's HRM competence and those factors that lead management to decide whether this competence is context specific or context generalizable and, hence, transferable. A third implication is the need to reconsider the assumption that the critical groups of employees at affiliate level are either expatriates or white-collar workers. On a more general level, Taylor *et al.* argue that further research is needed into the determinants of the context generalizability of a resource and the ways in which managers can judge whether a particular resource is useful beyond the context in which it was created.

The research quoted above has a strong North American influence. This highlights an important issue in IHRM research in general: the hegemony of the USA. Because of the extensive influence of US multinationals and the power of the US academic tradition in defining the nature of research into HRM in general (Brewster 1998), US researchers have had a defining influence on research into IHRM. Not only is the vast mass of research into the topic conducted in the USA and focused on US MNEs, but the US texts have tended to 'set the agenda'. Arguably, the balance needs to be corrected. International organizational experience pre-dates even the establishment of the USA. There are now ever greater numbers of countries with substantial international organizations based there and ever more internationally operating organizations which are not. In some parts of the world, such as the Arab states and the Pacific region, the influence of locally based MNEs is becoming crucially important. And, of course, the European experiment adds a different flavour to the concept of internationalization. One of the key missions of the European Union (EU), the dismantling of the barriers to the international movement of goods, labour and capital within Europe, has led to a substantial increase in cross-border trade in a region which was already well down that road. It is, therefore, unsurprising to note the extensive growth in the amount of research into IHRM now being conducted in Europe (Brewster and Scullion 1997). Conceptually, although one of the originating texts in the field of IHRM was European (Torbiörn 1982), the time is now perhaps right to see whether these European researchers have a new perspective to offer.

Over half of the chapters in this book consider issues relating to the broader scope of SIHRM, ranging from a consideration of the role of HRM in strategic decision-making, linkages between international business strategy and international HRM and key SIHRM policies and practices in the areas of international staffing, rewards and performance management. The book presents a uniquely European perspective on some of the key SIHRM issues facing organizations today. Many of the chapters contain the results of empirical research using a variety of methods. Hence, the book contributes to the debate about the most appropriate way of undertaking research in IHRM.

The nature of expatriation

An understanding of the management of expatriates is of growing importance because of the recent rapid increases in global activity and global competition (Young and Hamill 1992). As multinational enterprises (MNEs) increase in number and influence so the role of expatriates in those MNEs grows in significance (Dowling *et al.* 1994). Indeed, the effectiveness of these expatriates and, therefore, the management of this group of employees are recognized as major determinants of success or failure in international business (Tung 1984). The human and financial costs of failure in the international business arena are more severe than in domestic business (Dowling and Schuler 1990; Forster 1998) – even if recent research in Europe shows that such failures may well be less common than is sometimes argued (Harzing 1995). Indirect costs for the organization, such as a loss of market share and damage to overseas customer relationships may be considerable (Zeira and Banai 1984); and will be exacerbated by the effect on the confidence of the local employees in the MNE. The evidence is clear: despite advances in our understanding since the point was first made (Desatnick and Bennett 1978; Tung 1984), many companies underestimate the complex nature of the HRM problems involved in international operations and business failures in the international arena may often be linked fairly directly to the poor management of expatriates.

Research on international staffing has identified a number of principal reasons for employing HQ expatriates in MNEs: a perceived lack of availability of management and technical skills in some countries; control of local operations (Torbiörn 1985; Brewster 1991); to maintain trust in key foreign businesses following large international acquisitions; for representation (Brewster 1991); and for management development purposes (Hamill 1989).

The use of expatriates can, therefore, resolve a number of problems for an international enterprise. However, the use of expatriates also creates several areas of problems. These problems include, first (at least in the view of many organizations), the fact that the use of expatriates is a very costly practice. High salaries to persuade good individuals to work outside their own country are compounded by extensive benefits, moving costs, expense accounts and substantial administrative expertise for a relatively small, if crucial, group of employees. It has been estimated that an expatriate costs three or four times as much as the employment of the same individual at home (Copeland and Griggs 1985; Brewster 1988; Hiltrop and Janssens 1990). This is gaining increasing attention from companies where cost control is seen as an important issue – and there are few where it is not. Second, expatriates are commonly reported to face significant adaptation problems in their new environment which make it difficult to operate effectively, particularly during the early stages of their international assignments. Unsuccessful expatriate adjustment, personally, by the family, or in terms of inadequate performance, leading to early repatriation, have been commonly reported – in American studies in particular. A more common problem may be that of underperformance while in post. The problem of cost versus performance encapsulates the major issue in the management of expatriates for the organization.

Recruitment and selection

Research into the recruitment and/or selection of expatriates has generally been focused on the more 'visible' aspects such as the criteria used in such decisions. Much of the early work on expatriation was concerned with this issue. A consistent finding was that work competence was seen as the crucial factor by MNEs (Ivancevich 1969; Hays 1971, 1974; Miller 1973; Howard 1974; Lanier 1979; Tung 1981, 1982; Zeira and Banai 1984, 1985), by the expatriates themselves (Gonzales and Neghandi 1967; Hays 1971; Harris 1973; Hautaluoma and Kaman 1975; Bardo and Bardo 1980; Hawes and Kealey 1981; Zeira and Banai 1984, 1985) and by host country nationals (Zeira and Banai 1985). It was widely argued that too little attention was paid to the expatriate's ability to adjust to working in the new situation: the ability to be successful in one environment does not necessarily imply that the person will be successful in all circumstances. Mendenhall and Oddou (1985) identified a major problem area in expatriate selection as the ingrained practice of operating with the 'domestic equals overseas performance equation'. Factors such as language skills and international adaptability are rarely found to be key criteria, though there is some evidence that these have more importance for European organizations (Tung 1982; Brewster 1991). There has been less attention paid to the methods of selection (though see Harris and Brewster, forthcoming) or to the selection systems.

Adjustment

The issue of expatriate adjustment to their new situation has been explored in more recent studies (see, as examples, Black and Stephens 1989; Black *et al.* 1991; Bird and Dunbar 1991; Brewster 1993; Suutari and Brewster 1998). Attempts have been made to identify three elements of adjustment: intercultural interaction, work and job responsibilities (Black 1988; Black *et al.* 1991); or to add to those a fourth, emotional adjustment (Janssens 1992). Studies by Tung (1981), Black (1988, 1990), Mendenhall and Oddou (1986) and Ronen (1989), bring together the dimensions of expatriate success, identifying five categories of attributes of success:

- job factors;
- relational dimensions;
- motivational state;
- family situation;
- language skills.

The complexity of the expatriate's role and the required level of adjustment has been summarized as a paradox (Brewster 1993), with expatriates being expected to adjust to the host culture sufficiently well to be effective, but to remain sufficiently independent to act as a representative of headquarters.

Preparation and training

In reviews of expatriate preparation and training (see, for example, Black and Mendenhall 1990; Brewster and Pickard 1994) it is clear that much preparation is focused on creating an ability to understand and adjust. US MNEs tend to use pre-departure training programmes less frequently than the European and Japanese firms (Tung 1982). Expatriates themselves are very positive about the value of training programmes (Brewster and Pickard 1994; Suutari and Brewster 1998). Other forms of preparation – briefings, shadowing, look–see visits – are more frequent than formal training programmes (Brewster 1991; Scullion 1993) and may be more cost-effective.

Performance evaluation

One issue gaining ever more attention is the question of performance evaluation. Given that expatriates are among the most expensive people that an organization employs, it is surprising how little is known about the assessment of their performance and contribution. Of course, it involves a complex range of issues (Schuler *et al.* 1991) and research to date suggests that rigorous performance appraisal systems for expatriates are far from universal (Brewster 1991; Schuler *et al.* 1991). The assessment of expatriate performance requires an understanding of the variables that influence an expatriate's success or failure in a foreign assignment. It has been argued that the three major variables include the environment (culture), job requirements, and personality characteristics of the individual (Schuler *et al.* 1991). Problems in cultural adjustment can impact on work performance but are rarely considered when assessing an expatriate's performance in a new job (Mendenhall and Oddou 1988). An objective appraisal of subsidiary (and expatriate) performance is likely to be highly complex, given the possible conflict between global and subsidiary objectives, the problem of non-comparability of data between subsidiaries and the volatility and variability of the international markets. This already problematic relationship is further complicated by the necessity of reconciling the tension between the need for universal appraisal standards with specific objectives in local units, and to recognize that more time may be needed to achieve results in markets which enjoy little supporting infrastructure from the parent company (Schuler *et al.* 1991).

Repatriation

The repatriation of expatriates has been identified as a major problem for multinational companies (Harvey 1989; Johnston 1991; Scullion 1993), but is still comparatively under-researched (Pickard and Brewster 1995). Concern over re-entry has been cited as a significant reason affecting expatriate performance (Scullion 1993). The problem has been emphasized in recent years, particularly in Europe, because the expansion of foreign operations has taken place coincident with a rationalization of HQ operations. In the leaner HQ operations of today's world there are few spaces for expatriates to 'fill in' while the organization seeks a more permanent position for them. From the repatriate perspective, other problems associated with reintegrating into the home country are loss of status, loss of autonomy, loss of career direction and a feeling that international experience is undervalued by the company (Johnston 1991). Where companies are seen to deal unsympathetically with the problems faced by expatriates on re-entry, other individuals will be more reluctant to accept the offer of international assignments (Scullion 1993). Many expatriates leave their company on return (Adler 1986) with the consequent loss of investment and expertise. Yet while it is widely accepted that the costs of expatriate turnover are considerable, very few firms have formal repatriation programmes to assist those involved and their families to achieve a successful repatriation.

Merely managing some of these issues better will not resolve the problems for international organizations because the situation is changing in some crucial ways. There are changes in the MNEs, in the host locations, and in the expatriates themselves (Brewster and Scullion 1997).

Significant changes in international organizations

In the increasing number of trading blocs throughout the world, and most obviously in the EU, the growth in international business is less among the giant 'blue chips' (which are often reducing their numbers of expatriates) than in smaller or newer organizations in the international arena. These newer organizations will include, for example, some of the giants that privatization has recently freed to compete outside the country of origin. But there are also increasing numbers of small organizations which are beginning to treat the total European market as their own local market. In both cases the experience of internationalization is limited.

Among the larger and more traditionally international players there have also been changes: a much more competitive environment (D'Aveni 1995) forcing an increasing attention to cost reduction and cost-effectiveness. Since expatriates are among the most expensive people any organization employs and the measurement of expatriate performance is, to say the least, uncertain, this has had a direct effect on the way organizations view them. This has been made more difficult to handle by the reorganization of MNEs and the consequent reduction in the size of headquarters' operations. Among other effects, a move towards organizing on the lines of business streams and a reduction in the number of people in corporate international human resource management departments has meant a significant change in the way expatriates are handled. More than a few MNEs have lost the central expertise in the management of expatriates that had been built up over many years.

In non-commercial organizations expatriation has also grown. More and more international governmental and 'non-governmental' organizations, international aid organizations and charities employ an increasing number of international employees. The growth in their work also seems likely to be linked to a growth in expatriation. There has been almost no research into expatriation or the management of expatriates in these non-commercial organizations.

Change in host locations

For commercial organizations, at least, the proportion of expatriates going from the developed world to the Third World has reduced. This has been created to some extent by an increasing unwillingness on the part of the poorer countries to continue taking foreign expatriates, whom they see as required only because the MNEs have failed to train up and provide jobs for local employees. The greater part of the change, however, has come through a growth in expatriation which does not follow the traditional pattern of developed to underdeveloped country. There has been some increase in expatriates moving in the other direction as the underdeveloped countries develop their own international operations. There has been a substantial increase in transfers between developed countries caused by extensive European and Japanese investments in the USA and cross-border developments in new world trading blocs, particularly, of course, in the EU.

These developments have taken place alongside a substantial growth in international joint ventures and in licensing and franchising. Each of these organizational forms has led to an increase in the number of expatriates. The fact that the type of expatriate assignment involved has some important differences from the traditional assignment exacerbates the lack of information here.

Changes in the expatriate population

Changes in the employing organizations and in the host countries have occurred alongside changes in the expatriate population. The traditional, middle-class, crusty, career expatriate can still be found, but much more rarely. Expatriates will more often do one assignment and then return home, occasionally undertaking a second assignment later in their career. More of them are well educated, with degrees or MBAs. One consequence is that they are more likely to see a foreign assignment as part of a career: expecting to come back to headquarters in an improved position and ready to negotiate and argue about their contracts.

Although there is still only a small proportion of female expatriates (Adler 1986; Scullion 1994; Harris 1995) the number of women expatriates is increasing. Fewer partners, male or female, are prepared to accept a 'trailing' role – not working, but expected to act as support to their MNE employed partner and even as (typically) 'hostess' for corporate functions. Partners now more frequently have their own career or expect to work in the new country.

The growth of international trade in Europe, especially among these organizations, has led to a growth in the overall number of expatriates (Brewster 1993). European researchers have responded with a significant increase in explorations of the subject, often going into areas uncovered in the US texts. This book offers some of the best of recent examples of that research.

Content guidelines

Our text aims to provide a uniquely European perspective to the key debates and challenges facing both practitioners and researchers in the area of IHRM. The core theme relates to SIHRM's role in achieving the balance between differentiation and integration among the units of an international organization. Critical to this outcome are the issues of the links between international business strategy and SIHRM, SIHRM policies and practices and the influence of exogenous and endogenous variables. Expatriation remains a critical factor in international staffing strategies and is therefore included as a dominant theme, although it is recognized that this forms a subset of an overall SIHRM orientation. The chapters are grouped together to address these central themes.

Part I Relation between international business strategy and SIHRM

The need for HR practitioners to be involved at the strategic level of business has long been a core tenet of models of strategic HRM in domestic settings (see, for example, Beer *et al.* 1984, Storey 1989, 1995, Schuler 1992). The same can be seen to hold true for SIHRM. In a world where competitive advantage is strongly linked to the management of human resources, the interplay between an organization's international business strategy and SIHRM can influence the attainment of the concerns and goals of the international enterprise (Kobrin 1992). The influence can be two-way, with the strategic orientation of the organization impacting on the international management issues, policies, practices and vice versa. Two chapters in Part I contribute new perspectives to the issue of linkage between international business strategy and SIHRM by exploring the role of HR in the strategic decision-making process from a Belgian perspective, and identifying the key components of SIHRM in relation to medium-sized firms in the Irish Republic.

The added value of the HR department
Dirk Buyens and Ans de Vos

A new model of the added value of HRM in strategic decision-making is presented in Chapter 2, using a Belgian research base. The model permits the HR function to be profiled using two variables: HR roles, referring to the domains in which HRM can add value, and HR positions, referring to the degree of involvement of HRM in decision-making processes. This provides a more dynamic picture of the actual nature of strategic HRM and stresses the need for HRM to be present at all levels of decision-making. An HR function which only works at the strategic level will be seen to lose much of its added value according to the results of the research. Likewise, one which operates only at the administrative level will be seen to provide an incomplete service for the strategic business needs of the company. Although the model is developed from a national base, it is considered useful as a tool for analysing the role of HRM in providing value-added in an international context. Assessing where the various HR functions are positioned on this model within an international organization will allow for a more realistic appraisal of the contributions of each unit. Is it appropriate for each HR unit within an international organization to be working at the strategic level, or should this be reserved for the headquarters' unit? How does each unit's positioning on the model align with the international orientation of the organization or its primary response to the differentiation vs. integration dilemma?

International HRM in medium-sized MNEs: evidence from Ireland
Hugh Scullion

Chapter 3 looks at IHRM in medium-sized MNEs based in the Irish Republic. The author addresses the specific nature of internationalization of organizations within the Irish Republic, which is seen to be highly concentrated within traditional and resource-based sectors and to consist of rapidly increasing acquisitional growth strategies. This type of internationalization strategy is seen to conflict with traditional models of stages of internationalization (Adler and Ghadar 1990) as it leapfrogs the early stages of the process. Research evidence reported in the chapter into IHRM within such MNEs reveals a number of features which have rarely been reported before. These include differences in international staffing policies, where marketing and public relations (PR) considerations influence the choice of parent country nationals (PCNs) over host country nationals (HCNs) for staffing of subsidiaries in firms working in the finance sector. Overall, however, the research showed that most of the organizations relied heavily on expatriates as a result of being in the early stages of internationalization, in line with current theory (Edstrom and Galbraith 1977; Punnett and Ricks 1992). A major focus of IHRM policy and practice in Irish MNEs was the need to develop a cadre of international managers to allow for the future development of internationalization strategies. The chapter reinforces the need for organizations to adopt SIHRM policies and practices which reflect the specific international business issues facing each firm. In this respect there is no 'right way' to internationalize the management of people; each strategy needs to be tailored to the current context of internationalization.

Part II Balancing differentiation with integration

The chapters in this section all address aspects of one of the most hotly debated topics in IHRM: the need for any MNE simultaneously to exploit the advantages of operating as a global organization while responding to and learning from the different environments in which it operates. The authors of these chapters explore elements of these necessary dualities (Evans and Doz 1992), going, to the relief of all serious researchers, beyond the trite and meaningless mantras of 'think global, act local'. Our contributors take a more careful and research-based look at what is happening in a number of specific areas in order to contribute to the debate.

MNE staffing policies for the managing director position in foreign subsidiaries: the results of an innovative research method
Anne-Wil Harzing

The determination of staffing choices in an international organization represents a critical component of its strategy in relation to the balance between differentiation and integration. In order to balance the needs of co-ordination, control and autonomy, organizations have a number of options to choose from in terms of deciding an appropriate mix and flow of parent country nationals (PCNs), third country nationals (TCNs) and host country or local nationals (HCNs). There is extensive theoretical writing about the reasons underlying such choices, but there is little empirical evidence to support prevailing assumptions. The studies by Tung (1981, 1982, 1987) and Kopp (1994) provide the main sources of empirical evidence.

Chapter 4 presents European-based research using an innovative desk research method sampling 1,746 subsidiaries in 22 countries to determine the nationality and hence the categorization (PCN, TCN, HCN) of the managing director of each unit. Anne-Wil Harzing's imaginative study provides a greater depth of analysis than has previously been undertaken, initially differentiating MNE staffing policies according to country of origin of headquarters, industry and subsidiary country. Further exploration of the data enabled differentiation by size of the MNE, measured by the number of employees and age of the MNE. The research highlights the limitations of considering Europe as a homogeneous whole with respect to MNE policies. Distinct clusters of countries were identified which shared similar policies in respect to staffing of subsidiaries. Analysis by industry again identified clear differences in staffing policies. The chapter explores in depth the possible reasons for such findings, comparing the empirical results with existing theoretical assumptions about appropriate SIHRM policies for various international business strategies.

Localization as an ethical response to internationalization
John Hailey

Continuing with the theme of choice of staffing policies in order to obtain the best balance between differentiation and integration of units, Chapter 5 raises serious questions about the ability and commitment of some multinationals to identify and develop host country managers in their foreign operations (Hailey 1992). Indeed, it has been argued that the failure of the localization process to create new generations of skilled local staff to take over key positions may in part reflect the self-fulfilling nature of ethnocentrism (Banai 1992). The counter-argument, that ethnocentrism may be a rational and effective policy in many cases, has also been made (Mayrhofer and Brewster 1996). John Hailey develops this theme. He argues that the growing pressure from different stakeholders builds a greater expectation for both multinationals and international agencies to make the most cost-effective and ethical use of all resources. This includes the way they manage their international human resources, employ expatriates and develop local management talent.

Moving beyond the general debate about the reasons for sending expatriates, Hailey looks at the actual implications of having expatriate and local staff working together. Previous research has indicated the detrimental consequences of tensions which can exist between local staff and expatriate managers (Armstrong 1987; Hailey 1996a, b). If strategic international business requirements suggest a need for expatriates, what can be done to ensure the most effective use of all the human resources in the organization, including local staff? The author considers whether the tension between local staff and expatriate managers can be resolved through the use of innovative ways of generating commitment, harmony and a sense of common purpose among expatriate and local staff around the world. The perceptions of staff working in overtly value-driven international non-profit development agencies were examined. These are organizations that emphasize their caring, participative and ethical approach to work. Yet despite this, the research still suggested that relations between local staff and expatriate development workers are strained and counter-productive. This raises the question as to whether the continued use of expatriates is both cost-effective and ethical, thus suggesting that localization may need to be more closely examined as an alternative, ethical and efficacious response to internationalization.

A critical component in ensuring maximum return from human resources throughout the whole international organization lies in the design of performance and reward systems. The next three chapters consider some of the overarching issues relating to the goal of designing SIHRM policies and practices in this area which are in line with corporate business goals, while allowing for sensitivity to business, cultural and other influences at subsidiary unit level.

International reward systems: to converge or not to converge?
Paul Sparrow

This chapter considers the forces for and against convergence in international rewards and compensation systems. Three key factors are explored in order to understand and integrate knowledge: those that lead to distinctive national patterns of HRM, those that are making national business systems more receptive to change; and the processes through which new policies and practices are delivered. Paul Sparrow makes the point that differences in international reward are not just a consequence of cultural differences, but also of differences in institutional influences, national business systems and the role and competence of managers in the sphere of HRM. The critical and yet highly dynamic influence of national business systems (defined as a combination of the role of the state and financial sectors, national systems of education and training, employment and tenure expectations and national cultures) is revealed by an examination of the different natures of reward and compensation systems in Europe, Japan and the USA.

Despite evidence of distinct national (and regional) patterns of reward management, three overarching themes are identified: a shift from job-based to person-based HR systems; the transfer of social costs and risks away from organizations; significant threats to the psychological contract with fragmentation and individualization of the reward–effort bargain. Sparrow argues that the impact of these trends will be moderated by two key processes. The first relates to the complex productivity equations upon which managers draw when making decisions that affect the location of investment, and the employment conditions and flexibility demands that might be tied into the investment. The second concerns the evolution of labour markets and the maturing behaviour that accompanies this, which can make apparently cheap labour markets far more expensive than expected.

Global or multi-local? The significance of international values in reward strategy
Paola Bradley, Chris Hendry and Stephen Perkins

Chapter 7 develops the theme of the impact of cultural differences on international reward policies. The authors argue that studies of cultural differences suggest that reward system design and management needs to be tailored to local values to enhance the performance of overseas operations. However, they view cultural difference studies as too generalistic and failing to provide an adequate guide to the design and management of reward systems. They propose that it is necessary to incorporate attention to corporate and industry effects, since the companies within national legal structures and managing specific business environments, design the reward systems and have to cope with problems involved in managing them. The chapter describes a pilot project for a larger study which will view reward systems through the lens of particular MNEs in particular contexts. This project aims to identify key cultural value sets and their impact on international strategic reward issues for multinational corporations, within the context of national, industry and organizational differences.

Performance appraisal of host country employees: Western MNEs in China
Niklas Lindholm, Marja Tahvanainen, Ingmar Björkman

The literature identifies a number of significant constraints on strategic performance measurement and management in MNEs. These include the possible conflict between global and subsidiary objectives, the problem of non-comparability of data between subsidiaries, the volatility of the international market and the variable levels of market maturity. These factors make objective appraisal of subsidiary (and expatriate) performance highly complex. Further, it is important to reconcile the tension between the need for universal appraisal standards with specific objectives in local units, and to recognize that more time may be needed to achieve results in markets which enjoy little supporting infrastructure from the parent company (Schuler *et al.* 1991). Following the theme of the debate concerning the balance between localization and standardization of international HRM policies and practices, Chapter 8 addresses the issue of the extent to which performance appraisal should be adapted to suit local conditions. The authors use research evidence from MNEs operating in China to address the issues of the extent to which Western MNEs have implemented standardized performance appraisal practices for their local professionals and managers in China and what their experiences have been in implementing such practices. The research discovered a high degree of standardization in performance appraisal practices in MNEs in China for a number of business, control and other factors. It revealed, however, several key facets of Chinese work culture which acted against the implementation of a standard approach. Included in these were the aspect of 'face', the role of hierarchy and group orientation in communication difficulties between subordinate and manager. As a result, it was seen to be necessary to alter some aspects of a Western-style performance appraisal system to allow for local sensitivities.

Part III Contemporary issues in expatriation

The contributors to Part III explore expatriation as a subset of SIHRM. These chapters address all stages of the expatriation cycle: selection, preparation, adjustment, repatriation. In contrast to the predominantly descriptive literature in this area, the aim of this section is to present new evidence and develop theories, frameworks and models from a European perspective.

Strategic staffing in multinational companies: a resource-based approach
Jaime Bonache and Zulima Fernández

Research into the recruitment and/or selection of expatriates has generally been focused on the more 'visible' aspects of these issues such as the decision criteria. Mendenhall and Oddou (1985) identified a major problem area in expatriate selection as the ingrained practice of operating with the 'domestic equals overseas performance equation'. Technical expertise and domestic track record are by far the two dominant selection criteria. Factors such as language skills and international adaptability come further down the list in all studies, though there is some evidence that these have more importance for European organizations (Tung 1982; Brewster 1991). There has been less attention paid to the strategic antecedents of the appointment decision (i.e. whether an expatriate was the appropriate way to fill the assignment anyway) or to the manner in which the appointment is made. There has been very little research since the seminal work of Perlmutter and Heenan (1974) into the question of when it is appropriate to use expatriates (see also Ondrack 1985; Mayrhofer and Brewster 1996). Indeed, much of the literature fails to question either the use of expatriates or the reality of the manner of their appointment. It should not be assumed that the majority of multinationals adopt a systematic and coherent approach to selection (Robinson 1978; Harris 1997). In many MNEs staffing and selection processes are still rather informal with responses being reactive rather than proactive (Brewster 1991). Arguably, a consistent human resources strategy that fits the organization's overall business strategy is much more difficult to achieve with this type of ad hoc approach.

These issues are the focus of Chapter 9. Jaime Bonache and Zulima Fernández explore the selection processes of a number of Spanish international organizations and argue that there is a need for a strategic assessment of the circumstances of the foreign subsidiary prior to the selection being made. Applying a categorization of strategic roles of subsidiaries based on the work of Penrose (1959), these authors utilize the theoretical framework of the resource-based theory of the firm to identify the necessary types of knowledge transfer needed in each instance and hence the type of selection strategy required. The in-depth nature of their analysis presents challenges to conventional ways of thinking about expatriate selection, particularly in providing an innovative method of adopting a strategic approach to expatriate selection.

International assignments across European borders: no problems?
Vesa Suutari and Chris Brewster

Chapter 10 explores the issues of adjustment, focusing on Finnish expatriates moving to other European countries. There is an assumption both in the literature and in company practice that such 'close' transfers should be largely problem-free. The evidence is that this varies by culture and transfers can be problematic within developed and nearby countries as well as across the other side of the world. The research presented in the chapter also questions the existing groupings of categories of adjustment, arguing the need for a disaggregation of some of the areas, for example, the inclusion of 'leadership style' as a feature of adjustment.

Irish expatriates in Moscow: exploratory evidence on aspects of adjustment
Michael Morley, Christopher Burke and Geraldine Finn

In Chapter 11 the authors address the extent to which frameworks of international adjustment, developed primarily in the North American context, are applicable to the European context by examining the adjustment of Irish expatriates in Moscow. In general, a positive relationship existed between role clarity, host country national interaction, quality of the working environment, degree of autonomy of the subsidiary and work adjustment. The level of company support was also seen to be linked to work satisfaction. However, the study found that aspects of cultural novelty, previous international experience, role novelty and role discretion did not seem relevant to Irish expatriates in Moscow. A detailed understanding of the context of adjustment in each case is therefore seen to be important in determining which variables are most likely to cause problems.

An integrative framework for pre-departure preparation
Hilary Harris and Chris Brewster

Much of the work on expatriate preparation and training is built on the importance of the ability of the expatriates (and their families) to understand the nature of adjustment as described in Chapters 10 and 11. There has therefore been a concentration on issues of cross-cultural training among writers in this area (Tung 1981; Mendenhall and Oddou 1986; Black and Mendenhall 1989). However, the evidence is that the majority of organizations sending people abroad do not invest in adequate pre-departure preparation, whether through training or some other alternative. The negative effect on adjustment and performance in the international role has been documented through research into expatriate failure rates discussed earlier in the introduction. Chapter 12 explores the reasons for the lack of investment in pre-departure preparation and proposes an integrative framework which will allow organizations to tailor pre-departure programmes to the needs of each individual expatriate, taking into account both job and individual variables, together with assessment of existing level of competence.

Repatriation and career systems: Finnish public and private sector repatriates in their career lines
Tuomo Peltonen

Existing research into repatriation has traditionally focused on the problems of readjustment for returning expatriates. This approach concentrates on the socio-psychological processes of adjustment and coping, studying repatriation as a cultural transition in which expectations of smooth return and career development facilitate any problems inherent in re-entry. The second approach is related to expatriate policies and transnationalism. Repatriation is set within the strategic context of the international HR operations of a firm. In a truly global learning organization international career moves have become part of normal work life and the individual rather than the organization is expected to take care of the management of transitions.

In Chapter 13, Tuomo Peltonen claims that both perspectives lack critical features, for instance, the adjustment approach tends to lack sensitivity to contextual factors such as industry and historical heritage of the firm. On the other hand, the tendency to focus on strategic processes related to repatriate learning becomes problematic due to the tendency to use globalism as a prescription and to neglect individual level practical problems related to the return from an international assignment. The author situates repatriation in the context of career development and explores the organizational logic behind repatriate career outcomes. In order to do this, research was carried out to investigate the career lines of different categories of Finnish expatriates from the time they entered the organization to the international assignment and beyond. In this way, the author argues that re-entry position allocations are in fact the result of latent rankings which will result in a more permanent division into central and less central individuals.

Women in international management: why are they not selected?
Hilary Harris

International management has long been a masculine preserve in Europe as it has in the USA (Adler 1984). Indeed the evidence suggests that women in British MNEs are not making as much progress in international management as those in US multinationals (Adler 1991; Scullion 1992). The lack of willingness to recruit and develop women as international managers is worrying: recent research suggests that women can be as successful internationally as men (Adler 1987, 1991; Jelinek and Adler 1988; Barham and Devine 1991; Harris 1995). Although there is still only a small proportion of female expatriates (Adler 1986; Scullion 1994; Harris 1995), the numbers of women expatriates are increasing.

Chapter 14 takes an alternative perspective to existing research into women in international management. The paucity of women has been attributed primarily to factors external to the home country organization such as: women's own lack of interest; dual-career couple constraints; host country managers' and clients' prejudice. The theme developed in this chapter is the need to focus on the home country organizational selection process for international managers as a key determinant of participation rates of women in international management appointments. It argues that the notion of 'fit' in the context of male-dominated international assignments is likely to be gender biased unless selection systems are carefully designed. A typology of international management selection systems is presented which conceptualizes the relationship between features of selection processes and resultant outcomes in terms of ease of entry to international appointments for women.

Part IV New research perspectives on IHRM

Throughout the book, alternative research methodologies are utilized in an effort to capture unique aspects of SIHRM. The debate about the most effective ways of undertaking international and cross-cultural research is extensive and continues to reveal sharp differences of opinion among academics. Academics and researchers are divided at a domestic level by their conflicting views on the nature of the world (ontology) and how it can be researched (epistemology). These fundamental philosophical and methodological divisions continue to exert a significant influence on choice of research methodology at an international level. In addition, however, undertaking research at an intercultural or international level raises separate issues of parochialism. Boyacigiller and Adler (1991) provide a powerful demonstration of the strength of parochialism inherent in US-based organizational theory and academic and management education. They argue that despite a large body of research substantiating the cultural diversity of values and the impact of such diversity on organizational behaviour (e.g. Hofstede 1980; Kelley and Worthley 1981; Laurent 1981; Lane and DiStefano 1988), most American-based organization theories appear implicitly to assume universality. In order to increase the internationalism of management research, the authors make several recommendations: first, that researchers indicate the national and cultural characteristics of their sample; second, that cross-national research is carried out to encourage scholars to create theoretical and methodological approaches not predicated solely on single culture; third, that scholars study foreign organizations on their own terms (idiographic research). By developing thick descriptions of other cultures (Geertz 1973) they increase the types of organizational forms and environmental contexts with which they are familiar. Finally, they recommend the use of multinational and multicultural research teams to facilitate the recognition of cultural biases in theory development.

Earley and Singh (1995) categorize existing research forms in the international management literature into four, based on two dimensions: relevance to international management; relevance to intercultural management. The international dimension embraces the examination of a cultural or national system as a gestalt, whereas the intercultural dimension embraces the component relationships within the cultural system. In the unitary form, emphasis is placed on a single instance of a phenomenon, i.e. trying to understand a single cultural group or nation on its own terms and using its own constructs. The gestalt form focuses on examining a system as a whole. Relationships among variables are examined as they occur across different cultural or national systems. Constructs and hypothesized relationships are derived from general principles rather than from the systems themselves.

Interpretations of findings from a given cultural or national system must be developed with reference to specifics of the system so as to test the universality of a given principle. The reduced form emphasizes breaking a system down into components in order better to understand the functioning of processes within it. An example could be the study of a specific process such as reward allocation with regard to a specific feature of the system (individualism vs. collectivism). This form assumes that individual relationships are meaningful taken out of context and that out of context relationships can be placed back into a complex cultural system without loss of meaning. In line with the gestalt form, theoretical relationships are typically arrived at deductively and are based on general principles researchers observe in various cultural systems.

The hybrid form utilizes aspects of both the gestalt and the reduced perspective. Earley and Singh (1995) identify the features of a hybrid form as follows: first, in developing research questions, researchers study gestalt systems to identify their important aspects. Second, hypothesized relationships are derived across systems and are not necessarily unique to a given system. Third, constructs and relationships are assumed to be separable from the system in which they are embedded, but the mapping back onto an existing system may not be simply linear or additive. Fourth, specific relationships are interpreted in terms of reduced parts of the system but with reference to the general system (p. 332). The hybrid form is seen to represent the most promising way forward for international management research in that it works to develop a meaningful model by understanding how and why differences exist *vis-à-vis* nation or culture rather than just identifying differences. The hybrid form of necessity encourages a wide range of research methods to be employed to arrive at a comprehensive understanding of the research topic. The authors quote research by Van Maanen and Barley (1984) into an assessment of occupational communities. This illustrated the complementary mixing of ethnographic observation, conceptualizations derived from within a given system extended onto other systems, and the development of a general theoretical model that captures general principles across many systems.

Qualitative research strategies in international HRM
Christine Mattl

Methodological and theoretical issues arising from the use of qualitative research strategies in international HRM form the basis of Chapter 15. The author used a qualitative research methodology in a research project based in Vienna which looked at the differences and similarities in co-operative patterns of work groups in different cultures and countries. Some of the critical points arising from this approach include: the researcher's culture as an anchor point; the conceptualization of culture; the language of interviewers and interviewees; approaches to analysis; the art of interpretation of cultural clues.

The contribution of this book

As we hope is clear, the book is distinctive in two significant ways. First, the chapters present new or current material, largely unavailable elsewhere, drawn from sites which have until now been largely unresearched. This means that some of the chapters are presenting unfinished work, but the findings to date are, we believe, sufficiently sound and sufficiently challenging to be worth presenting here. The contributions cover a wide range within the specific area of IHRM and are in several cases breaking new ground. Some of the chapters present new and innovative research methodologies. Second, the book is distinctive in that it has known and experienced contributors, as well perhaps one or two new names, from a dozen different European countries. The chapters present material that is either rooted in the experience of European organizations or takes an unashamedly European view of the topic. The difference between the traditional European environmentalist paradigm of research into HRM and the traditional US universalist tradition has been noted elsewhere (Brewster 1998). This book adds to the analyses of SIHRM and expatriation which are available to us from the US literature. This is certainly not to deny the validity or inspiration of the US material. Many of our contributors refer extensively to that work and all of them have been influenced by it. However, we believe that the work in this book adds to the coverage of that material by providing European examples and goes beyond it by presenting different approaches, different research methodologies and different subjects for analysis.

Acknowledgements

Half of the chapters here were originally presented as papers at a conference on the international transfer of employees run by EIASM, the European Institute for Advanced Studies in Management, at Turku University in Finland. We would like to express our appreciation of Graziella Michelante of EIASM and Satu Lähteenmäki of Turku for making that such a valuable and interesting experience. We are grateful to many of the colleagues with whom we have worked for their help in the development of our ideas. We would also like to thank the reviewers who commented on our original proposal. While we have not accepted all of their suggestions, their comments and critique were of great value in clarifying what we wanted to achieve with the book and helping us to steer our contributors.

We are sure that the amount of work on the topic being carried out in Europe, and reflected in that conference and the wider list of chapters offered here, is evidence of an increasing interest in this important area of research into international human resource management.

Finally, we would also, as ever, like to express our gratitude to Kim Fitzgerald at Cranfield School of Management. Without her, this book would still be in our minds rather than in your hands.

Hilary Harris and Chris Brewster
March 1998

Note

1 We have preferred the terminology of multinational enterprise (MNE) to the perhaps more familiar term multinational corporation (MNC) because we want to include intergovernmental, public sector and not-for-profit organizations in our analysis.

References

Adler, N.J. (1984) 'Women in international management: where are they?', *California Management Review* 26(4): 78–89.
—— (1986) *International Dimensions of Organizational Behaviour*. Boston: PWS-Kent.
—— (1987) 'Women as androgynous managers: a conceptualisation of the potential for

American women in international management', *International Journal of Intercultural Relations* 3(4): 407–36.

—— (1991) *International Dimensions of Organizational Behaviour*, Boston: PWS-Kent.

Adler, N.J. and Bartholomew, S. (1992) 'Managing globally competent people', *Academy of Management Review*, 6: 52–64.

Adler, N.J. and Ghadar, F. (1990) 'Strategic human resource management: a global perspective', in R. Pieper (ed.) *Human Resource Management in International Comparison*, Berlin/New York: De Gruyter, pp. 235–60.

Armstrong, A. (1987) 'Tanzania's expert-led planning: an assessment', *Public Administration and Development* 7: 261–71.

Banai, M. (1992) 'The ethnocentric staffing policy in multinational corporations: a self-fulfilling prophecy', *International Journal of Human Resource Management* 3: 451–72.

Bardo, J.W. and Bardo, D.J. (1980) 'Dimensions of adjustment for American settlers in Melbourne, Australia', *Multivariate Experimental Clinical Research* 5(1): 23–8.

Barham, K. and Devine, M. (1991) *The Quest for the International Manager: A Survey of Global Human Resource Strategies*, London: Economist Intelligence Unit.

Beaumont, P. (1991), 'Human resource management and international joint ventures: some evidence from Britain', *Human Resource Management Journal* 1(14): 90–101.

Beer, M., Spector, B., Lawrence, P., Mills, D. and Walton, R. (1984) *Human Resources Management*, New York: Free Press.

Bird, A. and Dunbar, R. (1991) 'The adaptation and adjustment process of managers on international assignments', Stern Working Paper, New York University.

Black, J.S. (1988) 'Work role transitions: a study of American expatriate managers in Japan', *Journal of International Business Studies* 30(2): 119–34.

—— (1990) 'The relationship of personal characteristics with the adjustment of Japanese expatriate managers', *Management International Review* 30(2): 23–51.

Black, J.S., Gregerson, H. and Mendenhall, M. (1993) *Global Assignments*, San Francisco: Jossey-Bass.

Black, J.S. and Mendenhall, M. (1989) 'A practical but theory-based framework for selecting cross-cultural training methods', *Human Resource Management* 28: 511–39.

Black, J.S. and Mendenhall, M. (1990) 'Cross-cultural training effectiveness: a review and a theoretical framework for future research', *Academy of Management Review* 15(1): 113–36.

Black, J.S., Mendenhall, M. and Oddou, G. (1991) 'Toward a comprehensive model of international adjustment: an integration of multiple theoretical perspectives', *Academy of Management Review* 16: 291–317.

Black, J.S. and Stephens, G.K. (1989), 'The influence of the spouse on American expatriate adjustment in overseas assignments', *Journal of Management* 15: 529–44.

Boxall, P. (1995) *The Challenge of Human Resource Management*, Harlow: Longman.

Boyacigiller, N. and Adler, N. (1991) 'The parochial dinosaur: organizational science in a global context', *Academy of Management Review* 16(2): 262–90.

Brewster, C. (1988) 'Managing expatriates', *International Journal of Manpower* 9(2): 17–20.

— (1991) *The Management of Expatriates*, London: Kogan Page.

— (1993) 'The paradox of expatriate adjustment: UK and Swedish expatriates in Sweden and the UK', *Human Resource Management Journal* 4(1): 49–62.

— (1998) 'Different paradigms in strategic HRM: questions raised by comparative research', in P. Wright, L. Dyer, J. Boudrear and G. Milkovitch (eds) *Research in Personnel and HRM*, Greenwich CT: JAI Press.

Brewster, C. and Pickard, J. (1994) 'Evaluating expatriate training', *International Studies of Management and Organisation* 24(3): 18–35.

Brewster, C. and Scullion, H. (1997) 'Expatriate HRM: an agenda and a review', *Human Resource Management Journal* 7(3): 32–41.

Copeland, L. and Griggs, L. (1985) *Going International*, New York: Random House.

D'Aveni, R.A. (1995) *Hyper Competitive Rivalries: Competing in Highly Dynamic Environments*, New York: Free Press.

Desatnick, R.L. and Bennett, M.L. (1978) *Human Resource Management in the Multinational Company*, New York: Nichols.

Dowling, P.J. (1986) 'Human resource issues in international business', *Syracuse Journal of International Law and Commerce* 13(2): 255–71.

Dowling, P. and Schuler, R. (1990) *International Dimensions of Human Resource Management*, Boston: PWS-Kent.

Dowling, P.J., Schuler, R.S. and Welch, D. (1994) *International Dimensions of Human Resource Management*, 2nd edn, Belmont CA: Wadsworth.

Earley, P.C. and Singh, H. (1995) 'International and intercultural management research: what's next?', *Academy of Management Journal* 38(2): 327–340.

Edstrom, A. and Galbraith, J. (1977) 'Transfer of managers as a coordination and control strategy in multinational organizations', *Administrative Science Quarterly* 22: 248–63.

Evans, P. and Doz, Y. (1992) 'Dualities: a paradigm for human resource and organisational development in complex multinationals', in V. Pucik, N.M. Tichy and C. Barnett (eds) *Globalising Management: Creating and Leading the Competitive Organisation*, New York: Wiley.

Evans, P., Doz, Y. and Laurent, A. (eds) (1989) *Human Resource Management in International Firms: Change, Globalization, Innovation*, London: Macmillan.

Evans, P. and Lorange, P. (1989) 'The two logics behind human resource management' in P. Evans, Y. Doz and A. Laurent (eds) *Human Resource Management in International Firms*, London: Macmillan.

Forster, N. (1998) 'The effects of international job moves on employees' work performance', *Journal of Occupational Psychology* (forthcoming).

Galbraith, J.R. (1987) 'Organization design', in J. Lorsch (ed.) *Handbook of Organization Behavior*, Englewood Cliffs NJ: Prentice-Hall, pp. 343–57.

Geertz, C. (1973) *The Interpretation of Cultures*, New York: Basic Books.

Ghoshal, S. (1987) 'Global strategy: an organizing framework', *Strategic Management Journal* 8: 425–40.

Gonzales, R.F. and Neghandi, A.R. (1967) *The United States Executive: His Orientation And Career Patterns*, East Lansing: MSU Graduate School Of Business Administration.

Hailey, J. (1992) 'Localisation and expatriation: the continuing role of expatriates in developing countries', EIASM Workshop, Cranfield, September.

—— (1996a) 'The expatriate myth: cross-cultural perceptions of expatriate managers', *International Executive* 38: 2.

—— (1996b) 'Breaking through the glass ceiling', *People Management*, 11 July.

Hamill, J. (1989) 'Expatriate policies in British multinationals', *Journal of General Management* 14(4): 18–33.

Harris, H. (1995) 'Women's role in international management', in A.W.K. Harzing and J. Van Ruysseveldt *International Human Resource Management*, London: Sage.

—— (1997) 'Developing a typology of international manager selection systems: effects on women's participation rates', paper presented at the EIASM Conference on International HRM, Turku, Finland, March.

Harris, H. and Brewster, C. (1998) 'The coffee machine system: how international selection really works', *International Journal of Human Resource Management* (forthcoming).

Harris, J.C. (1973) 'A science of the South Pacific: analysis of the character structure of the Peace Corps volunteer', *American Psychologist* 28: 232–47.

Harvey, M.G. (1989) 'Repatriation of corporate executives: an empirical study', *Journal of International Business Studies*, Spring: 131–44.

Harzing, A.-W.K. (1995) 'The persistent myth of high expatriate failure rates', *International Journal of Human Resource Management* 6(2): 457–75.

Hautaluoma, J.E. and Kaman, V. (1975) 'Description of Peace Corps volunteers' experience in Afghanistan', *Topics In Culture Learning* 3: 79–96.

Hawes, F. and Kealey, D. (1981) 'An empirical study of Canadian technical assistance: adaptation and effectiveness on overseas assignment', *International Journal of Intercultural Relations* 5: 239–58.

Hays, R.D. (1971) 'Ascribed behavioural determinants of success–failure among US expatriate managers', *Journal of International Business Studies* 2(1): 40–6.

—— (1974) 'Expatriate selection: insuring success and avoiding failure', *Journal Of International Business Studies* 5(1): 25–37.

Hendry, C. and Pettigrew, A. (1990) 'Human resource management: an agenda for the 1990s', *International Journal of Human Resource Management* 1(1): 17–44.

Hiltrop, J.M. and Janssens, M. (1990) 'Expatriation: challenges and recommendations', *European Management Journal*, March: 19–27.

Hofstede, G. (1980) *Culture's Consequences: International Differences in Work-Related Values*, London: Sage.

Hossain, S. and Davis, H.A. (1989) 'Some thoughts on international personnel management as an emerging field', in A. Nedd, G.R. Ferris and K.M. Rowland (eds) *Research in Personnel and Human Resources Management – International Human Resources Management*, Greenwich CT: JAI Press.

Howard, C.G. (1974) 'The returning overseas executive: cultural shock in reverse', *Human Resource Management* 13(2): 22–6.

Ivancevich, J.M. (1969) 'Selection of American managers for overseas assignments', *Personnel Journal* 18(3): 189–200.

Janssens, M. (1992) 'International job transfers: a comprehensive model of expatriate managers' cross-cultural adjustment', paper presented at EIASM Conference on Industrial Staffing and Mobility, Cranfield, September.

Jelinek, M. and Adler, N.J. (1988) 'Women: world-class managers for global competition', *Academy of Mangement Executive* 2(1): 11–19.

Johnston, J. (1991) 'An empirical study of repatriation of managers in UK multinationals', *Human Resource Management Journal* 1(4): 102–8.

Kelley, L. and Worthley, R. (1981) 'The role of culture in comparative management: a cross-cultural perspective', *Academy of Management Journal* 25: 164–73.

Kobrin, S.J. (1992) 'Multinational strategy and international human resource management policy', unpublished paper, Wharton School, University of Pennsylvania.

—— (1994) 'Is there a relationship between a geocentric mind-set and multinational strategy?', *Journal of International Business Studies*, third quarter: 493–511.

Kochan, T., Batt, R. and Dyer, L. (1992) 'International human resource studies: a framework for future research', in D. Lewin *et al.* (eds) *Research Frontiers in Industrial Relations and Human Research*, Madison WI: Industrial Relations Research Association.

Kopp, R. (1994) 'International human resource policies and practices in Japanese, European and United States multinationals,' *Human Resouce Management* 33(4): 581–99.

Lado, A. and Wilson, M. (1994) 'Human resource systems and sustained competitive advantage: a competency-based perspective', *Academy of Management Review* 19: 699–727.

Lane, H. and DiStefano, J. (1988) *International Management Behaviour*, Scarborough, Ontario: Nelson.

Lanier, A.R. (1979) 'Selecting and preparing personnel for overseas transfers', *Personnel Journal* 58(3): 106–63.

Laurent, A. (1981) 'Matrix organizations and Latin cultures', *International Studies of Management and Organization* 10(4): 101–14.

—— (1986) 'The cross-cultural puzzle of international human resource management', *Human Resource Management* 25: 91–102.

Mayrhofer, W. and Brewster, C. (1996) 'In praise of ethnocentricity: expatriate policies in European multinationals', *International Executive* 38(6): 749–78.

Mendenhall, M. and Oddou, G. (1985) 'The dimensions of expatriate acculturation: a review', *Academy of Management Review* 10: 39–47.

—— (1986) 'Acculturation profiles of expatriate managers: implications for cross-cultural training programs', *Columbia Journal of World Business* Winter: 73–79.

—— (1988), 'The overseas assignment: a practical look', *Business Horizons* September–October: 78–84.

—— (1991) *International Human Resources Management*, Boston: PWS-Kent.

Miller, E.L. (1973) 'The international selection decision: a study of some dimensions of managerial behaviour in the selection decision process', *Academy of Management Journal* 16(2): 239–52.

Nedd, A., Ferris, G.R. and Rowland, K.M. (1989) *Research in Personnel and Human Resources Management – International Human Resources Management*, Greenwich CT: JAI Press.

Ondrack, D. (1985) 'International human resource management in European and North American firms', *International Studies of Management and Organization* 15(1): 6–32.

Penrose, E.T. (1959) *The Theory of Growth of the Firm*, Oxford: Blackwell.

Perlmutter, H.V. (1969) 'The tortuous evolution of the multinational corporation', *Columbia Journal of World Business*, January–February: 9–18.

Perlmutter, H.V. and Heenan, D.A. (1974) 'How multinational should your top managers be?', *Harvard Business Review*, November–December: 121–32.

—— (1979) *Multinational Organization Development*, Reading MA: Addison-Wesley Longman.

Pickard, J. and Brewster, C. (1995) 'Repatriation: closing the circle', *International HR Journal* 4(2): 45–9.

Porter, M.E. (1986) 'Changing patterns of international competition', *California Management Review* 28(2): 9–40.

Prahalad, C.K. and Doz, Y. (1987) *The Multinational Mission: Balancing Local Demands and Global Vision*, New York: Free Press.

Pucik, V. (1984) 'White collar human resource management in large Japanese manufacturing firms', *Human Resource Management* 23: 257–76.

—— (1992) 'Globalization and human resource management', in V. Pucik *et al.*, *Globalizing Management*, New York: Wiley.

Punnett, B.J. and Ricks, D.A. (1992) *International Business*, Boston: PWS-Kent.

Robinson, R.D. (1978) *International Business Management: A Guide to Decision Making*, 2nd edn, Illinois: Dryden Hinsdale.

Ronen, S. (1989) 'Training the international assignee' in I. Goldstein (ed.) *Training and Career Development*, San Francisco: Jossey-Bass.

Rosenzweig, P.M. and Nohria, N. (1994) 'Influences on human resource management in multinational corporations', *Journal of International Business Studies*, second quarter: 229–51.

Scherm, E. (1995) *Internationales Personalmanagement*, Munchen, Wien.

Schuler, R.S. (1992) 'Strategic human resource management: linking the people with the strategic needs of the business', *Organizational Dynamics*, summer: 18–32.

Schuler, R.S., Dowling, P.J. and De Cieri, H. (1993) 'An integrative framework of strategic human resource management', *International Journal of Human Resource Management* 4: 717–64.

Schuler, R.S., Fulkerson, J.R. and Dowling, P.J. (1991) 'Strategic performance measurement and management in multinational corporations', *Human Resource Management* 30: 365–92.

Scullion, H. (1992) 'Strategic recruitment and development of the international manager: some European considerations', *Human Resource Management Journal* 3(1): 57–69.

—— (1993) 'Creating international managers: recruitment and development issues', in P. Kirkbride (ed.) *Human Resource Management in Europe*, London: Routledge.

—— (1994) 'Staffing policies and strategic control in multinationals', *International Studies of Management and Organization* 3(4): 86–104.

Shaw, Ben B., Deck, John E., Ferris, Gerald R. and Rowland, Ken M. (1990) *Research In Personnel And Human Resource Management – International Human Resources Management* Greenwich CT London: JAI Press.

Storey, J. (ed.) (1989) *New Perspectives on Human Resource Management*, Routledge: London.

—— (1995) *Human Resource Management: A Critical Text*, Routledge: London.

Sundaram, A.K. and Black, J.S. (1992) 'The environment and internal organization of multinational enterprises', *Academy of Management Review* 17: 729–57.

Suutari, V. and Brewster, C. (1998) 'The adaptation of expatriates in Europe: evidence from Finnish companies', *Personnel Review* (forthcoming).

Taylor, S., Beechler, S. and Napier, N. (1996) 'Towards an integrative model of strategic international human resource management', *Academy of Management Review* 21(4): 959–85.

Torbiörn, I. (1982) *Living Abroad: Personal Adjustment and Personnel Policy in the Overseas Setting*, New York: Wiley.

—— (1985) 'The structure of managerial roles in cross-cultural settings', *International Studies of Management and Organization* 15(1): 52–74.

Tung, R.L. (1981) 'Selection and training of personnel for overseas assignments', *Columbia Journal of World Business* 16(1): 68–78.

—— (1982) 'Selection and training procedures of US, European and Japanese multinationals', *California Management Review* 25(1): 57–71.

—— (1984) 'Strategic management of human resources in the multinational enterprise', *Human Resource Management* 23(2): 129–43.

—— (1987) 'Expatriate assignments: enhancing success and minimizing failure', *Academy of Management Executive* 1(2): 117–25.

Van Maanen, J. and Barley, S. (1984) 'Occupational communities: culture and control in organizations', in B. Staw and L. Cummings (eds) *Research in Organizational Behavior*, vol. 6, Greenwich CT: JAI Press.

Weber, Wolfgang and Festing, Marion (1991) 'Entwicklungstendenzen Im Internationalen Personalmanagement: Personalfuhrung Im Wandel', *Gablers Magazin* 2 S: 10–16.

Young, S. and Hamill, J. (1992) *Europe and the Multinationals*, Aldershot: Gower.

Zeira, Y. and Banai, M. (1984) 'Selection of expatriate managers in MNEs: the host environment point of view', *International Studies of Management and Organization* 15(1): 33–51.

—— (1985) 'Present and desired methods of selecting expatriate managers for international assignments', *Personnel Review* 13(3): 29–35.

Part I

Relation between international business strategy and SIHRM

2   The added value of the HR department

Dirk Buyens and Ans de Vos

Introduction

This chapter explores the added value of human resource management (HRM) in general and more specifically in decision-making processes. The new competitive reality facing organizations calls on new and different capabilities. How can one create an organization which adds value to its clients, investors and employees? And how can HRM help to realize this? What is the role of HRM in the organization of tomorrow? When the importance of flexibility and productivity is emphasized, how can HRM add significant value to the strategic decision-making process? Is there a role for HRM at this strategic level? Or is its added value rather situated at the level of the implementation of these strategic decisions?

Over the last ten to twenty years, a decrease in administrative practices of the HR department and a growing focus on specialist services such as staffing, rewarding, planning, training and labour relations may be observed. As the economic environment becomes more complex and the organization's capacity to change has become a crucial issue, there is a growing accent on the strategic role of HRM in helping the organization to survive (see e.g. Brown 1991; Thornburg 1993; Mabey and Salaman 1995; Paauwe 1995; Prahalad 1995; Spencer 1995; Yeung *et al.* 1995; Scherm 1996; Ulrich 1997).

This strategic objective of HR has been much debated and discussed: 'HR has to become a strategic partner in the organization'; 'there is a meaningful role for HR at the top table'. But where do these propositions fit into the reality of a company's policies? What does this 'strategic mission' of HR mean in the Belgian reality? In many companies, personnel administration and sometimes even HR services are being outsourced to specialist organizations. But does this tendency imply that the released capacity of the HR department is filled by activities at the strategic level or does it simply mean that the department is shrinking?

Literature review

Spencer (1995) distinguishes three main domains in which HRM may have an added value for the organization. He argues that the importance of this added value differs between these three domains (Figure 2.1). According to Spencer, HR's main added value is situated in the strategic domain and second in HR services. Administration is the HR domain with the least added value. However, the costs spent on these three domains, that is to say their importance in terms of expenditure of time and money, are often reversed. In order to increase its added value, HR has to refocus its activities by outsourcing costly but less value-creating activities (Figure 2.2).

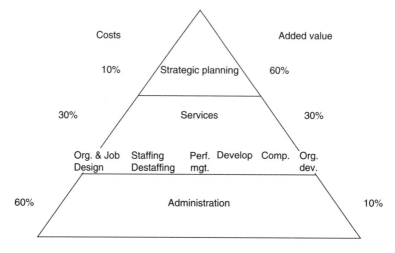

Figure 2.1 Costs and added value of three activity domains of HRM
Source: Spencer 1995

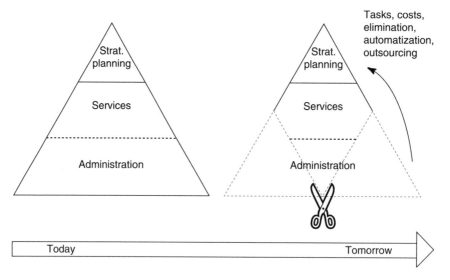

Figure 2.2 Refocusing HR activities
Source: Spencer 1995

Spencer (1995) clearly favours the strategic role of HRM in the organization. But this does not mean that other HR domains have to be neglected; for example, the outsourcing of administration should not mean a neglect of this area. Personnel administration remains an important area of responsibility for HRM. Furthermore, the facts and figures provided by personnel administration form an important base from which to develop HR policies in other domains and to evaluate their effectiveness.

Another model for the added value of HRM is provided by Ulrich (1997), Ulrich *et al.* (1995) and Yeung *et al.* (1995). They distinguish four key roles for the HR professional. HR has to deliver results in each of these domains, since the four of them are equally important. This model is presented in Figure 2.3. The two axes represent the focus and the activities of the HR professional. The focus may be short term or long term: HR professionals have to be operational and strategic. Their activities vary from managing processes (HR tools and systems) to managing people. This second axis constitutes an important difference to Spencer's model, where the focus is almost exclusively on HR processes. The combination of the two axes results in four HR roles.

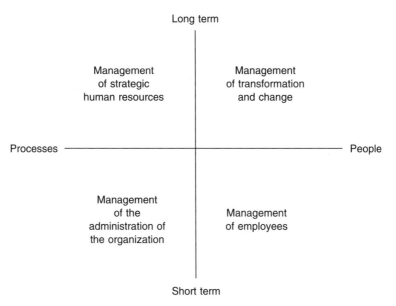

Figure 2.3 HR roles
Source: Ulrich 1997

1   *Management of strategic human resources*: this role is focused on the synchronization of HR strategies and practices to the business strategy. In this role, the HR professional is a strategic partner who helps to realize the business strategy by translating it into concrete HR practices.
2   *Management of transformation and change*: a second key role in which HR professionals can deliver value to the organization. HR professionals have

to assist in the identification and implementation of change processes, being catalysts as well as guards of cultural transformations.

3   *Management of the employees*: this role refers to the daily problems, expectations and needs of employees. HR professionals have to stimulate the employees' contribution to the success of the company by understanding their specific needs and ensuring that these are met.

4   *Management of the administration of the organization*: the HR professional has to ensure that the administrative processes concerning hiring, rewarding, training, evaluation, promotion, etc. are designed and delivered efficiently and correctly. Ulrich (1997) accentuates the importance of this role. Although many organizations and HR professionals tend to underestimate it due to a growing focus on strategic HRM, the successful deliverance of administrative aspects of HR will prove to be an added value for the organization.

Shared responsibility for each role

Ulrich (1997) stresses that these multiple HR roles are not the responsibility of the department alone. HR professionals have the responsibility and accountability to ensure that the deliverables of each role are fulfilled. Nevertheless, accomplishing the goals and designing the process for achieving them are different issues. HR professionals do not have to fulfil all four roles themselves. Depending on the processes designed to reach the goal, the work may be shared by line managers, outside consultants, employees, technology, or other delivery mechanisms for HR activities. The allocation of HR activities to different parties will vary depending on the organization. An example of shared HR responsibilities is represented by Figure 2.4.

When discussing the added value of the HR department, the areas in which HRM can deliver value is not the only relevant issue. In today's organization, where flexiblilty, creativity and innovation are key issues, the process of decision-making, discussion and communication throughout the whole organization becomes more important (see, for example, Cyert and Williams 1993; Jacobs 1994; Noorderhaven 1995). By being involved in these strategic processes, the HR department can have an impact on the decision-making process. This goes further than an involvement in the implementation of a decision made by others (situated within one of the areas described by Ulrich 1997; see, for example, Laabs 1992; Caudron 1994; Anthony 1995). The method and stage at which the HR department is involved in strategic decision processes can therefore be considered as a second relevant criterion in the discussion about added value of the HR department.

Ulrich (1997) does not mention this involvement of HRM in the organization's strategic decision-making processes. In his model, a strategic HR professional is someone who is involved in the strategic decision-making or someone who bases HR policies or HR activities on the strategy of the organization. Both forms of strategic HRM do not represent the same degree of involvement in the

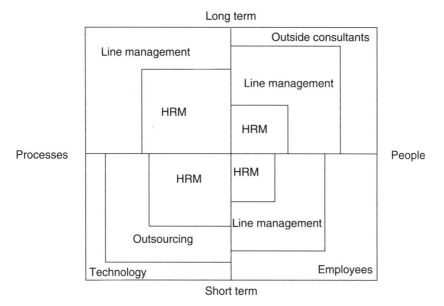

Figure 2.4 Shared responsibility for HR roles
Source: Ulrich 1997

strategic decision-making process. The earlier HR professionals are involved in this process, the greater their impact on the decisions. The stage of involvement is an important indicator of the integration and appreciation of HRM within the organization. However, this is often not a feature of strategic HRM models.

The same reasoning is true for the other HR roles, for example, HR as a change agent: what is the impact of HR professionals on the change process? Are they involved from the very first moment or is the role restricted to the implementation of decisions concerning change? Involvement is possible at different levels and stages in the organization's policy, although this does not mean that the added value of HRM at each level or stage is automatically the same.

These reflections have led to the development of our own model, which profiles the added value of HRM as a function of its involvement in the decision-making process and is inspired by the model of Cooke and Slack (1991). These authors developed a decision-making model consisting of seven phases, the essence of which is represented by Figure 2.5.

HRM can be involved at each of the seven stages distinguished by Cooke and Slack (1991). Our own model summarizes these stages in four moments of involvement in a decision process, varying from 'very early' to 'very late' (Figure 2.6).

Assuming that the decision process starts with the observation of a discrepancy between the actual situation and the desired situation, HRM is *value-driven* if the HR professional is involved at this first stage. HRM as an *intelligent toolbox* refers to the HR professional who shapes the change process by creating instruments

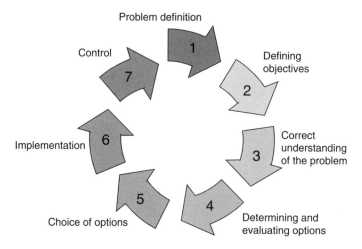

Figure 2.5 Decision-making model
Source: Cooke and Slack 1991

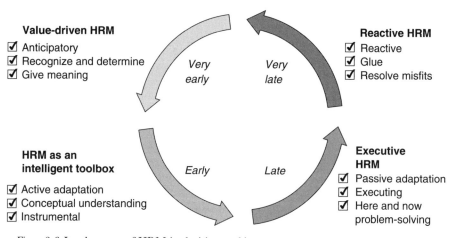

Figure 2.6 Involvement of HRM in decision-making processes

and supporting the line managers responsible for the implementation. If the involvement in a decision is restricted to the implementation of HR activities without any active input, it is called *executive HRM. Reactive HRM* implies that the HR professional is consulted if things go wrong or do not work out as expected.

If the HR professional wants to add value to the decision-making process, an anticipative, value-driven involvement is important but not sufficient. An active presence during the whole change process is necessary, whereby each role demands specific aptitudes which allow the HR professional to recognize and fill in the opportunities of each position.

Method

Research was carried out to assess the added value of the HR function in Belgium and to test the applicability of the model developed regarding the involvement of HRM in strategic decision-making processes.

Chief executive officers (CEOs), HR directors and line managers were all interviewed in order to obtain a complete picture of the added value of HR in a specific organization. The perception and attitudes of all three groups towards HR's roles, responsibilities and deliverables were seen to be essential in ensuring that a true picture of the extent of HRM's added value was revealed.

The participating organizations were selected based on the following parameters in order to obtain a varied sample, representative of the variety of organizations in the Belgian context:

1 Sector in which the company has its main activities.
2 Nationality of the mother company.
3 Geographical location.
4 Number of employees.
5 Life cycle of the company.
6 Technology.
7 Experience/age of the persons interviewed.

The purpose of the study was to picture the visions of CEOs, HR directors and line managers across organizations, not to make an in-company comparative study. Therefore, these three groups were not systematically interviewed within the same organization. A second reason for this option was that we wanted to ensure a maximum of openness by the participants. This openness might be diminished if participants expected their answers to be compared with those of other (superior) persons in the organization.

In total, 100 HR directors, 50 CEOs and 150 line managers were interviewed. All CEOs were interviewed individually. Fifty per cent of the HR directors were interviewed individually, while the other half were invited to forums to discuss the questions in small groups. Line managers were seen in groups of twenty and were asked to describe the added value of HRM in their organization.

The interviews and forums were structured using a questionnaire containing a number of open questions on the added value of HRM and the role of HRM in strategic decision-making.

The HR directors were asked to answer the following questions:

• What is the added value of HRM in your company today?
• Tomorrow?
• What is the involvement of HRM in decision-making processes?

In addition to these questions, some models were shown and discussed with the participant. For the CEOs the main questions were the same as for the HR directors, but some additional questions were asked concerning the importance of the HR department relative to others. Line managers only answered the broad question: What is the added value of HRM in your company?

All interviews with CEOs and HR directors were recorded and transcribed. The responses from the line managers were also transcribed. A content analysis was carried out on all responses. For each question, the responses of the participants were listed together and grouped in function of their content. With reference to the added value of HRM, responses were categorized along the four HR domains distinguished by Ulrich (1997). The responses concerning the involvement of HRM in decision-making processes were structured against our own model. In the analysis, a distinction was made between the three interviewed samples: HR directors, CEOs and line managers. Their responses were analysed separately and compared afterwards.

Results and discussion

The aim of our empirical research was to map the added value of the HR function in Belgium. Underlying the structured interviews with HR directors and CEOs were the models discussed earlier.

Added value of HRM

The questions in the first part of the interview concerned the added value of HRM. The objective was to examine whether the four areas distinguished by Ulrich (1997) could be found in a sample of companies located in Belgium.

The analysis of the answers of the participating HR managers, CEOs and line managers supported Ulrich's model. Their answers could be structured along the four HR domains distinguished by Ulrich.

HRM as a strategist

Most of the HR directors and CEOs interviewed see the translation of the business strategy into HR practices as an important role for HRM. HRM has to develop an HR strategy based on the business strategy. It has to realize this business strategy by developing and implementing an adequate people management policy. This role was less stressed by the line managers in our sample.

HRM as change agent

HRM has to provide the balance between the necessity of change processes and the capacity of the employees. A professional management of change processes may increase its effectiveness. HRM also has to focus on the management of human potential from a long-term perspective. Change management is commonly recognized as an important issue. Participants acknowledged the importance of a well-managed change process in which HRM would play a significant role.

HRM as employee champion

Most of the interviewed participants, especially the CEOs and HR directors, accentuated the importance of the human dimension of HRM. HRM can realize an important added value by stressing the human face of the organization. The importance of the human capital gets recognized more and more and HRM plays an important role in its development. As such, HRM must act as the heartbeat of the organization.

HRM as personnel administrator

Although many of the HR practices referred to in this area tend to be outsourced in many of the organizations in our sample, HRM still has an important responsibility here. For example, since personnel costs are a substantial part of the global costs, it is very important to manage them carefully. Although technical aspects can be outsourced, the role of HRM is to manage the personnel administration and to develop an HR strategy not only based on the business strategy, but also on the facts and figures provided in this area. Second, an important added value of HRM is situated in its knowledge of the law concerning social–juridical affairs. Many line managers situated HR's main added value in this domain, referring to specialist services such as selection and training.

We may conclude that, according to the participants in our sample, HRM can deliver value within different areas, ranging from administration to strategy formulation. Line managers saw the added value of HRM to be mainly within the provision of HR services, while HR managers as well as CEOs stressed the importance of strategic HRM. The three groups indicated that the added value of HRM is not restricted to the strategic domain, but there are several other areas in which this added value can be and has to be delivered. This confirms the multiple-role model designed by Ulrich (1997).

Involvement of HRM in strategic decision-making

Ulrich's model does not provide any information about the degree of involvement of HRM in strategic decision-making processes within the organization. This aspect was investigated by asking the participants to position HRM on our model. Their responses allowed us further to specify the four positions.

Value-driven HRM

An early involvement of the HR professional will enable them to utilize their profound knowledge of human resources and gives them the recognition necessary to influence the organization's policies from an HR perspective. The added value of HR professionals are formally recognized by their membership of the executive committee. Although this is neither a necessary nor sufficient condition, many HR directors stressed their informal and amicable relationship with other directors as the main reason for their early involvement, while other HR directors were members of the executive committee without having any substantial influence on the decisions taken by it. This early involvement can create an added value in three main domains by: influencing the organization's strategic decisions; indicating opportunities and initiating decision processes; safeguarding the basic values of the company, which are the cement of the organization.

HRM as an intelligent toolbox

The HR professional is involved early in a decision, though not from the first conceptualization. Still, HRM is actively involved since the information about a decision is received quite early. HRM's role consists in preparing employees for changes by creating an appropriate culture. Another role of HR at this stage includes the concrete development of tools necessary for implementing decisions. Although HR professionals are not the architect of decisions, their role in the concrete development of decisions is considered indispensable. As such, HRM becomes the architect of a workable translation of the decision while its execution becomes the responsibility of the line managers.

Executive HRM

The HR professional is not always actively involved at the first stages. It often happens that the HR role starts when the elaboration of a decision has already been carried out. The HR professional has to communicate decisions taken by the general management and to inform the employees about them. Labour relations are an important aspect here. An important task at this stage is the deliverance of diverse HR services, such as selection and training, necessary for the successful implementation of a decision.

Reactive HRM

It often happens that HRM has to intervene when the consequences of a decision do not turn out as expected. The HR professional has to pick up the pieces in order to reclaim the situation. Although often, seemingly, a thankless task and without much involvement, this role is as important as the others. Reacting late is better than reacting too late. HRM can create added value by reacting very fast and immediately paying attention to things when they appear to be going wrong. In this way, HRM creates credibility at the administrative level, which may help it to gain greater influence in strategic decisions.

The CEOs in our sample stressed the importance of an early involvement of HRM. Especially in organizations where employees are the only resources, the early impact of HRM is considered important by top management. But the representation of the function at the first stage is not always fulfilled by the HR director. Several CEOs said that they took the responsibility for HRM at the first stage themselves.

Although the majority of the HR directors considered a very early involvement of HRM to be of primary importance, they often emphasized that the main part of their daily activities was situated at the latter stages.

The finding that HRM is not always involved from the first moment is confirmed by the data of a quantitative research conducted earlier into the HR function in Belgium (Buyens *et al.* 1996). This study is part of a research project on HR policies and practices in Europe. The results indicate that 52 per cent of the 400 participating HR directors were involved in strategy formulation, whereas 24 per cent had an advising role and 18 per cent were involved during the implementation stage. A small minority (6 per cent) were not involved at all in strategy formulation or implementation. Another relevant question in this research concerned the membership of the HR director of the executive committee. Only 52 per cent of the participating HR directors indicated that they were members of executive committees.

The involvement of HRM at the different stages is summarized by Figure 2.7. As already emphasized, there is only an integrated HRM if the HR professional is involved at each of the four stages. There has to be a continuous involvement. As one HR manager stated: 'We have to be involved at an early stage, but in the meantime, we have to be present on the floor, to detect what is going on there and to react quickly when something goes wrong.'

Involvement at a value-driven level only creates value if HRM is also involved during the stages of elaboration, implementation and follow-up. When the operational aspect is neglected, the chance of a successful realization of the decision in practice is diminished. But HRM can only gain a meaningful position in the whole organization if it is also recognized as a valued partner at a higher position. At this stage, its responsibility reaches further than the communication

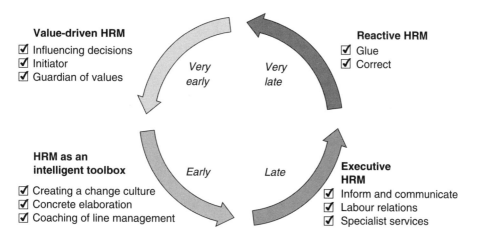

Figure 2.7 The added value of HRM at different moments of involvement in decision-making processes

of decisions and the prevention of fire. The successful fulfilment of these activities serves as an argument for an earlier involvement: 'We are very good at managing fires. But when they only know us that way, they will only use us that way. We have to become proactive in our attitude. We also have to realize fire prevention.' We also found this emphasis on a continuous involvement in the interviews with CEOs.

Clearly there are some mediating factors which determine at which stage the HR professional will be involved in the decision process. First, the subject of the decision proved to be an important mediator. The less related a decision is to HR issues, the less the HR professional will be involved at the first stage. Technical decisions often seem to be taken without involvement of the HR professional, although they can have severe implications for the employees. Besides the nature of the decision, much will depend on the HR professional: credibility is an important indicator of involvement in the organization. This credibility is not only related to the experience and the professional competence of the HR professional, but also to personality and social skills. Finally, the specific relationship of the HR professional with the management team at different levels in the organization will influence actual involvement.

An integrated model for the added value of HRM

One important conclusion of our study is that HRM should care for the employee as a human being. The added value of HRM is not only situated at the strategic level, in service delivery or administration, but also in the concern for employees and their satisfaction. Both HR directors and CEOs recognize the importance of the human resources for the effective functioning of the organization. We also emphasized that the role of HRM in the organization as such is no indicator of its involvement in the decision-making process. By making the link between the four domains in which HRM may deliver value and the four positions of HRM in decision processes, we developed an integrated model for the added value of HRM. This model is represented in Figure 2.8.

The employee is depicted in the core of the circle, as a pivot on which HR policies have to be based. In the complex organization of today, the attention to the employee as a human threatens to be lost, even in HRM. In aspiring towards recognition as a strategic partner, HRM must not forget its primary reason for existence: human resource management. The four domains in which HRM can offer added value for the organization are centred around this core. An integrated HRM which delivers value to the organization implies that this added value is created in each of the domains. In order to have an impact on the decision processes, the HR professional has to be involved in decisions as early as possible. We can distinguish four positions depending on the moment at which HRM is involved with the four HR areas. The exterior circle is not static, but moves around the four HR roles, indicating that each HR role can be more or less involved in a decision process.

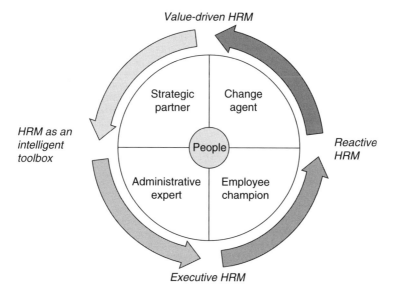

Figure 2.8 An integrated model for the added value of HRM

HR professionals cannot restrict themselves to one position. It is important to be flexible in terms of interventions in a decision process. Sticking to one position risks the danger of losing contact with the policies upstream and with the reality downstream. As such, the HR professionals work away happily on an island, but the added value created in this way threatens to decrease if there is no link with the whole. This is true for all four positions.

Excesses

A one-side-oriented HRM threatens to be stereotyped in the position in which it is comfortable to work, as became clear when analysing the negative examples of HR activities lacking added value. The excesses resulting from this situation are shown in Figure 2.9 on page 44.

The dreamer

The HR professional who works only at a value-driven level risks losing touch with reality. As a consequence, HR decisions are taken without acknowledgement of real needs. The danger exists that desire for power becomes a goal in itself, with 'being part of top management' as the final target. Such HR professionals will lose their credibility in the long term: at the base because the decisions in which they are involved do not correspond with the expectations towards an effective HRM; at the top because their input will prove not to be founded on real insight and daily HR practices. The facts and figures necessary for sound strategic decision-making are missing.

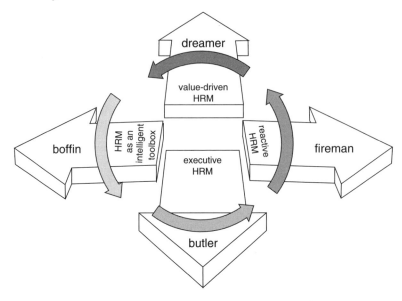

Figure 2.9 Excesses as a consequence of a one-sided involvement of HRM

The boffin

HRM as an intelligent toolbox implies the danger that HR tools and concepts are formulated missing a link with daily HR needs or HR policies at a higher level. The development of concepts becomes an end in itself. Such HR professionals are so busy modelling reality that they forget the reality which goes beyond the model. This leads to solutions for non-existent problems and the development of systems and tools in which the anticipatory element and attention to workability in practice are missing. HR professionals who are valued for their competence in developing HR tools will lose credibility when they do not go beyond this safe domain.

The butler

The HR professionals who only carry out tasks, risk being forgotten in HR decisions and lose the recognition to deliver a significant input earlier in the decision process. An executive HRM is important, but those who completely neglect the more conceptual work will evolve into a purely supporting function. Such HR professionals will be butlers who serve on demand, following orders without having any input themselves. They will be recognized for their special-ism, but when their activities are restricted to implementation they will be stereotyped and forgotten when decisions are taken upstream.

The fireman

The HR professionals who wait in their offices until a fire has to be extinguished without inplementing fire prevention will be neglected in the strategic management of the organization and will lose any impact on the decision process. HRM becomes purely reactive, a function without meaningful content that exists only to react in emergency situations. When HR professionals restrict themselves to this position, their actions will involve only the treatment of symptoms without attacking the underlying causes. Therefore they will lack recognition. The 'acting on demand' of the previous phase becomes here a 'reacting on command'. HRM becomes a last treatment, used in the case of dysfunctioning elements.

Conclusion

As the results of our research indicate, the added value of the HR function cannot be described by simply classifying it in one distinct category. At least two criteria are involved here: the domain in which the HR function can add value and the involvement of HRM in decision processes. A differentiated vision concerning HRM is required.

One of the first conclusions made during our interviews concerned the enormous diversity in HR policies and HR activities within the participating organizations, and correlating with this the different accents concerning the added value of HRM and its involvement in decision-making processes. The added value of HRM clearly is not and cannot be restricted to one domain.

The CEOs and HR directors in our sample stressed the importance of integrated involvement of HRM through the whole decision-making process. The main challenge is to add value during the four stages. Strategic HRM means more than involvement at the first stage of a decision-making process. It also involves the development and implementation of HR tools. Even reactive HRM can be strategic. In order to realize an integrated strategic HRM, the HR professional needs sound business knowledge, together with social skills and professional expertise.

We may conclude that the added value of HRM in a specific organization will depend not only on the roles it fulfils, but also on the way in which it is involved in the whole organization. The HR roles and positions vary among organizations. There is no such thing as 'the one and only' added value of HRM.

Few HR departments have reached a full integration of HRM. The research design used to illustrate the HR function allows some insight into the complex organizational reality in which HR has to deliver value. Although in most cases the other actors recognize the relevance and importance of good management of human resources within an organization, HRM often remains a subject that misses a direct link with profit and is therefore not judged to be necessary to many of the strategic decisions made at the top. This is not only a matter of culture. HRM often puts itself in this position by leaving unused the objective information ('facts and figures') it has at its disposal. In order to be recognized throughout the organization, HRM first has to recognize the added value of its activities in terms of deliverables to the organization's profit.

The developed model is a tool which allows the mapping of the HR function in a real organization. Once this picture has become clear, it can be used in the next stage as an instrument to indicate result domains for HRM and to evaluate its functioning or to screen future employees of the department.

As indicated already, the added value of the HR function is relative, varying between companies. A next step in the research should be examination of the variables which come into place in order to predict the added value and involvement of HRM in a specific organization: which circumstances existed in relation to a highly involved versus an almost neglected HRM? When these variables are detected, the research model can be further developed and used in practice not only to evaluate the HR function, but also to change it in the desired direction by working on such variables.

References

Anthony, R.J. (1995) 'Human resources in the front', *HR Focus*: 6–7.

Brown, D. (1991) 'HR is the key to survival in the 90s', *Personnel*: 68: 5–6.

Buyens, D., Vandenbossche, T. and Van Schelstraete, S. (1996) Internationaal Strategisch Human Resource Management (ed.) *Personeelsbeleid in België*, Dendermonde: Jaarboek HR Magazine, Nieuwe Media Groep.

Caudron, S. (1994) 'HR leaders brainstorm', *Personnel Journal*: 173(7): 54–61.

Cooke, S. and Slack, N. (1991) *Making Management Decisions*, 2nd edn, New York: Prentice Hall.

Cooper, Gary L. and Rousseau, Denise (1996) *Trends in Organizational Behavior*, Chichester: Wiley.

Cyert, R.M. and Williams, J.R. (1993) 'Organizations, decision making and strategy', *Strategic Management Journal*, special issue.

Jacobs, R.W. (1994) *Real Time Strategic Change*, San Francisco: Berrett-Koehler.

Laabs, J.J. (1992) 'HR adds value to board of directors', *Personnel Journal*: 71(11): 12–15.

Mabey, Christoper and Graeme Salaman (1995) *Strategic Human Resource Management*, Oxford: Blackwell.

Noorderhaven, N.G. (1995) *Strategic Decision Making*, Wokingham: Addison-Wesley.

Paauwe, J. (1995) 'Kernvraagstukken op het gebied van strategisch HRM in Nederland', *M&O*: 369–89.

Prahalad, C.K. (1995) 'How HR can help to win the future', *People Management*: 1(1): 34–36.

Scherm, E. (1996) 'Heeft de personeelsafdeling nog toekomst?', *HRM-select*: 5–13.

Spencer, Lyle M. (1995) *Reengineering Human Resources: Achieving Radical Increases in Service Quality with 50% to 90% Cost and Head Count Reductions*, New York: Wiley.

Thornburg, L. (1992) 'HR leaders tell how they make their companies better', *HRMagazine* 38: 49–57.

Ulrich, D. (1997) *Human Resource Champions, The Next Agenda for Adding Value to HR-Practices*, Boston: Harvard Business School Press.

Ulrich, D., Brockbank, W., Yeung, A.K. and Lake, D.G. (1995) 'Human resource competencies: an empirical assessment', *Human Resource Management* 34(4): 473–95.

Warnick, S. (1993) 'HR doesn't have to be a paradox', *Personnel Journal* 72: 30–38.

Yeung, A., Brockbank, W. and Ulrich, D. (1995) 'Lower cost, higher value: human resource function in transformation', *Human Resource Planning* 17: 1–16.

3 International HRM in medium-sized MNEs

Evidence from Ireland

Hugh Scullion

Introduction

There is a growing literature on the field of international HRM (IHRM). However, much of it has been devoted to large multinational or transnational companies and in particular to the study of expatriates in these organizations. Yet many organizations are now faced with the prospect of becoming international if they are to survive in an increasingly global economy (Benito and Welch 1994) The evidence suggests that the majority will be of small or medium size and the growing research emphasis on the internationalization strategies of small and medium-sized enterprises (SMEs) reflects the growing importance of SMEs in most economies (Mulhern 1995). However, relatively little attention has been given to the HRM issues arising from the internationalization of such organizations, despite the growing evidence that smaller firms appear to experience significant problems and high failure rates in the process of internationalization (Loustarinen *et al.* 1994).

The aim of this chapter is to explore the field of IHRM in the context of the internationalization of Irish business. The chapter begins with a brief discussion of the nature of IHRM and considers why it is important to research this area in an Irish context. The internationalization strategies of Irish firms are examined and finally the chapter considers some empirical evidence on the HR practices of international Irish firms. IHRM may be defined as: 'the human resource management issues and problems arising from the internationalization of business, and the human resource management strategies, policies and practices which firms pursue in response to the internationalization process' (Scullion 1995: 352).

Reviews of the literature have suggested that international HRM is more complex than domestic HRM and that the complexities of operating in different countries and employing different national categories of workers are the main factors that differentiate domestic and international HRM, rather than any major differences between the HRM functions performed (Dowling *et al.* 1994).

Brewster and Scullion (1997) identify a number of reasons why an understanding of IHRM is of growing importance at the present time:

1   Recent years have seen rapid increases in global activity and global

competition, which has resulted in an increase in the number and influence of multinational enterprises (MNEs) (Young and Hamill 1992).

2   The effective management of human resources internationally is increasingly being acknowledged as a key source of competitive advantage in international business (Edwards *et al.* 1996).

3   It is increasingly recognized that the effective implementation of international business strategies will depend on the ability of companies to develop appropriate human resource strategies for the recruitment and development of their 'international managers' (Bartlett and Ghoshal 1992).

4   There is growing evidence to suggest that the human and financial costs of failure overseas are more severe than in domestic business and that many companies underestimate the complex nature of the HRM problems involved in international operations (Tung 1984).

5   The advent of the Single European Market and the rapid growth of Irish direct investment abroad mean that IHRM issues are increasingly important concerns for a far wider range of companies than the traditional giant MNEs, particularly among the growing number of smaller and medium-sized enterprises (SMEs) that have significantly internationalized their operations in recent years (Scullion 1995).

International HRM in an Irish context is particularly pertinent for several reasons. First, recent research suggests the emergence of a growing number of Irish-owned MNEs (Donnelly 1996). Given the current economic climate of steady growth, low inflation and interest rates, Irish companies are reported to be increasingly internationalizing, primarily through overseas acquisitional activities (Chapman Flood 1993). Second, Irish MNEs, while large in national terms, are small to medium sized when compared with other European and North American MNEs. Despite evidence suggesting that SMEs are becoming increasingly 'internationalized' (UN 1993), the internationalization of small to medium-sized MNEs is still a relatively underdeveloped research area. Indeed, research suggests that SMEs expanding overseas often face such HRM constraints as a lack of managerial capability and limited foreign experience (UN 1993). Third, many Irish MNEs are relatively new to the international scene. With the exception of a few companies, such as CRH and Smurfit, that pioneered the route to internationalization in the 1970s, the majority of Irish MNEs have only begun to diversify into overseas markets since the early 1980s. As Forster and Johnsen (1996) highlight, a further under-researched area is the management of expatriates within newly internationalized companies. Finally, much of the previous research to date has focused on large MNEs from large advanced economies, while little is known of small to medium-sized MNEs from small and/or 'late industrialized' economies such as Ireland.

Within Irish-based research there is virtually no previous research on the IHRM policies and practices of indigenous companies. Indeed, the majority of Irish-based research hitherto has either centred on the role of HRM in foreign-owned MNEs (Gunnigle 1992; Monks 1996) or, alternatively, on issues of convergence between the HRM practices of foreign and domestic companies (Kelly and Brannick 1985; Enderwick 1986; Roche and Geary 1997). Moreover, Dineen and Garavan (1994) argue that the growth in HRM research is largely the result of a growth in the number of foreign-owned MNEs within the Irish economy. In an attempt to redress this imbalance, this chapter will focus on outlining some empirical findings concerning the IHRM practices of Irish companies. First, we seek to locate IHRM in an Irish context by considering the internationalization strategies of Irish businesses.

International HRM in an Irish context

As the internationalization of Irish business gains momentum, IHRM has become firmly fixed on the agendas of a growing number of Irish companies. Evidence suggests that the number of Irish-owned enterprises investing overseas has been increasing, particularly since the mid-1980s (OECD 1994). Research conducted by the United Nations in the early 1990s identified seventeen indigenous small to medium-sized transnationals[1] within Ireland (UN 1993). More recent research into the approach of Irish companies to industrial relations identified a conservative estimate of twenty indigenous MNEs (Donnelly 1996).[2] As Table 3.1 highlights, Irish MNEs are predominantly located within what Lynch and Roche (1995) define as 'traditional' and 'resource-based' sectors of Irish industry. The sectoral location of these Irish MNEs would, at first sight, seem to support O'Malley's (1985) 'late industrialization' thesis. The basic premise of this thesis is that, as a result of Ireland's late industrialization, 'barriers to entry for latecomers' have constrained and shaped the internationalization of indigenous industry. O'Malley (1992: 36) argues that barriers to entry have resulted in the 'clustering' of Irish international companies either into sectors involving the processing of local produce or sectors with 'non-traded activities' which afforded a 'significant degree of natural protection against distant competitors'. Large in domestic terms but small in international terms, Irish international firms are either 'the survivors of many years of intensifying competition or else they are relatively young companies which were established in a competitive environment' (O'Malley 1992: 45). (See Table 3.1.)

Internationalization strategies of Irish companies

While the number of Irish companies that are internationalizing are reported to be increasing, evidence suggests that the pace of overseas business expansion is also accelerating. As Figure 3.1 indicates, the acquisitional activity levels of Irish companies have been rapidly increasing since 1990, reaching record levels in 1996. Most of the acquisitional activities were found to be located in overseas markets. In 1996, 60 per cent of completed acquisitions by Irish companies were outside domestic markets, of which the UK accounted for the largest proportion, followed by the US and other European countries (Chapman Flood 1996). The recent acceleration in internationalization is widely attributed to an increase

Table 3.1 Irish-owned MNEs by sector, size and European sites, 1994

Name	Main activity	Group employment	Location of other European sites
CRH plc	Building materials	14,000	UK, Belgium, Germany, Netherlands, Spain
Kerry Group	Dairy and food	9,500	UK, Germany
Avonomore Foods plc	Dairy and food	6,348	UK, Belgium, Germany, Hungary
Waterford Foods plc	Dairy and food	3,224	UK
Golden Vale	Dairy and food	2,250	UK, Denmark, France, Netherlands
Greencore plc	Dairy and food	1,840	UK, Belgium
Glen Dimplex plc	Electrical appliances	4,800	UK, Belgium, Germany
Fyffes plc	Exporter of food produce	3,000	UK, France, Germany, Netherlands, Spain, Eastern Europe
An Bord Bainne	Exporter of dairy produce	2,300	UK, Belgium
Allied Irish Banks plc	Financial services	16,000	UK
Bank of Ireland plc	Financial services	12,000	UK, Eastern Europe
Waterford Wedgewood	Household goods	9,000	UK, France, Eastern Europe
Fitzwilton plc	Industrial holding	5,000	UK
James Crean plc	Industrial	2,185	UK, Netherlands

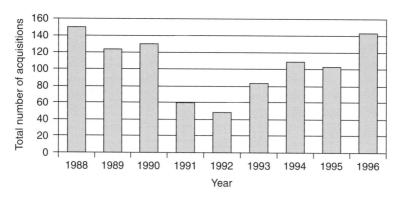

Figure 3.1 Acquisitional activity of Irish companies, 1988–96
Source: Chapman Flood 1996

in the purchasing power of indigenous companies, the ready availability of significant venture capital and the ability to extract a quick return on acquisitions (*Sunday Business Post* 1996).

Acquisitional growth strategies are the most prevalent means of internationalization among Irish companies. After organic growth strategies, mergers and joint ventures are the least popular methods of internationalization (Chapman Flood

1993; Donnelly 1996). As O'Malley (1992: 38) notes, Irish companies have predominantly 'engaged successfully in international markets in the form of taking over foreign firms and becoming multinational companies'. Irish companies, in the main, tend to pursue small to medium-sized overseas acquisitions, many of them 'bolt-ons' to existing operations. The rationale suggested includes ease of integration, the minimization of risk, the consolidation of market share and a rapid return on investments (*Sunday Business Post* 1996). As the chief executive of a large manufacturing Irish MNE explained: 'by and large "greenfielding" takes a lot longer in order to get your money back. We found it much easier, much quicker to actually go off and buy an existing business' (fieldnotes, Donnelly, 1996).

However, recent reporting suggests a change in this trend with a number of Irish companies, including the Bank of Ireland, Allied Irish Banks, CRH and Independent Newspapers announcing their largest ever acquisitions in 1996 (*Irish Times* 1996). Recognized as progressively important and having different requirements from foreign-owned firms, internationally trading indigenous companies have recently become the direct focus of state industrial policy initiatives (*National Development Plan 1994–1999*). The internationalization of Irish companies is expected to continue, given the limitations of domestic markets, the further opening of the economy, the shift in state policy toward the development of indigenous companies in international markets, the growing need to locate facilities close to the main overseas markets and the need to achieve critical mass to compete in the deregulated markets of the twenty-first century.

Strategy and international HRM

One area of international business research has concentrated on identifying the methods by which firms seek to penetrate foreign markets and the rationale for adopting their chosen foreign market entry strategy (for example, McKiernan 1992). Scandinavian research has attempted to explain the process of internationalization in terms of well-defined stages, with firms moving sequentially from exporting to licensing and then to foreign direct investment, with each step involving greater commitment to the internationalization process (Johanson and Vahlne 1977; Johanson and Mattsson 1988). Such approaches to internationalization have problems with recent developments in international business. First, these models have been complicated by rapid growth, in the last decade, of collaborative arrangements such as international joint ventures and strategic alliances (Hendry 1994). Second, with the upsurge in international joint ventures and acquisitions in the last decade (Hamill 1992), many firms were able effectively to leapfrog the internationalization process. This is particularly significant in the Irish context, given the primary role of acquisitions in the foreign market entry strategies of Irish firms.

One of the central issues concerning companies with overseas operations is the balance between globalizing forces and local market responsiveness (Bartlett and Ghoshal 1989). Problems of control are exacerbated in international companies when operations are dispersed over considerable geographic and cultural distances and the environment is complex and heterogeneous (Baliga and Jaeger 1984). Edstrom and Galbraith (1977) suggest three modes of control: personal or direct control, bureaucratic control which relies on recording and reporting, and control by socialization, where the functional behaviours and rules are learned and internalized by individuals. It has been argued, however, that control modes may change as the firm's strategy evolves over time. During the early ethnocentric or home country focused stage of a firm's international involvement, parent country expatriates exercise tight control. As strategy becomes host country focused or polycentric, there is a marked decline in the number of expatriates abroad and their function shifts to the communication and co-ordination of strategic objectives. Finally, with globalization and the evolution of a globally focused or geocentric strategy, there is a need for a broad range of executives with international experience (Adler and Bartholomew 1992).

There is growing evidence to suggest that the international HRM policies of firms organized on a multi-domestic basis differ from globally integrated firms (Kobrin 1992; Schuler *et al.* 1993). Other researchers have suggested linkages between product life cycle stage/international strategy and HRM policy and practice. (Milliman *et al.* 1991). The concept of strategic international human resource management (SIHRM) is defined as: 'human resource management issues, functions and policies and practices that result from the strategic activities of multinational enterprises and that impact the international concerns and goals of those enterprises' (Schuler *et al.* 1993: 720).

With the emergence of SIHRM came a growing recognition that the success of global business depends more importantly on the quality of the MNE's human resources and how effectively the enterprise's human resources are managed and developed (Bartlett and Ghoshal 1992).

International HRM: some Irish empirical evidence

This section summarizes the results of a small-scale pilot study which examined the IHRM practices of five leading Irish international companies. The study was based on semi-structured interviews with the human resource or personnel director, based at corporate headquarters. The majority of the interviews were conducted in the early 1990s, with some follow-up interviews in 1996. These companies were specifically chosen to represent both the manufacturing and service sectors. Three of the companies were international service companies (two in the financial services sector and one in air transportation). The other two were manufacturing multinationals (both in the clay, cement and glass sector). All reported rapid growth of their international business operations in recent years.

There are four areas normally encompassed by the term international HRM. This section considers each in turn. The first is international staffing, the area which to date has enjoyed the bulk of research on IHRM. The second is expatriate performance and assessment. The third focuses on IHRM policies such as recruitment, selection, training and repatriation. The fourth examines international management development. The main focus of this chapter is on the management of expatriates. The issues of staffing and international management development are discussed in a broader context related to the internationalization strategies of the companies.

International staffing policies and practice

International companies face three alternatives with respect to the staffing of management positions abroad: the employment of parent country nationals (PCNs), host country nationals (HCNs), or third country nationals (TCNs). The choice between the various alternatives is influenced by several factors, both internal and external to the international firm, which are discussed below. As Scullion (1995) outlines, there are a number of options open to MNEs with respect to their staffing policies: ethnocentric, polycentric, geocentric, mixed and ad hoc. Companies with ethnocentric predispositions will tend to favour the employment of PCNs, while companies with a polycentric value system will tend to employ HCNs (Heenan and Perlmutter 1979). In regiocentric or geocentric international firms, overseas management positions may be staffed by TCNs. In practice, geocentric staffing policies are unusual even in the giant MNEs. Evidence suggests that in general Irish-owned MNEs tend not to adopt a geocentric approach to the management of their overseas operations, favouring instead a mix between the ethnocentric and polycentric approaches (Donnelly 1996).

The international business strategy of the firm also influences staffing policies at the subsidiary level. Multinational integration strategies require a greater use of PCNs in order to control and co-ordinate integrated activities (Porter 1986). Multi-domestic or nationally responsive strategies would require the use of HCNs to ensure sensitivity to local market and cultural considerations (Scullion 1993). The availability of local management talent in host countries and government restrictions on the employment of parent country nationals are other factors influencing the choice of staffing policy, as are the relative costs of the alternatives. The characteristics of the subsidiary will also have an impact. The employment of PCNs will be greater in new subsidiaries, particularly in the start-up phase. Similarly the employment of PCNs will be greater in greenfield sites as compared with acquisitions and in subsidiaries which are strategically important to the international company (Hamill 1989).

There was considerable variation in the international staffing practices of the Irish companies interviewed. This was not surprising given the range of factors influencing the choice of staffing policy as discussed above. The financial service companies had a very clear ethnocentric policy, with a strong preference for the employment of PCNs in senior management positions abroad. By contrast, the employment of HCNs was the preferred policy in the two manufacturing companies. In the air transportation company there was no fixed policy and considerable variation across countries in staffing policy and practice.

There was a considerable contrast in the approach to international staffing between the two financial services companies. This was illustrated sharply by their very different staffing practices following major international acquisitions by both companies in the 1990s. One of the financial services companies chose to manage the new international acquisition with a senior management team comprising both parent-country nationals and host-country nationals. The main rationale for using Irish expatriates in this case was for development purposes: to develop future senior managers with the international management perspective and capability to run an increasingly international business. A very different approach was followed by the other financial service company. Post acquisition, it decided to continue with the practice of HCN managers running the business. The company was very concerned with ensuring a non-hostile takeover and felt that for political reasons it was appropriate to continue with local managers rather than bringing in expatriates. In addition, the company was very satisfied with the quality and the performance of the HCN senior management in the acquired company.

The financial service companies also had a number of branches abroad, in addition to their recently acquired businesses, particularly in the US and UK. In contrast to the staffing approach in the acquired banks, the senior management of the foreign branches were usually Irish expatriates. This is linked to the strategic marketing approach of the companies to focus on the extended domestic markets in the UK and US, and the strong preference expressed by some major customers that top managers in host countries should be parent-country nationals. In this context public relations and marketing were usually the key roles. Previous research had mostly ignored this factor because it concentrated mainly on very large multinationals and had tended to neglect the service sector (Brewster 1991).

As the two manufacturing companies moved beyond the early phase of internationalization and adopted a highly decentralized approach to their international business, they shifted towards a polycentric staffing policy. A number of advantages of this approach were identified which were consistent with findings in the literature (Dowling *et al.* 1994):

1   Local managers were more sensitive to local culture and local market trends.
2   It helped to maintain the local identity of the business.
3   It helped to recruit and retain high quality HCN managers.
4   HCN managers generally cost less than PCN managers.
5   This approach was a better fit with the decentralized business approach.

Despite the tendency towards polycentrism in the two manufacturing companies, both firms continued to employ a growing number of expatriates. Similarly, in the air transportation company, there was a growing use of expatriates in the 1990s, following a period in the 1980s when there was a move away from expatriate staffing in favour of HCNs which was largely on cost grounds. The study identified a number of reasons for employing expatriates in Irish MNEs which were consistent with recent European research (Banai 1992; Brewster and Scullion 1997):

- the lack of available management skills in some countries;
- to retain control of local operations;
- the need for specific product and business knowledge;
- the training and development of local staff;
- international assignments were increasingly seen as a central part of management development.

The increase in the use of expatriates in practice can be linked to the rapid increase in the pace of internationalization experienced by Irish companies, together with the development of new international business areas. This finding is consistent with the argument that an ethnocentric approach is particularly appropriate in the early stages of the internationalization process (Zeira 1976). A major challenge for the Irish companies in the next decade will be to adjust the staffing policies to the international evolution of the firm (Scullion and Donnelly 1998).

The performance of expatriate managers

An important issue in the international HRM literature is expatriate failure, which is usually defined as the premature return of an expatriate manager (Dowling and Welch 1988). The literature suggests that expatriate failure remains a significant problem, particularly for US multinationals, ranging between 25 and 40 per cent (Mendenhall and Oddou 1985). Recent research suggests that these figures are somewhat exaggerated (Harzing and Van Ruysseveldt 1995) and that expatriate underperformance is a far more frequent problem than failure of the type that requires repatriation (Scullion 1995). A major conclusion which emerges from the present study is that the expatriate failure rate in Irish companies is similar to other European countries and is considerably lower in comparison with US companies. None of the five companies reported expatriate failure rates in excess of 5 per cent and the majority (four out of five) had rates of around 1 per cent. Four reasons were given for the low Irish expatriate failure rate. First, Irish managers were felt to be more international in their orientation and more internationally mobile than some of their foreign counterparts. Second, international assignments were generally seen to be a key part of the overall management development process. Third, Irish MNEs were seen to be developing effective HRM policies in response to internationalization. Fourth, the relatively small numbers of expatriates involved in smaller MNEs and the personal knowledge of managers resulted in more reliable selection.

Family-related problems were identified as the major reason for poor performance on an international assignment in Irish MNEs, a finding which is consistent with recent European research (Brewster and Scullion 1997). In practice, however, Irish companies paid little attention to the family factor in relation to their selection decisions, notwithstanding the importance of this factor to the success of the international assignment (Mendenhall and Oddou 1987). Finally the research illustrated the complexity of the issues surrounding the question of performance measurement in MNEs (Schuler *et al.* 1991). An important finding was that despite the growing tendency to see expatriates as key human assets, the criteria used for the performance appraisal of international managers had, in practice, received relatively little attention and none of the companies had introduced separate appraisal systems for expatriate managers.

Repatriation

A significant finding of the present study was the identification of the repatriation of managers as a significant problem for Irish international companies. Whereas none of the five companies reported serious concerns with the performance of expatriates, four of the five companies said they faced or anticipated significant problems regarding the re-entry of expatriate managers. The research highlighted that concerns over re-entry may lead to low morale and a higher turnover of expatriates (Harvey 1989; Scullion 1994). A key problem for the Irish international firms was finding suitable posts for repatriates of similar status and responsibility to those they had held abroad. It was anticipated that the repatriation problem would become more acute in future years because some companies expected to continue to expand overseas at the same time as undertaking rationalization of domestic operations, thereby limiting opportunities at home. The research also highlighted other problems associated with re-entry such as loss of status, loss of autonomy, loss of career direction and a feeling that international experience is undervalued by the company (Johnston 1991).

Despite concerns about the costs of expatriate turnover, none of the Irish companies had introduced formal repatriation programmes to assist managers and their families with repatriation difficulties. Similarly, none of the companies had introduced mentor systems designed to assist the career progression of the expatriate manager. However, three measures were introduced to minimize the repatriation problem. The first was to reduce the duration of the international assignment as it was generally felt that repatriation problems were more acute in longer assignments. Second, companies were paying greater attention to the career planning of expatriates, and in particular were planning the return of expatriates earlier. Third, one of the financial service companies had begun to offer sabbaticals to some senior expatriates on completion of their international assignment.

International HRM policies

Three of the five companies (the air transportation company, one manufacturing company and one of the financial services companies) claimed to have well-developed policies covering the recruitment, selection, pre-departure briefing, repatriation and compensation of expatriates. The other two were operating with a more limited set of guidelines in these areas.

Recruitment and selection

The high costs of expatriate failure have highlighted the importance of effective recruitment and selection procedures to the international firm (Tung 1982). A key recruitment issue is whether firms recruit internally or externally and an important selection issue is whether the criteria used for selecting expatriates should be different from that used for domestic appointments (Scullion 1994). None of the five Irish companies recruited externally for expatriate positions. They had a clear preference to recruit internally from their existing pool of management. Two main advantages of internal as opposed to external recruitment were cited by the companies. The first was knowledge of the individual and the family, which was particularly important for companies establishing new international operations in the early phase of the internationalization process. The second was the growing tendency to use international assignments for career development purposes.

In terms of the selection criteria used for international assignments, domestic track record and general management and technical skills were the main factors considered. However, four of the five companies also took into account a wider range of factors including cultural empathy, family situation, previous international experience. Foreign language ability was important for younger graduates and the development potential of the graduate was increasingly important. For more senior expatriate appointments, the ability to operate independently and to develop cross-cultural leadership skills were seen as key factors. However, while all companies felt that the effective selection of managers was vital to successful performance abroad, only one of the companies had introduced psychological testing for expatriates. It was felt that the candidates for such jobs would be well known to the company in a relatively small organization. This suggests that there is a case for focusing on the personal development of key players in SMEs who have the potential to lead the internationalization process.

International briefing and training

An effective briefing on the nature of the international assignment prior to departure was also regarded as important to the success of an international assignment (Ronen 1989; Brewster 1991). All the companies conducted briefings which usually involved interviews with senior managers to clarify the key objectives of the assignment. In addition, there was sometimes the opportunity to hold discussions with former and current expatriates who had knowledge of the country in question. This latter form of briefing was particularly valued by the managers because they could ask questions and learn from the experiences of their predecessors.

None of the companies had established their own cultural awareness training programmes. This was partly because the two most important foreign markets, the US and the UK, were not felt to be so culturally dissimilar to the domestic culture. The relatively small size of the Irish companies was also a factor here.

There were limited resources available at the corporate headquarters for training and development (Scullion and Donnelly 1998). Three of the companies used external training organizations to help prepare their managers for international assignments. One of the financial services companies sent senior international managers to courses run by business schools in the US. Four of the five companies adopted the approach of encouraging the manager and the spouse to visit the area prior to the acceptance of the assignment. This was felt to be an effective way of giving the managers and their spouses some real understanding of the conditions in the foreign country and the nature of the challenges they would face in living in a foreign environment.

International management development

The effective implementation of global strategies depends, to a large degree, on the existence of an adequate supply of internationally experienced managers (Adler and Bartholomew 1992). Scullion (1992) identified shortages of international managers as an increasingly important problem for British multinationals. There were growing concerns among some Irish MNEs that shortages of international managers and restrictions on managerial mobility were recently emerging as significant constraints on the internationalization and growth strategies of Irish companies. In some cases the shortage of host-country national managers shaped their preference for acquisitional growth strategies, with the retention of existing management a key factor. Shortages of qualified HCN managers was a particularly acute concern for the manufacturing MNEs due to the very rapid internationalization of their business in recent years.

There was also growing recognition of the importance of developing effective international management development programmes (Scullion 1997). Four of the five companies reported that they were spending more on international management education, particularly for top and senior management. The companies used a combination of internal and external international development programmes, one interesting feature of which in the case of the banks was the use of leading foreign business schools in Europe and the US. Two of the five companies (one manufacturer and one financial services company) had introduced international HR planning; however, this development was at a relatively early stage in these companies. Due to the smaller size of the Irish multinationals a more informal approach to management development was possible which allowed the companies to focus on the personal development of managers who were identified to be key players in the internationalization process. The key international HR issue facing the Irish firms was the need to develop the next generation of top managers with the capacities to run an international business. International management development, succession planning and international career planning were seen as vital areas for the corporate human resource function in the international firm (Scullion 1998, forthcoming).

Conclusions

The argument presented in this chapter suggests that international HRM is becoming increasingly important, not only in the traditional giant MNEs but also among a growing number of medium-sized firms which have internationalized their operations in recent years. The preliminary evidence presented in this chapter suggests that a number of Irish MNEs, in this case among the largest Irish firms, have few serious problems regarding expatriate performance or expatriate management. The repatriation of expatriate managers back to Ireland was identified as a growing problem for Irish MNEs. The recruitment and retention of high quality HCN managers was a vital component of international HRM strategy in those companies committed to the policy of using local managers to manage the acquired international businesses. More generally, the integration of the acquired foreign businesses was a key challenge facing Irish MNEs.

In general, all of the Irish companies in the present study were effective in international HRM, despite the failure to follow best practice in some areas such as the use of sophisticated selection methods and tailored training programmes to suit the needs of a particular foreign assignment. There are two main reasons to explain this paradox. First, the use of internal recruitment in companies which have a relatively small population of expatriates facilitates the development of self-selecting, highly motivated expatriate populations. Second, the current selection and training procedures are adequate for the time being because they are only dealing with a limited number of international assignments. However, these procedures may become less effective as the nature of the firm's international involvement changes and the expatriate population grows (Forster and Johnsen 1996). This suggests that further empirical research is required which charts the international HRM problems and issues that Irish companies face when they develop through the various stages of the internationalization process.

While our study examined the IHRM practices of five Irish international companies, there is clearly a need for more extensive in-depth case study research that would allow cross-case comparisons. This type of research is needed in order to develop more sophisticated theoretical frameworks for identifying the range of variables which impact upon human resource choices in international activities. The present study provides in a limited way some indication of the rich potential in this direction. There is also a need for more extensive use of the longitudinal approach to provide a deeper understanding of the dynamics of the internationalization process (Benito and Welch 1994). A recent unpublished study suggested that theories of internationalization which have been developed from research in large MNEs do not adequately explain the approaches used in smaller firms (Creaner and Monks 1996). This conclusion is supported by the findings of the present study and suggests the need for a new research agenda to establish better information about the role and management of HRM across frontiers in small and medium-sized firms, as well as in giant MNEs, to clarify and measure current developments and to place them in the context of more adequate theories of international HRM.

Notes

1 In this case, SMEs were defined to be any enterprise with a home base (head office or parent firm) in a developed country that operates at least one affiliate in another country and whose employment level in its home country is fewer than 500 people.
2 This figure excludes those companies whose overseas operations are located outside Europe. Irish international companies were identified as wholly Irish-owned firms (i.e. over 50 per cent shareholding within Ireland) employing 1,000 or more employees worldwide and with at least two operating sites within Europe – one of which could be in Ireland itself.

References

Adler, N.J. and Bartholomew, S. (1992) 'Managing globally competent people', *Academy of Management Executive* 6: 52–64.

Baliga, B.R. and Jaeger, A.M. (1984) 'Multinational corporations: control systems and delegation issues', *Journal of International Business Studies* 2: 25–40.

Banai, M. (1992) 'The ethnocentric staffing policy in multinational corporations: a self-fulfilling prophecy', *International Journal of Human Resource Management* 3: 451–72.

Bartlett, C. and Ghoshal, S. (1989) *Managing Across Borders: The Transnational Solution*, Boston: Harvard Business School Press.

—— (1992) 'What is a global manager?' *Harvard Business Review*, September–October: 124–32.

Benito, R.G. and Welch, L.S. (1994) 'Foreign market servicing: beyond choice of entry mode', *Journal of International Marketing* 2: 7–27.

Brewster, C. (1991) *The Management of Expatriates*, London: Kogan Page.

Brewster, C. and Scullion, H. (1997) 'Expatriate HRM: a review and an agenda', *Human Resource Management Journal* 7(3): 32–41.

Chapman Flood (1996) *Acquisition Surveys 1993–96*, Dublin: Chapman Flood.

Creaner, J. and Monks, K. (1996) 'Entering the international market: opportunities and choices in human resource practices', Research Paper Series, Dublin City University Business School.

Dineen, D. and Garavan, T. (1994) 'Ireland: the emerald isle – management research in a changing European context', *International Studies of Management and Organisation* 24(1–2) 137–64.

Donnelly, N. (1996) 'The management of industrial relations in Irish-owned multinational companies: some exploratory findings', paper presented at the First Conference on Management Research in Ireland, University College Cork, 12–13 September.

Dowling, P.J. and Welch, D. (1988) 'International human resource management: an Australian perspective', *Asia-Pacific Journal of Management* 6(1) 39–65.

Dowling, P.J., Schuler, R.S. and Welch, D. (1994) *International Dimensions of Human Resource Management*, 2nd edn, California: Wadsworth.

Edstrom, A. and Galbraith, J. (1977) 'Transfer of managers as a coordination and control strategy in multinational organizations', *Administrative Science Quarterly* 22: 248–63.

Edwards, P.K., Ferner, A. and Sisson, K. (1996) 'The conditions for international human resource management: two case studies', *International Journal of Human Resource Management* 7(1) 20–40.

Enderwick, P. (1986) 'Multinationals and labour relations: the case of Ireland', *Journal of Irish Business and Administrative Research* 8: 1–11.

Forster, N. and Johnsen, M. (1996) 'Expatriate management policies in UK companies new to the international scene', *International Journal of Human Resource Management* 7(1) 179–205.

Gunnigle, P. (1992) 'Management approaches to employee relations in greenfield sites', *Journal of Irish Business and Administrative Research* 3(1) 20–36.

Hamill, J. (1989) 'Expatriate policies in British multinationals', *Journal of General Management* 14(4) 18–33.

—— (1992) 'Cross-border mergers, acquisitions and alliances in Europe', in S. Young and J. Hamill (eds) *Europe and the Multinationals*, London: Edward Elgar.

Harvey, M.G. (1989) 'Repatriation of corporate executives: an empirical study', *Journal of International Business Studies*, spring: 131–44.

Harzing, A.-W.J. and Van Ruysseveldt, J. (1995) *International Human Resource Management*, London: Sage.

Heenan, D.A. and Perlmutter, H.V. (1979) *Multinational Organisation Development*, Reading MA: Addison-Wesley.

Hendry, C. (1994) *Human Resource Strategies for International Growth*, London: Routledge.

Irish Times (1996) 'A record year for the big business in Irish businesses', 28 December.

Johanson, J. and Mattsson, L.G. (1988) 'Internationalization in industrial systems – a network approach', in N. Hood and J.E. Vahlne (eds) *Strategies in Global Competition*, London: Croom Helm.

Johanson, J. and Vahlne, J.E. (1977) 'The internationalization process of the firm – a model of knowledge development and increasing foreign commitment', *Journal of International Business Studies* 8(1) 23–32.

Johnston, J. (1991) 'An empirical study of repatriation of managers in UK multinationals', *Human Resource Management Journal* 1(4) 102–8.

Kelly, A. and Brannick, T. (1985) 'Industrial relations practices in multinational companies in Ireland', *Journal of Irish Business and Administrative Research* 7: 98–111.

Kobrin, S.J. (1992) 'Multinational strategy and international human resource management policy', unpublished paper, Wharton School, University of Pennsylvania.

Loustarinen, R.K., Korhonen, H., Jokinen, J. and Pelkonen, T. (1994) *Globalisation of Economic Activities and Small and Medium-sized Enterprise Development*, Helsinki: Helsinki School of Economics.

Lynch, J. and Roche, F. (1995) *Business Management in Ireland: Competitive Strategies for the 21st Century*, Dublin: Oak Tree Press.

McKiernan, P. (1992) *Strategies of Growth*, London: Routledge.

Mendenhall, M.E. and Oddou, G. (1985) 'The dimensions of expatriate acculturation: a review', *Academy of Management Review* 10: 39–47.

—— (1987) 'Expatriate selection, training and career pathing: a review and critique', *Human Resource Management*, fall: 331. XX.

Milliman, J., Von Glinow, M. and Nathan, B. (1991) 'Organizational life cycles and strategic international human resource management in multinational companies: implications for congruence theory', *Academy of Management Review* 16: 318–39.

Monks, K. (1996) 'Global or local? HRM in the multinational company: the Irish experience', *International Journal of Human Resource Management* 7(3) 721–35.

National Development Plan 1994–1999, Dublin: The Stationery Office.

O'Malley, E. (1985) 'The performance of Irish indigenous industry: some lessons for the 1980s', in J. Fitzpatrick and J. Kelly (eds) *Perspectives on Irish Industry*, Dublin: Irish Management Institute.

— (1992) 'Problems of industrialisation in Ireland', in J.H. Goldthorpe and C.T. Whelan (eds) *The Development of Industrial Society in Ireland*, Oxford: Oxford University Press for the British Academy.

Mulhern, A. (1995) 'The SME sector in Europe: a broad perspective', *Journal of Small Business Management* 30(3) 83–7.

OECD (1994) *Reviews of Foreign Direct Investment: Ireland*, Paris: OECD.

Porter, M. (1986) *Competition in Global Industries*, Boston: Harvard Business School Press.

Roche, W.K and Geary, J.F. (1997) 'Multinationals and industrial relations practices', in T.V. Murphy and W.K. Roche (eds) *Industrial Relations in Practice*, Dublin: Oak Tree Press.

Ronen, S. (1989) 'Training the international assignee', in I. Goldstein (ed.) *Training and Career Development*, San Francisco: Jossey-Bass.

Schuler, R., Dowling, P.J. and De Cieri, H. (1993) 'An integrative framework of strategic international human resource management', *International Journal of Human Resource Management* 4(4) 717–64.

Schuler, R.S., Fulkerson, J.R. and Dowling, P.J. (1991) 'Strategic performance measurement and management in multinational corporations', *Human Resource Management* 30: 365–92.

Scullion, H. (1992) 'Strategic recruitment and development of the international manager: some European considerations', *Human Resource Management Journal* 3(1) 57–69.

—— (1993) 'Creating international managers: recruitment and development issues', in P. Kirkbride (ed.) *Human Resource Management in Europe*, London: Routledge.

—— (1994) 'Staffing policies and strategic control in British multinationals', *International Studies of Management and Organisation* 3(4) 86–104.

—— (1995) 'International human resource management', in J. Storey (ed.) *Human Resource Management: A Critical Text*, London: Routledge.

—— (1997) 'The key challenges for international HRM in the 21st Century', in *Association of European Personnel Managers Handbook*, London: Institute of Personnel Managers.

—— (1998) *The Role of the Corporate Human Resource Function in the International Firm* (forthcoming).

Scullion, H. and Donnelly, N. (1998) 'International HRM: recent developments in Irish multinationals', in K. Monks, J. Walsh and W.K. Roache (eds) *Human Resource Management in Ireland: A Critical Text*, Dublin: Oak Tree Press.

Sunday Business Post (1996) 'A record year for mergers and acquisitions', 29 December.

Tung, R.L. (1982) 'Selection and training procedures of U.S., European and Japanese Multinationals', *California Management Review* 25(1) 57–71.

—— (1984) 'Strategic management of human resources in the multinational enterprise', *Human Resource Management* 23(2) 129–43.

United Nations (UN) (1993) *Small and Medium-sized Transnational Corporations: Role, Impact and Policy Implications*, New York: UN Publications.

Young, S. and Hamill, J. (1992) *Europe and the Multinationals*, London: Edward Elgar.

Zeira, Y. (1976) 'Management development in ethnocentric multinational corporations', *California Management Review* 18(4) 34–42.

Part II

Balancing differentiation with integration

4 MNE staffing policies for the managing director position in foreign subsidiaries

The results of an innovative research method

Anne-Wil Harzing

Introduction

Virtually every publication on expatriate management starts with two issues. First, over the last three decades it has become almost 'traditional' to open an article on expatriate management by stating that expatriate failure rates are (very) high. In a recent article (Harzing 1995b) it was argued that there is in fact very little empirical proof for the persistent claim of high expatriate failure rates when measured as premature returns. A second issue that usually draws the attention is multinational enterprise (MNE) staffing policies. Do companies employ parent country nationals (PCNs), host country nationals (HCNs) or third country nationals (TCNs) as (top) managers in their subsidiaries and in which circumstances is one option favoured above another? Although many publications focus on the advantages and disadvantages of using expatriates as opposed to local managers and indicate the factors influencing MNE staffing policies (see e.g. Hamill 1989; Dowling and Schuler 1990; Hendry 1994; Hodgetts and Luthans 1994; Mead 1994; Borg and Harzing 1995; Briscoe 1995; Fatehi 1996), there are surprisingly few empirical studies that examine MNE staffing policies. All of the above publications refer to Tung (1981, 1982, 1987) in this respect. Although Tung's study was a primer in the field, it is now more than fifteen years old. Recently, Kopp (1994) compared international human resource policies in Japanese, European and US multinationals.[1] One of the issues studied was the nationality of top managers in overseas operations. Kopp's study confirmed Tung's finding that Japanese companies employ the largest number of PCNs in their subsidiaries, US companies the smallest, while the number of PCNs in subsidiaries in European companies lies between these two extremes. Kopp's study did not differentiate among host countries, however, while neither Tung's nor Kopp's study takes industry effects into account. Further, as will be shown later in this chapter, both studies do not differentiate among European countries, neither when looking at headquarters, nor when looking at subsidiaries.

In view of these observations above, the issue of MNE staffing policies would seem to benefit from large-scale systematic comparisons. However, large-scale comparisons almost inevitably involve mail surveys and international mail surveys are plagued by low response rates (Harzing 1996b), a problem that seems to have exacerbated over time. While Tung's survey had response rates varying from 12 per cent for European MNEs to 32 per cent for Japanese, Kopp needed two mailings to get an 8.8 per cent response rate. This chapter therefore provides such a large-scale comparison by using an innovative research method. The next two sections describe this research method and the sample that was obtained. The remainder of the chapter is devoted to an analysis and discussion of differences in MNE staffing policies along various dimensions.

Research method

In the author's research into control mechanisms in MNEs, data were collected by means of an international mail survey (for a discussion of the practicalities of international mail surveys and a description and analysis of the large differences in response rates between countries, see Harzing 1996b, 1997). Questionnaires (some 1,650 in total) were sent out to subsidiaries of MNEs in 22 countries. As personalization of the letter is usually thought to increase response rates (e.g. Dillman 1978; Yu and Cooper 1983; Jobber 1986; Harvey 1987; Fox *et al.* 1988; LaGarce and Kuhn 1995), the name of the managing director/CEO/president of the subsidiary was written down while verifying the addresses. During this process, which took over two months of full-time work, some pleasant distraction was found in guessing the nationality of the managing directors. It seemed surprisingly easy in most cases to guess their nationality simply based on their names (mostly both first and last names were available). Only later did it become apparent that these data could be a valuable source of information in themselves and we noted down systematically whether the managing director was thought to be a PCN, an HCN or a TCN. The research method for this study therefore consisted of 'guessing' the nationality of the managing director from his or her name and subsequently classifying the managing director as PCN, HCN or TCN. A full justification of why this research method could be valid in general can be found in Harzing (1995c). For this particular study, sufficient justification can be found in considering the number of successful classifications in a sub-sample of the original sample. As indicated in the introduction, the author's study on control mechanisms involved a mail questionnaire to 1,650 subsidiaries. On this questionnaire the respondents were asked to indicate their nationality, which provided a check on the original classification by name alone. Out of 287 questionnaires returned, a verification was not possible in 69 cases because the respondent preferred to remain anonymous, the respondent was not the person to whom the questionnaire was sent, the respondent's name was unavailable, or the respondent's name could not be classified in the first place. Out of the remaining 218 cases, 212 had been classified correctly. In six cases the respondent turned out to be a TCN instead of a PCN or HCN. So in fact less than 3 per cent of the cases were classified incorrectly.

The two previous studies on MNE staffing policies asked HQ managers to either indicate whether a particular region was 'primarily staffed' by certain types of employees (Tung 1982) or to indicate the overall percentage of PCN, HCN and TCN managers (Kopp 1994). A specific problem with the first approach is that the answer is never completely accurate. Our data show that most companies use PCNs as well as HCNs in many regions so, although easier for the respondent, this type of question loses many possibly important details. In addition, not all companies are likely to have detailed data on the nationality of managers of their subsidiaries readily available. More importantly, however, even if they have these data, not all respondents are likely to take the trouble to consult them, especially if nationality policies are only one of the many issues in the questionnaire, as was the case in both Tung's and Kopp's study. So what are the respondents indicating:

- the actual situation?
- their most recent experience in this respect?
- the experience that made the largest impression?
- an answer that they think is socially desirable?
- stated company policy, while the reality gradually emerged to be different? (Neghandi and Welge's 1984 study showed large differences between stated policy and actual practice).

Of course the same basic problem applies for all mail questionnaires, where the researcher has no opportunity to verify or explore answers. Although we certainly do not want to question the overall validity of Tung's and Kopp's studies, we do feel that in the case of staffing policies our research method will provide data that are at least as accurate as questionnaire data. We verified what actually happened in subsidiaries, measuring emergent rather than espoused strategy. Our research method also permits the collection of a much larger sample than would be feasible by sending out questionnaires, let alone by using interviews. In total, the names of 1,746 managing directors of MNE subsidiaries were classified. The total number is somewhat higher than the number of subsidiaries indicated above as participating in the actual survey because for various reasons ten headquarters were excluded from the survey.

As readers might be concerned about how the research method was used in practice, some specific examples will be given below. In many cases the choice was simple: Is Carlos Gonzales de Castejon Spanish or Swedish? Is Mikko Tanhuanpää Finnish or German? Is Diarmuid O'Colmain Irish or French? Of course some combinations of headquarters and subsidiary countries proved to be more difficult than others. What about the difference between Swedish/Finnish/Danish/Norwegian names, between Singaporean and Japanese names, between German/Austrian/Swiss names, and last but not least between American and British names? For the first three groups assistance was sought from a Finnish, a Japanese and a German citizen respectively. They were able to classify more than 70 per cent of the names without having any doubts. Scandinavian names, for instance, are not so similar as the reader might think at first sight.[2] Names that evoked any doubts remained unclassified.

The really difficult task involved American/British names, so we decided to call in the help of a larger number of people. A list of names was sent to two email mailing lists – one with a dominant American audience (Aibnet) and one with a dominant British audience (Management Research). Subscribers were asked whether they could classify any of the names as either British or American. Apart from a sizeable number of reactions which called the research method preposterous and cast doubts on the author's future academic career, no useful suggestions were received from American subscribers. The British subscribers for the larger part did not seem to be bothered about the research method and were very helpful. For most of the names, unanimous votes (varying from five to ten reactions) were received, while for others the votes were more mixed. It was decided to classify only the names with unanimous votes, while the others remained unclassified. All in all, 80 per cent to 85 per cent of the names were classified by the author herself, sometimes helped by the fact that the same names would occur in different country combinations, while another 10 per cent were classified by 'assistants'. As indicated above, the names that could not be identified unambiguously remained unclassified.[3]

Sample

As indicated above, the sample consists of the names of managing directors of subsidiaries of MNEs that were included in the author's mail survey on control mechanisms in MNEs. The headquarters were originally selected from the Fortune Global 500 list (1994), choosing industries that included at least fifteen companies. The industries selected were: electronics/electric equipment, computers/office equipment, motor vehicles (or parts), petroleum (products), food and beverages, pharmaceuticals, paper and chemicals. As the questionnaire was tailored to manufacturing companies, no service companies were included.[4] The industries were selected partly for their presumed international orientation (global, multidomestic, transnational) as this was one of the independent variables in the survey.

The majority of research on MNEs – no matter on what subject – involves companies of North American origin, which is of course not surprising as the majority of researchers have the same origin. If other companies are included, these will most likely be Japanese. If European companies are included in the research design, they are usually lumped together into one big group, sometimes even without identifying the different countries. The fact that Europe is very heterogeneous has long been accepted and is common knowledge among Europeans. Most American researchers, however, continue to regard Europe as a monolith, especially in the field of MNE staffing policies. In this survey, it was decided to have an over-representation of European companies (nearly 49 per cent of the total 136 headquarters) in order to be able to analyse at the level of different European countries. The European countries included with the

Table 4.1 Country of origin of headquarters included in the sample

Study	USA	Japan	Europe	Belgium	Finland	France
Tung	80	35	29	???	none	none
Kopp	24	34	23	none	none	3
Harzing	44	26	66	none	9	13

	Germany	Italy	Netherlands	Norway	Sweden	Switzerland	UK
Tung	???	none	???	???	???	???	???
Kopp	3	1	2	none	1	none	13
Harzing	11	none	4	none	11	5	13

number of firms between brackets are: UK (13), France (13), Germany (11), Sweden (11), Finland (9), Switzerland (5) and The Netherlands (4). Other European countries were not included because they had only one or two MNEs in the selected industries. Japan takes up 19 per cent of the total with 26 firms, while 44 US firms make up the remaining 32 per cent. If we compare this sample with those by Tung and Kopp (see Table 4.1), we see that more than half of Kopp's European sample consists of UK firms. Tung did not indicate the number of responses per country. However, the total number of European companies in Tung's sample is less than half of the number included in this sample.

The subsidiaries in this sample are located in 22 different countries. The countries have been purposefully selected in order to provide a large amount of cultural variance, measured in terms of their scores on Hofstede's dimensions (1980, 1991).[5] Included in the survey are an Anglo (USA, UK, Ireland), a Germanic (Germany, Austria, Switzerland), a Nordic (Finland, Sweden, Denmark, Norway, The Netherlands), a Latin-European (France, Spain, Italy, Belgium), a Latin-American (Brazil, Mexico, Argentina, Venezuela) and a Far Eastern (Japan, Hong Kong, Singapore) cluster (see also Ronen and Shenkar 1985). Eastern European countries have not been included because they do not yet host enough full-blown subsidiaries to provide adequate response rates, though this might change rapidly in the next few years. The data available thus allow us to make comparisons on MNEs' staffing policies, with the country of origin of headquarters, the type of industry and the location of the subsidiary as independent variables.

Results

In the first subsection, we differentiate MNE staffing policies according to the country of origin of headquarters, the type of industry and the country of location of the subsidiary. To reduce the level of complexity, the 9 headquarters countries, 8 industries and 22 subsidiary countries are clustered into homogeneous subgroups. This cluster analysis shows that subgroups previously used by Tung and Kopp might be inadequate as they underestimate the diversity within Europe. A second subsection then tests whether the results found in the univariate analysis are still valid when using logistic regression analysis, a multivariate type of analysis that takes interaction between the independent variables into account.

Description

In the total sample, 36 per cent of the managing directors are PCN, 60.5 per cent HCN and the remaining 3.5 per cent TCN. On average, MNEs seem to prefer HCNs to PCNs for the highest level position in their subsidiaries. As we will see in the remainder of this section, however, this general picture conceals large differences in staffing policies between countries and industries. As the percentage of TCNs is very small,[6] we will focus on the distinction between HCNs and PCNs in the remainder of this chapter. What can be indicated, however, is that most TCNs are employed in subsidiaries of American multinationals in the pharmaceutical industry located in Hong Kong or Singapore. Table 4.2 shows the percentage of HCNs for various industries, countries of origin of headquarters and the country of subsidiary location.

Country of origin of headquarters

To allow comparison with previous studies, we first investigated whether different staffing policies could be identified when looking at the 'traditional' division in the location of headquarters: Japan, Europe and the USA. Both Tung's and Kopp's studies found that Japanese companies have the lowest and US companies the highest percentage of HCNs, while European companies fall between these two extremes. Table 4.3 shows that this study confirms these findings.

As can be seen in Table 4.2, however, there are major differences in staffing policies between companies from various European countries. It was therefore decided to perform a k-means cluster analysis to investigate whether even more homogeneous clusters could be formed. The three cluster solution, shown in Table 4.3, has a chi-square value that lies slightly below the chi-square value of a cluster solution in which each country forms its own cluster (163.032, p < 0.000). However, the chi-square value of our three-cluster solution lies considerably above the chi-square value of the three-cluster solution that distinguishes between Japan, Europe and the USA only. Our clusters are therefore considerably more homogeneous.

Industry

A second variable that could possibly explain differences in staffing policies between MNEs is the type of industry, a variable that has unfortunately not been isolated in previous studies. A k-means cluster analysis produced significantly different groups when the number of clusters was set at 3. A four-cluster solution

Table 4.2 Percentage of HCNs in various industries, subsidiary countries and countries of origin of headquarters

Industry	% of HCNs	Subsidiary country	% of HCNs
		Hong Kong	25.0
Motor vehicles and parts	44.2	Japan	34.0
Petroleum (products)	55.6	Singapore	34.5
Electronics, electr. equipment	59.5	Brazil	45.3
Chemical (products)	61.6	Venezuela	45.7
Pharmaceutical	63.8	USA	45.8
Computers, office equipment	66.1	Argentina	48.7
Paper (products)	71.3	Mexico	50.0
Food & Beverages	77.2	Spain	59.5
		Germany	64.0
Country of origin	*% of HCNs*	Netherlands	64.4
of headquarters		UK	64.7
		France	65.9
Japan	38.5	Switzerland	68.1
Germany	40.0	Austria	73.6
Netherlands	55.2	Belgium	75.9
Switzerland	62.1	Italy	75.9
Sweden	64.7	Sweden	81.8
Finland	65.9	Denmark	82.4
UK	70.1	Norway	88.7
France	74.8	Finland	96.4
USA	77.0	Ireland	100.0

Table 4.3 Percentage of HCNs in various country clusters

Japan		Europe		USA	
Mean	N	Mean	N	Mean	N
38.5%	273	62%	999	77%	478

Chi-square 110.116 (p <0.000), all group means significantly different (p < 0.000)

Germany and Japan		Finland, Netherlands Sweden, Switzerland		USA, UK, France	
Mean	N	Mean	N	Mean	N
39%	443	63.4%	541	75.5%	766

Chi-square 158.321 (p <0.000), all group means significantly different (p < 0.000)

Table 4.4 Percentage of HCNs in various industry clusters

Motor industry		Other industries		Food and paper industry	
Mean	N	Mean	N	Mean	N
44.2%	190	61.6%	1,185	74.5%	373

Chi-square 50.514 (p < 0.000), all group means significantly different (p < 0.000)

produced a slightly higher chi-square (53.844, p < 0.000), but two of the clusters did not differ significantly from each other. Table 4.4 summarizes the results for the three clusters that were identified. The automobile sector forms a cluster of its own, with a low percentage of HCNs. At the other end we find the food and paper industry with a relatively high percentage of HCNs. The other industries (electronics, computer, petroleum, pharmaceutical and chemical) all fall in the same cluster with a percentage of HCNs that closely resembles the average percentage of HCNs for the sample as a whole.

Subsidiary country

The subsidiary country, that is the country in which the subsidiary is located, has been identified by Tung as an important factor in explaining differences in staffing policies. In exploring the effect of the location of the subsidiary, again the 'traditional division' as used by Tung is first examined (Kopp's analysis did not differentiate according to subsidiary location). Table 4.5 shows the percentage of HCNs for these different regions. It can be seen the USA cluster does not differ significantly from the Latin American cluster.

Returning to the original 22 countries in the sample (see Table 4.2, p. 73), we can see that the Far East and Latin/South America do indeed cluster together. The USA, however, does not seem to form a cluster of its own, but instead falls in the middle of the Latin American cluster. Although all European countries show a higher percentage of HCNs than all Far Eastern and (Latin) American countries, they do differ quite a lot among themselves. Spain lies closest to the Latin American cluster, in which we find some of its former colonies. At the other end of the scale, we find the Scandinavian countries clustering together. Ireland is a very special case, as all managing directors in the sample are HCNs. The other European countries do not seem to form 'logical' clusters.

Using a k-means cluster analysis, several cluster solutions were explored, varying from two to six clusters. Although Kruskal–Wallis analyses provided significant chi-square values (p < 0.000) for each solution, a five-cluster solution provided both a chi-square that was close to a solution where each country formed its own cluster (191.400 vs. 197.645) and groups means that were all significantly different from each other.[7] The second part of Table 4.5 shows the different cluster means for a five-cluster solution.

Table 4.5 Percentage of HCNs in various subsidiary country clusters

Far East		Latin/South America		Western Europe		USA	
Mean	N	Mean	N	Mean	N	Mean	N
32.5%	166	47.6%	233	71.3%	1,220	45.8%	131

Chi-square 140.763 (p < 0.000), USA cluster and Latin American cluster not significantly different (Z= -0.337, sig. 0.736).

Far East		(Latin/South) America		Spain, France, UK, Germany, Switzerland, Netherlands		Denmark, Sweden, Belguim, Austria, Italy		Ireland, Finland, Norway	
Mean	N	Mean	N	Mean	N	Mean	N	Mean	N
32.5%	166	47%	364	64.2%	721	77.5%	373	94.4%	124

Chi-square 191.400 (p < 0.000), all group means significantly different (p < 0.01 or better)

Further exploration

To explore possible interaction effects between the three variables described above, a binomial logistic regression analysis was conducted. This regression analysis showed that all three independent variables are highly (0.000) significant, but that the country variables (country of origin of headquarters and country of location of subsidiary) have a substantially higher explanatory power than the industry variable. Looking at the different instances of the independent variables, we see that German and Japanese MNEs are significantly less likely and French, UK and US MNEs significantly more likely than average to have an HCN as the managing director for their subsidiaries, which confirms our conclusions in the previous section. With regard to industries we see that not only the motor industry but also the petroleum industry have a significantly lower than average chance of having an HCN as managing director. The fact that nearly 75 per cent of the cases in the petroleum industry are subsidiaries from UK, US or French MNEs might have confounded this effect in the previous univariate analysis. MNEs in the food industry are significantly more likely than MNEs in other industries to have an HCN as managing director for their subsidiaries. With regard to subsidiary countries, the three countries that form the Far Eastern cluster are all significantly (0.000 level) less likely to have an HCN than average. With lower levels of significance, the same goes for the five countries that form the (Latin/South) American cluster. At the other end of the spectrum we see the Scandinavian countries that have a significantly (at the 0.01, 0.02, 0.06 and 0.07 level respectively) higher than average chance of having an HCN for managing director. Apart from the petroleum industry, these results therefore completely confirm our results from the univariate analysis.

Several other data were extracted from address books or annual reports: the year of foundation of both headquarters and subsidiaries, and the number of employees of both the MNE as a whole and of the subsidiary in question. These variables were also entered into the stepwise regression analysis. Further, two additional variables were created: relative age (year of foundation of subsidiary – year of foundation of headquarters) and relative size (number of employees of subsidiary/number of employees of total MNE). Only two of these six variables, the number of employees of the MNE as a whole and the year of foundation of subsidiary, proved to offer a significant contribution to the model. The larger the number of employees of the MNE and the more recently the subsidiary has been founded, the lower the chance of an HCN as managing director.

Interestingly, some of the country and industry effects changed by including these variables. Finnish multinationals now have a (marginally significant) lower chance to have HCNs in their subsidiaries. Previously, this effect was confounded by the fact that Finnish MNEs are usually rather small (on average 16,417 employees, the smallest MNEs in this sample). The reverse goes for Germany, whose lower than average chance of having HCNs is no longer significant. This can be explained by the fact that German MNEs are the largest in the sample (159,827 employees on average). The computer industry now shows a significantly higher than average chance of having an HCN for managing director, an effect that was previously confounded by the age of most of the subsidiaries in this industry (average year of foundation 1974, compared to 1959 for the total sample) The reverse effect (older subsidiaries, average year of foundation 1944) explains why the effect of the food industry is now less significant. The motor industry combines large MNEs (219,350 on average, the largest in this sample) with relatively recently established subsidiaries (1969 on average). Including these two variables drastically reduces the industry effect, which is no longer significant. Finally, although the effect (positive or negative) of the coefficients remains the same, most of the differences for subsidiary country are no longer significant when the number of employees of the MNE and the year of foundation of the subsidiary are included.

Discussion

This section will discuss what can be concluded regarding MNEs staffing policies from the data presented above. First, the facts that can be deduced from the previous analysis will be summarized. Subsequently, we will try to find the reasons behind these facts. Some of these reasons can be found in previous research, others can be found in the author's ongoing research about control mechanisms in MNEs, while the remainder could provide an agenda for future research.

The facts

The first fact that emerges unambiguously from the data above is that Europe should not be considered as a homogeneous whole with respect to MNE's staffing policies. MNEs from the small European countries – Finland, Sweden, Switzerland and The Netherlands – seem to have staffing policies that are rather similar. German MNEs, however, resemble the Japanese far more closely than any of the other Europeans. At the other end of the spectrum we find that French and British MNEs share a common staffing pattern – that is, a rather large percentage of HCNs heading their subsidiaries. This is similar to US MNEs. These different patterns persist if we take the difference in industry distribution in the various country clusters into account.

Looking at the subsidiary level, we also have to conclude that Europe cannot be considered as homogeneous. Patterns within Europe at subsidiary level are not as clear as at HQ level. We can distinguish, however, a cluster with two Scandinavian countries (Finland and Norway) that has a significantly higher percentage of HCNs heading subsidiaries than other European countries. Ireland joins this cluster as there do not seem to be any PCNs in Irish MNE subsidiaries, at least not in the function of managing director. The two other Scandinavian countries (Denmark and Sweden) are very close, but form a cluster with Belgium, Italy and Austria, while the remaining European countries (Spain, France, UK, Germany, Switzerland, The Netherlands) form a cluster of their own. Though no immediately obvious patterns can be distinguished, the former cluster seems to contain mostly smaller and the latter cluster a relatively large number of bigger European countries. Corresponding with earlier research, Far Eastern and Latin American clusters were clearly distinguishable. Both clusters had a very low percentage of HCNs in their subsidiaries. The USA, however, which is usually considered separately, was shown not to differ from other American (whether Central and South American) countries with regard to the number of HCNs in its subsidiaries.

Many industry sectors have broadly similar staffing policies. At the low HCN end, however, the motor industry stands out clearly, while the same goes for the food industry and to a lesser extent for the paper industry at the high HCN end. Although these differences might be partly explained by the fact that German/ Japanese MNEs dominate the motor industry and UK/US/French firms dominate the food industry, an industry effect has nevertheless been shown to persist. However, the logistic regression analysis also identified petroleum as an industry with a lower chance of HCNs, while electronics and to a lesser extent the computer industry have a significantly higher chance of HCNs.

In the logistic regression analysis, the size of the MNE, measured by the number of employees and the year of foundation of the subsidiary, have also been shown to have a significant impact on the chance of encountering an HCN as managing director. Old subsidiaries of small MNEs are more likely to have a local managing director, while young subsidiaries of large MNEs are more likely to have an expatriate managing director. Interestingly, the inclusion of size and age influences the explanatory power of some of the industry and country variables. Although the effect (positive or negative) of the coefficients does not change, some coefficients become more significant (Finnish MNEs, computer and electronics industry) or less significant (German MNEs, motor and food industry, and most subsidiary countries).

The reasons

Although these 'facts' might be very interesting in themselves, knowing the reasons behind the differences in staffing policies would make them more useful. This section will therefore discuss various issues that could explain these different staffing policies. Previous research will be the starting point in the first subsection. Subsequently, the issues that can be tested in the author's ongoing research about control mechanisms in MNEs are summarized. A final section will then provide a tentative agenda for future research.

Previous research

Expatriates as a control mechanism

A possible explanation for different staffing policies in different HQ clusters might be the preferred way of controlling an organization in various countries. Bartlett and Ghoshal (1989) indicate that the 'typical' control strategy of Japanese companies is centralization, which involves a heavy use of expatriates, while American MNEs rely on formalization, thus having less need of expatriates. Neghandi and Welge (1984) found that US MNEs relied more on both formalization and reports (output control) than German and Japanese firms. This is highly consistent with the results from this study as formalization and output control are both impersonal control mechanisms, while direct supervision and socialization are personal control mechanisms in which expatriates can play a key role (see also Harzing 1994). A similar point is put forward by Ferner (1995) who states that 'Japanese or German firms rely more on informal face-to-face control processes compared with the predominance of formal, system-based controls in Anglo-Saxon and French companies'. In this case the conformity with the results described above is complete (Japanese/German MNEs low percentage of HCNs, UK/US/France high percentage of HCNs).

Expatriate failure

The relatively low number of expatriates sent out by American MNEs could also be attributed to the fact that American expatriates seem to have larger problems (or at least higher premature re-entries) in foreign assignments than Japanese and European expatriates (Tung 1982; Kobrin 1988). This would not explain, however, why French and British firms have the same staffing pattern as far as the number of outgoing PCNs are concerned. Further, one might wonder whether American expatriates actually experience larger problems than, for instance, Japanese expatriates, or whether they are just less likely to fulfil the assignment in spite of these problems as committed Japanese expatriates would do. It should also be noted that for American expatriates an international assignment often means going several thousand kilometres across one of the oceans, while for Europeans it might be just moving 150 kilometres south (although it is questionable whether the expatriate would actually move in this case). Problems of American expatriates might therefore lie more in the specific circumstances and their unwillingness to accept a less than optimal employment situation than in fact that they would be unsuitable for an international assignment because of their personal characteristics.[8]

Strategic orientation

Significantly different staffing policies in the motor industry (lower percentage of HCNs) and food industry (higher percentage of HCNs) could be explained by the very different strategic orientation of these industries. The motor industry has often been classified as global (Doz 1986; Porter 1986; Prahalad and Doz 1987; Harzing 1996a), while the food industry is the prototype of a multidomestic industry (Porter 1986; Bartlett and Ghoshal 1989; Ghoshal and Nohria 1993; Harzing 1996a). In a global industry, integration prevails over local responsiveness, while the opposite is true for a multidomestic industry (see Prahalad and Doz 1987 for a discussion of the integration/responsiveness framework). It is of course easier to be responsive to the local market and culture when employing mostly local managers. On the other hand expatriation is a very effective way to integrate various subsidiaries into a common corporate policy. In an earlier publication (Harzing 1995a), we have already argued that an ethnocentric staffing policy (mainly PCNs) would fit global industries, while a polycentric strategy (mainly HCNs) would fit multidomestic industries. However, different strategic orientations cannot explain the higher chance of HCNs in the electronics and computer industries, both of which are normally considered to be global or integrated (Doz 1986; Harzing 1996a; Porter 1986; Prahalad and Doz 1987; Bartlett and Ghoshal 1989).

Cultural differences

An often-mentioned characteristic to explain different staffing policies in different subsidiary countries is cultural difference (see e.g. Boyacigiller 1990). Generally the argument is that the larger the cultural distance, the higher the proportion of PCNs in top management positions in subsidiaries. This study clearly supports this idea as the largest numbers of expatriates are found in Far Eastern and Latin American countries, which viewed from the US and Western European headquarters would indeed seem to be rather different culturally. Also, although it was not incorporated in the logistic regression models, cultural distance was shown to have a significant negative influence on the chance of encountering an HCN as managing director.

Lack of qualified local personnel

Another issue that is often mentioned to clarify different staffing policies for different subsidiary countries is the amount of locally qualified personnel available (Tung 1982; Hamill 1989; Boyacigiller 1990). In less developed countries fewer qualified personnel are available or more importantly (biased) personnel managers at headquarters might think this is the case. In fact most countries nowadays contain at least a highly educated elite (see e.g. the large number of companies transferring software programming to Indian employees). In this sample it could explain the high amount of PCNs in Latin America, although countries such as Brazil and Mexico can hardly be unambiguously qualified as less developed. The argument is of course even less tenable for the other cluster with a large number of PCNs, namely the Asian cluster.

Experience effects

The larger chance of an HCN in an older subsidiary is easily explained by experience effects. Many MNEs use expatriates in the start-up phase, but gradually move to local managers (Youssef 1973; Tung 1982; Hamill 1989). To our best knowledge no study has yet investigated the effect of the size of the MNE on its staffing policy.

Current research

Expatriates as control mechanism

One of the reasons discussed in the previous section, namely the preferred way of controlling an organization, is the focal point of the research project for which the nationality data were accumulated in the first place. In this project, four types of control mechanisms are distinguished: personal centralized control, formal bureaucratic control, output control and control by socialization and networks (see Harzing 1994 for a more extensive description). In view of the discussion above, we would expect the German/Japanese clusters to show the highest levels of personal types of control, while the USA/UK/France cluster should show the highest level of impersonal types of control. Preliminary analyses of the data show that the German/Japanese cluster scores significantly higher (using Sheffe's test) than the two other groups on personal centralized control, while the USA/UK/France sample scores significantly higher on formal bureaucratic control. The difference in output control is in the predicted direction (higher for USA/UK/France), but is not significant, while for control by socialization and networks the highest scores are found in the small European group. These results, combined with the observations above, provide a reasonable amount of support for the influence of the preferred type of control mechanism on staffing policy.

In many cases, expatriates are seen as a direct way to control subsidiaries. This would be more necessary when the subsidiary is performing under par. We would therefore expect subsidiaries with a lower than average profitability to 'attract' PCNs to get subsidiaries in line again. Although this relationship would of course benefit from a longitudinal analysis, in a cross-sectional analysis we would expect subsidiaries headed by a PCN to perform below average. This proved indeed to be the case: profitability was lower in subsidiaries that had a PCN as managing director (t-value 2.67, p <0.01, two tailed).

Strategic orientation

The type of international strategy (global, transnational or multidomestic) is one of the most important independent variables in the author's survey on control mechanisms. Relating this to the industry effect described in the previous section, we might expect companies that follow global strategies to have a higher incidence of PCNs as managing director than firms that follow multidomestic strategies. Although the results were not statistically significant, they were in the expected direction. Related to the type of strategy is dependence on either HQ or other subsidiaries, measured in terms of intra-company sales and purchases. In HQ-dependent subsidiaries a large percentage of purchases and sales comes from or goes to headquarters. In subsidiary-dependent subsidiaries, other subsidiaries in the group are the subsidiary's main trading partner. We would expect HQ-dependent subsidiaries to have more PCNs than subsidiary-dependent subsidiaries. This hypothesis is indeed confirmed by the available data (t 1.997, p < 0.05).

Lack of qualified local personnel

With regard to subsidiary countries, we would expect respondents in Latin American countries to attach a higher importance to position filling as a reason for expatriation, since highly qualified local personnel might not be available. The results of the author's survey indeed show that the importance of expatriation because of position filling is felt to be highest in Latin America, closely followed by Asia, while Europe and the USA score lower in this respect. The results are not statistically significant though, probably due to the small sample size in some of the categories.

Future research

Country of location of subsidiary

One of the most remarkable results of this study is that all Irish subsidiaries have a local as managing director. Future studies could first investigate whether this finding is replicated when a larger sample is considered (this sample consisted of only 43 Irish subsidiaries) and second try to find a reason for this peculiarity. Scandinavia turned out to be a region with a very high number of locals in foreign subsidiaries, regardless of the country of origin of the headquarters. High cost of living and a poor climate might make the Scandinavian countries undesirable to expatriates. Future research could pay special attention to this region. At the host country level, government restrictions on the employment of PCNs are a very important influential factor that should be included in future studies.

Country of origin of headquarters

With regard to the clusters of headquarters, one of them consisted solely of small European countries; countries that combine a small home market with a relatively high percentage of MNEs, while exports and imports are large relative to the GNP. Future studies could investigate whether other small European countries with broadly the same characteristics as Norway, Belgium, Denmark and Austria show the same staffing policies. A problem in this respect is that these countries have a smaller amount of MNEs than the countries that were included in the survey (which was in fact the reason why they were not included in the first place) and that company and industry peculiarities could become too dominant.

Industry

Although industry did seem to have an effect on staffing policies, this was not very strong and the reasons were inconclusive. Perhaps future research could identify a number of industry characteristics that are publicly available. Concentration and integration could be used as measures of globalization, while advertising intensity might be a measure for multidomestic orientation (see Kobrin 1991; Ghoshal and Nohria 1993). Growth of the industry might also be an important factor, though the exact relationship with staffing policies is ambiguous.

Structural characteristics

Two structural variables, the size of the MNE and the year of foundation of the subsidiary, proved to add significant explanatory power. Unfortunately, in this sample these data were available for only a small proportion of cases. Future studies might try to verify these data for a larger number of cases, so that the findings could be verified. Additional structural characteristics that might be of influence are the type of subsidiary (sales/service, production/assembly/R&D) and the entry mode (greenfield or acquisition). Production, assembly or R&D subsidiaries are more likely to have an expatriate as managing director as they are of vital importance for headquarters and are more likely to experience personal control from there. Greenfield subsidiaries will also be more likely to have an expatriate as managing director as they have to be started up from scratch. Headquarters are unlikely to interfere personally with well-established acquired subsidiaries as long as they achieve satisfactory results. Finally, a greater percentage of ownership increases the company's bargaining power and hence the likelihood that a PCN will be accepted as managing director. Figure 4.1

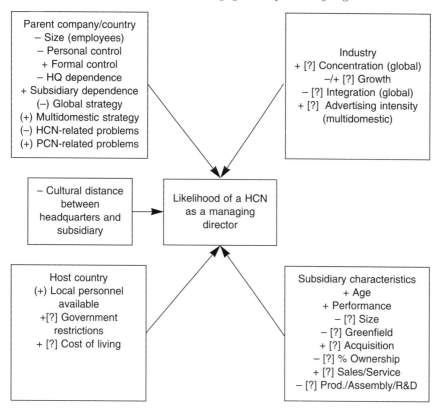

Figure 4.1 Summary of the influences on MNC staffing policies

summarizes the reasons behind the different staffing policies and their influence on the likelihood of an HCN as managing director. Reasons that have not been investigated either in previous research or the author's own study include a hypothesized relationship followed by [?]. For the reasons that were tested, the relationship has been put between brackets if the result was in the expected direction, but not significant.

Of course many of these effects interact with each other. For example, sales/ service subsidiaries are likely to be small and though the size of the subsidiary did not have explanatory power in this sample it has been argued before that it leads to a higher percentage of HCNs (Hamill 1989). On average, acquisitions will be older than greenfield subsidiaries and they might be more appropriate in a multi-domestic industry where knowledge of the local market is important. Previous studies have shown that UK companies have the largest number of acquisitions and Japanese companies the smallest (Wilson 1980; Kogut and Singh 1988; Cho and Padmanabhan 1995). Added together, these factors point in the same direction: a greater chance of an HCN as managing director. To separate these different influences, a very large scale and systematically constructed sample will have to be investigated. It should be clear by now that desk research is the only way to achieve this goal.

Figure 4.1 can easily be linked with some recent attempts to model IHRM. The model of Schuler *et al.* (1993) links various exogenous and endogenous factors to SIHRM issues, functions and policies/practices. Since staffing is one of the SIRHM policies/practices and many of our independent variables resemble their exogenous and endogenous factors, our model can be seen as a further specification of their general model. Two other recent models (Rosenzweig and Nohria 1994; Taylor *et al.* 1996) mainly focus on the similarity between subsidiary HRM practices and headquarters HRM practices. Virtually all of the independent variables included in these models can also be found in Figure 4.1. This is not surprising since the factors that favour the use of an HCN as managing director will also favour an adaptation of overall HRM practices to local circumstances, since both imply an emphasis on local responsiveness/embeddedness. Rosenzweig and Nohria's (1994) study even provides strong evidence for this link, since the presence of expatriates is negatively related to the extent to which subsidiary HRM practices resemble local practices.

Conclusion

The conclusions of this chapter with regard to MNE's staffing policies are summarized in Figure 4.1. In addition, two general conclusions can be drawn from this study. First, it might be very dangerous either to consider Europe as an undifferentiated group in research projects or to generalize findings from one or two European countries to a 'European pattern'. The country of origin effect might not be as strong in all research domains as it seems to be in MNE staffing policies. However, when selecting European countries in a research project, it might be wise to include at least Germany, the UK and one of the smaller European countries and, if possible, to analyse the data at country level.

Another important conclusion is that it would probably be a good idea to consider desk research methods in international management research to a larger extent than has been done so far. The research method used above does not claim to be able to give answers to all questions about staffing policies. However, this type of research can give a sound start in describing differences between countries and industries. Some of the differences can be explained by available knowledge, others cannot. However, as indicated above, these types of data might at least help us to formulate sensible hypotheses that can then be tested by using mail surveys, interviews or case studies. It is the author's firm conviction that academics should reflect on their decisions very carefully before sending out questionnaires or performing interviews to collect data that could possibly be gathered in another way. Otherwise we might find that we have spoiled the market when we really need data that can only be acquired via insiders.

Knut Aulund, Lennart Svensson and Pekka Palermää are Norwegian, Swedish and Finnish nationals respectively.

Notes

1 There is a handful of other studies that discuss the choice between expatriate and local managers (Franko 1973; Youssef 1973; Hamill 1989; Scullion 1991). Unfortunately, these studies focus on very limited samples (e.g. two subsidiaries of one American MNE or only British MNEs) and provide very fragmented empirical information.

2 As a challenge to the reader, try to classify the next three names: Knut Aulund, Lennart Svensson and Pekka Palermää. The correct answers – they identified them- selves – can be found at the end of the chapter (see page 84).

3 One of the anonymous reviewers was interested to know how the method could be used with MNEs from Latin American and Arab countries. The essentials would be the same. However, some specific problems might occur with Latin American emigrants in the USA; are they PCNs or HCNs? Identification would not be a problem in most other countries, except for Spain and Portugal. For Arab countries, the main problem would be that very few Western researchers (including the author) are familiar with Arab languages. As the example of Japan in the study shows, this does not necessarily preclude correct classifications. Of course, calling on the assistance of Arab academics could be a solution in this case.

4 The fact that no service companies are included in this study limits the ability to generalize the findings of this chapter. An attempt to remedy this problem by including companies from a service sector (banking) ran into problems. Less information was available in address books on service companies so that some of the analyses in this chapter could not be executed. It was therefore decided to leave these data out altogether. What can be concluded from the data that were available is that the general patterns described in this chapter did not change and that the banking sector on average employed even more PCNs as managing directors than the motor industry. As one of the anonymous reviewers suggested, a high percentage of PCNs in the service sector might be attributed to their representational function.

5 Although Hofstede's work has elicited some criticism, it is largely accepted as a helpful though crude way to quantify cultural differences (see Harzing and Hofstede 1996 for a discussion of the various critiques and the extensive use of Hofstede's dimensions in other studies; see Søndergaard 1994 for a summary of reviews, replications and citations).

6 Note that the actual percentage of TCNs might be underestimated as the adequate classification of TCNs is a weakness of this research method. All of the six misclassifica- tions were TCNs. If we extrapolate this finding in a linear way, the actual percentage of TCNs might lie around 5.5 per cent, but still constitutes a minority. In the question- naire of the author's survey that was completed by corporate HRM managers, the average percentage of TCNs lay around 5 per cent, with the highest percentage of TCNs in Asia.

7 The six-cluster solution placed Hong Kong in a separate cluster that was not signifi- cantly different (Z= -1.009, sig. 0.313) from the cluster with the other two Far Eastern countries. The four-cluster solution groups the four Scandinavian countries together with Ireland, while the remaining European countries form a separate cluster.

8 I am grateful to an anonymous reviewer for pointing this out to me.

References

Bartlett, C.A. and Ghoshal, S. (1989) *Managing Across Borders. The Transnational Solution,* Boston MA: Harvard Business School Press.

Borg, M. and Harzing, A.W.K. (1995) 'Composing an international staff', in A.W.K. Harzing and J. Van Ruysseveldt *International Human Resource Management,* London: Sage, pp. 179–204.

Boyacigiller, N. (1990) 'The role of expatriates in the management of interdependence, complexity and risk in multinational corporations', *Journal of International Business Studies* 21(3): 357–81.

Briscoe, D.R. (1995) *International Human Resource Management*, Englewood Cliffs NJ: Prentice Hall.

Cho, K.R. and Padmanabhan, P. (1995) 'Acquisition versus new venture: the choice of foreign establishment mode by Japanese firms', *Journal of International Management* 1(3): 255–86.

Dillman, R. (1978) *The Total Design Method*, New York: Wiley.

Dowling, P.J. and Schuler, R.S. (1990) *International Dimensions of Human Resource Management*, Boston: PWS-Kent.

Doz, Y. (1986) *Strategic Management in Multinational Companies*, New York: Butterworth-Heineman.

Fatehi, K. (1996) *International Management*, New Jersey: Prentice Hall.

Ferner, A. (1995) 'Country of origin effects and human resource management in multinational companies', work in progress paper, Coventry: Industrial Relations Research Centre, University of Warwick.

Fox, R.J., Crask, M.R. and Kim, J. (1988) 'Mail survey response rate: a meta analysis of selected techniques for inducing response', *Public Opinion Quarterly* 52: 467–91.

Franko, L. (1973) 'Who manages multinational enterprises?', *Columbia Journal Of World Business* 8(2): 30–42.

Ghoshal, S. and Nohria, N. (1993) 'Horses for courses: organizational forms for multinational corporations', *Sloan Management Review*, Winter: 23–35.

Hair, J.F., Anderson, R.E., Tatham, R.L. and Grablowski, B.J. (1979) *Multivariate Data Analysis*, New York: Macmillan.

Hamill, J. (1989) 'Expatriate policies in British multinationals', *Journal of General Management* 14(4): 18–33.

Harvey, L. (1987) 'Factors affecting response rates to mailed questionnares: a comprehensive literature review', *Journal of the Market Research Society* 29: 341–53.

Harzing, A.W.K. (1994) 'Organizational bumblebees: international transfers as a control mechanism in multinational companies', paper presented at the doctoral tutorial of the 20th annual meeting of the European International Business Academy, Warsaw, 11–13 December.

—— (1995a) 'Strategic planning in multinational firms', in A.W.K. Harzing and J. Van Ruysseveldt *International Human Resource Management*, London: Sage, pp. 25–50.

—— (1995b) 'The persistent myth of high expatriate failure rates', *International Journal of Human Resource Management* 6(2): 457–75.

—— (1995c) 'MNE staffing policies: in search of explanations for variety', paper presented at the 21st annual meeting of the European International Business Academy, Urbino, 10–12 December.

—— (1996a) 'Environment, strategy, structure, control mechanisms, and human resource management', company report of doctoral research project, Maastricht: University of Limburg.

—— (1996b) 'How to survive international mail surveys: an inside story', conference proceedings of the 22nd EIBA conference, Stockholm, 15–17 December, pp. 313–39.

—— (1997) 'Response rates in international mail surveys: results of a 22 country study', *International Business Review* 6(6): 641–65.

Harzing, A.W.K. and Hofstede, G. (1996) *Planned Change in Organizations and the Influence of National Culture*, Greenwich CT: JAI Press.

Hendry, C. (1994) *Human Resource Strategies for International Growth*, London: Routledge.

Hodgetts, R.M. and Luthans, F. (1994) *International Management*, New York: McGraw-Hill.

Hofstede, G. (1980) *Culture's Consequences. International Differences in Work-Related Values*, London: Sage.

—— (1991) *Cultures and Organizations. Software of the Mind*, Maidenhead: McGraw-Hill.

Jobber, D. (1986) 'Improving response rates in industrial mail surveys', *Industrial Marketing Management* 15: 183–95.

Kobrin, S.J. (1988) 'Expatriate reduction and strategic control in American multinational corporations', *Human Resource Management* 27: 63–75.

—— (1991) 'An empirical analysis of the determinants of global integration', *Strategic Management Journal* 12: 17–31.

Kogut, B. and Singh, H. (1988) 'The effect of national culture on the choice of entry mode', *Journal of International Business Studies*, Fall: 411–32.

Kopp, R. (1994) 'International human resource policies and practices in Japanese, European and United States multinationals', *Human Resource Management* 33(4): 581–99.

LaGarce, R. and Kuhn, L.D. (1995) 'The effect of visual stimuli on mail survey response rates', *Industrial Marketing Management* 24: 11–18.

Mead, R. (1994) *International Management. Cross Cultural Dimensions*, Oxford: Blackwell.

Morrison, D. (1974) 'Discriminant analysis', in R. Ferber (ed.) *Handbook of Marketing Research*, New York: Wiley, pp. 2442–57.

Neghandi, A.R. and Welge, M. (1984) *Beyond Theory Z: Global Rationalization Strategies of American, German and Japanese Multinational Companies, Advances in International Comparative Management*, Greenwich CT: JAI Press.

Porter, M.E. (1986) 'Competition in global industries: a conceptual framework', in M.E. Porter *Competition in Global Industries* Boston: Harvard University Press, pp. 15–56.

Prahalad, C.K. and Doz, Y.L. (1987) *The Multinational Mission*, New York: Free Press.

Ronen, S. and Shenkar, O. (1985) 'Clustering countries on attitudinal dimensions: a review and synthesis', *Academy of Management Review* 10(3): 435–54.

Rosenzweig, P.M. and Nohria, N. (1994) 'Influences on human resource management practices in multinational corporations', *Journal of International Business Studies* 25: 220–51.

Schuler, R., Dowling, P.J. and De Cieri, H. (1993) 'An integrative framework of strategic international human resource management', *Journal Of Management* 19(2) 419–59.

Scullion, H. (1991) 'Why companies prefer to use expatriates', *Personnel Management* 23(11): 32–5.

Søndergaard, M. (1994) 'Hofstede's consequences: a study of reviews, citations and replications, *Organization Studies* 15(3): 447–56.

Taylor, S., Beechler, S. and Napier, N. (1996) 'Toward an integrative model of strategic international human resource management', *Academy of Management Review*, 21(4): 959–65.

Tung, R.L. (1981) 'Selection and training of personnel for overseas assignments', *Columbia Journal of World Business* 15: pp. 68–78.

— (1982) 'Selection and training procedures of U.S., European, and Japanese Multinationals', *California Management Review* 25(1): 57–71.

— (1987) 'Expatriate assignments: enhancing success and minimizing failure', *Academy of Management Executive* 1(2): 117–25.

Wilson, B. (1980) 'The propensity of multinational companies to expand through acquisitions', *Journal of International Business Studies* 12: 59–65.

Youssef, S.M. (1973) 'The Integration of local nationals into the managerial hierarchy of American overseas subsidiaries: an exploratory study', *Academy of Management Journal* 16(1): 24–34.

Yu, J. and Cooper, H. (1983) 'A quantitative review of research design effects on response rates to questionnaires', *Journal of Marketing Research* 10: 36–44.

5 Localization as an ethical response to internationalization

John Hailey

Introduction

Research into the issues of internationalization and the way organizations adapt to the challenges of working in different countries and cultures must increasingly include evidence not just from the corporate sector but also from public or not-for-profit sectors. Most researchers have focused on the way multinational companies have responded to working internationally. However, the experience of major multilateral agencies such as the United Nations or leading international non-government organizations (INGOs) such as the Red Cross, Oxfam or CARE can also shed valuable light on the internationalization process.

Such development agencies operate throughout both the developed and the developing world. The Red Cross is represented in most countries; World Vision operates in nearly a hundred different countries, while PLAN International directly employs nearly 5,000 staff in 33 different countries. Not only are these agencies operating in poor, turbulent environments, but they do so with limited resources. It many ways their ability to mobilize and motivate staff in such difficult conditions and diverse cultures is an object lesson for many multinationals.

In the current competitive environment, international development agencies and multinational companies face growing pressure to make the most cost-effective and ethical use of their resources. Multinationals are under pressure from shareholders to increase dividends, managers are expected to build market share or achieve global economies of scale, while pressure groups and the media articulate growing concern for social values, the environment and sustainable development. In 1996, for example, Shell was faced with a welter of criticism both from European environmentalists over their plans to dismantle the Brent Spar oil platform and from social activists concerned at their continued investment in Nigeria and their tacit support for the Nigerian military regime.

Development agencies and INGOs face an equally difficult balancing act. Some of these are acted out in public, as seen by the budget crises facing the UN system, while many agencies struggle with major strategic dilemmas in private. INGOs are increasingly under pressure to decentralize their activities, be less operational, and increasingly work in participative ways through a variety of partners in the South, while ensuring quality, value for money and promoting the value of their work to politicians, official donors and private sponsors, as well as the local community with whom they want to work. Such INGOs have to balance the demands and conditions imposed by their donors in the industrialized countries of the North with the growing pressure to indigenize their operations in the South and promote a more responsive, participative way of working with local communities.

Faced with the challenge of trying to succeed in this competitive environment, both types of organizations recognize that the way they manage and motivate their staff is key to their success in working internationally. This perception has been shaped by the work of different researchers and commentators who have examined how they manage their staff around the world and argued for the introduction of a clear international human resource strategy (Dowling and Schuler 1990; Hendry 1994; Scullion 1995; Welford and Starkey 1996).

The continued employment of expatriates is still an important element in such strategies, despite their cost and being a possible source of tension. The response of many human resource strategists is that expatriates still play a valuable role as a source of expertise, corporate control, and international learning. Moreover, they would argue that tension can be reduced through innovative ways of generating commitment, shared values and common purpose. This chapter reviews some of the ethical and operational issues of the continued use of expatriates and attempts to test the role of shared values and commitment in reducing tension between expatriates and local staff by comparing and contrasting the perceptions towards expatriates of staff working in profit-driven multinationals with the attitudes of local staff in overtly value-driven, non-profit development agencies.

The evidence suggests that although these organizations publicly emphasize shared values, commitment and an ethical, participative approach to their work, it appears that relations between local staff and expatriate development workers are still strained and dysfunctional. This in turn raises the question as to whether the continued use of expatriates is both a cost-effective and ethical use of organizational resources, and suggests instead that the localization of senior posts is an ethical and efficacious response to internationalization.

Localization: a cost-effective alternative

On the one hand there are the direct costs of employing expatriates and their families, including relocation expenses, accommodation and special allowances; added to which are difficulties of recruiting good expatriates willing and able to work away from home, let alone the recruitment and training costs. Recent studies argue for increased investment in more sophisticated expatriate recruitment and selection processes, as well as in comprehensive cross-cultural training (Janssens 1995; Harvey 1996). There are also the financial costs of expatriate mistakes. Thus, for example, Armstrong (1987) in a highly critical article on expatriates in Tanzania noted how they drew up plans that ignored local realities and resulted in costly mistakes. He also demonstrated how expatriates made unnecessary, and therefore costly demands on limited local resources and staff time.

On the other hand there are the opportunity costs of failing to develop local management talent and not promoting staff who understand the local market and political environment, can work effectively in the local cultural context, develop long-term relationships with local customers and suppliers, and build a network of local contacts. Furthermore, there is also the cost and consequences of the personal tensions and cross-cultural misunderstandings that may jeopardize relations between expatriates and local staff. Research in Southeast Asia which reviewed the perception of local staff highlighted some of the problems faced by expatriates as outsiders and their failure to adapt to the local business culture (Hailey 1996a). Local managers were concerned at the short-termist nature of the expatriate timescale and their perceived lack of long-term commitment. They were suspicious that expatriates made decisions to suit their careers rather than for the good of the business. Moreover, many expatriates were perceived as being culturally insensitive with inappropriate training or interpersonal skills which resulted in their failure to build mutual trust with local staff or develop profitable contacts within the local business community.

There was also resentment by local staff at the continued employment of expatriates, not just because of their questionable performance, but also because of their perceived power, perks and salary. This resentment of the perks and privileges enjoyed by many expatriate managers is fuelled by the belief of many local managers that there is a 'glass ceiling' of expatriates that blocks their own career ambitions and reduces chances of promotion (Hailey 1996b). When combined together these tensions have a detrimental impact on organizational morale, staff commitment, public image and relations with the local business community.

Expatriation and localization: the research dilemmas

Yet despite the cost, both direct and indirect, of the continued use of expatriates, all the evidence points to the growing demand by multinational firms and international agencies for expatriate staff who can work internationally. Most recruitment specialists and consultancies suggest that multinationals expect to recruit more international executives and employ more expatriates. This is supported by the evidence of researchers who have noted a continued demand for expatriates and staff with overseas experience (Torbiörn 1994; Scullion 1995; Harvey 1996). Multinational firms explain this trend in terms of their expanding role in the global marketplace and their consequent need to transfer skills and expertise to different locales, as well as expose their staff to a global perspective and be able to co-ordinate systems and strategies around the world (Hailey 1996a). Yet there is evidence to suggest that this trend may be partly explained by a degree of resistance by some local staff to work in such a multinational environment or be transferred overseas (*The Economist* 1995).

However, our understanding of the reasons behind this ongoing investment in expatriate staff, rather than in developing indigenous talent, is not helped by the dearth of research on the performance and perceptions of local staff and the limited analysis of the 'non-performance' of localization policies. The small body of research that does exist includes contradictory evidence as to the attitude of local staff to their expatriate managers. One study examined the extent of the negative perception of local staff towards their expatriate managers and concluded that such tensions could have an impact on productivity and profitability (Hailey 1996a). Another study based on research in Hong Kong indicated that local staff felt that expatriate managers were more supportive than their local counterparts (Selmer *et al.* 1994).

Other research has analysed the obstacles to effective localization experienced by a multinational operating in West Africa and the failure of a new generation of local managers to provide for their succession (Hailey 1994). The issue of localization and succession was also examined by Cohen (1992) in his study of 'failed retention' in Kenya, and by Leach (1993) in her analysis of expat/counterpart relations and their implications for the future role of expatriates in development projects. Vance and Ring (1994) focused on the need to invest in developing the skills and confidence of the host country workforce, rather than merely investing in the training of expatriate staff.

The overall lack of research in this area can be contrasted with the extensive literature on the role, recruitment, training and performance of expatriates employed by both development agencies (Fry and Thurber 1989; Hancock 1989) and multinational firms (Brewster 1991; Black *et al.* 1992; Mamman 1995; Scullion 1995; Harvey 1996). As Leach suggests, much of the literature is fundamentally flawed in that it limits itself almost exclusively to a discussion of expatriate concerns and 'ignores the importance of local inputs and local personnel' (Leach 1993: 316). Consequently, our analysis of the consequences of expatriation is rather one-sided, and our understanding of the complex dynamics of the localization process is still fairly hazy.

Thus to recap, we have a situation where international organizations face competing, often contradictory demands from different stakeholders. There is now greater public accountability and therefore awareness of the need to balance efficiency with ethical use of all resources. There is growing evidence to suggest that expatriates are an increasingly expensive and even counter-productive human resource that could be managed more effectively or replaced by host country nationals. Yet expatriates and international executives continue to be employed in growing numbers. However, because of the lack of research in this area it is unclear whether this is because of their expertise and the lack of a local skill base, or whether it is because the continued use of expatriates is part of the process of building a global, learning corporate culture. Is it because, as suggested earlier, local staff are unwilling to work internationally, preferring instead the security of their domestic working environment? Or is it, as many local staff would suggest, because of the colonial mentality of many multinational organizations and the perception that they do not trust local staff?

Localization: an issue of trust and ethics

The issue of trust and commitment is something that has taxed managers and researchers alike. Historically, there existed an implicit bond of trust between those who owned a business and the managers they employed to run it. Rather than being formally defined or prescribed, this bond of trust was reinforced by a variety of socialization processes which would have informally influenced and modified managerial behaviour, thereby achieving a form of 'cultural control' (Child 1984). As agents of the owners and shareholders bound in this relationship of trust, managers would be expected to demonstrate a degree of commitment to their employers and the good of the organization generally. In return, the owners or shareholders implicitly promise security of employment or career advancement.

However, by the late 1980s the nature of this relationship had changed, partly because of increased job insecurity, partly the disintegration of traditional managerial norms and partly the increasing 'professionalism' of managerial work; all of which contributed to the breakdown of the informal mechanisms that had traditionally existed to shape managerial behaviour. Organizations increasingly resorted to a variety of formal systems and procedures designed to prescribe and monitor managerial practice on a day to day basis. Consequently, trust could no longer be taken for granted and the employee–employer relationship changed accordingly. This exposed both the importance and fragility of the traditional relationship of trust and among other things highlighted its importance as a key factor in operationalizing effective localization strategies.

In a review of the issue of trust in international human resource management (IHRM) and the implications for localization strategies, Hope and Hailey (1995) argue that the real issue facing multinationals as to whether they localize their international management is not about the availability of management skill but more a matter of trust. The level of trust that international employers have in the abilities and integrity of local managers is key to our understanding of why international organizations do or do not promote local staff.

Similarly, the evidence in a study by Chan Kim and Mauborgne (1993) emphasized that firms need to trust their local managers if such subsidiaries are to grow and remain profitable. This study focused on how multinationals handle relations with their increasingly autonomous subsidiary operations. Their findings suggest that multinationals need to find innovative ways of generating trust and commitment among local managers because prescribed instrumental systems were proving ineffective in such a multinational environment. They conclude that multinationals should not rely on formal incentive schemes, performance appraisal mechanisms, or other such systems to reward or punish their local managers. Instead they argue that any international organization should encourage an element of 'due process' by improving interpersonal communication and strengthening information flows in such a way that local managers feel empowered, respected and trusted.

Whether people trust each other, and in particular whether colleagues trust each other at work, is a core ethical consideration. The fact that the issue of trust lies at the heart of the relationship between many international organizations and their local staff suggests that the dynamic between expatriates and local staff has an ethical dimension. Moreover, the perceived lack of trust between local staff and expatriate managers noted in the research (Hailey 1996a), raises questions as to the ethics of continuing to use such an expensive 'alien' resource while overlooking the training needs of local staff. This, in turn, raises wider issues for consideration. There is the moral question as to whether it is ethical to misuse organizational resources in this way. There is also the concern whether this behaviour abuses an 'international fundamental right' (Donaldson 1989).

Donaldson's (1989) influential work into the ethics of international business has posited that society as a whole has the 'right' to expect that such businesses will enhance the general interests of consumers, employees and other key stakeholders within that society. Based on this premise, local staff can legitimately argue that they have a 'fundamental right' to be given the same opportunities as any expatriate staff and it is therefore unethical to deprive them of training opportunities, promotion or personal support.

This concern that multinationals were not making effective and therefore ethical use of the host country workforce was explored by Vance and Paderon (1993). They argued that multinational companies had a moral responsibility to train host country workers because of the duties they acquired operating as a business institution in many different countries. These duties include responsibilities:

- to assist expatriates in the successful execution of their assignment;
- to avoid any semblance of discriminatory treatment based upon racial or ethnic prejudice;
- to encourage the treatment of local staff as members of equal status and help integrate them in the local economy;
- to provide opportunities for personal growth and foster personal enlightenment and self-enrichment;
- to help individuals develop useful marketable skills;
- to contribute to the development of a more functional national labour skill base and help develop employment and managerial talent within the host country;
- to introduce effective long-term strategies that create enduring value for a maximum number of stakeholders.

These are all powerful arguments for seeing localization of the host country workforce as a legitimate, ethical and efficacious strategy for any international organization. One of the conclusions from the review of the literature on trust and ethics is that it appears that effective localization is also ethical localization. It is as much about promoting trust between colleagues as about giving local staff equal opportunities with expatriates and making cost-effective, sustainable and therefore ethical use of a key organizational resource.

Whether this rather pious conclusion is reflected in reality is debatable. All the evidence points to multinational companies and international organizations having to devote time to balancing competing demands and resolving conflicts between stakeholders. The tension between local staff and expatriates is merely one example of this phenomenon. However, it is debatable whether many multinationals have the time or motivation to look for innovative, value-driven ways of handling local managers, as advocated by Chan Kim and Mauborgne (1993), or promoting trust between international staff as proposed by Hope and Hailey (1995). Yet all their evidence would suggest that the formal tools and prescribed personnel systems associated with HRM are not effective in such an international setting. Therefore, if as the research suggests, multinationals should employ ethical, value-driven ways of promoting a degree of localization and handling local–expatriate relations, then it would seem appropriate to review the experience and perceptions of staff working for overtly value-driven organizations such as international development agencies.

Localization and international development agencies

The role of these agencies and INGOs has grown rapidly over the last fifteen years with the diversion of aid funds away from governments to non-government organizations. They are increasingly important players in the aid sector which in 1997 had a turnover of nearly US$60 billion. INGOs include among their number strategic alliances such as Oxfam International or the Save the Children Alliance and major transnational non-profit making organizations such as PLAN International or World Vision. PLAN, for example, has a global headquarters in the UK, a funding base in nine different industrialized countries and 4,800 employees in 1994 working in 33 different developing countries. World Vision has its international headquarters in California and employs over 5,000 staff in nearly a hundred different countries. In Europe major INGOs include DanChurchAid and Radda Barnen in Denmark, Misereor and EZE in Germany, NOVIB and HIVOS in The Netherlands, and ActionAid and Oxfam in the UK.

Most of these INGOs publicly espouse ethical values, as they were established to alleviate suffering, relieve poverty, promote justice and facilitate sustainable development. Most of them emphasize their caring, participative and ethical approach to their work and, as a consequence, one would expect that in such a value-driven environment they would have championed ethical, value-driven ways of promoting local staff and alleviating expatriate–local tensions.

In an attempt to test this, a study was undertaken of local staff employed or funded by such INGOs in sub-Saharan Africa and South Asia. They were all employed in responsible management positions and had been participants of specialist courses run by Cranfield University's International Development Centre. These courses are designed to improve the strategic understanding and management capability of specialist development workers and NGO staff. The survey approach, sample size and gender mix were similar to those used in earlier research in Southeast Asia (Hailey 1996a). The questionnaire was modified somewhat to suit the needs of the sector and followed up with semi-structured interviews with further clarification through email. Thus, the responses are directly comparable with the earlier survey of attitudes and perceptions of local multinational managers to their expatriate bosses.

Despite the fact that the studies were undertaken in two very different sectors, with one group of respondents from major for-profit multinationals and the other from value-driven, non-profit aid agencies, it was somewhat dispiriting to discover so much common agreement. Both groups commented adversely on the perks and privileges of expatriates, the difficulties arising from the failure of expatriates to adjust their management style and tensions caused by cultural misunderstandings and insensitive expatriate behaviour. The one area where there was a difference of opinion was that most of the local staff employed by development agencies felt that expatriates had a valuable role to play in terms of the diversity of experience and skills, while the local staff of multinationals were highly critical of the role and performance of most expatriate managers.

The positive attitude of most local staff working for development agencies towards their expatriate colleagues was based on two distinct issues. First, expatriates had skills and experience in the effective management of development projects that were missing locally. For example, expatriate staff had the under- standing and specialist knowledge to introduce systematic, yet participative, planning procedures, as well as being seen as effective problem solvers. Second, they could handle donor relations and ensure aid funding was not jeopardized. They had the knowledge and experience as well as the cultural confidence to negotiate with donors over terms and conditions, as well as having an insight into donor procedures and systems. As a result, expatriates were invaluable in ensuring the financial sustainability of many non-government organizations and development agencies.

The two studies elicited very similar responses in terms of the perceptions of local staff to expatriates, their terms and conditions, attitude and management style. However, it is a matter of some concern that the feedback from local staff on the attitude and style of expatriate staff was so negative and mirrored many of the comments of the local multinational managers. A number of common themes ran through their responses: that expatriates do not trust local staff; that they were patronizing and still reflected colonial, even racist, attitudes; that they were insensitive to local cultural mores and indifferent to personal needs.

Trust

At least half the respondents commented on the lack of trust displayed by expatriates in their local counterparts. Typical of the respondents' comments was that in their reports to donors expatriates 'portray an image of local staff being incompetent' or that 'local staff are lazy and not committed'. Respondents felt that many expatriate development workers had a fixed image of local staff being 'not reliable, lacking commitment and not trustworthy', and as a result 'don't seem to trust local staff or involve them in decision-making . . . and only have faith in other expatriates'. There were many similar comments to this effect, all of which echo the views of local managers employed by multinationals that were exposed in the earlier study. This suggests that the issue of trust lies at the heart of the relationship between local and expatriate staff.

Ethics and values

While concern about trust may lie at the heart of relationships, even in such value-driven organizations, there was also anxiety at the contradictory ethical stance of many expatriates. Thus, while they may be critical about local staff in reports, they were very happy to use local staff in a 'fixit' or intermediary role to resolve problems, deal with corrupt officials or mediate with government departments. Respondents also commented on the 'two-faced' ethics of some expatriates in that they would rely on the rulebook where convenient, yet breach procedures with impunity when it suited their own needs. For example, the use of organization vehicles was commonly cited as an example of such hypocrisy, with expatriates commonly appropriating them for their own use while denying access to local staff. There was also concern that while aid agencies espoused high levels of accountability and participation in the way they worked with local communities, these values did not transfer to the way they worked with local staff. Thus, many respondents felt there was one stance for public consumption and another for the way they worked internally.

Attitude and respect

Apart from contradictory values and the apparent lack of trust, relations were further aggravated by the attitude of many expatriates. Nearly two-thirds of those interviewed felt that in some way expatriates behaved in a patronizing and even colonial manner. One respondent went so far as to comment that 'I strongly believe that the expatriate phenomenon is one of the most insidious forms of neo-colonialism', and concluded by suggesting that expatriates remained because of the colonial mentality of the aid donors and their failure to listen to the criticism of their expatriate nominees. This was partly explained in that expatriates were perceived to be 'watchdogs of donor money', a perception which runs counter to any genuine partnership or participatory approach to decision-making. Moreover, some expatriate development workers were criticized for being patronizing in their relations with their local colleagues. This was well defined by one respondent as being when expatriates resort to 'frequent and excessive praise when a local manager had accomplished even the smallest task'.

Work practices

Respondents commonly perceived expatriate development workers as hard-working but inflexible in their approach. This was because many expatriates stuck closely to procedures and the 'rulebook' and were 'very particular with fine details'. This provoked one respondent to comment that expatriates were merely 'robots' who were unable to make decisions appropriate to the situation or the cultural context. Another issue that seemed to be the cause of much tension was the failure of expatriates to recognize that local staff have a whole set of obligations that are inherent in their culture. Expatriates all too often appeared cynical or indifferent to the demands placed on local staff arising from family obligations or their requests to take time off for funerals, weddings or illness. Such cultural insensitivity seems to beset most expatriate–local relations and further jeopardizes any hope of building a genuine relationship of trust.

Pay and perks

There was obvious concern among local staff working for INGOs at the salary gap between expatriates and locals, with one estimate that the highest paid local received only one-tenth of his expatriate counterpart's salary. One respondent commented that it was commonly the situation that a junior expatriate earned more than the local 'boss' and could therefore influence decisions far more than would have been possible if paid as a local in a similar post. As with multinational expatriates, there was anger that 'the quality and the quantity of the package differed so vehemently'. Many expatriates continued to receive free or subsidized accommodation, education for their children, medical cover and provision of guards and security, which, interestingly, had become a perk that provoked the envy of local staff. However, some respondents noted that with the increasing number of mature volunteer expatriates arriving through VSO or Peace Corps the range of perks and privileges enjoyed by expatriates varied considerably. Many volunteers lived in difficult conditions with little financial support, which in turn had a knock-on effect of depressing the pay and career expectations of local staff.

This brief review of the feedback of local staff and their perceptions of expatriates highlights some of the concerns felt by local staff at the attitude and behaviour of expatriates and raises questions about why are they still employed at great expense. The fact that they were employed by international development organizations with clearly espoused ethical values and extensive experience of working in many different countries and cultural settings seems to have made little difference. The evidence from both studies would suggest that there are deep-rooted tensions, many of which revolve around whether such international organizations trust their local staff or have invested sufficiently in the selection and training of expatriate staff.

Discussion and conclusion

In the current competitive environment, international agencies and multi-national companies face growing pressure from different stakeholders. There is pressure from shareholders to increase dividends, while pressure groups and the media articulate concern for social values, the environment and sustainable development. As a result both multinationals and international agencies are expected to make the most cost-effective and ethical use of all resources. This includes the way they manage their international human resources, employ expatriates and develop local management talent. This chapter has drawn on existing research which reviewed some of the negative effects of continuing to employ expatriates. While there are obvious constraints on studies of this kind in terms of the limited sample size, the spread of respondents and interpretative biases, the findings all point to the detrimental consequences of the ongoing tensions that exist between local staff and expatriate managers.

There is a well-established thread through much of the human resource literature that argues that in an international organizational setting tensions may be resolved by generating trust, harmony and a sense of common purpose among all staff – expatriates and local staff alike. In an attempt to explore this logic the staff of overtly value-driven organizations were questioned. Yet in spite of all the espoused values of these organizations, the relations between local staff and expatriate development workers were clearly strained and counter-productive.

This raises the question as to whether the continued use of expatriates is both cost-effective and ethical. While there is an obvious need for high quality skills and expertise in complex international organizations, it is debatable whether the continued reliance on expatriate staff is an ethical and efficacious response to internationalization. There is sufficient evidence to suggest that multinational companies and international development agencies need to invest more in developing the skills, confidence and capabilities of local staff. As one respondent succinctly commented, 'If an organization can afford expatriates then they can afford to train locals.'

The economic and operational logic of promoting local staff and developing indigenous talent is obvious. It is based around their knowledge of and contacts in the local community, their experience and understanding of local markets, the cultural setting or the local economy. Local managers are more likely to speak the vernacular language and be culturally assimilated. They can take a long-term perspective on the organization's operations in the local community and make a career commitment to developing activities. This contrasts with the limited perspective of expatriates on short-term contracts whose commitments and loyalties lie elsewhere.

An underlying issue that runs through the research into the relationship between expatriates and their local colleagues, irrespective of the values and remit of the organization involved, is the long-term impact of the breakdown in trust between both parties. As has already been noted, the issue of whether managerial staff trust each other is both an operational concern and a major ethical consideration.

This state of affairs is aggravated by the derogatory, patronizing attitude of many expatriates which, as one respondent reminded us, is reflective of 'the most insidious form of neo-colonialism'. At one level such behaviour breaches a basic human right in that it smacks of intolerance and racism. At another level it is legally discriminatory in that it is an attack on what Donaldson (1989) would see as an 'international fundamental right'. If one accepts such a point of view then local managers could legitimately argue that they have a 'right' to be given the same opportunities as any expatriate and that it is both illegal and unethical to treat them differently or deprive them of impartial management support, training or promotion opportunities. Therefore, unless expatriates can be proven to be justifiable and cost effective, or there is a sea change in their attitude and behaviour, then the elimination of expatriates is possibly the only economically viable and ethically sustainable strategy that organizations can adopt to pursue sustainable internationalization.

References

Armstrong, A. (1987) 'Tanzania's expert-led planning: an assessment', *Public Administration and Development* 7: 261–71.

Black, J.S, Gregersen, H. and Mendenhall, M. (1992) *Global Assignments*, San Francisco: Jossey-Bass.

Brewster, C. (1991) *The Management of Expatriates*, London: Kogan Page.

Chan Kim, W. and Mauborgne, R. (1993) 'Making global strategies work', *Sloan Management Review*, spring: 11–27.

Child, J. (1984) *Organisation*, London: Harper & Row.

Cohen, J. (1992) 'Foreign advisers and capacity building: the case of Kenya', *Public Administration and Development* 12(5): 493–510.

Donaldson, T. (1989) *The Ethics of International Business*, Oxford: Oxford University Press.

Dowling, P. and Schuler, R. (1990) *International Dimensions of Human Resource Management*, New York: PWS-Kent.

The Economist (1995) 'Managing on the frontier', 24 June.

Fry, G.W and Thurber, C.E. (1989) *The International Education of the Development Consultant*, Oxford: Pergamon.

Hailey, J. (1994) 'Localising the multinationals: limitations and problems', in S. Segal Horn (ed.) *The Challenge of International Business*, London: Kogan Page.

—— (1996a) 'The expatriate myth: cross-cultural perceptions of expatriate managers', *The International Executive* 38(2): 255–71.

—— (1996b) 'Breaking through the glass ceiling', *People Management*, 11 July.

Hancock, G. (1989) *The Lords of Poverty*, London: Macmillan.

Harvey, M. (1996) 'The selection of managers for foreign assignments', *Columbia Journal of World Business*, winter: 103–18.

Hendry, C. (1994) *Human Resource Strategies for International Growth*, London: Routledge.

Hope, V. and Hailey, J. (1995) 'Beyond human resource management: internationalisation, localisation, and building trust', paper presented at the Academy of International Business annual conference, Bradford University.

Janssens, M. (1995) 'Intercultural interaction: a burden on international management', *Journal of Organisation Behaviour* 16(2).

Leach, F. (1993) 'Counterpart personnel, a review of the literature with implications for education and development', *International Journal of Educational Development* 13(4): 315–30.

Mamman, A. (1995) 'Socio-biographical antecedents of intercultural effectiveness', *British Journal of Management* 6(2): 97–114.

Scullion, H. (1995) 'International HRM', in J. Storey (ed.) *Human Resource Management: A Critical Text*, London: Routledge.

Selmer, J. Kang, I. and Wright, R. (1994) 'Managerial behaviour or expatriate versus local bosses', *International Studies of Management and Organisation* 24(3): 48–63.

Torbiörn, I. (1994) 'Operative and strategic use of expatriates in new organisations and market structures', *International Studies of Management and Organisation* 24(3): 64–78.

Vance, C.M. and Paderon, E.S. (1993) 'An ethical argument for host country workforce training and development in the expatriate management assignment', *Journal of Business Ethics* 12: 635–41.

Vance, C.M. and Ring, P.S. (1994) 'Preparing the host country workforce for expatriate managers: the neglected side of the coin', *Human Resource Development Quarterly* 5(4): 337–53.

Welford, R. and Starkey, R. (1996) *Business and the Environment*, London: Earthscan.

6 International rewards systems

To converge or not to converge?

Paul R. Sparrow

Introduction

An analysis of the business and academic literature presents a confusing picture for the practitioner. We see evidence both of international convergence around best practice coupled with an increasingly sophisticated awareness of the distinctive nature of rewards policies and behaviour across countries. Therefore the agenda being pursued by HRM academics now focuses on the need to understand and integrate knowledge about three sets of factors (Sparrow and Hiltrop 1997): those that lead to distinctive national patterns of HRM; those that are making national business systems (and the HRM policies they encourage) more receptive to change; and the processes through which new policies and practices are being delivered. In order to review the issues associated with this debate, this chapter is split into three main sections, each of which addresses a fundamental question:

1 What is the range of factors that creates distinctive sets of reward policy, practice and employee behaviour across countries?
2 What are the transitions that currently impact the debate about rewards flexibility in the USA, continental Europe and Japan?
3 Do these transitions suggest any overarching or convergent trends?

Factors that create distinctive national rewards systems

The reasons for confusion among international managers and academics about the role of national culture in the rewards field are obvious. Sparrow and Hiltrop (1997) noted that when considering HRM from a European perspective four clear sets of cross-national factors could be seen to shape policy and practice at the organizational level. HRM practices (with rewards policies and practices being just one example) are located within an external environment of national culture value systems, varying institutional influences and factors, powerful but distinctive national business systems, structures and labour markets, and variations in the role and competence of HRM decision-makers. Not surprisingly, the scope for national differences in rewards systems is broad. Each set of factors in turn includes a number of influences that may be seen to shape organizational policy and practice or employee behaviour. The most important institutional influences and their impact on rewards systems behaviour are shown in Table 6.1.

The important national business system influences on rewards policy, practice and resultant employee behaviour are shown in Table 6.2.

The important factors that influence rewards behaviour relating to the role and competence of managers in the sphere of HRM are shown in Table 6.3.

Finally, but by no means least, national culture creates distinct patterns of HRM because of its influence on rewards behaviour. These are summarized in Table 6.4.

Given the range of influences detailed in Tables 6.1 to 6.4, it is not surprising that when employees are asked about the desirability of such issues as performance-related pay, flexible benefits, competence or skill-based pay, changes in bonus levels, share options and the like, it is very difficult to fathom how much of their answer is due to a reflection of national culture *per se* and how much is a product of other influences such as institutional, business system and HRM actor competence factors. This is an important and very practical distinction for international HRM managers to be able to make. Consider a multinational organization that wants to introduce a competence-based pay system worldwide which will require an upwards appraisal process. If national managers agree or disagree with this specific policy because they perceive that the people who make the HRM decisions (personnel managers, line managers or subordinates) are not competent enough, the new rewards practice may still work if the firm deals with

Table 6.1 Institutional influences on rewards behaviour

Level of provision of social security and welfare	Shapes the reward–effort bargain and the power of pay differentials
Scope of labour legislation and its recency of codification	Creates new codes of conduct through issues such as sex discrimination, equal pay for equal work, and minimum wages
Employer–employee bias in legislation	Influences expectations of rewards enhancement
Role of trades unions as a mediating party and level of collective bargaining in the employment relationship	Shapes factors such as pay relativities between skills groups and plants
Level of corporate responsibility and penalty for redundancy	Influences the strength with which claims for pay advancement might be pursued
Overall level of organizational autonomy that such an institutional pattern engenders	

Table 6.2 Business system influences on rewards behaviour

Degree of state ownership	Influences the extent to which pay rates may be regulated and controlled
Average size of organizations	Influences the level of formality built into wage systems
'Life expectancy' of organizations and the typical duration of employee tenure	Influences the centrality of short-term and hard contractual financial incentives or longer term, non-monetary and implicit rewards
Fragmentation or integration of the economy around core industrial sectors	Influence the benchmark pay comparators and the value of industry-specific skills in the labour market
Corporate performance criteria engendered by the national business system	Influence the range of stakeholders who have a say in wealth creation and distribution, and the extent to which short- or long-term return on investments are favoured

Table 6.3 HRM actor competence influences on rewards behaviour

Extent to which there is strategic integration of HRM decisions either through direct representation, decision-making participation and formal process	Influences the strength of signals and messages about corporate performance as potential mediators of performance and rewards expectations
Level of decentralization and devolvement of HRM powers to line managers	Influences the extent to which managers are comfortable, capable or skilled in handling individual reward negotiations
Level of contracting out or externalization of rewards planning systems	Influences the degree of flexibility or not of the organization to manipulate basic issues such as grade structures and market–pay comparator groups
Degree of professional and career allegiance of HR managers to the function as a consequence of their career routes, and the level of experience in HRM decision-making and line management exposure	Influences the level of technical insight into the mechanics of rewards systems, and the importance and degree of attention given to legislative, fairness and equity concerns in the operation of pay systems

Table 6.4 Cultural value orientation influences on rewards behaviour

Differences in the attitudes and definitions of what makes an effective employee and the associated qualities that are recruited, trained and developed	Influence the effort put towards, and value of, specific competences within the labour market
Different styles and attitudes to the giving of face-to-face feedback and associated behaviours in interview, communication, negotiation and participation processes	Influence the extent to which power and influence over rewards issues will be ceded to one-to-one fora
Differences in internal career anchors	Influence the attractiveness of different advancement and mobility patterns within labour markets
Different expectations of the manager–subordinate relationship and their impact on performance management and motivational processes	Influence the perceived validity and attractiveness of performance-related pay systems, incentive programmes
Differential concepts of distributive justice, socially healthy pay and the individualization of reward	Set many of the expectations around the new rewards equation

the issues of skill and credibility. If national managers agree or disagree because the national business system in which they operate tends to reinforce specific corporate performance criteria which sideline this concept of effectiveness, then changes in corporate governance or control systems may save the day. If the issue is one of legislative influence which rules against the adoption of a certain practice, then the firm may be limited in extension of the programme worldwide or may finds ways round the letter of the law. However, if the objection is due to the cultural values held by individual employees, then there is a real problem. Values are predictive of behaviour and if the policy is counter-cultural it will either simply be rejected locally, or be modified in a way which the organization did not intend, or even worse apparently adopted but operated on a totally different set of behavioural and decision rules. The international HRM manager needs to know which HRM policies are values free and which are values linked.

In truth, we have not yet addressed such a simple issue. This is because much of the historical discussion of comparative rewards management has concentrated on three descriptive issues (Atchinson 1990):

- wage level (average level of remuneration);
- wage structure (the pattern of differentials or relativities within an organization);
- wage form (the mix of elements that make up the remuneration package and the variety of benefits).

Distinctive national positions across all three forms of comparison are easy to summarize. For example, in the USA, wage level is an important decision. This is because it is both seen as an important factor in organizational competitiveness and is a natural consequence of a reliance on highly active external labour markets. Therefore, the need to know what the competitors are paying is an important issue and is achieved through the collection of labour market data by wage surveys. At the other end of the scale, wage level decisions carry far less weight in countries such as Australia, Thailand and (until recently) New Zealand. This is because wage levels are more prone to be controlled through incomes policies or commissions which attempt to link and associate wage levels to productivity improvements. A principle of 'comparative wage justice' exists whereby legislative and collective practice agreements tend to establish common rates for the job and maintain set parities (Whitfield 1988). Decisions about wage structure are also seen to be distinctive. These determine the differentials between jobs or employees within an organization. Wages, it was argued, may be differentiated on the basis of the job, a combination of output of the organization and the job, or the skills and abilities input by the individual. US organizations rely quite strongly on a combination of job and output based systems, with complex and structured job evaluation processes acting as a basis for determining wage structure, aided by increasing attention to the need for more performance or output related measures. In contrast, Japanese organizations favour input systems, which differentiate pay on the basis of the education, experience and seniority of the employee. The particular job that an individual is performing at any one time is not seen as important. Bradley *et al.* (Chapter 7, this volume) analyse the significance of cultural values in designing rewards policies. As Table 6.4 shows, the mechanisms through which national culture orientations influence rewards behaviour deserve more investigation. Nonetheless, we must not pursue the 'cultural determination' issue unquestioningly. This chapter is intended to remind us of the limits that must be placed around such descriptions and prescriptions of comparative practice in the light of recent business transitions.

Transition management: linking rewards issues to developments in national business systems

The business press headlines remind us that in many parts of the world such stereotyped reward and payment systems are coming under intense pressure to change. Despite our insights into the factors that make rewards management distinctive across countries, it has become easy to argue that the nature of work and organizational life is best understood as a subset of the political economy and that this is where most of the new people and rewards management developments will be driven from. Our understanding about rewards policies and practices and the national business system within which they reside is being built up on an increasingly international and comparative basis. Employees and employers alike are increasingly aware that there is a competition between the different forms of capitalism and their associated mindsets and that each of these systems looks at the content and role of HRM in very different ways (Sparrow and Hiltrop 1994). The role of the state and financial sectors, national systems of education and training, employment and tenure expectations and national cultures combine to create 'national business recipes', each driven by its own 'dominant logic of action' (Whitley 1992). Therefore the development and success of specific managerial structures and HRM practices – such as ideologies about motivation, reward and commitment – are strongly determined by the degree of integration between and support from the institutional arrangements in a country (Lane 1992). This stream of work argues, for example, that any progress that has been made towards a new territory and role for HR practitioners in the UK is at best fragile and subject to becoming 'unlocked' or 'dislocated' by the marked changes in markets and technology that we now witness (Knights *et al.* 1992). More importantly, as we break away from the American assumptions about high performance practices and look towards other parts of the world such as Europe and the Far East in order to gain insights into best practice, there is a growing understanding about the importance – and dominating rule – of national business systems in setting the context for rewards management. In order to highlight the need to understand the business system context, we can consider the situation in continental Europe, Japan and the USA. This reveals:

1 The extent of change around the world warns us to avoid becoming too obsessed by comparative differences in rewards management.
2 A range of higher level factors above the operation of national culture that must shape our thinking about the topic of rewards management in an international context.

Transitions in continental Europe

In Europe we hear calls to break up national business systems in the pursuit of flexibility. Germany has been the centre of much attention and there is evidence of significant change in some areas of the employment relationship, with the Bundesverband der Deutschen Industrie (BDI) arguing that enterprise is blighted by high tax, wages and welfare costs. While the German labour market is portrayed as being inflexible, its companies certainly are not. To counter the export abroad of around 2 million jobs from manufacturing and an increase in unemployment to 4.5 million, Germany has attempted to balance cuts in pension funds, unemployment pay, redundancy protection, health insurance and sickness benefit and more flexible work hours by positive attempts at job creation. From 1990–96, ABB shed 59,000 jobs in western Europe and created 56,000 jobs in Asia and eastern Europe.

There is pressure to break up the 40,000 *Tarifverträge* that regulate German pay and compensation negotiations. Recent years have witnessed major developments towards flexibility across Europe, with labour reforms in Spain in May 1997 and the IG Chemie trade union in Germany finally agreeing in June

1997 to allow Hoechst, Bayer and BASF to cut wages by up to 10 per cent in difficult economic periods. However, the 1997 EU Joint Resolution on Growth and Employment avoided use of the word 'flexible' when describing labour market plans, adopting alternative adjectives of 'adaptable', 'responsive' and 'employment-friendly' (Naudin 1997).

In an OECD study (Lehrman Brothers 1994), EU countries were scaled in terms of how difficult it is to dismiss employees. Countries such as Portugal, Spain and Italy scored above 14 on a 16-point scale. Germany, Finland and Sweden scored around 10. The UK scored 2. Despite the jobs predicament in France, its labour markets are more flexible than is often portrayed. On the one hand it has tenured public sector jobs, tax disincentives to return to employment and a minimum wage. On the other hand, employers have failed to reinvest enough of their retained profits in new plant and equipment to create sufficient jobs (Naudin 1997) to counter demographic population growth (preferring to invest in high yield government bonds). Attitudes to flexibility are understandably ambiguous in France:

1   Wages have lagged behind growth in productivity for more than a decade.
2   Wages have only grown by an average of 0.2 per cent a year throughout the 1990s.
3   The 1997 minimum wage is lower in real terms than it was in 1985 and is widely bypassed by 50 per cent of French industry through subsidized contracts and branch agreements.
4   For more than 40 per cent of the workforce, significant pay rises are tied to individual performance.

There has then been some wage flexibility in Europe but, the critics argue, not enough.

Japanese transitions

Japan is frequently presented as a target for the break-up of national rewards systems and is used to remind us that disillusionment knows no national borders. Its social contract, based on lifetime employment and seniority based pay, is slowly breaking down as forces of internationalization, global competition, demography, slowed economic growth and the collapse of investment banks begin to bite. Salaries and earnings in Japan peak at age 50–54 (compared to 45–49 in the UK), but by the year 2000 a quarter of the Japanese workforce will be aged 55 or older, creating high fixed cost. This is especially so as much of the apparently variable bonus is awarded almost automatically on the basis of age. The seniority based wage system meant that employees could depend on high and virtually guaranteed twice-annual bonuses (amounting to 23 per cent of total compensation).

The chairman of the Japan Federation of Employers Association (Nikkeiren) today urges pay restraint in wage and bonus demands and states that Japanese companies employ 1.2 million excess workers. Deregulation is expected to lead to 10 per cent job losses in the finance, public administration and construction sectors, and Japan has changed from being a role model for HRM policies and practices to becoming a major target for those who argue for the break-up of national business systems (Wood 1994). A survey of the Tokyo Chamber of Commerce and Industry conducted in October 1996 (Nakamoto 1997) found that while 53 per cent of firms still wished for a lifetime employment system, 35 per cent did not. Of firms, 40 per cent had introduced performance related pay (PRP), but felt that the system was not yet working properly; 10 per cent had introduced PRP systems that were now effective; 20 per cent were considering such systems; only 30 per cent had no plans to go down this route.

Flexibility is now an issue in Japan. Although wage increases are flexible, the annual wage bargaining ritual known as *shunto* (or spring labour offensive) in practice used to mean that wages increased uniformly across sectors as awards were made irrespective of productivity. According to the Japanese Ministry of Labour in 1996, although basic wages increased by only 3 per cent (accounting for 72 per cent of total compensation), average final monthly wages increased by 7 per cent (Dawkins 1997). However, 1997 saw divergence from the uniform agreements, with profitable firms like Toyota offering well above the average, but Nissan and Honda falling behind. For the first time in recent history, financial markets dropped harmonious practices and share prices of internationally competitive exporters increased while several organizations have faced bankruptcy. Within companies, the seniority based wage system has come under threat. Honda and Sony have introduced pay systems that place greater emphasis on performance. Mitsubishi has allowed the pay of managers of the same age to vary by plus or minus 10 per cent and many firms are introducing Western-style performance related pay schemes. Sony and Honda run formal merit-based systems. Matsushita has introduced the first tiered wage system in Japan which differentiates between those following a lifetime employment 'contract', newcomers who want to bring forward and forgo the substantial retirement benefits, and those with specialist skills in demand who wish to contract out of most age and service related benefits. Employees are offered the option of receiving their pension as part of their salary rather than as a lump sum at the end of their careers. Term limits for managerial posts and voluntary redundancy programmes have become a common feature. Again, inbuilt rigidities make a difficult situation worse. Japanese workers tend to suffer significant wage cuts when they change jobs. A mid-career job move results in only 70 per cent of the salary of those who stick with the company. Moreover, the tradition of recruiting generalist graduates means that employees who are forced to change jobs find themselves with few transferable technical skills.

Transitions in the USA

Tensions mount worldwide and everywhere we see a questioning of the status quo. The US business model has come in for much praise in recent years because of its superior job creation record in comparison with Europe. However, this flexibility has not been achieved without price. In the first five years of the 1990s, 3.1 million US workers lost their jobs through redundancy and reorganization. The erosion of employment in its more traditional sense and the continued pressure on employers to maintain current staffing levels is expected to continue. In 1991 the American Management Association (AMA) surveyed 1,142 organizations that had downsized (Academy of Management Survey 1995). The limited success and many negative side effects of the strategy were clearly evidenced. Sadly, the 1995 AMA survey saw 'a continuation, if not an acceleration of many of these trends' (Mroczkowski and Hanaoka 1997: 58). Of US organizations, 29 per cent expect further to trim their workforces, the highest proportion since the surveys began in 1987. The use of alternative strategies to stave off redundancies (demotions, transfers, recruitment moratoriums) has declined from 70 per cent of organizations to 43 per cent. A recent survey of 400 US Conference Board organizations shows that 70 per cent expect to continue downsizing (Mirvis 1997). It is seen as an essential way of maintaining cost control, profitability and improved productivity. Political economists contribute to the analysis of obstacles facing rewards and performance management practitioners in the US context by arguing that sustained developments in HRM, and in particular significant improvements in the efficiency of rewards systems, become near impossible while there are 'financial systems that fail to reward companies making hard-to-measure investments in their workforce, and macroeconomic policies that penalise companies that try to provide long term commitments to their employees' (Levine 1995: 2). However, despite such qualms there is evidence of convergence in practice between Japanese and US organizations. The Japanese process of gradual adjustment of employment levels (*Koyochosei*) and the strategies pursued by 'best practice' US organizations attempting to pursue proactive downsizing and work system redesign (Mroczkowski and Hanaoka 1997) are felt to bear many similarities.

Overarching themes or convergent trends?

In the introduction it was asked whether these business transitions suggest any overarching themes in the rewards flexibility debate. There are three such trends that are leading, on the surface at least, to a break-up of distinctive national patterns of HRM. At the very least this makes national rewards systems more receptive to change and in reality creates the possibility of a renewed process of convergence in organizational thinking about best practice in the rewards field. The three themes are:

- a shift from job- to person-based HR systems;
- the transfer of social costs and risks away from organizations;
- significant threats to the psychological contract and a fragmentation and individualization of the reward–effort bargain.

Shift from job- to person-based systems.

The task facing HR and rewards practitioners at the millennium is being made more difficult because much of their armoury is based upon and targeted at job-based systems (Lawler 1994). These include the pay systems that compare different jobs in terms of their complexity and place labour market valuations on jobs by comparing like with like, and selection systems that match the person to the job based on assumptions of predicted performance. But the rhetoric from the management gurus is that the end of the 'job' is nigh. Organizations, for example, are experiencing high levels of rewards failure because most of their pay systems do not reflect strongly enough strategic thrusts towards quality, team working and competition based on time. The rewards systems – and most of the other job-based personnel management systems – break down under pressure from technological change and downsizing. These changes have combined to reduce the 'half-life' of the technical and functional skills associated with a task-based view of the job and therefore the job evaluation systems. This distorts appraisal systems and leads to a breakdown of the pay-for-performance relationship. As organizations reallocate knowledge, information, power and rewards in response to this failure, a shift to person- as opposed to job-related performance management systems becomes inevitable because the evolving set of tasks and activities built into internal roles can no longer be accurately priced in the labour market. According to this argument, it is no longer jobs which have value, but people. The implications for rewards systems are immense, because most US textbooks imply that the job is the basic differentiator of wages in an organization. This is an assumption that is increasingly being challenged.

Transfer of social costs

A second phenomenon of the 1990s has been a continued transfer of responsibility for social cost from organizations to either the state or the individual, and from the state to the individual. Brewster (1998) and Sparrow and Hiltrop (1994) point to the transfer of costs and risks from the state and the organization to the individual within Europe. Several cases have drawn attention to this issue. The decision by Renault to move production away from Vilvoorde in Belgium provided some powerful insights into corporate behaviour. Employment had already fallen from 217,000 in 1982 to 140,000 by early 1997. Facing a FFr5 billion deficit in 1997, Renault (along with Peugeot) had asked the French government for assistance to help pay for an early retirement scheme to shed 40,000 employees aged over 51. The French Finance Minister, Jean Arthuis, stated that the state could no longer pay for such subsidy (Tillier 1997). The closure of a whole plant in France was seen as politically unacceptable. The Belgian government was given one day's notice of the decision on Vilvoorde. The Vilvoorde plant had only opened in January 1995 and carried large technological investments in a computerized, laser-controlled parts store. By most measures it was a profitable plant. The 1994 investment was accompanied by an agreement between unions and management on a flexible working system with nine-hour shifts and variable working days per month. However, although the average net pay of Belgian and French workers at Renault is about the same, Belgian social security contributions are higher, so labour costs at Vilvoorde are 25 per cent higher than in plants in northern France. Closing the Vilvoorde plant will amount to savings of FFr850 million a year, with the same level of production of Clio and Megane cars being achieved by 1,900 workers in French and Spanish factories, compared to 3,100 workers in Belgium. Renault shares increased in value by 25 per cent on the announcement.

Therefore one inevitability in such a period is that the overall HRM agenda and the specific compensation and benefits issues continue to be set – and are being increasingly driven – by institutional behaviour at the level above the organization. For example, in the USA it is calculated that if corporations were now to pay as much tax as they did in the 1950s, the US government would gain $250 billion extra revenue a year, enough to wipe out the entire budget deficit (Korten 1995). Organizations will not pay for social policy. Within the EU, estimates suggest that in the UK the hidden economy is now worth about £80 billion, or 12 per cent of GDP (up from 6 per cent to 8 per cent of GDP in the mid-1980s). At a cost to the treasury of £20 billion a year, it represents a third of all annual tax revenues. States will allow considerable degrees of 'self-help' as long as they do not siphon off too much revenue.

The 'transfer of social costs' agenda includes not just the loss of employment but also the pauperization of many sectors of remaining employment, as jobs are deskilled, working hours are reduced and terms and conditions are deregulated. Western societies are once again considering whether they must provide basic incomes and, if so, who funds them. They are wondering whether it should be accepted that people may have to be paid not to work, and therefore continue to shift the funding of public welfare from taxation of income to taxation of indirect expenditure and consumption. The agenda raised by this transfer of social costs, originally stated in the mid-1980s (Sparrow 1986), could be restated today (see, for example, Kossek *et al.* 1997). A range of problems plays on the minds of rewards consultants and strategists. The 'transfer of social costs' issue is influencing employee rewards behaviour in a number of ways, as shown in Table 6.5.

Changing psychological contract

A related issue therefore has been the arrival of a 'new deal'. Academics talk of a changing 'psychological contract', a term which is used to capture a very wide range of changes around the nature and process of the employment relationship within organizations (Rousseau 1990, 1995; Ehrlich 1994; Morrison 1994; Herriot and Pemberton 1995). The 'contract' is portrayed as an open-ended agreement about what the individual and the organization expect to give and receive in return from the employment relationship. Psychological contracts represent a dynamic and reciprocal deal. New expectations are added over time and the contract changes as perceptions about the employer's commitment

Table 6.5 Impact of transfer of social costs on rewards behaviour

Rise, fall and need for management of true measurement of the levels of unemployment	Influence the degree of insecurity and requirement for immediate financial rewards
An exchange of free time for increased consumerism	Means that employees will not automatically trade off free time for pay because of the increasing attractions and cost of staying in touch with a consumer society
Creation of increasingly productive households	Whereby processes of wealth creation and income substitution blunt the value and incentives created by rewards from employment
Pursuit of jobless economic growth	Whereby careers, progression systems and rewards expectations become constrained to a narrower range of people, given that young employees enter the organization later and older employees leave it earlier
Limitations of economic and monetarist assumptions about employee rewards behaviour	Whereby financial incentives are seen to limit motivational power or link to productivity because of the breach in the psychological contract of employees
Pauperization of employment and increased social divisions	Large segments of the workforce become estranged; traditional social expectations of advancement and the traditional exchange of financial security for compliance
Need for more inventive work sharing, new forms of wealth distribution, alternative forms of work organization and fundamental changes in work values	Needed to accommodate all of the above shifts in behaviour

evolves. These unwritten individual contracts are therefore concerned with the social and emotional aspects of the exchange between employer and employee. A Conference Board (1997) report based on 92 US and European organizations, including IBM, Amoco, Fiat and Philips, found that while 27 per cent denied that an implicit deal had ever existed and 6 per cent believed that they still offered a paternalistic relationship, 67 per cent acknowledged that they no longer had a contractual or tacit understanding with employees that promised a secure job in return for dedicated service. The majority of firms, after a period of denial, perceive that there is low morale, a trust gap and a desire for a new set of HRM tools, practices and priorities at the millennium.

The perceived breach of the psychological contract in the USA and UK has been well documented (Sparrow 1998), but we now see the issue raised in continental Europe and Japan. Such different perceptions highlight the need to understand the different national frames of reference for HRM. At a recent Anglo-French British Council meeting, French HR directors and employment ministers spoke of the need to offer *employabilité*, defined as the creation of competitive competences in the wider labour market. Yet the British and French participants differed wildly in terms of the means through which the creation of such employability should be pursued, the employee relations strategy deployed and the pace at which they thought it legitimate that organizations should challenge the psychological contract of employees (MacLachlan 1996). The perceived breach of contract in Japan is summarized by Nakamoto (1997: 18): 'Japan is in the midst of a tumultuous transition from a community based on sharing to one based on contracts . . . Now companies are saying "you have to be loyal while you are employed but we won't take care of you for life anymore" (Kiyotsugu Shitara, General Secretary Tokyo Managers Union).

Moderating factors

Complex productivity equations

Not only should the debate in Europe be seen in the wider context of business transitions facing Japan and the USA, but the assumption that high wage and high social cost countries such as Germany, France and Sweden are destined to see a fundamental break-up of their social contracts is also a little naive. Insight is needed into two processes that moderate the wage flexibility debate:

1 The complex productivity equations that managers draw upon when making decisions that affect the location of investment and the employment conditions and flexibility demands that might be tied into the investment.
2 The evolution of labour markets and the maturing behaviour that accompanies this which can make apparently cheap labour markets far more expensive than expected.

Therefore a discussion of the important contingencies that surround rewards flexibility decisions (in terms of pay policies or labour cost considerations) forms the last topic of this review of international and comparative rewards issues. The availability, cost and quality of qualified staff vary massively between countries, forcing organizations to develop country-by-country rewards strategies that may contrast starkly or apparently fly in the face of the global transitions outlined above.

Despite the issue of social costs overriding moves towards flexibility in some instances – such as the Renault case – as some German firms have demonstrated, decisions over factory location depend on a variety of factors in addition to labour costs, such as productivity, plant flexibility, closeness to customers and the technical content of the work. A recent flexibility negotiation at Osram, the light bulb manufacturer which is part of the Siemens group, demonstrated how German financial flexibility can be outweighed by other considerations. Production was in danger of being transferred from Augsburg to Bari in Italy, where labour costs were 40 per cent cheaper. However, analysis showed that the output per person in the German plants was twice that in the US plants and it takes thirty-eight times as many people to produce a light bulb in China than it does in Germany, partially cancelling out China's fifty-fold advantage on labour costs (Marsh 1997). IG Metall agreed to an extension in plant operation time. Not surprisingly, in Germany the recent trend has been to trade off reductions in take-home pay by providing more time off work. In a complex deal, Ford Germany intends to save £74 million a year through more flexible work levels, adjustment of shift times and reductions in overtime. The carrot for workers is that they end up with more time off. Already working a 37.5 hour week with 30 days holiday and 10 'free' shifts a year, when they can stay away from work, the deal provides an additional 15 free shifts a year earned through work practice flexibility. Such a deal suits German work values.

Maturing labour markets

Moreover, where national business systems are in transition, rewards policies and issues become complicated by the increased currency carried by either foreign education or foreign company training. Such maturing labour market behaviour is typical of the social, psychological and moral readjustments of a country in transition. Many of these problems have been evidenced in studies of labour market maturation in eastern Europe and China. For example, in the Czech Republic, Hungary and Poland the staffing, recruiting and retaining of skilled managers is often a problem. There are not enough local managers with sufficient levels of experience or who have not been conditioned by old management methods (Lee 1995). In the Czech Republic a recent survey found that 90 per cent of firms experience some sort of recruitment difficulty (Koubek and Brewster 1995). It often takes up to six months to fill a middle management job in Hungary, for example, while in Poland, Western firms have to extend the assignments of their own expatriates until qualified local applicants are found (Redman *et al.* 1995). The staffing process in an international joint venture (IJV) requires the partner to understand the local labour market of the host country, as well as the fit between the desired organizational culture and the national culture. The shortage of staff may be exacerbated by Western companies being able to pay salaries that are exorbitant by local standards (Pullar-Strecker and Papp 1994). Rewards systems also create pressures. Performance evaluation and management is therefore another issue. The IJV has to decide how to evaluate both IJV managers and local staff. Inappropriate control of performance is seen to result if the foreign partner offloads incompetent managers onto the IJV, or if appraisal and reward systems do not fit in with local custom and practice. Pay levels historically were much lower in the Czech Republic than in the West and pay differentials were much narrower. Personal connections were an important way of ensuring rewards. Appraisal schemes today are still relatively new. The Czech Republic has adopted Western rewards systems quite widely, with variable pay and profit sharing systems tied to performance gaining ground (Koubek and Brewster 1995).

Similar transitional issues have been seen in China. A more complex and mature labour market is emerging as the psychological contract is redefined. On the one hand greed, personal hopes of advancement and the need to maintain security in a high-risk economic environment have reinforced a job-hopping mentality, while on the other, firms find they are competing for a scarcer supply of the new value-added workforce. Firms are now having to differentiate between managers of different worth, background and age and to learn how to respond to them. As these firms seek more creative and cost-effective combinations of recruitment, retention, welfare and pay systems, new HRM developments are being forced into the system. Inhouse training now carries more currency than academic qualifications and is boosting the employability of workers, leading to relatively high attrition rates. Rather than leaving to take their technical knowledge back to a Chinese agency or government operated firm, which was a problem in the mid-1980s (Davidson 1987; Holton 1990), Chinese employees now move increasingly to other competitive firms. Reports of talent raiding by new joint ventures became prevalent by the mid-1990s, as the official cap of pay rates of 20 per cent to 50 per cent more than state-owned enterprises (SOEs) was breached. By the mid-1990s, 3M China was paying a premium of 160 per cent to 260 per cent of salary to attract even ordinary clerks in relation to local wage rates (Hua 1994). In order to avoid losing staff pay reviews are held twice or thrice yearly. Foreign-invested enterprises have been allowed considerable latitude in developing their own incentive systems and non-cash bonuses to compensate for the cap on basic wages such as extended vacation, study trips and house purchase schemes became a feature of the labour market (Casati 1991).

Turnover rates similar to those experienced in Hong Kong became a possibility and some of the better performing Chinese SOEs found themselves doubling or tripling benefit packages of key staff. In the longer term, competitive wage rates, a positive work environment and incentives for personal growth are seen as the best defence against this labour competition (Business Asia 1993). This suggests that the early comparative management studies of rewards practice in China (such as Chow and Shenkar 1989), showing that only rudimentary compensation systems existed and those that did lacked focus on performance management issues, may soon become a relic of history. The same problem can be extrapolated to much comparative work.

Conclusions

This chapter has argued that the tradition for descriptive analysis of wage level, structure and form in the international rewards field now needs to be developed by a more sophisticated analysis. In the first instance, this requires consideration of three dynamics. The first is the range of factors that create distinctive patterns of rewards behaviour. Four frames of reference have been outlined: the legislative context; the influence of national business systems, the role and competence of HRM actors; the influence of national culture. In order to help international HR managers to understand the constraints on employee behaviour across international operations, we need to partition the influence of the four sets of influence. Implicitly, therefore, we need a stronger theoretical basis from which to examine the issue of cultural determinism, an issue that is picked up by Bradley *et al.* in Chapter 7 of this volume. However, there are grounds to challenge both the validity and future relevance of the cultural determinism perspective.

A second perspective that must be considered is the range of business transitions that are breaking up national rewards systems. The situation in continental Europe, the USA and Japan has been considered and one conclusion is that radical change is being considered at the organizational level. This analysis highlights three overarching themes that characterize the debate in Europe, the USA and Japan. First, we can see a shift from job- to person-based HR systems, a trend which breaks the historical comparative patterns of wage structure. Second, there is a clear process of transfer of social costs and risks away from organizations and the state. This is creating new employee behaviour patterns and will shift the labour market power of those groups that still have central core skills once the transfer of costs has been fully comprehended. Third, there are significant threats to the psychological contract and a fragmentation and individualization of the reward–effort bargain.

All three themes return attention to the dynamics of individual behaviour and reactions. Therefore, we need far better cross-cultural insight into these three processes, which means that research must focus on the causal links between cultural values and HR behaviour at the individual level. The need for such understanding is reinforced by the analysis of some of the processes through which rewards flexibility may be pursued by organizations – such as decisions to shift investment from one plant to another or investment in apparently cheaper foreign labour markets. This showed that countries, though faced with similar competitive pressures and business transitions, are still pursuing distinctive policy trajectories. Again, the agenda for comparative management research is clear. The new policy trajectories provide a convenient route for national culture still to show its head. We therefore need to analyse the way in which national culture influences both the approaches to and attitudes towards flexibility and new forms of work organization and the various trade-offs these entail (such as trading non-work time or work sharing for pay, or qualification integrity for multi-skilling choices). Similarly, we need to understand the cultural influence on employee behaviour in maturing and evolving labour markets. Such focused and applied analysis will enable international HR managers to know exactly when to converge practice or not, and around which issues.

References

Academy of Management Survey (1995) *Corporate Downsizing, Job Elimination and Job Creation*, New York: AMA.

Atchinson, T.J. (1990) 'Impressions of compensation in the Pacific Rim', in *Research in Personnel and Human Resources Management, Supplement Two*. New York: JAI Press.

Brewster, C. (1998) 'Flexible working in Europe: extent, growth and the challenge for HRM', in P. Sparrow and M. Marchington (eds) *Human Resource Management: The New Agenda*, London: Pitman.

Business Asia (1993) 'Raiders on the bund', *Business Asia*, autumn: 8.

Casati, C. (1991) 'Satisfying labor laws – and needs', *China Business Review*, July–August: 16–22.

Chow, I.H.-S. and Shenkar, O. (1989) 'HR practices in the People's Republic of China', *Personnel*, December: 41–7.

Conference Board (1997) 'Implementing the new employment compact', *HR Executive Review*.

Davidson, W.H. (1987) 'Creating and managing joint ventures in China', *California Management Review*, 24(4): 77–94.

Dawkins, W. (1997) 'Old structure ends in tiers', *The Financial Times*, 9 May: 20.

Ehrlich, J.C. (1994) 'Creating an employer–employee relationship for the future', *Human Resource Management* 33(3): 491–501.

Herriot, P. and Pemberton, C. (1995) *New Deals: The Revolution in Managerial Careers*, Chichester: Wiley.

Holton, R.H. (1990) 'Human resource management in the People's Republic of China', *Management International Review* 30: 121–136.

Hua, D. (1994) 'Feeling the strain', *China Economic Review*, April: 25.

Knights, D., Morgan, G. and Murray, F. (1992) 'Business systems, consumption and change: personal financial services in Italy', in R.D. Whitley (ed.) *European Business Systems: Firms and Markets in their National Context*, London: Sage.

Korten, D.C. (1995) *When Corporations Rule The World*, New York: Berrett-Koehler.

Kossek, E.E., Huber-Yoder, M., Castellino, D., Heneman, R.L. and Skoglind, J.D. (1997) 'The working poor: locked out of careers and the organisational mainstream?', *Academy of Management Executive*, 11(1): 76–92.

Koubek, J. and Brewster, C. (1995) 'Human resource management in turbulent times: HRM in the Czech Republic', *International Journal of Human Resource Management* 6(2): 223–48.

Lane, C. (1992) *Management and Labour in Europe*, Aldershot: Edward Elgar.

Lawler, E.E. (1994) 'From job-based to competency-based organisations', *Journal of Organisational Behaviour* 15: 3–15.

Lee, S. (1995) 'Money talks, talent walks', *Business Central Europe*, April: 33.

Lehrman Brothers (1994) *Jobs Study*, Paris: OECD.

Levine, D.I. (1995) *Reinventing the Workplace: How Business Employees Can Both Win*, Washington, DC: Brookings Institution.

MacLachlan, R. (1996) 'Liberté, Egalité and now employabilité, *People Management* 2(24): 16.

Marsh, P. (1997) 'A shift to flexibility', *The Financial Times*, 21 February: 14.

Mirvis, P.H. (1997) 'HRM: leaders, laggards and followers', *Academy of Management Executive* 11(2): 43–56.

Morrison, D. (1994) 'Psychological contracts and change', *Human Resource Management* 33(3): 353–72.

Mroczkowski, T. and Hanaoka, M. (1997) 'Effective rightsizing strategies in Japan and America: is there a convergence of employment practices?', *Academy of Management Executive* 11(2): 57–67.

Nakamoto, M. (1997) 'Revolution coming, ready or not', *The Financial Times*, 24 October: 18.

Naudin, T. (1997) 'Flexibility can bend job rules', *The European* 371, 19 June: 17–18.

Pullar-Strecker, T. and Papp, B. (1994) 'Manager wanted', *Business Central Europe*, January: 7–9.

Redman, T., Keithley, D. and Szalkowski, A. (1995) 'Management development under adversity? Case studies from Poland', *Journal of Management Development* 14(10): 28–43.

Rousseau, D.M. (1990) 'New hire perceptions of their own and their employer's obligations: a study of psychological contracts', *Journal of Organisational Behaviour* 11: 389–400.

—— (1995) *Psychological Contracts in Organisations: Understanding Written and Unwritten Agreements*, Thousand Oaks CA: Sage.

Sparrow, P.R. (1998) 'New organizational forms, processes, jobs and psychological contracts: resolving the issues', in P. Sparrow and M. Marchington (eds) *Human Resource Management: The New Agenda*, London: Pitman.

—— (1986) 'The erosion of employment in the UK: the need for a new response', *New Technology, Work and Employment* 1(2): 101–12.

Sparrow, P.R. and Hiltrop, J.M. (1994) *European Human Resource Management in Transition*, London: Prentice Hall.

—— (1997) 'Redefining the field of European human resource management: a battle between national mindsets and forces of business transition', *Human Resource Management* 36(2): 201–20.

Tillier, A. (1997) 'Renault cuts and runs from Belgium', *The European*, 6 March: 17.

Whitfield, K. (1988) 'The Australian wage system and its labour market effects', *Industrial Relations*, spring: 149–65.

Whitley, R.D. (ed.) (1992) *European Business Systems: Firms and Markets in their National Context*, London: Sage.

Wood, C. (1994) *The End of Japan Inc.*, New York: Simon and Schuster.

7 Global or multi-local? the significance of international values in reward strategy

Paola Bradley, Chris Hendry and Stephen Perkins

International reward strategy: beyond the Tower of Babel

This chapter describes a pilot project to identify key cultural value sets and their impact on international reward issues for multinational enterprises (MNEs), within the context of national, industry and organizational differences. However, in reviewing the literature on the influence of cultural values, it quickly becomes apparent that this is an unsatisfactory and partial way to see the determination of reward systems and levels of rewards. This leads us to take a radical and somewhat unusual approach to international rewards as a research problem and to propose a methodological solution which could have significant implications for the conduct of international studies of HRM from both a theoretical and practical point of view.

We begin by identifying some of the key cultural value issues described in the literature which impact on rewards. We then proceed to a discussion of national, industry and organization-specific effects which are likely to mediate the effect of these key values. Finally, we set out a procedure for investigating the consequences of these factors and offer some preliminary evidence from a sample of MNEs on the implications for international reward strategy in resolving current 'hot issues'.

Background to the study

Much of the writing on international reward strategies focuses on expatriates (Armstrong and Murlis 1994; Torrington 1994) and by implication concerns organizations with ethnocentric staffing policies (Heenan and Perlmutter 1979). This has no doubt been because of the proportionately high cost of these individuals to MNEs. However, this overfocus on expatriate issues has tended to distort treatments of international HRM generally (Hendry 1994). Many organizations are now looking to reform their approach to international reward strategy in broader terms, to design compensation programmes appropriate for specific cultural traditions (Sparrow and Hiltrop 1994).

The issues are similar in some respects to those in marketing when decisions are made to adopt either global or multi-local marketing strategies. From the point of view of simplification, global policies would be ideal, but there are undoubtedly some cultural aspects which would make implementation, understanding and effectiveness different between countries. Increasingly, researchers and practitioners are concluding that the exportability of management theories and practices is determined by the comparability of the cultural values between the importing and exporting nation (Bigoness and Blakely 1996). For example, Mamman *et al.* (1996: 3) observe: 'Depending on their cultural backgrounds, it would seem that employees will perceive criteria for pay systems differently. Thus organizations operating across borders should take these potential differences into account when rewarding their employees.'

The question of cultural values goes to the heart of the purpose of reward strategies, which is to deliver corporate performance. This chapter and the intended research is therefore concerned with the broader question of reward strategies in MNEs where local cultural values impact on the delivery of corporate performance.

Towards a model of national culture and rewards

International values and reward policy

Values help to determine what we think is right and wrong, what is important and what is desirable (Schiffman and Kanuk 1993). Values will therefore affect how management practices are interpreted by members of a society. Values have a profound effect on the actions of individuals because of our readiness to defend core cultural values (Cartwright and Cooper 1996). Triandis and Berry (1980) suggest using an emic–etic distinction when discussing business practices. Emic refers to culture-specific aspects of values, concepts or behaviours that are non-transferable. Etic practices, on the other hand, are culture common, i.e. transferable. Our research is particularly concerned with identifying the former – that is values which are not common and could potentially cause problems with respect to reward strategy.

When employees from one culture work in an organization operating another culture's management practices, differences between the two cultures may become 'painfully evident' (Gaugler 1988). Harris and Moran (1992), in studying the different motivational factors in a comparison of East Asian and Western cultures, found a range of fundamental differences which, if not appreciated by an MNE, could potentially affect performance in subsidiaries.

One of the attributes of culture is that it can foster a type of ethnocentrism whereby practices or activities that do not conform to an individual's view of conducting business are viewed negatively. There are undoubtedly different 'realities' and views of the world and MNEs are likely to increase their chance of success by understanding the socio-cultural system of the regions in which they operate. They need to be sensitive to different cultural values when designing their performance management systems and reward policy. However, sensitivity of a particular managerial function to cultural or value differences depends on the importance of direct exchange between that function and the cultural environment. Functions such as human resources and marketing, for example, demand more interaction with the local culture than, say, finance (Bradley 1991), and are therefore more culturally sensitive.

Not all researchers believe that cultural differences affect management practices (Harpaz 1990; Terpstra 1992). The normative literature on international performance management and rewards makes the assumption that there is a set of policies that can and should be applied universally. Nevertheless, there are certain facets of national culture which appear to be deeply rooted and consequently will have an impact on management practices (Torrington 1994). When reviewing international comparisons of HR practices (Gaugler 1988; Fillella 1991; Brewster and Larsen 1992; Sparrow *et al.* 1994), it is evident that the various activities of HR management are differently weighted and carried out. Multinational enterprises need to be aware of which HR practices can be transferred abroad effectively (Schuler *et al.* 1993). For example, values relating to individualism, informality, materialism and time orientation are likely to have an effect on human resource practices such as appraisal and compensation (Ronen 1986; Adler 1991; Phatak 1992). In other words, culture affects HRM, but not all HR practices equally.

In a study of matched Chinese and UK companies (Easterby-Smith *et al.* 1995), there was a marked difference between them with regard to pay and reward systems, but consistency within each country, which the researchers directly attributed to 'deep seated differences between the two countries with regard to attitudes towards rewards'. The likely impact on performance that such practices might have – whether derived from the global parent or adapted to the locality – needs to be considered. More specifically, the effect that practices have on host country nationals and the cumulative effect on performance of the MNE subsidiary in the host country need to be key in decision-making. Evidence suggests that if management practices are inconsistent with deeply held values, this can negatively affect performance. Conversely, management practices which reinforce national cultural values are likely to result in greater self-efficacy and higher performance (Kotter and Heskett 1992; Earley 1994). The implication for MNE managers is that to achieve high performance outcomes it is better to adapt to local cultural conditions (Newman and Nollen 1996).

Cultural dualities and their reward implications

Various writers have attempted to classify the main cultural dimensions appropriate for international comparisons. Hofstede's work based on an extensive study of employees in IBM subsidiaries (1980) has undoubtedly been the most influential, originally yielding four dimensions (latterly Hofstede 1991 added a fifth). Hampden-Turner and Trompenaars (1993) identified seven key dimensions and Bento and Ferreira (1992) six. Between these classifications, there is a degree of overlap.

Bento and Ferreira (1992) have produced the most detailed review of the potential impact on rewards of different cultural values. Based on the work of Hofstede (1980), Martin *et al.* (1983) and Schein (1985), Bento and Ferreira (1992) identified the cultural assumptions which would have relevance for compensation plans and organized them into five dualities. They suggest that these five taken together comprise a 'cultural lens' through which to view the different interest groups' underlying assumptions regarding reward systems. The dualities are:

- equality versus inequality;
- certainty versus uncertainty;
- controllability versus uncontrollability;
- individualism versus collectivism;
- materialistic versus personalistic foregrounding.

In addition to the dualities comprising their 'cultural lens', there are three other dimensions which are likely to impact on reward systems:

- short-term versus long-term orientation;
- emphasis on people, ideas or action;
- emphasis on abstractive or associative modes of information processing.

The following discussion explores these assumptions and their implications for reward systems. We should note that in many cases these are speculative. The purpose of the field research is to establish the nature and impact of cultural values on reward systems in practice in specific organizations.

Equality versus inequality

Originally proposed by Martin *et al.* (1983) and subsequently developed by Bento and Ferreira (1992), this duality affects the assumptions about desired range of diversity in pay, likelihood of differences in performance and how closely pay should relate to hierarchic level. In the USA differentials between the pay of those at top and bottom of the organization may be up to one hundred times, whereas in Europe differentials are more modest. Henzler (1992) introduced the term 'socially healthy' top pay levels.

The equality assumption would support an egalitarian culture, a flat hierarchy, small power distance relationships, decentralized decision-making and small differentials in status and compensation. Small differences in pay and benefits and/or participatory schemes (e.g. gainsharing) would be culturally appropriate (Gomez-Mejia and Welbourne 1991). Conversely those scoring highly on the inequality dimension believe people vary in their ability and skill. Measuring and comparing these forms the basis for allocation of positions, responsibilities and rewards. Employees will accept inequalities of rewards based on predetermined criteria such as age and seniority (Lincoln and Kallenberg 1990) so high differentials will not be unusual. Reward systems designed in such a way that subordinates could earn more than the superior would probably not be tolerated. The equality assumption thus indicates how values can affect the quantum of socially acceptable pay.

Certainty versus uncertainty

This dichotomy concerns variability in the environment. Referred to as 'uncertainty avoidance' by Hofstede (1980), it describes the degree to which members of a society are threatened by uncertain and ambiguous situations and how they react. In a high certainty culture organizational structures and processes will be designed to create predictability of the working environment. Key features are many rules, standardization, specialization and attention to detail. There is likely to be low turnover and clearly defined career paths as individuals will be motivated by security and belongingness. It is likely therefore that reward systems with any element of risk will not be preferred, so fixed rather than variable pay programmes will be in place. Likewise any elements of competition will not be favoured (Mamman *et al.* 1996). Conversely, in a high uncertainty culture there is less structuring of activities. Flexibility and high turnover are perceived to be beneficial. In this case, values affect the structure of pay, especially the role of incentives. (Since incentive schemes are likely to increase differentials, there would appear to be an association between 'certainty' and 'equality' values.)

Controllability versus uncontrollability

This duality also relates to the above certainty–uncertainty assumptions. The variability in the environment may be seen as desirable or undesirable, but what also matters is the extent to which it is believed to be within individuals' or organizations' control. This construct (internal or external locus of control, Rotter 1966) affects the way causality is attributed and the allocation of responsibility, blame and rewards. In high controllability cultures, human resources are seen to be the key factor in creating or changing environments. Conversely, in high uncontrollability cultures emphasis is placed on adaptive strategies to cope with environments which are seen as inherently unpredictable. The key is to collect as much relevant information as possible to improve prediction. The underlying assumption in this dimension will particularly affect performance management systems.

Individualism versus collectivism

Ties between individuals in individualistic cultures are loose. Conversely in collectivist cultures there is strong cohesiveness of groups. In business, this dimension will be reflected in the nature of the employer–employee contracts (Hofstede 1980). This dimension influences beliefs about motivation, the relationship between employees and the company and the ethical choices when individual and collective goals conflict. It will therefore affect performance appraisal and compensation, especially the appropriateness of individual or group-based reward measures (Bento and Ferreira 1992).

In highly individualistic cultures (Hofstede 1980) people are driven by self-interest. The best source of security for individuals is their market value and they will therefore prefer performance related rewards. In collectivist cultures (Hofstede 1980) people derive important benefits from belonging to a group or organization. They are prepared to put group goals before their own. Collectivists would not prefer individualized performance related pay because they hold in high regard the view that others have of them (Bond and Hwang 1986). In such circumstances, if their performance did not lead to high pay they would lose face. They are likely to prefer reward systems which do not create competition, for example, those based on seniority and qualification (Mamman *et al.* 1996). Again, certain values (like certainty, controllability and collectivism) may reinforce one another.

Materialism versus personalistic foregrounding

This duality originates from gestalt psychology where it is known as fore-grounding and backgrounding. The relevance of organizational context is in understanding whether individuals see people and their relationships in the foreground and material actions and outcomes in the background, or the reverse. This is relevant for reward system design as it concerns focus of attention. It bears some similarity to Hofstede's (1980) dimensions of high and low masculinity and the dimensions of universalism versus particularism (rules versus relationships) proposed by Hampden-Turner and Trompenaars (1993). This affects the extent to which masculine values predominate (acquisition of money at the expense of others) as compared with showing sensitivity and concern for others' welfare. In cultures with materialistic foregrounding monetary incentives are regarded as a high source of motivation and relative measures of performance (forced rating distributions) are acceptable. In cultures where personalistic foregrounding predominates the focus is on the process, on 'being and becoming'. Personal relationships are more important than monetary reward.

Short-term versus long-term time horizon

This is a more recent dimension added by Hofstede (1991). It marks a dimension concerning attitudes and beliefs about time. On the one hand there are Western-style concepts and on the other notions of long-term time orientation adapted from the Confucian idea of virtue versus truth. Cross-cultural misunderstandings can occur because of differences in the concept of time. In the USA, for example, time is a commodity to be controlled for financial gain ('time is money'). In other cultures this is considered vulgar and offensive (Taoka and Beeman 1991). Closely related to this is the cultural view of the future. For example, in the UK there is a major assumption that in business individuals can influence future events. Long-term incentive plans are designed with this in mind, with a view to motivating future performance. In other countries, such as in Latin America, there is a much more fatalistic view which could affect the success of similar plans.

According to research carried out by Bond (1988), respondents with a long-term orientation are more concerned with the future. Plans should be evaluated in terms of the future benefit to be gained by a project or activity. For short-termists or past-oriented people, plans need to be evaluated in the context of societal customs and traditions and firmly based on past experience. This adds an interesting dimension to the debate on whether bonuses should be rewards for past action or incentives for future performance. Ironically, given the interest in designing such schemes, the North American orientation to short-termism may mean that employees do not view long-term performance pay systems favourably.

Emphasis on people, ideas or action

This distinction is based on the work of Bhagat *et al.* (1990). In cultures where people are emphasized it is the quality of interpersonal relationships which is important. In cultures where ideologies are emphasized, sharing common beliefs is more important than social group membership. In cultures where action is emphasized, what is done is more important than what is said. These factors are likely to have an effect on the appropriateness of reward philosophies. In particular it will impact on issues of equity and equality, differentials and status.

Abstractive or associative modes of information processing

These dimensions were proposed by Bhagat *et al.* (1990) and Hampden-Turner and Trompenaars (1993). In cultures where associative modes of information processing are emphasized, processing is dependent on the context. In abstractive cultures there is a factual inductive approach to information processing, independent of context. The approach taken will impact on the nature of truth and reality and the way these are determined. This is likely to have an impact on the applicability of different performance measures linked to rewards and the role of appraisals.

In summary, it will be apparent that a number of the dualities proposed relate to the distinction between high-context and low-context cultures (Hall 1976) in the extent to which the preservation of harmonious social relationships is a prime value.

Problems with cultural research

Research on cultural differences presents inherent problems. Making attributions, then, from values to the design and acceptability of reward systems may consequently be ill-judged and unreliable.

First, the concept of culture is diffuse and complex. It is difficult both to define and measure (Ronen 1986). Most of the literature on cultural differences research is based on findings from questionnaire surveys. Because of the international nature of the studies, response rates (at less than 10 per cent) are even lower than would normally be expected from domestic surveys. These relatively small samples can adversely affect the ability to draw generalized conclusions.

Second, value measures are usually ipsative, that is it is usually possible to determine the importance of one value dimension relative to another, but not to determine the absolute intensity with which certain values are held (Hambrick and Brandon 1987). It is not only methodological problems such as the lack of suitable tools for measuring intensity that present difficulties.

Third, related to this there are problems in translating interpretations of the impact on rewards based on polarized extremes to situations which are likely to be far less extreme. In the case of the dualities of Bento and Ferreira (1992) and Hofstede (1980), it is easier to suggest what the likely implications are for reward issues at each of the extremes of the dualities, but much harder to propose what the effects would be where a culture would be scored in the middle – which is, for example, neither wholly individualistic nor collectivist.

Fourth, to complicate matters further, most countries are not homogeneous with respect to culture. Rather they are an aggregation of subcultures. Criticisms lodged particularly against Hofstede's research have focused on the fact that it neglects cultural diversity (Hollingshead and Leat 1995). In order to make valid generalizations, Leeds *et al.* (1994) emphasize that 'whatever are described as mainstream cultural traits are best considered as a central tendency or average. Individuals will differ to the extent to which they share the values associated with any particular country.'

Fifth, another frequent criticism is that such research produces static results, although cultures evolve. Whether adopting the premise that national cultures are converging (Child 1981) or will remain diverse over time (Hofstede 1980; Dowling and Schuler 1990), the fact remains that they have an internal dynamic, are exposed to external influences (through immigration) and MNEs may have an impact on local culture. Certainly, MNEs seek to reduce the complications of their environment, with cultural peculiarities being a major source of such complexity. Therefore reviews must be conducted regularly to ensure applicability over time.

A sixth and final problem is that dimensions of culture may be culture specific. In the research cited, the value dichotomies are largely derived from particular Western concepts. In effect, this type of research is susceptible to a hermeneutic circle effect, in that no observation or description is free from the observers' own presuppositions and projection of their values onto the phenomena. More precisely, would the eight values outlined above be recognized as significant in all cultures?

Ultimately, however, there is one central practical problem which limits the value of culturally focused studies in interpreting specific HR practices. That is, how does one reconcile the complex and potentially contradictory effects of culture which, as the previous discussion suggests, are multi-faceted? This leaves the way open to casually attributing reward patterns and effects to aspects of culture that are, in fact, poorly defined, empirically uncertain and practically inseparable.

Beyond culture: national, industry and corporate effects

While the work of Hofstede (1980) introduced a new sensitivity to the appreciation of national culture in the context of MNE operations, it has also encouraged a crude stereotyping of cultural values in psychological terms divorced from institutional, legal and economic factors. It is not enough to look solely to cultural difference studies to guide the design and management of reward systems. Other considerations dictate that it is also necessary to look to national, corporate and industry effects. Pennings (1993), for example, notes that values and beliefs about compensation are a function of corporate, industry and market culture as well as national culture. What is required, therefore, is not solely an ideographic approach to the research, where an understanding of behaviour is sought only through individuals' culture or subjectivity. There are undoubtedly other factors that also need to be taken into consideration when trying to understand which reward strategies would be appropriate to manage performance. A comprehensive view of the factors that are likely to impact on the design of reward systems is likely to comprise the following:

- the corporate culture of the MNE (including industry effects);
- parent country of origin effects contributing to corporate culture and reward strategy;
- developmental issues for the MNE and strategic objectives informing reward policy in the particular location;
- expatriate and local labour markets;
- local cultural sensitivities (a more pragmatically useful term than 'values');
- legal and institutional factors in the host country which directly impact on reward management.

Ultimately, the choice of management practices in an MNE will be determined by the resolution of the conflict between 'opposing pressures for internal consistency and for isomorphism with the local institutional environment' (Rosenzweig and Nohria 1994). HRM practices, in particular, are subject to these dual pressures. On the one hand, for example, seeking internal consistency by developing common compensation and benefits policies would facilitate the movement of employees across borders and preserve internal equity. On the other hand, pressures to conform to local practices may be too great to ignore.

Ferner (1997) characterizes three possible directions that 'isomorphism' can take. The first, cross-national isomorphism, occurs when country of origin practices are introduced into the host country operations. In this case it could be that practices will be counter-cultural or alien to the host country nationals. The opposite is local isomorphism. DiMaggio and Powell (1983) suggest three reasons that impel affiliate HRM practices to resemble local practices

- where local laws and regulations compel isomorphism ('coercive isomorphism');
- where adoption of local practices is perceived to be important in improving competitiveness ('normative isomorphism');
- where adopting local practices is an attempt to fit in ('mimetic isomorphism').

Rosenweig and Nohria (1994), in a study of HR practices in 249 affiliates of foreign-based MNEs, found that benefits significantly resembled local practice, whereas executive bonuses were almost equally adapted to local and parent practices. Overall, rewards for the rank and file were more locally specific, whereas those affecting executives were relatively closer to the parent.

A third theoretical model proposed by Ferner (1997) is that of 'internal isomorphism', a hybrid of the national and local models. Here it is suggested that the interaction of host and parent produces a variety of different approaches, the parent acting as the blueprint and the different hosts mediating this.

It is evident that there are a number of national, industry and organizationally specific factors which will impact on the extent to which different practices can be designed to be 'global or multi-local'. In the case of executive performance management, this is relatively free of host country regulation and management concern will be focused on striving for cross-national isomorphism. In contrast, pay determination of manual operatives is likely to be highly regulated and the interest of subsidiary policy coherence is less important.

National and industry effects

As already discussed by Sparrow in Chapter 6 of this volume, at the macro level, there are national business systems and economy effects which operate both in the host country and in the parent MNE's country of origin. The key elements of national business culture infrastructure as defined by Garrison (1994) are:

- the extent to which factors of production (location, physical, human and financial resources) differ from country to country;
- the extent to which their economies differ in terms of manufacture, service and agriculture;
- the human–machine balance, productivity and competitiveness levels;
- the country's welfare state.

Alongside these factors there is national legislation which can be viewed as a significant reflector of cultural values (Hofstede 1980). Pieper (1990) suggests that the main difference between HRM in the USA and Western Europe is a result of the extent to which practices are influenced and determined by state regulations. It is not only regulatory legislation that influences HRM, but also the role of the state in social security provision (Brewster 1995), as compared, say, with the insurance burden which is carried by firms in the USA and inflates pay bills.

Trade union membership and influence varies country by country, but is always significant (Brewster 1995). It is not only the degree of membership that is of importance, but also the status of unions in terms of recognition. In many European countries union recognition for collective bargaining is required by law. In most European countries union functions such as pay bargaining may be carried out at industry or national level rather than at the company level, thus reducing the role of individual management's input. As the current trend towards decentralized pay bargaining progresses (to become more in line with the current UK situation) this influence is likely to wane in the future.

Ferner (1997) argues that there has been insufficient evidence to date to determine how far national differences in business systems inform the behaviour of MNEs from different countries. He suggests that two of the factors which are likely to impact on MNE behaviour are national systems of corporate governance and corporate control. Financial control systems have direct implications for performance management and pay determination. Where elaborate systems of control geared to short-term financial performance predominate, as in the UK and USA, globally standardized performance evaluation is likely to operate. Conversely, in countries like Germany and Japan, formal control systems are far less significant and informal performance management processes predominate. This has obvious implications for performance management in, for example, a German subsidiary of a British MNE (and vice versa).

National business systems and economy effects may, in turn, be moderated by sectoral factors (Ferner 1997). In globalized industries (such as vehicles, chemicals or electronics), the MNE is likely to be more globally integrated, with corporate policies overriding local cultures. In more fragmented industries (such as food and drink and clothing), global effects are far weaker, competitive factors are more localized and HR policies are likely to be adapted to the host country.

Finally, labour markets (both expatriate and local), which are a central issue in the determination and design of rewards, are structured by all of the previous macro influences, as well as by the organization-specific factors below.

Corporate effects

The relative effect of national values on reward systems will also depend on organization-specific factors:

*   the degree of centralization or decentralization;
*   role of the line;
*   the composition of the line (expatriates or nationals);
*   growth patterns;
*   degree of technological sophistication;

- strength of 'corporate branding' (for example, the strength of corporate image may make it easier for firms like Coca-Cola or McDonald's successfully to adopt global reward strategies, regardless of national culture).

Rosenzweig and Nohria (1994) argued that the 'lifeblood that supplies the affiliate with people and ideas' is a significant influence on whether HR practices resemble local or parent HR practices. They defined the lifeblood of organizations in terms of three dimensions:

- the affiliate's dependence on the parent for technical and managerial know-how;
- the proportion of expatriates;
- the frequency of communication with the parent.

Relatively high levels for any of these were positively correlated with HR practices more closely resembling the parent than local practices. This finding reinforces the observations made by Walsh (1996), in a study of 13 British multinationals, that information gathered from subsidiaries was crucial in HR policy formulation. In particular the remuneration of overseas subsidiary management was characterized by a high degree of control and co-ordination associated with widespread monitoring of performance.

The management culture of the MNE parent can have a powerful effect on foreign subsidiaries. This has been demonstrated to be the case in Japanese MNEs (Tsurumi 1986) and Swedish MNEs (Hedlund and Aman 1984) where the parent companies export their corporate philosophies. This contrasts with the findings of Guest and Hoque (1996), however, in a study of 14 UK-based MNE subsidiaries, that national ownership had an unexpectedly small impact on the type of HR practices found. They suggest that managers from highly regulated countries, when freed from formal constraints, may make unpredictable choices. Such discrepancies may be explained by the stage of growth of the multinational and the extent of foreign trade in which the MNE engages (Japanese MNEs in general being in an early growth stage compared with many US and UK MNEs, Hendry 1994). The method of subsidiary founding may also have an impact on the adoption of global or local HR strategies. Greenfield sites are not only less like local firms than the parent at the time of their founding compared with acquisitions; they also persist in their differences (Rosenzweig and Nohria 1994).

Company strategy and performance: the forgotten dimension

From the foregoing we conclude that it is necessary to adopt a perspective which incorporates attention to cultural values in behavioural terms and to the institutional, legal and economic factors which frame these. Both levels are necessary. However, both styles of enquiry are equally deficient if they fail to take account of people and firms within specific socio-cultural systems and in the context of specific problems faced by MNEs. Generalized descriptions of the macro-environment may be just as weak a guide to actual company behaviour as cultural simplifications based on surveys are to individual behaviour.

This points to a different approach to research in international HRM. The firm is the point of intersection at which cultural values and institutional pressures get worked out (Hendry 1991). HR practices are a primary lightning conductor – none more so than rewards (along with employee–industrial relations) since they embody enormously complex and diverse assumptions about the relations between people. Rewards also have the added significance that they are the expression of corporate attitudes towards performance. It may not be true for all aspects of HRM, but research into rewards internationally would surely benefit from a more issue-based approach. This means as an initial step identifying the 'hot' issues that MNEs face in designing and managing reward systems in different parts of the world, while also taking account of the particular stage of development and strategic objectives of the MNEs concerned.

The identification of 'hot topics' that are giving problems, or which involve attempts to change reward systems, provides a comprehensive focus for study through each of the six levels of analysis outlined above. Moreover, this view from the 'inside out' focuses attention on company strategy and performance, which is often the forgotten dimension in investigations into international HRM.

Not only does this 'issues-based' approach have the practical merit of addressing the real concerns of managers in MNEs, it also provides a more rigorous and comprehensive focus for study through each of the six levels of analysis. The focus on 'hot topics' serves to expose the cultural, institutional and organizational factors which bear on the company and its reward system in a particular country or region. It functions in the same way as 'critical incident' methodology, or as Kurt Lewin recommended for the study of organizations, it seeks to understand something and the environment in which it exists by trying to alter it (in this case, through a change in reward structure or strategy). It is a pragmatic methodology which generates observable behaviours and actions. Thus, one makes observations of values when something is being changed and in the process sees other influences coming into play, instead of the barren procedure of asking what people's values are and extrapolating from these in a way which ignores how practical contingencies may affect action.

The research study

The first step is to identify current reward issues faced in a sample of MNEs. Ideally, to allow generalizable statements to be made, one would like a sample that is comparable in terms of country of origin, stage of development and type of business, covers the same set of countries and exposes a number of recurrent issues. Such a project clearly implies a substantial scale and many companies. At this stage, therefore, we are conducting a pilot study with a sample group of five multinational enterprises drawn from the Strategic Remuneration Research Centre (SRRC) sponsor group. (The SRRC, based at City University Business School, is sponsored by a consortium of 30 blue-chip multinationals to undertake a wide ranging programme of research on reward strategies of which this study is a part.)

In the first stage of this project, which is described here, we have identified a series of 'hot reward issues' with senior HR managers or compensation and benefits specialists who have responsibility for international remuneration in the five pilot firms. Discussions will then probe these issues relating to different locations in order to bring out the values and institutional factors involved as well as those to do with the corporation itself. The analysis of these discussions uses the 'narrative' method (Gunnarsson 1997) to understand how managers construe and then seek to resolve the conflicting demands of the six sets of factors, or levels of analysis.

Revelatory storytelling: the narrative method

Espoused company practice, referred to by Brown and Duguid (1991) as canonical practice, can distort the picture of what really happens in firms. Rather than relying on documentation of company policy on international reward practices, an issues-based approach asks individuals to describe their perceptions of presenting problems and their resolution, and where possible seeks to observe how these problems are resolved in the field. Such an ethnographic approach, comprising a combination of observation and semi-structured interviews, allows an explanation of individuals' actions and events. It serves to uncover the various cultures and subcultures which inform systems of meanings, beliefs and values and consequent decisions which may not be evident on the face of events.

Individuals make decisions on the basis of a set of 'justified beliefs' (Brown and Duguid 1991). In order to construct a coherent sequence of events to relate to an interviewer as to how a decision has been made, in effect they provide a causal map of their experience. This story is likely to reflect the complex social web within which decisions take place. By examining multiple perspectives or versions of events the researcher can uncover and analyse issues of social construction.

The narrative method is a way of viewing action through language. Speech itself is governed by social norms and conventions (Gunnarsson 1997). The key feature of this type of research is that it emphasizes how action is forged through language and how language is a vital component of organizational cognition (Bryman 1989). The narration provides a method for examining decision-making, by providing insights into the normative context in which it takes place. The narrative method is especially relevant for applying to decisions and 'hot issues' where they are likely to involve a disruption of convention or equilibrium. Because proposed changes affecting rewards are likely to be contentious, they fit this requirement admirably. We can then observe how problems are resolved and the factors that people are having to manage their way through, by what they say:

> The narrative mode of cognition will be used . . . when there is something
> puzzling, abnormal or unusual in a situation; when the ends and identity
> of a company is questioned or have to be revised . . . By explicating the
> abnormal or unusual in a situation it hints at dilemmas concerning beliefs
> about the control of choices.
>
> (Gunnarsson 1997: 3)

Qualitative research such as this captures the processual aspects of organizational
reality (Bryman 1989). The rich picture it gives us is gained both by emphasizing
individuals' interpretation and representing context.

In this study there are three different perspectives of the 'hot' topic which need
to be examined: the head-office perception of the presenting 'hot' topic; the
'on the ground' local perception of the 'hot' topic; and the actual discussion
to resolve the issue itself. First, we ask the corporate HR specialist and the local
representative independently to tell us the story of what they perceive the
presenting problem to be. We then observe the discussions leading to the decision
on how to deal with the hot topic. Finally, we will return to the corporate and
local interviewees to ask them to narrate their perception of the resolution
of events. In practice, however, it may not always be possible to be party to
proceedings at all stages, so it may be necessary to rely on participants' narration
of events afterwards.

In two of our six pilot MNEs we have been invited to observe the actual
discussion of the international focus groups specially convened to resolve the
presenting issue. In the other three organizations we will have to rely on narratives
recounting the discussion after the event. In all cases, we are able to tape record
discussions. Once we have gathered all the evidence we will be able to exercise
some post-hoc control of our sample by focusing on countries that are common to
our six MNEs generating issues and deriving other distinguishing criteria which
emerge.

Individual company stories: the parent perception of the 'hot' topic

The first phase in the pilot study has been to uncover the presenting 'hot' issues.
The senior head office HR or compensation and benefits managers tackling
the issue in each of our six MNEs were asked to describe the problem that the
company is facing and to proffer their perceptions of the relevant factors which
will affect its resolution. The following provides an outline of the 'hot issue' in
each case.

Company A: a prestige international hotel group

In this organization the majority of operations are overseas and not dominated
by the home base; in other words, the concept of 'expatriate' has little meaning
since movements of key personnel occur all over the group and the board is

drawn from all parts of the world. A few years ago the company adopted the maxim 'Think global – act local'. Now there is a new paradigm at the company, 'Think local – act global'. This marks a significant turnaround from a central philosophy to being culturally sensitive locally in working with local staff.

Currrently, the company is torn between maintaining the current market rate policy for remunerating general managers and moving to what it considers a 'philosophically fair' scheme which is more in keeping with its new paradigm. Thus the 'hot' issue facing the company concerns regional market rates for general managers versus considerations of internal equity – managers of similar sized hotels being paid similar rates irrespective of location or continuing to be paid to reflect the local market rate.

A general manager will be over 35 and have trained with the company for at least ten years. The company has a policy of moving managers around every two to three years to ensure that they remain fresh in their careers. Although not explicitly stated, there is an understanding that it is acceptable to refuse only one move because mobility is a central part of the company culture.

At present the company remunerates its general managers with base pay using the local market rate, determined by examining competitor rates, other international chains and local hotels. Rates can vary widely according to region. The total package will include a bonus and benefits calculated using this basic rate, so any differentials will be compounded. The differential in salaries has been an issue of growing concern. In the past, salaries were lower and differences were not so marked, but salary escalation since the late 1980s has caused the gulf to widen and the improvement in the world economy since 1992 has brought the subject to the fore. The issue of regional disparities has become a topic at the area meetings held for general managers.

A commonly cited rationale for regional differentials is that they reflect differences in local costs of living. However, for hotel general managers this argument is not so pertinent. They are housed in the hotel, all meals are provided and they have full access to leisure facilities. Therefore they have very little exposure to external costs.

One solution would be to pay everyone the same amount, but that would run counter to the market, and not just the labour market. The real problem is the ownership structure of the hotels. As in the hotel industry generally, the company acts as an operator, not owner, for 80 per cent of the hotels in its portfolio. For a fixed fee and a percentage commission, a hotel chain typically contracts with the owners to run their hotels for fifteen to twenty years. General managers are employed by the company, but paid by the owner. All other hotel staff are employed by the owner, but are recruited by the general manager. As the general managers are paid by the owner any attempts to increase their pay on the grounds of equity or some other criterion will directly affect the owner's pay bill and profit. Owners will make comparisons locally and if an operator company tries to impose higher rates of pay in the short term it will sour relations and in the longer term lead them to look elsewhere for a managing firm.

The key determinant which affects this issue and its resolution is therefore the strategic objectives of the local owners and the pressure of the local labour market, moderated by corporate philosophy. In other words, it is likely to have little to do with cultural values, unless these arise in managers' feelings about status derived from their country of origin.

Company B: a large telecommunications company

A major task facing the company in the next year is to resolve the need for a common grading system across all countries. On the surface it appears that one system is currently in use. This was designed through a common job evaluation, but it has become increasingly evident that different parts of the business in different product areas have evolved the system differently and some have dropped it altogether. If it were a language, they would all be using the same words, but the meanings would be different. The increasing number of international transfers has resulted in pressures from managers to have all employees on a common system. In addition, stock options entitlements and eligibility for inclusion in major incentive plans are allocated according to grade. As disparities emerge, so employees are beginning to voice serious concerns.

In some countries the system is already in place, but is in need of repair. In others, there is a lack of both the structure and the expertise to design it. The expertise lies particularly in the USA and there is therefore an inherent danger that the US model gets imposed. The issue is compounded by the fact that the organization is structured as a matrix and different countries and business units are at varying stages of readiness to embark on a change programme. Some regions and business units have indicated that they would be satisfied with an improved version of the current American grading model; others are indicating that they require a radically different solution. Because of the decentralized structure there is very little resource and authority to drive any initiative centrally and the different parts of the business cannot all be counted on to be involved in the process.

The key factors affecting reward management in this case appear to be both the decentralized corporate culture of the company and different developmental stages of the product business units impacting on readiness to change. Again, the problem does not derive from cultural values, although its resolution may play on individuals' cultural preferences and involve an imposed cultural model.

Company C: a petrochemical company

In this company two main presenting issues have been highlighted. The first is in France where there is a company-specific reward structure, *la participation*, involving sharing regional profits with employees, which is embedded in practice but dysfunctional for the company. The problem here is that the company is not run on regional lines, but as a national business. This is a clear case of the legal and institutional factors in the host country impacting on reward management (and not culture in an individual behavioural sense).

The second problem is in the Far East, where the dynamic labour market means the company ends up training staff for other employers. Retention is a problem across the company, but especially for the marketing function. New recruits learn from the company and then leave. The problem is that the company needs to consider who or what they are training for, effectively making individuals marketable through training. The 'hot' issue for the company is how to manage, respond and retain through rewards in this region, without upsetting internal equity. This is an example of the developmental stage of the MNE, as compared with competitors in the region, affecting reward management decisions, where being first into the market may mean unwittingly providing skills for others subsequently.

Company D: a large telecommunications company

A recent merger has forced the company to look at what needs to be common to pull things together in the operating subsidiaries and what can remain independent. There are now three UK subsidiaries, one US and one rest of world.

The current 'hot issue' facing the company concerns share plans. The focus on this particular issue has been driven by the need to retain options as a corporate glue and to bring some communality to the operating units. US plans typically do not have performance criteria attached to share options, whereas in the UK investors react negatively to plans structured without them. The American subsidiary, in the words of the senior specialist, is 'running scared' at the type of performance measures which the UK institutions favour. The company is about to do battle on this topic, having lodged three different plans with shareholders for approval. Three plans were needed to pick up the different needs of the UK, US and rest-of-world subsidiaries. One cultural difference between the UK and the USA, which has become evident during the debate surrounding this issue, has been the different views that exist about differentials, equity and 'making lots of money'. The solution seems to be to stick with options in the USA but to put performance criteria on half of the options, the rest being treated as part of the overall basic package. The key factor at play here does appear to be the difference in value sets in the different regions.

Company E: a large pharmaceutical company

The problem in the company at the moment is the way the US subsidiary's executive compensation levels are viewed by UK main board members. Relevant values in the USA are around wealth creation and expectations of what bonus schemes should deliver. Share options are an accepted way of making individuals very wealthy over time and there is an expectation that this is what they are designed for. This causes friction with the UK parent. The problem is exacerbated by the fact that the US company contributes approximately 50 per cent of the profitability. They think of themselves as autonomous and benchmark themselves against other large US companies rather than subsidiaries of UK-based companies. This issue causes backroom friction rather than being given overt airplay, but it is nevertheless a problem as it puts a drag on both trust and relationships. The key factor which seems to be affecting reward management for this issue, as with company D, is differences in local cultural values around the quantum of rewards and how these are allocated.

Discussion

The six levels of analysis we have identified as appropriate to this study are:

1   the corporate culture of the MNE (including industry effects);
2   parent country of origin effects contributing to corporate culture and reward strategy;
3   developmental issues for the MNE and strategic objectives informing reward policy in the particular location;
4   expatriate and local labour markets;
5   local cultural sensitivities;
6   legal and institutional factors in the host country which directly impact on reward management.

Bearing in mind that we have so far only heard one side of the story (the home country specialists' view of the problem), we can only make some tentative observations in relation to these six factors. Nevertheless, they are quite revealing.

For companies A and B, the overriding factors contributing to the problem seem to be centred on the corporate culture of the MNE itself (1) and local strategic objectives (3). For company A, it is the ownership/operating relationship within the company shaping local strategic objectives which is critical. It may be that local cultural sensitivities (5) come into play in the form of owners' risk for return expectations in different countries, which affect how much they are willing to spend on individuals' pay packages, or through managers' own feelings about status which derive from cultural origins. Similarly, for company B it is the decentralized structure and 'don't trust it if it wasn't invented here' culture (1) which seems to be driving the hot issue, in a company characterized by distinctive product business units following different growth patterns (3).

For company C, the first presenting issue is evidently the result of legal and institutional factors (6), whereas the second stems from labour market dynamics (4) contingent upon the company's strategic objectives in that location (3).

It is only companies D and E that appear to be tackling issues which arise directly as a result of differences in local cultural sensitivities or value sets (5). The perceived fairness of quantum of rewards and the risk–return balance in the USA compared with other countries appears to be driving their hot reward issues.

During 1998, we will have interviewed all the relevant parties and observed the decision-making process in these companies. However, we can begin to see what factors drive international reward strategy.

Much of the drive for globalization in reward practices seems to be pragmatic. Fiscal, institutional and market pressures often override what a company wants to do. This is then compounded by post-hoc rationalization, driven by external pressures on a local basis. The parent may set some philosophical parameters, but this is tempered with local sensitivities. For example, as pointed out by one of our interviewees, in India, the chairperson in a company will only be paid up to a maximum multiple of the lowest paid worker. In order to circumvent this, commission is paid. The key thing is to know where a compromise has been made.

Undoubtedly, the benefit of a global reward system is that you only have to design it once. However, it is possible to export compensation at a number of levels: principles, levels and quantum. Few take it down as far as the last category. The degree to which companies can adopt global policies depends on a variety of things including the environment. There are evidently many factors to take into consideration, all of which may be key. Organizations may have to make compromises. What is important is to know what people want and to go through the process. It is only through discussions that the opposing pressures for convergence and divergence can be resolved. We may hypothesize, then, that those organizations that take time to talk through a problem will produce better solutions, because they expose more of the factors (including cultural values) which impact on it.

Conclusion

We believe that, to date, research and literature on international reward policies have been over-focused on expatriate rewards. There is now a need to look at international reward strategies in terms of what they deliver for corporate performance. Studies of 'cultural differences' suggest that reward system design and management needs to be tailored to local values to enhance the performance of overseas operations. However, cultural difference studies are too generalistic and fail to provide an adequate guide to the design and management of reward systems. It is necessary to incorporate attention to corporate and industry affects, since the companies within national legal structures and managing specific business environments, design the reward systems and have to cope with the problems involved in managing them.

Finding a suitable way to investigate such a complex set of factors is a methodological challenge. The study currently underway is attempting to tackle this by viewing reward systems through the specific lens of particular MNEs in particular cultural contexts, as they face and deal with 'hot' reward issues, using narrative methodology as a tool to interpret the different voices in the 'Tower of Babel'.

References

Adler, N. (1991) *International Dimensions of Organizational Behavior*, Boston MA: PWS-Kent.

Armstrong, M. and Murlis, H. (1994) *Reward Management: A Handbook of Remuneration Strategy and Practice*, 2nd edn, London: Kogan Page.

Bento, R. and Ferreira, L. (1992) 'Incentive pay and organizational culture', in W. Bruns (ed.) *Performance Measurement, Evaluation, and Incentives*, Boston MA: Harvard Business School Press.

Bigoness, W. and Blakely, G. (1996) 'A cross-national study of managerial values', *Journal of International Business Studies*, 4th quarter: 739–53.

Bhagat, R., Kedia, B., Crawford, S. and Kaplan, M. (1990) 'Cross cultural issues in organizational psychology: emergent trends and directions for research in the 1990s', in C. Cooper and I. Robertson (eds) *International and Organizational Psychology*, Chichester: Wiley.

Bond, M. (1988) *The Cross-cultural Challenge to Social Psychology*, Newbury Park CA: Sage.

Bond, M. and Hwang, K. (1986) 'The social psychology of Chinese people', in M. Bond (ed.) *The Psychology of the Chinese People*, Hong Kong: Oxford University Press, pp. 213–66.

Bradley, F. (1991) *International Marketing Strategy*, Hemel Hempstead: Prentice Hall.

Brewster, C. (1995) 'Towards a "European" model of human resource management', *Journal of International Business Studies*, 1st quarter: 1–21.

Brewster, C. and Larsen, H. (1992) 'Human resource management in Europe: evidence from ten countries', *International Journal of Human Resource Management* 3(3): 409–34.

Brown, J.S. and Duguid, P. (1991) 'Organizational learning and communities of practice: towards a unified view of working, learning and innovation', *Organization Science* 2(1): 40–57.

Bryman, A. (1989) *Research Methods and Organization Studies*, London: Routledge.

Cartwright, S. and Cooper, C. (1996) *Managing Mergers, Acquisitions and Strategic Alliances: Integrating People and Cultures*, Oxford: Butterworth-Heinemann.

Child, J. (1981) 'Culture, contingency and capitalism in the cross-national study of organizations', in L. Cummings and B. Staw (eds) *Research in Organizational Behaviour*, New York: JAI Press.

DiMaggio, P. and Powell, W. (1983) 'The iron cage revisited: institutional isomorphism and collective rationality in organizational fields', *American Sociological Review* 48: 47–160.

Dowling, P. and Schuler, R. (1990) *International Dimensions of Human Resource Management*, Boston: PWS-Kent.

Engel, J., Warshaw, M. and Kinnear, T. (1983) *Promotional Strategy*, 5th edn, New York: Irwin.

Earley, P. (1994) 'Self or group? Cultural effects of training on self-efficacy and performance', *Administrative Science quarterly* 39: 89–117.

Easterby-Smith, M., Malina, D. and Yuan, L. (1995) 'How culture sensitive is HRM? A comparative analysis of practice in Chinese and UK companies', *International Journal of Human Resource Management* 6(1): 31–59.

Ferner, A. (1997) 'Country of origin effects and HRM in multinational companies', *Human Resource Management Journal* 7(1): 19–37.

Filella, J. (1991) 'Is there a Latin model in the management of human resources?', *Personnel Review* 20(6): 15–24.

Garrison, T. (1994) in Garrison, T. and Rees, D. (1994) *Managing People across Europe*, Oxford: Butterworth-Heinemann.

Gaugler, E. (1988) 'HR management: an international comparison', *Personnel* 65(8): 24–30.

Gomez-Mejia, I. and Welbourne, T. (1991) 'Compensation strategies in a global context', *Human Resource Planning* 14(1): 29–42.

Guest, D. and Hoque, K.. (1996) 'National ownership and HR practices in UK greenfield sites', *Human Resource Management Journal* 6(4): 50–75.

Gunnarsson, J. (1997) 'Innovations in decision models in firms that internationalise their markets: a narrative approach', 12th Workshop on Strategic Human Resource Management, 24–25 March, Turku, Finland.

Hall, E. (1976) *Beyond Culture*, New York: Anchor Press/Doubleday.

Hambrick, D. and Brandon, G. (1987) 'Executive values', in D. Hambrick (ed.) *The Executive Effect: Concepts and Methods for Studying Top Managers*, Greenwich CT: JAI Press.

Hampden-Turner, C. and Trompenaars, F. (1993) The Seven Cultures of Capitalism, London: Piatkus.

Harpaz, I. (1990) 'The importance of work goals: an international perspective', *Journal of International Business Studies* 21(1): 75–93.

Harris, P. and Moran, R. (1992) *Managing Cultural Differences*, Houston TX: Gulf.

Hedlund, G. and Aman, P. (1984) *Managing Relationships with Foreign Subsidiaries: Organization and Control in Swedish MNEs*, Stockholm: Mekan.

Heenan, D. and Perlmutter, H. (1979) *Multinational Organization Development*, Reading MA: Addison-Wesley.

Hendry, C. (1991) 'International comparisons of human resource management: putting the firm in the frame', *International Journal of Human Resource Management* 2(3): 415–40.

—— (1994) *Human Resource Strategies for International Growth*, London: Routledge.

Henzler, A. (1992) 'The new era of Eurocapitalism', *Harvard Business Review* 70(4): 57–68.

Hofstede, G. (1980) *Cultures Consequences: International Differences in Work-related Values*, Beverly Hills CA: Sage.

—— (1991) *Cultures and Organizations: Software of the Mind*, Maidenhead: McGraw-Hill.

Hollingshead, G. and Leat, M. (1995) *Human Resource Management: An International and Comparative Perspective*, London: Pitman.

Kotter, J. and Heskett, J. (1992) *Corporate Culture and Performance*, New York: Free Press.

Kuruvilla, S. (1995) 'National industrialization strategies and their influence on patterns of HR practice', *Human Resource Management Journal* 6(3): 22–41.

Leeds, C., Kirkbride, P. and Durcan, J. (1994) 'The cultural context of Europe: a tentative mapping', in P. Kirkbride (ed.) *Human Resource Management in Europe: Perspectives of the 1990s*, London: Routledge.

Lincoln, J. and Kallenberg, A. (1990) *Culture, Control and Commitment: A Study of Work Organization and Work Attitudes in the USA and Japan*, Boston MA: Cambridge University Press.

Mamman, A., Sulaiman, M. and Fadel, A. (1996) 'Attitudes to pay systems: an exploratory study within and across cultures', *International Journal of Human Resource Management* 7(1): 101–21.

Martin J., Feldman, M., Hatch, M. and Sitkin, S. (1983) 'The uniqueness paradox in organizational stories', *Administrative Science quarterly* 29: 438–53.

Newman, K. and Nollen, S. (1996) 'Culture and congruence: the fit between management practices and national culture', *Journal of International Business Studies*, fourth quarter: 753–79.

Pennings, A. (1993) 'Executive reward systems: a cross-national comparison', *Journal of Management Studies* 30(2): 261–80.

Pieper, R. (1990) *Human Resource Management: An International Perspective*, Berlin: Walter de Gruyter.

Phatak, A.V. (1992) *International Dimensions of Management*, 3rd edn, Boston MA: PWS-Kent.

Ronen, S. (1986) *Comparative and Multi-national Management*, New York: Wiley.

Ronen, S. and Shenkar, O. (1985) 'Clustering countries on attitudinal dimensions: a review and synthesis', *Academy of Management Review* 10: 435–54.

Rosenzweig, P. and Nohria, N. (1994) 'Influences on human resource management practices in multinational corporations', *Journal of International Business Studies*, 2nd quarter: 229–51.

Rotter, J. (1966) 'Generalised expectancies for internal versus external control of reinforcement', *Psychological Monographs* 80: 3–43.

Schein, E. (1985) *Organizational Culture and Leadership*, San Francisco: Jossey-Bass.

Schiffman, L. and Kanuk, L. (1994) *Consumer Behaviour*, 5th edn, Englewood Cliffs NJ: Prentice Hall.

Schuler, R., Dowling, P. and De Cieri, H. (1993) 'An integrative framework of strategic international human resource management', *International Journal of Human Resource Management* 4(4): 717–64.

Sparrow, P. and Hiltrop, J.-M. (1994) *European Human Resource Management in Transition*, Hemel Hempstead: Prentice Hall.

Sparrow, P., Schuler, R. and Jackson, S. (1994) 'Convergence or divergence: human resource practices and policies for competitive advantage world-wide', *International Journal of Human Resource Management* 5(2): 267–99.

Taoka, G. and Beeman, D. (1991) *International Business: Environments, Institutions and Operations*, New York: HarperCollins.

Terpstra, V. (1992) *International Dimensions of Marketing*, Boston MA: PWS-Kent.

Tilghman, T. (1994) 'Beyond the balance sheet: developing alternative approaches to international compensation', *ACA Journal*, summer: 36–49.

Torrington, D. (1994) *International Human Resource Management: Think Globally Act Locally*, Hemel Hempstead: Prentice Hall.

Triandis, H.C. and Berry, J. W. (eds) (1980) *Handbook of Cross-cultural Psychology, Vol. 2 Methodology*, Boston MA: Allyn and Bacon.

Tsurumi, Y. (1986) 'Japanese and European multi-nationals in America: a case of flexible systems', in K. Macharzina and W. Stahle (eds) *European Approaches to International Management*, New York: Walter de Gruyter.

Walsh, J. (1996) 'Multinational management strategy and human resource decision making in the Single European Market', *Journal of Management Studies* 33(5): 634–48.

8 Performance appraisal of host country employees

Western MNEs in China

Niklas Lindholm, Marja Tahvanainen and Ingmar Björkman

Introduction

Performance appraisal is today a central element in many Western companies' strategic human resource management (HRM). Although there is no universally accepted model of performance appraisal, it often includes a definition of the employee's objectives, monitoring and measuring of the performance, feedback on the results and, possibly, rewards and plans to improve future performance (Mabey and Salaman 1995). Research has indicated that, provided the design of the performance appraisal is appropriate, it tends to have a positive effect on company performance (Williams 1991). However, while there has been extensive research on performance appraisal in a domestic context, much less work has been conducted on the international dimensions (Vance *et al.* 1992; Dowling *et al.* 1994). In particular, few studies have investigated the performance appraisal practices of Western companies' operations in developing countries.

One of the essential questions facing a multinational enterprise (MNE) overseas is the extent to which the management of human resources is, and in fact should be, adapted to local conditions. The answer to this question is far from self-evident and several studies have analysed the extent to which subsidiary practices resemble those of local firms (localization) as opposed to those of the foreign parent organization (standardization) (e.g. Beechler and Yang 1994; Rosenzweig and Nohria 1994; Hannon *et al.* 1995). In this chapter we will analyse one particular HRM practice, performance appraisal, in one country, the People's Republic of China.

Recent research (e.g. Lasserre and Ching 1996; Southworth 1996) indicates that MNE executives view management of human resources as a key challenge for Western companies in China, where foreign companies are faced with low levels of managerial and professional skills among their employees. The local employees also tend to be unaccustomed to the concept of individual responsibility for the success of their own, their unit's, and their company's operations (Child 1991; Björkman 1994). A performance appraisal system in which specific individual and group goals and development plans are agreed upon and subsequently followed up might constitute an important vehicle for enhancing MNE performance in China. However, to date little research has been conducted on the use of Western-type performance appraisal systems in China. Therefore, our research aims at answering the following two questions:

1   To what extent have Western MNEs implemented standardized perform- ance appraisal practices for their host country professionals and managers in China?
2   What experiences have expatriate managers had when implementing such practices for their local subordinates?

We will report the findings from two consecutive studies: first, an interview based survey of 70 Chinese–Western joint ventures and wholly owned subsidiaries; second, an in-depth case study of the implementation of a performance appraisal system in one Western MNE.

Literature review

Standardized versus localized HRM practices

In the international business literature, MNE strategy has often been conceptual- ized in terms of global integration versus local responsiveness (e.g. Doz and Prahalad 1981; Prahalad and Doz 1987). A similar framework has been proposed for HRM policies and practices in MNEs (Schuler *et al.* 1993). Researchers have typically analysed the extent to which subsidiary HRM practices resemble those of local firms as opposed to those of the MNE parent organization (e.g. Beechler and Yang 1994; Rosenzweig and Nohria 1994). The MNE standardization– localization framework is used in the present study.

But why does a certain MNE unit have a localized or standardized HRM practice? At least four different kinds of explanations (and arguments) can be forwarded: economic, control, institutional and cultural. From an economic point of view, MNEs may be expected to standardize certain management practices because they are seen as the most efficient way to operate in the local environment. Additionally, standardization may lead to lower transaction costs between different parts of the MNE. Standardization of policies and practices may also be viewed as a way for headquarters to control foreign subsidiaries (Martinez and Jarillo 1989). Several institutional explanations (see DiMaggio and Powell 1983) are possible. First, expatriate managers and headquarters executives tend to have set views of the kind of HRM practices that are efficient. As a consequence, they may attempt to introduce patterns of operation from their home organization when functioning in overseas settings (Brooke and Remmers 1970; Bartlett and Ghoshal 1989). Second, for a number of HRM practices, the local coercive pressures through host country legislation and existing labour practices are likely to be strong (Rosenzweig and Nohria 1994). Additionally, rooted in their own past, local managers have institutionalized views about management practices which may influence their suggestions and actions in the local MNE units.

A number of scholars have argued strongly that the way in which human resources are managed must fit in with the cultural environment. Thus, MNEs are encouraged to adapt the HRM policies and practices to the local environment (Mendonca and Kanungo 1994). Localized HRM practices may result both from proactive MNE decision-makers who adapt policies and practices to local conditions and from a process of problem-driven experiental learning (Cyert and March 1963) where managers change 'unsuccessful' organizational policies and practices.

Performance appraisal

Performance appraisal (PA) is currently used in the majority of large Western companies. Traditionally, appraisal schemes have concentrated on past and current performance. The main motivation for introducing an appraisal system used to be to provide a basis for wage increases or new levels of merit pay. Today, performance appraisal processes are often associated with the identification of training needs and long-term potential. The most sophisticated forms of performance appraisal systems, where the personal objectives of the appraisee are agreed upon and the outcomes of the appraisal are linked to training and development (and sometimes also to financial bonuses), are called 'performance management systems' (Holdsworth 1991).

In most Western companies employees are appraised by their immediate manager. The process can be as simple as filling out a narrative report once a year about an employee's quality and output of work, or it may involve sophisticated measurement techniques, such as simple rankings, ratings, behavioural checklists, critical incidents and/or comparisons with objectives (Sparrow and Hiltrop 1994).

Although some empirical research has indicated that HRM practices in MNEs tend to adhere more closely to host country practices than those in the MNE's home country operations (Rosenzweig and Nohria 1994), this may not be the case regarding performance appraisal. In a study of 168 international joint ventures with a US parent firm, it was found that parent firms typically employed the same performance appraisal practices in their joint ventures as in their divisional headquarters (Anderson 1990). More empirical research is clearly needed on the extent to which MNEs from different Western countries standardize and localize their performance appraisal systems in their units abroad. The present chapter aims to fill some of this gap.

Several authors have pointed to the culturally induced problems in standardizing performance appraisal in the Asian units of Western MNEs. For instance, based on a study of 707 managers in the USA, Indonesia, Malaysia and Thailand, Vance *et al.* (1992) argue that significant management style differences between countries hamper the transferability of performance appraisal practices across borders. Pucik (1988) analyses the problems in implementing Western performance appraisal systems in Japan. The research revealed problems related to language (most MNEs used English), the use of individualistic goal setting and the use of manager–subordinate appraisal discussions with host country nationals.

Mendonca and Kanungo (1994) maintain that performance appraisal practices with a more confrontational mode of feedback during the appraisal discussion may not be effective in developing countries where 'face saving' is important. In addition, employee involvement, which is critical to performance appraisal practices, may be problematic in authoritarian societies (see Hofstede 1991).

In conclusion, a number of scholars have suggested that there may be significant problems in the use of standardized MNE performance appraisal practices in foreign units. Unfortunately, very little research has been conducted on this issue.

Performance appraisal in China

Several studies have been conducted on the management of people in MNE units in China (e.g. Von Glinow and Teagarden 1988; Child and Markóczy 1993; Child 1994). While there seems to be little research focusing specifically on the performance appraisal practices in MNEs in China, empirical work by Child (1991,1994; Child and Markóczy 1993) does suggest that Western appraisal practices have been transferred with only limited success to Chinese–Western joint ventures. Several studies have been published on HRM practices in domestic Chinese companies, frequently with the intention of pointing to differences between Chinese and Western practice and thus (explicitly or implicitly) arguing for limitations in the transferability of HRM practices between countries (Warner 1986, 1993; Child 1994; Easterby-Smith *et al.*, 1995).

Performance appraisal is widely practised in Chinese state-owned enterprises (Zhao 1986; Easterby-Smith *et al.* 1995; Nyaw 1995). According to Nyaw (1995), the unique feature of Chinese performance appraisal practices is that they place great emphasis on the 'moral' aspect, such as political attitude, team spirit and diligent work for the motherland. In China, appraisal is often carried out through self-evaluation and 'democratic' sounding of opinions. In practice, this means that an employee writes a self-evaluation and these comments are reviewed by superior managers and then transferred to the employee's personal file. It is common to gather opinions from a wide range of employees in order to strive for a 'democratic' evaluation (Easterby-Smith *et al.* 1995).

The differences between Chinese and Western performance appraisal practices seem to encompass both evaluation criteria, appraisal methods and sources of appraisal. Table 8.1 summarizes these differences.

Chinese culture and performance appraisal

It has been argued that certain central features of Chinese culture are strong determinants of managerial practices and organizational behaviour (Lockett 1988). Four features of Chinese culture are usually singled out as important in understanding management practice and thus also the effects of introducing Western performance appraisal practices for host country employees in China:

Table 8.1 Performance appraisal practices in Chinese and Western companies

	Chinese	Western
Evaluation criteria	Broad evaluation criteria related to task but also to 'moral' and ideological behaviour	Performance criteria related to specific objectives of task
Appraisal discussion	No appraisal discussion, limited interpersonal feedback	Appraisal discussion common, direct feedback on performance
Sources of appraisal	Self-evaluation and democratic sounding of opinions by peers and subordinates	Usually immediate manager

Source: Easterby-Smith *et al.* 1995

- respect for age and hierarchy
- group orientation
- 'face';
- importance of relationships (*guanxi*) (Lockett 1988).

First, the respect for age and hierarchy may influence the Western type of performance appraisal discussions, as local subordinates are unlikely to engage in candid discussions with their expatriate managers. Respect for authority tends to result in centralized decision-making and acceptance of hierarchy. Furthermore, respect for hierarchy tends to hinder the development of individual responsibility and initiative (Child 1991), which are central ingredients in Western performance appraisal practices.

Second, Chinese individuals tend to identify themselves as part of a specific group, team or unit, and an important distinction is made between 'insiders' and 'outsiders' (Gabrenya Jr and Hwang 1996). It is conceivable that this collective orientation on the part of Chinese employees may render it more difficult for expatriate managers to set individual objectives and goals for their subordinates.

Third, the role of 'face' and harmony is a significant aspect of social life in China. The manager who criticizes a subordinate, whether in private or in the presence of others, can cause that subordinate to 'lose face'. However, in this situation the managers also lose face because they made the subordinate lose face. The issue of face may complicate the direct feedback between expatriate managers and subordinates which is often assumed in Western performance appraisal practices.

Fourth, another central aspect of Chinese culture is the importance of relationships (*guanxi*). A common perception is that *guanxi* customarily deals with mutual favours and 'string pulling' between organizations and authorities (Bond 1991; Child and Markóczy 1993). However, relationships may also be of importance within organizations in the sense that good relationships can promote open and frank communication between manager and subordinate (Gao *et al.*

1996). In Western performance appraisal practices appraisal discussion and direct communication and feedback take a crucial role since evidence suggests that the effect of feedback can serve both to direct and to motivate performance (Locke and Latham 1984).

Research methodology

This chapter reports on two studies of performance appraisal in MNE units in China. Study 1 consists of semi-structured interviews carried out by the third author and two collaborators during 1996 in 63 manufacturing Chinese–Western joint ventures and 7 wholly owned subsidiaries located in different parts of the country. In each company, a minimum of one and a maximum of three managers were interviewed. The sample covered a range of industries, from the manufacturing of telecommunication equipment to the production of shoes and textiles. The companies had an average of 5.8 expatriates. Table 8.2 contains the characteristics of this sample.

The interviewee was usually the general manager and/or the human resources manager. Although the majority of the interviewees had been recruited from the Western company, there were also some who had been transferred from the local partner and some who had been externally recruited in China or elsewhere. A written questionnaire was used to collect data on the degree of localization and MNE standardization of the companies' HRM practices. The respondents were then asked to describe, among other things, the performance appraisal system used in their company. They were also told to elaborate on the experiences with these HRM practices for host country managers and professionals.[1] The main objective of this study was to increase our knowledge of the degree of MNE standardization and localization of HRM practices for host country professionals and managers in Western MNEs in China, and to describe company experiences with these practices. The study revealed a need for a more in-depth analysis of

Table 8.2 Sample profile in Study 1 (n = 70)

	Categories	*No. of companies*
Parent nationality	US	14
	European	63
	Other Western	3
Ownership of the (main) Western parent	<50%	10
	50%	11
	>50–80%	36
	80–100	13
Employees	−100	24
	100–500	30
	500–1000	7
	1000–	8
	missing value	1

the implementation of standardized performance appraisal systems in China. Therefore, a case study was undertaken of a European MNE's performance appraisal practices in its Chinese operations.

The case study was conducted by the first and second author. The primary means of collecting case data was personal interviews. Twenty one expatriates and two Chinese employees were interviewed in China. All interviewees held a managerial position and had mainly local subordinates. They represented different job categories and different organizational levels. The Western expatriates had been in China from six months to eight years, 2.7 years on average. In the interviews, preplanned topics and questions were used to guide the discussion as suggested by Patton (1994). The interview guides, although not identical, both covered HRM practices with a special focus on performance appraisal. In reference to this, interviewees were asked questions regarding objective setting, performance appraisal, usage of appraisal information and their experiences regarding the implementation of the performance appraisal for the Chinese employees. The interviews lasted between forty-five minutes and four and a half hours and were all recorded with permission of the interviewees (Yin 1994). The tapes were transcribed. The validity of the analysis was further improved by the first author's one and half years of experience working for the HR function of the case company in China.

Standardization versus localization of performance appraisal

During the interviews in Study 1, a self-reporting technique was used. In each company, the highest ranking interviewee (72.8 per cent of which were expatriates) was asked to fill in a questionnaire. The respondents were asked to answer the following questions concerning the HRM practices: 'Compared to the MNE's home country operations, the [HRM practices] are very similar (1) . . . very different (7).' The same questions were asked with regard to the local companies. Table 8.3 reports the respondents' answers.

There was a much higher degree of MNE standardization than localization of performance appraisal practices (statistically significant at <0.001, independent t-test, two-tailed test). Thus, the results were similar to those reported by Anderson (1990) on US international joint ventures. It may be noted that performance appraisal was much more standardized and somewhat less localized than the other HRM practices for which data were collected (methods and criteria used for recruitment, amount and content of management and professional training, relative importance of financial bonuses and criteria employed to determine the bonuses, criteria used to select people for promotion).

Most of the respondents in Study 1, in particular the Western interviewees, maintained that it is necessary from a competitive point of view to introduce Western-style HRM policies and practices in China. Based on the interviews carried out in Study 1, it appears that the use of formal performance management systems is currently increasing among Western investment enterprises in China. A

Table 8.3 Degree of MNE standardization and localization of HRM practices in the sample companies (scale: very similar (1), very different (7) to (i) practices in the MNE's home country operations; (ii) practices in local firms) (n = 61–70)

	Standardization	*Localization*
Methods used to appraise the performance of local professionals and managers	3.34	5.07
Criteria used to appraise the performance of local professionals and managers	3.09	5.23
Overall measure of other HRM practices	3.86	4.96

number of MNE units have already introduced formal periodic appraisal systems. In the companies that have a formal appraisal system, following common Western practices, the superior typically carries out a performance appraisal interview/ discussion with the subordinate. However, all interviewees maintained that there were difficulties in implementing a fully standardized Western performance appraisal system. The performance review discussions in particular were found to differ significantly from the expatriates' prior experience in Western countries. There is also some indication in the data presented in Table 8.3 that, compared to performance criteria used by Western MNEs in China, methods used to appraise host country employees were somewhat more localized and less MNE standardized. Experiences in using Western performance appraisal systems in China will be discussed in more depth in the case study presented below.

Implementation of Western-style performance appraisal

This case study examines a large European MNE with extensive operations around the world. The MNE is a leading international high-tech group with over 38,000 employees in 45 countries. In 1995, a performance management (PM) system was launched to replace the variety of systems that had been in use so far. The aim was to implement the PM system in a standardized way throughout the global operations. Some localization of the process was allowed, as long as the modifications were made within the PM framework. The company's PM system was based on PM discussions between the manager and the subordinate. In the annual or biannual discussions, the issues of performance review, objective setting and training and development matters were covered. The discussions were documented. For documentation purposes standard forms (in English) have been developed by the MNE headquarters for global use. Comparison with pre-agreed performance objectives is the only measurement technique suggested. Depending on the employee's position, the meeting of objectives could be linked to financial bonuses.

In spite of the fact that the company had been operating in China for over ten years, until 1994 it employed only a few people in China. As a consequence of a strategic decision to enhance local presence and the rapid growth of company sales in China, the number of employees had risen to over 1,000 in 1997. These employees worked for joint ventures and representative offices in several locations around the country. The MNE headquarters had proposed that the PM system should be used in China in line with their global strategy. Many (yet far from all) of the MNE managers in China, including Chinese managers, implemented the standard performance management process. They commenced PM discussions with their subordinates and used the standard PM documentation. These attempts were supported by the company's HR function in China, which offered managers training sessions on how to use the PM system.

Objective setting

A few of the Western managers set similar types of objectives for their Chinese subordinates as they set for subordinates of any other nationality. For example, a sales director said that he set goals derived from the budget (e.g. net sales and profitability) and objectives such as market entry, acquirement of x number of new customers and customer satisfaction. Furthermore, some of the interviewees stated that the difficulty level of the goals was not dependent on the nationality of the subordinate.

Nature and number of objectives

However, a majority of the interviewees stated that they have had to modify both the nature and the number of goals for their host country subordinates, apparently at least partly in order to avoid a possible loss of face if the goals are not achieved. In local Chinese companies objectives are often set so low that they will certainly be met. This behaviour is consistent with the importance of 'face' in China (Bond 1991); by exceeding the goals, those in charge will 'gain face'. As related by a Western manager:

> It has been interesting to follow how for example the local company X sets objectives for its performance. To make sure that budgets and objectives are exceeded, they [managers in the company] assume year after year that there will be no growth anymore. Basing the budgets and objectives on this assumption results, after a year, in good looking newspaper headlines which state how much indeed the company exceeded the goals!

One Western manager explained that the goals she sets for her local subordinates in China are more concrete than the goals she sets for her subordinates from Western countries. Furthermore, the writing of specific job descriptions for local employees and explaining them was regarded of utmost importance. Job descriptions were typically updated during PM discussions. Several expatriate managers told that their subordinates have been very pleased about getting a specific job description and objectives. A comment by a Chinese interviewee supports this: 'A lot of [Chinese] people like to have clear goals and boundaries.'

These findings are consistent with cross-national research on managerial values, which has found that Chinese managers score very high on intolerance of ambiguity and on uncertainty avoidance (see Smith *et al.* 1996).

Another interviewee explained that for a Chinese subordinate he could only formulate less than half of the objectives that are normally set for someone in a similar position in his home country. Otherwise the locals regarded it as 'impossible' to achieve the objectives (though they would only seldom say so directly to their superior). This interviewee related the locals' fear of objectives to their tendency to avoid taking responsibility, an issue that arose from other interviews as well. A related matter that emerged clearly from the interviews was the seeming lack of initiative by local employees. If a task is not assigned specifically to a certain employee, the employee will seldom do it, in spite of having noticed that it needs to be done. A lack of initiative and responsibility taking on the part of Chinese employees has also been noted in earlier research (Child 1991; Björkman 1994).

Agreed objectives

Whereas in the MNE's home country the manager and the subordinate tend to decide on the performance objectives together, this appeared to be rare in China. One expatriate manager stated: 'The setting of objectives has in some cases been extremely one-way . . . however I think it is good that they know what is expected from them rather that omitting the system totally.'

One explanation, as told by a Chinese interviewee, is that: 'In China, the education starts from very young and you are told what to do. Therefore, as adults, Chinese also prefer to be told what they are to do.' A further explanation may be that the Chinese do not want to confront their manager and therefore they generally agree with anything suggested. In addition, many Western interviewees commented that although a Chinese person may say 'yes' it does not necessarily mean that he or she accepts the suggestion and is actually committed to it. Chinese employees' behaviour in the objective-setting process reflects the hierarchical nature of Chinese society (Lockett 1988; Bond 1991), where even in work relationships there tends to be a pattern of 'superior speaking and inferior listening' (Gao *et al.* 1996: 286).

Performance review

One part of the PM discussion is a review of the employee's performance during the preceding working period. During this discussion, the employees were also supposed to give feedback to their superiors on how they could have been helped in the job. Related to the performance review, two major issues arose from the interview data: difficulties involved in providing direct criticism and matters concerning the documentation of the performance management discussions.

Direct criticism

Although some had been exposed to performance appraisal in Chinese organizations, local employees were not accustomed to getting direct criticism. One Western interviewee commented that: 'I heard of one guy who decided to quit after the PM discussion . . . evidently he took feedback a little bit too personally.' Another Western manager maintained that if the superior gives negative feedback to a Chinese subordinate in a harsh way, the employee is likely to leave the company, having lost face in front of the manager.

The Chinese are not used to providing negative feedback, especially not to their superiors. As a Chinese interviewee explained: 'The Chinese employees, they don't like to talk very much to their bosses from Western countries. We are not very open people here.' A related comment regarding the standardized system was made by one of the company's Chinese HR managers: 'We should do some changes in the quite direct questions that are used in the appraisal forms . . . Chinese are not accustomed to receiving or giving direct feedback.'

These observations are related to the indirect and reserved communication patterns that have been observed in Chinese culture. The Chinese communication style has often been characterized as indirect, with individuals trying to minimize the loss of face and preserve harmonious relationships. According to Gao *et al.* (1996: 284): 'The Chinese say that when there are things left to be said there is room for "free advance and retreat".' In Chinese culture the listener must be able to understand indirect messages. Research has also established that direct feedback is particularly limited in hierarchical work relationships (see Gao *et al.* 1996). It is extremely difficult for Western expatriates to detect nonverbal clues and to second-guess local subordinates. Nevertheless, one interviewee stated: 'With most of my subordinates I had a good, thorough discussion which covered also negative issues. I was positively surprised. The discussions succeeded much better than what I had expected.' His perceived success may be explained by the fact that this expatriate had managed to build a good relationship with locals during his almost eight-year stay in China and thus he was able to achieve two-way interaction.

The importance of good relationships to two-way interaction between a Westerner and Chinese was brought up by a few of the interviewees and is directly related to the importance of relationships as applied internally in organizations. The importance of close relationships in China has been extensively elaborated upon in Goodwin and So-kum Tang (1996). The differences between communication with 'insiders' and 'outsiders' are stressed by Gao *et al.* (1996). While communication with insiders can be very personal and open, with outsiders the Chinese are more impersonal and closed.

The fact that the PM discussions and forms were in English was regarded as a potential problem, for example, by a Chinese manager: 'They are embarrassed if they choose some wrong words in English, I think English is one thing they are afraid of.'

Documenting the PM discussions

In the case company, the main purposes of documenting the PM discussion included: reminding the subordinate and the manager of the agreed performance objectives; providing a comparison point for the performance review; providing information for the HR functions different training needs and courses. As neutral as these purposes may seem, a few of the interviewees still mentioned their concern about the effects of documenting the PM discussion. The general impression was that this caused locals to neutralize their comments. As one expatriate pointed out: 'This is an issue that seems to create some concern . . . the completed PM forms should be kept only by the manager and the subordinate, and not be used by other parties'.

The concerns brought up by some locals may be related to the role of the local employees' personal file, *dang an*, which is still important in China. The file contains information of the employees' family background, education, work experience, political attitude and previous performance appraisals (Easterby-Smith *et al.* 1995). The file is not accessible to the employees themselves and is usually seen as a way in which Chinese organizations control employees (Child 1994). Local employees, especially with experiences in state-owned enterprises, may feel uncomfortable if their performance or comments regarding their superior are clearly documented; they may suspect that such information can be used against them. Another concern was that once something is agreed on paper, for example, performance objectives, the locals are reluctant to work for other objectives during that performance period.

Training and development plans

As the third central part in the case company's PM discussion, the manager and the subordinate were required to discuss the training that the subordinate needed in order to improve performance in the present job, as well as to discuss the subordinate's career aspirations. Standard practice in the MNE was that employees participate in drawing up their own training and development plans, even taking the major responsibility for such planning. This practice does not suit the Chinese culture. As one expatriate manager described: 'They expect [the manager] to think and decide for them what training they need; they think that how could they know it?'. Another expatriate manager had faced different difficulties when trying to make training plans: 'The problem is that they have so high expectations from us being a Western company . . . sometimes they do not understand that training can involve so many other aspects than just participation in courses.'

Regarding development, on the basis of the interview data it can be concluded that virtually all the Chinese employees expected extremely fast hierarchical progress. In spite of this fact, several interviewees noted that it was difficult to discuss long-term career plans with the appraisees. First, the Chinese employees seemed to expect ready-made career plans right from the beginning. Second, according to the interviewees, local employees seldom think about events more than a few months ahead. Therefore, if they did not see career progress taking place within six months of the PM discussion, they became impatient and dissatisfied and some of them might even leave the company, as one expatriate explained: 'The problem is that I can never get them to say what they aspire for . . . I ask them where they want to be and what they want to do in a year's time but just get avoiding answers . . . then they quit after half-a-year just because they were not promoted!'

Third, many locals expected to be promoted because of their age and/or tenure in the company. Promoting for age is typical in Chinese organizations. Many Chinese employees apparently suffered from a serious loss of 'face' when a younger person or a person with shorter tenure in the company made faster career progress than they did. As a result of such situations, some even decided to leave the companies (see also Child 1994). Fourth, although locals are eager for career progress they were, according to many of our interviewees, not willing to take the increased responsibility that normally comes with a higher position.

Cultural influences on the performance management system

Table 8.4 summarizes our interpretation of the central cultural influences on the performance management system in the case company.

As can be seen from Table 8.4, the findings of the case study concur for the most part with the literature on the influence of culture on management and organizational behaviour in China (see Lockett 1988). However, the importance of group orientation in Chinese culture was not found to have a major influence on the implementation of the performance management system. Research into Chinese organizations has revealed that Chinese employees may be uninterested in promotions (Weldon and Jehn 1993) at least partly because this may lead to

Table 8.4 Cultural influences on perceived problems with Western performance appraisal practices in China

	Face	Group orientation	Hierarchy	Relationships
Objective setting	Easy objectives		One-way objectives	
Performance review	Little criticism and feedback; language barriers		Scant upward feedback; few reactions on downward feedback	More open when close manager–subordinate relationship
Training and development plan			Expect ready-made training/career development plans	

exclusion from the present in-group. The present research showed no indication of this kind of behaviour on the part of the host country employees; on the contrary, most employees appeared focused on their own career development. It is conceivable that some career-oriented individualistic persons have been attracted to the MNE and/or that our results reflect a general trend towards more career-oriented individualistic values.

Summary and conclusions

The research reported in this chapter was aimed at answering two questions: first, the extent to which Western MNEs have implemented standardized performance appraisal practices for their local professionals and managers in China; second, what their experiences have been when implementing such practices. The interview-based survey of 70 Chinese–Western joint ventures and Western wholly owned subsidiaries show that there is a much higher level of standardization than of localization of performance appraisal practices. However, it should be pointed out that this research was restricted to local professionals and managers. Recent research by Goodall and Warner (1997) indicates that the degree of MNE standardization may be lower among blue-collar workers.

In order to augment our understanding of the experiences of introducing Western performance appraisal systems in China, an in-depth analysis of the operations of one Western MNE was carried out. Central features of Chinese culture were found to have an impact on the implementation and use of Western performance appraisal practices with host country nationals, implying some degree of localization. The study showed clearly that the issue of 'face' was crucial for Chinese employees and had implications for how to implement a performance appraisal system in China. For example, the Chinese employees expected the objectives to be set so that they were fairly easy to reach – thereby avoiding a loss of face for the subordinate. Therefore, some experienced expatriate managers relied more on informal discussions and daily interactions than on the formal objective-setting discussions to motivate their Chinese subordinates. The hierarchical nature of Chinese society also seemed to influence a number of elements of the MNE's performance management system. Moreover, the role of personal relationships was important. A good relationship between manager and employee fosters two-way communication about employee objectives, appraiser and appraisee performance, and career planning and development.

The research reported in this chapter may suggest a need for Western MNEs to make some adjustments to their appraisal practices to the Chinese context. There is a need to modify the style of communication in appraisal discussions. Blunt feedback on either the performance of manager or employee is not appropriate in the Chinese context and can result in deteriorating manager–subordinate relationships. The appraisal process documentation and forms should be translated into Chinese. There is a need to clarify the rationale of the performance appraisal system, both to appraisers and appraisees. Expatriates also tend to need training in how to handle appraisal discussions with Chinese employees. One could argue that this training is of even greater importance in China and other countries where the saving of face is more important than in individualistic societies where direct feedback on results and performance is more common. This would imply training in the art of giving feedback in a constructive and harmonious way. Moreover, the training of local human resources professionals seems to be necessary since they often lack experience working with Western concepts of management such as performance management systems.

The empirical data in this chapter have mainly dealt with expatriate (appraiser) experiences and perceptions of local subordinates. Future research should analyse the experiences from the point of view of those who are appraised – local employees. How do host country employees experience and perceive MNE performance appraisal practices? There is also a need for comparative studies of MNE performance appraisal practices in different host countries. Another interesting question to explore would be the differences between how Western expatriates and local supervisors implement the same performance appraisal system.

Note

1 See Björkman and Lu (1997) and Lu and Björkman (1997) for additional analyses based on the survey study.

References

Anderson, E. (1990) 'Two firms, one frontier: on assessing joint venture performance', *Sloan Management Review* 31(2): 19–30.

Bartlett, C.A. and Ghoshal, S. (1989) *Managing Across Borders: The Transnational Solution*, Boston MA: Harvard Business School Press.

Beechler, S. and Yang, J.Z. (1994) 'The transfer of Japanese-style management to American subsidiaries: contingencies, constraints, and competencies', *Journal of International Business Studies* 25: 467–92.

Björkman, I. (1994) 'Role perception and behavior among Chinese managers in Sino-Western joint ventures', in S. Stewart (ed.) *Advances in Chinese Industrial Studies*, vol, 4. Greenwich CT: JAI Press.

Björkman, I. and Lu, Y. (1997) *Managing the Human resources in Chinese–Western Joint Ventures*, Euro-Asia Centre Research Series, Insead Euro-Asia Centre, no. 46.

Bond, M.H. (1991) *Beyond the Chinese Face*, Hong Kong: Oxford University Press.

Brooke, M.Z. and Remmers, H.L. (1970) *The Strategy of Multinational Enterprise*, New York: Elsevier.

Child, J. (1991) 'A foreign perspective on the management of people in China', *International Journal of Human Resource Management* 2: 93–107.

—— (1994) *Management in China during the Age of Reform*, Cambridge: Cambridge University Press.

Child, J. and Markóczy, L. (1993) 'Host-country managerial behavior and learning in Chinese and Hungarian joint ventures', *Journal of Management Studies* 30: 611–31.

Cyert, R. and March, J. (1963) *A Behavioral Theory of the Firm*, Englewood Cliffs NJ: Prentice Hall.

DiMaggio, P.J. and Powell, W.W. (1983) 'The iron cage revisited: institutional isomorphism and collective rationality in organizational fields', American Sociological Review, 48: 147–60.

Dowling, P.J., Schuler, R.S. and Welch, D.E. (1994) *International Dimensions of Human Resource Management*, Belmont CA: Waldsworth.

Doz, Y.L. and Prahalad, C.K. (1981) 'Headquarters influence and strategic control in MNEs', *Sloan Management Review* 23: 15–29.

Easterby-Smith, M., Malina, D. and Yuan, L. (1995) 'How culture sensitive is HRM? A comparative analysis of practice in Chinese and UK companies', *International Journal of Human Resources Management* 6: 31–59.

Gabrenya, W.K. Jr and Kwang-Huo, Hwang (1996) 'Chinese social interaction: harmony and hierarchy on the good earth', in M. Bond (ed.) *The Handbook of Chinese Psychology*, Hong Kong: Oxford University Press, pp. 309–21.

Gao, G., Ting-Toomey, S. and Gudykunst, W.B. (1996) 'Chinese communication processes', in M. Bond (ed.) *The Handbook of Chinese Psychology*, Hong Kong: Oxford University Press.

Goodall, K. and Warner, M. (1997) 'Human resources in Sino-foreign joint ventures: selected case studies in Shanghai compared with Beijing', *International Journal of Human Resources Management* 8: 569–94.

Goodwin, R. and So-kum Tang, C. (1996) 'Chinese social relationships', in M. Bond (ed.) *The Handbook of Chinese Psychology*, Hong Kong: Oxford University Press.

Hannon, J., Huang, I.-C. and Jaw, B.-S. (1995) 'International human resource strategy and its determinants: the case of subsidiaries in Taiwan', *Journal of International Business Studies* 26: 531–54.

Hofstede, G. (1991) *Cultures and Organizations, Software of the Mind: Intercultural Cooperation and its Importance for Survival*, Chichester: McGraw-Hill.

Holdsworth, R. (1991) 'Appraisal', in F. Neale (ed.) *The Handbook of Performance Management*, Exeter: Short Run Press.

Lasserre, P. and Ching, P.-S. (1996) *Development of Managerial Resources in China*, Euro-Asia Centre Research Series, Insead Euro-Asia Centre, no. 36.

Locke, E. A. and Latham, G.P. (1984) *Goal Setting: A Motivational Technique that works!*, Englewood Cliffs NJ: Prentice Hall.

Lockett, M. (1988) 'Culture and the problems of Chinese management', *Organization Studies* 9: 475–96.

Lu, Y. and Björkman, I. (1997) 'HRM practices in China–Western joint ventures: MNE standardization versus localization', *International Journal of Human Resource Management* 8: 614–28.

Mabey, C. and Salaman, G. (1995) *Strategic Human Resource Management*, Oxford: Blackwell.

Martinez, J.I. and Jarillo, J.C. (1989) 'The evolution of research on coordination mechanisms in multination corporations', *Journal of International Business Studies* 20: 489–514.

Mendonca, M. and Kanungo, R.N. (1994) 'Managing human resources: the issue of cultural fit', *Journal of Management Inquiry* 3: 189–205.

Nyaw, M.-K. (1995) 'Human resource management in the People's Republic of China', in L.F. Moore and P.D. Jennings (eds) *Human Resource Management on the Pacific Rim*, Berlin: Walter de Gruyter.

Patton, M.Q. (1994) *Qualitative Evaluation and Research Methods*, 2nd edn, Newbury Park Sage.

Prahalad, C.K. and Doz, Y. (1987) *The Multinational Mission: Balancing Global Demands and Global Vision*, New York: Free Press.

Pucik, V. (1988) 'Strategic alliance with the Japanese: implications for human resources management', in F. Contractor and P. Lorange (eds) *Cooperative Strategies in International Business*, Toronto: Lexington Books.

Rosenzweig, P.M. and Nohria, N. (1994) 'Influences on human resource management practices in multinational corporations', *Journal of International Business Studies* 25: 229–51.

Schuler, R.S., Dowling, P.J. and De Cieri, H. (1993) 'An integrative framework of strategic human resource management', *International Journal of Human Resource Management* 4: 717–64.

Smith, P.B, Peterson, M.F, and Wang, Z.M. (1996) 'The manager as mediator of alternative meanings: a pilot study from China, the USA, and UK', *Journal of International Business Studies* 27, 115–37.

Southworth, D.B. (1996) 'FIEs in China: finding qualified personnel in China', *GBAktuell*, March: 15–21.

Sparrow, P. and Hiltrop, J.-M. (1994) *European Human Resource Management in Transition*, New York: Prentice Hall.

Vance, C.M., McClaine, S.R., Boje, D.M. and Stage, D.H. (1992) 'An examination of the transferability of traditional performance appraisal principles across cultural boundaries', *Management International Review* 32: 313–26.

Von Glinow, M.A. and Teagarden, M.B. (1988) 'The transfer of human resource management technology in Sino-US cooperative ventures: problems and solutions', *Human Resource Management* 27: 201–29.

Warner, M. (1986) 'Managing human resources in China: an empirical study', *Organization Studies* 7: 353–66.

— (1993) 'Human resource management "with Chinese characteristics"', *International Journal of Human Resource Management* 4: 45–65.

Weldon, E. and Jehn, K. (1993) 'Work goals and work-related beliefs among managers and professionals in the United States and the People's Republic of China', *Asia Pacific Journal of Human Resources* 31(1): 54–70.

Williams, S. (1991) 'Strategy and objectives', in R.A. Berk (ed.) *Performance Assessment: Methods and Applications*, Baltimore: Johns Hopkins University Press.

Yin, R. (1994) *Case Study Research: Design and Methods*, 2nd edn, Beverly Hills: Sage.

Zhao S.M. (1986) 'Human resources management in China', *Asia Pacific Journal of Human Resources* 32: 3–12.

Part III

Contemporary issues in expatriation

9 Strategic staffing in multinational companies

A resource-based approach

Jaime Bonache and Zulima Fernández

Introduction

In an influential paper in the international human resource management literature, Kobrin (1988) argued that US multinational enterprises (MNEs) were progressively reducing the number of international assignees in response to a need to reduce costs and due to the high rates of failure of expatriates. A decade later, it seems that this statement may not reflect the current practice of MNEs. According to the 1996 survey carried out by the consulting firm Organization Resources Counselors (ORC), from a sample of 546 MNEs (87 Asian, 108 European, 351 North American) the most common pattern among the majority of these companies, including the North Americans, is an increasing use of expatriates.

As a reflection of this increase in international assignees, there is an abundant number of studies about the way organizations manage their pool of expatriates. The studies cover different areas: selection, training, relocation and adjustment, pay and performance, career development, return. Of these practices, expatriate selection is perhaps the area which has received the most attention (see, for example, Tung 1981, 1982; Brewster 1991; Björkman and Gertsen 1993; Scullion 1994; Arthur and Bennett 1995). Studies on expatriate selection have focused mainly on the criteria which MNEs apply when assessing candidates for global assignments, the methods they use for selecting these candidates and the barriers to international mobility. In spite of their interest, these studies are often accused of being merely descriptive, developed in relative isolation from other expatriation policies and failing to connect expatriate selection to the company's international strategy (Brewster and Scullion 1997).

In view of these limitations, we attempt to base expatriate selection on a theoretical approach that allows us to link this policy with both the firm's strategic goals and other expatriation policies. This study addresses a fundamental question: What relationship exists between the MNE's international strategy and the expatriate's selection policy?

This question will be addressed within the conceptual framework of the resource-based view of the firm (e.g. Penrose 1959; Lippman and Rumelt 1982; Wernerfelt 1984; Barney 1991; Peteraf 1993). This theoretical model is chosen for two main reasons. First, because it enables us to provide a solid theoretical foundation for the expatriate selection policy; second, because of the importance this theory attributes to both human resources and the strategic design of HR practices.

We begin with a brief description of the resource-based view of the multinational firm. From this theoretical baseline, and relying on numerous examples from a set of Spanish multinationals, we will clarify the strategic role of international assignments. We will then propose a series of hypotheses regarding the way in which expatriates will be selected depending on the role they play within an organization's internationalization process. We will conclude with a discussion regarding the contribution of our work to expatriate HRM.

Resource-based view of the MNE enterprise

The resource-based view of the firm is basically a strategic theory. As such, it analyses the conditions under which firms can achieve positions of competitive advantage. According to this view, competitive advantage can occur only in situations of firm resource heterogeneity (resources are unevenly distributed and deployed across firms) and firm resource immobility (they cannot be transferred easily from one firm to another). A sustainable competitive advantage is achieved when firms implement a value-creating strategy that is grounded in resources that are valuable, rare, imperfectly imitable and non-substitutable (Barney 1991).

In the resource-based view, each enterprise is seen as a bundle of resources. These encompass all input factors that are owned or controlled by the firm and enter into the production of goods and services to satisfy human needs (Amit and Schoemaker 1993; Lado and Wilson 1994). They can be both tangible (financial and physical resources) and intangible (technology, reputation, organizational culture, human resources).

Some resources that provide the company with a competitive advantage in the firm's home country are also useful in other countries. According to Penrose (1959), firms expand in an effort to utilize their resources efficiently in the search for rents. In addition to providing an opportunity to derive additional rents from existing resources, internationalization also provides learning opportunities through exposure of the company to new cultures, ideas, experiences, etc., which can be used to create new expertise that complements and leverages its current knowledge. Hence, the simultaneous efforts to earn income from existing resources and to seek new resources to generate future income define the two basic dimensions of multinational expansion (Tallman and Fladmoe-Lindquist 1994). This view of internationalization is well illustrated by the expansion process of Zara, a Spanish textile company. In Spain this company developed the ability to complete a complex production process every fifteen days. This allowed it to offer stylish clothing every two weeks through its national network of shops at very reasonable prices. This capacity afforded Zara a leading position in its national market and became the driving force of its internationalization. The company expanded to those markets where demand for its products existed and where it could easily deploy its organizational resources (Belgium, France, Greece, Mexico, Portugal, USA). The company gradually enhanced its overall competitive capacity through the practices it learned in some of those markets (e.g. merchandising in New York). In sum, the company's resources – what it knows how to do better than its competitors – are what allowed and guided its international expansion.

During this exploitation and accumulation of resources, not all subsidiaries perform the same function. On the contrary, the most recent literature on corporate internationalization has also pointed out that there is internal differentiation among subsidiaries making up an MNE (Bartlett and Ghoshal 1989; Ghoshal and Nohria 1989; Martínez and Jarillo 1991; Gupta and Govindarajan 1991; Roth and Morrison 1992). Based on the extent (low versus high) to which subsidiaries develop the aforementioned two dimensions of internationalization, we can classify them into four categories: implementor, autonomous unit, learning unit, globally integrated unit (see Figure 9.1).

Implementor

Implementor subsidiaries apply the resources developed in the headquarters or other units of the organization to a specific geographic area. For example, the Spanish electrical firm Unión Fenosa, which also provides consulting in the electrical sector, began its international expansion eight years ago and is now present on four continents and in a total of twenty-one countries. The firm's strategy is based on exporting knowledge and experience gained in providing consulting to electrical firms.

Autonomous unit

Autonomous units are much less dependent on the human and organizational resources existing in the rest of the company's international network. In this case,

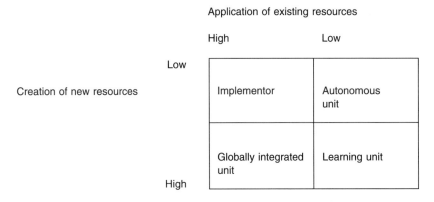

Figure 9.1 The strategic role of subsidiaries

internationalization is based more on the transfer of products or capital than on intangible assets (Gupta and Govindarajan 1991). The reason for this is that their environment is considered to be so idiosyncratic that the subsidiary has to develop expertise internally. This developed knowledge cannot then be transferred to other subsidiaries. Examples of this type of unit would be the Chinese subsidiary of the Spanish transportation company Alsa, or the subsidiary of the Banco Exterior de España in Cuba.

Learning unit

The learning unit acquires and develops new resources that may later be exported to other parts of the organization. An example of this type of unit is the US branch of Maphre, a Spanish insurance company. The reason for its location in the USA is the headquarters' interest in learning from the most competitive markets in order to transfer this knowledge to other units of the organization (including Spain).

Globally integrated unit

The globally integrated unit develops new expertise but also uses the resources generated in other subsidiaries or in the headquarters. Therefore, these subsidiaries best represent the modern subsidiary from a resource-based view. The Chilean subsidiary of the Spanish telephone company Telefónica belongs to this category. The company's management procedures were established in this subsidiary, yet, the firm soon recognized the limitations of its domestic resources. This was due to the fact that the Chilean subsidiary had to operate within a free market context, an environment that the headquarters did not know due to the highly regulated Spanish telecommunications market. In this situation, learning was a major objective and a significant part of the experience. Given the recent liberalization of the Spanish telecommunications market, the capabilities (in marketing, customer service, etc.) that the company built in the Chilean subsidiary have proved to be highly useful in the domestic market.

Knowledge

So far we have seen that within the set of resources that is transferred among the different units of the MNE there are tangible resources (financial resources, physical assets) and intangible resources (human resources, technology). It is increasingly recognized that intangible resources are more important to the firm both in value and as a basis for competitive advantage, and that knowledge is the most strategically important intangible resource (Grant 1996). Knowledge is the resource that potentially best satisfies the characteristics which are most important in establishing a competitive advantage over rivals (i.e. to be valuable, rare, imperfectly imitable and non-substitutable). Given that this concept plays an essential part in this work, it is necessary to define it with the utmost clarity.

In order to define knowledge some authors point to the meaning of this notion in philosophy (see, for example, Nonaka 1994; Grant 1996). As Nonaka (1994: 15) asserts: 'The history of philosophy since the classical Greek period can be regarded as a never-ending search for the meaning of knowledge.' Yet, the type of knowledge that is of interest in business does not necessarily agree with the type of knowledge with which philosophers are concerned. The latter – speculative knowledge – was clearly defined by Aristotle in *The Nicomachean Ethics*. This is focused on the understanding of the nature of things, simply for the sake of understanding. The 'speculative man' aims to have his notions conforming to the truth of things, not to bring things into harmony with his notions. Aristotle contrasts speculative knowledge with that which he defines as productive knowledge. In this type of knowledge, man is not interested in the unalterable nature of things (the nature of space, for example, or freedom), except insofar as this knowledge may be necessary to help him to be productive.

In the scope of business it is productive knowledge that is of interest; this knowledge enables the firm to add value to the incoming factors of production (Gupta and Govindarajan 1991). It may refer to input processes (e.g. purchasing skills), throughput processes (e.g. product designs, process engineering, technological and organizational knowledge) or output processes (e.g. marketing know-how, merchandising). Thus understood, knowledge differs from information, which is simply a statement of facts (i.e. external market data about key customers, competitors or suppliers).

For the purposes of this work, it is important to point out that productive knowledge has a series of characteristics:

Tacit or explicit knowledge

Knowledge can be tacit or explicit. This distinction is drawn from Polanyi (1966) who distinguished between these two types of knowledge on the basis of the observation that 'we can know more than we can tell'. Explicit knowledge can be codified (expressed in words and numbers) and easily communicated and shared in the form of hard data, manuals, codified procedures or universal principles. In contrast, tacit knowledge is deeply rooted in an individual's experience and only revealed through its application ('learning by doing'). As a result, tacit knowledge is not easily visible and expressible, making it difficult to imitate and transmit.

Hierarchical knowledge

Knowledge is organized according to a hierarchical structure (Grant 1995).[1] Some knowledge is very concrete and involves performing a certain task, whereas other knowledge is the integration of different types of expertise of a more specific nature. For example, a hospital's knowledge that allows it to treat heart patients depends on the integration of different lower level expertise such as diagnosis, cardiovascular surgery, post-operative care and other support know-how. In general, complex knowledge is more difficult to imitate and replicate in the market.

Generic and specific knowledge

Knowledge can be generic or specific. Generic knowledge can be applied in any company without losing value (for example, accounting expertise). Specific knowledge can be applied in the company proper but loses value in another organization. An example of this type of knowledge is an employee who knows a digit of the code that opens the company's safe. This information is highly valuable when combined with the knowledge of other employees, but its value diminishes outside the organization. As a result, the person who possesses this knowledge will lose most of his/her value upon abandoning the organization. Since a resource must be scarce and imperfectly mobile in order to be a source of competitive advantage, it holds that specific knowledge is more crucial than generic knowledge to explain the company's competitiveness and internationalization.

Context-specific and context generalizable knowledge

Knowledge can be context specific and context generalizable. As noted earlier, internationalization exposes the company to multiple markets in which different knowledge can be applied and developed. Depending on its usefulness outside the location where it is developed, knowledge can be context specific or context generalizable. If it is confined to its place of origin, it is context specific. If it is effective across countries, it is context generalizable (Taylor *et al.* 1996).

Individual and collective knowledge

Knowledge can be held individually or collectively (Prahalad and Hamel 1990). The generation or building of a particular type of knowledge depends only on a single individual (i.e. the ability to work in a particular language). Collective knowledge is the outcome of knowledge integration. It is the product of the co-ordinated efforts of many individual specialists who possess many different but complementary skills (Grant 1996). Both collective and individual knowledge can be explicit and tacit. An example of explicit collective knowledge (and hence a type of knowledge that can be objectified) is the organization's established human resource practices (performance appraisal procedures, selection methods, etc.). The organization's culture is an example of tacit collective knowledge. It is something which is manifested in the practice of an organization, but which cannot be objectified. Similarly, whereas 'numerical computation' is a case of explicit individual knowledge, 'negotiation skills' are an example of tacit individual knowledge.

Knowledge acquisition and generation

The process of obtaining and generating knowledge is gradual. A minimum amount of time is required to generate and assimilate new knowledge – what Dierickx and Cool (1989) call 'time-compression diseconomies'. This occurs even to acquire coded (and thus easily interpreted and transmitted) knowledge. In addition, acquisition of knowledge is path dependent, which means that the way in which the knowledge is gained affects the results that are eventually obtained.

Knowledge as information

Finally, Itami (1987) pointed out that knowledge, just like any other intangible asset, is characterized by the fact that its raw material is information possessed by the individuals and groups both within the organization and outside (for example, brand image and reputation become embodied in the company's customers and suppliers).

Thus information and people are two essential elements of intangible assets in general and of knowledge in particular. It is the people who have the experience, information and knowledge which are applied in the activities carried out by the company. From this perspective, we can discuss the role that expatriation policies play within corporate internationalization.

The strategic role of expatriation selection policy

The literature on the resource-based view has paid neither theoretical nor empirical attention to the strategic role of expatriation policies. Therefore, the principal basis on which to discuss the role of these policies from this theoretical perspective comes from the domestic literature (Wright and McMahan 1992; Wright *et al.* 1994). Building on this domestic literature, in Figure 9.2 we present a model suggesting that expatriation policies have two basic functions. The first is to identify and attract employees with the knowledge, skills and abilities required for the successful implementation of the strategy of the subsidiary. Having obtained this pool, the next aim of expatriation practices is to encourage expatriates to behave in a way that supports such a strategy. In this work we limit our attention to the first function of expatriation policies and, in particular, to expatriate selection.

In the analysis of expatriate selection we develop a contingency approach which draws on the following reasoning. First, we argue that the type of subsidiary partly determines the expatriate's strategic role. Second, we maintain that each strategic role requires different types of knowledge, skills and abilities on the part of expatriates. Finally, assuming a rational view according to which expatriate selection aims at supporting the subsidiary strategic role, we argue that the company will carry out different selection choices according to the subsidiary to which the expatriate will be assigned.

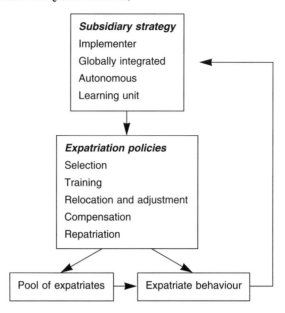

Figure 9.2 A model of the strategic role of expatriation policies

Reasons for using expatriates

According to Black *et al.* (1992), expatriates play three main strategic roles in corporate internationalization: control and co-ordination of operations (management function), transfer of skills and knowledge, managerial development. In Table 9.1, we reflect the percentage of expatriates that fall into these categories, according to the survey conducted by Price Waterhouse (1995) in a sample of a total of 180 European companies. Assignees performing management functions constitute the largest proportion of expatriates (56 per cent) in the surveyed companies, followed by skills transfer accounting for 28 per cent of expatriate assignments. We also see that there are two additional categories of expatriates: graduate trainees and career expatriates. This work will focus only on the first three categories.

Edstrom and Galbraith (1977) argued that expatriate roles depend on the company's international strategy. They noted that companies which integrated their operations globally assigned expatriates for reasons of co-ordination, while those which followed a multi-domestic strategy chose expatriates for control reasons. Since our analysis is carried out at the subsidiary level, our objective at this point will be to correlate the reasons for using expatriates to the types of subsidiary. Along these lines, we argue that while many expatriations involve more than one role, the relative importance of each varies by type of subsidiary.

Implementor subsidiaries exploit knowledge from other units. Most of the knowledge that is transferred among units is tacit (for instance, the capacities of a company's managers and employees to launch new products). Given that

Table 9.1 Roles of expatriates in European multinationals (n = 180)

What percentage of expatriates fall into the following categories?	*Percentage*
Management function	55.9
Transfer of skills and knowledge	28.0
Management development	11.2
Graduate trainees	3.8
Career expatriates	1.1

Source: Price Waterhouse 1996

such tacit knowledge cannot be codified or contained in manuals and can only be observed through its application, when a company decides to transfer tacit knowledge between different units it must assign employees to the foreign operations (Pucik 1992). Therefore, skills and knowledge transfer is expected to be a critical reason for using expatriates in implementor subsidiaries.

A significant presence of these knowledge transfer expatriates is also to be expected in the globally integrated units since there is a considerable input of knowledge into these subsidiaries. Along with transfer of knowledge, co-ordination is another reason to assign expatriates in globally integrated subsidiaries. For example, in its first phase of internationalization the Spanish textile company Zara wanted to ensure that its activities were co-ordinated in order to exploit the economies of scale that result from selling standardized products to the same global market segment. The firm only produces articles that can be sold in the nine countries in which it does business. To do so the headquarters chose to assign expatriates to start up operations and transferred them to different units in order to increase their knowledge of the network, their awareness of the impact of their decisions and to develop multiple contacts which would allow them to act as links between interdependent units.

In autonomous subsidiaries, there is no relevant transfer of knowledge from the headquarters to the subsidiary or vice versa. Therefore, there is little basis for using expatriates to transfer know-how. Moreover, the fact that the expatriates' expertise is not well suited to the subsidiary environment, together with factors such as expatriate costs, the motivation and aspirations of local employees or local governmental pressures, will make international assignments seem less attractive to the multinational firm. On this basis, it could be argued that these subsidiaries will tend to be directed not by expatriates but by local managers who speak the language, understand the country's culture and political system and generally belong to a social elite that permits the company more easily to penetrate the market. In addition, using local directors increases the company's acceptance by the government and trade unions in the host country.

In spite of these considerations, circumstances may exist (which can also be found in other types of subsidiaries) that force the company to opt for expatriate instead of local directors in order to ensure control of the subsidiary. For example, in situations of political risk (where an event is likely to occur that will change the profitability prospects of a specific investment), or cultural risk (when there is a large cultural distance between headquarters and subsidiary), the head-quarters need to process a lot of information. This may lead to the assignment of 'trustworthy' managers whose function will be to increase the channels of communication between the headquarters and subsidiary and to guarantee that head office interests are well represented in the subsidiary (Boyacigiller 1990). Thus, maintaining control is the main reason why the management of Banco Exterior de España assigned a Spanish expatriate to its subsidiary in Cuba.

Finally, learning units transfer knowledge from their unit to other units. The dominant pattern of international transfer will be one of managers from these units to another country (Black *et al.* 1992). On other occasions international transfers involving learning units may be more similar to the typical parent country expatriate pattern. This is the case of transfers to the US subsidiary of Maphre. Top management sees this subsidiary as the ideal unit for a manage-ment development process leading to organizational learning. What the manager learns about elements such as the US insurance market, local competitors and international competitors operating in a highly competitive market can later be transferred to Spain and other units and incorporated into future resources. Management development thus becomes the main reason for using expatriates in learning units.

Strategic choices in expatriate selection

Once we have analysed the reasons that a firm might have for assigning expatri-ates to each of its subsidiaries, we can examine expatriate selection. This process involves choosing qualified individuals to fill positions in the organization's international network. The organization faces several strategic choices during the selection process:

- internal recruitment vs. external recruitment;
- individuals vs. teams;
- technical qualifications vs. other selection criteria;
- extrinsic rewards vs. intrinsic rewards.

These are only an example of the choices that confront management when selecting expatriates. Other decisions which we do not include in our analysis would be, for example, whether to include the family in the selection process or whether psychological screening should be used. It is also important to note that these choices represent two opposite extremes on a continuum. The majority of the decisions fall somewhere in between these two extremes. Therefore, it becomes a question of emphasis, not exclusion. A review of the expatriation literature suggests the choices that are specified in Table 9.2.

Table 9.2 The strategic role of the subsidiary and selection of expatriates

	Implementor	*Autonomous unit*	*Globally integrated unit*	*Learning unit*
Main expatriates' roles	Transfer of knowledge	Control	Transfer of knowledge; co-ordination	Career development
Source of recruitment	Internal labour market	Internal labour market	Internal labour market	External labour market
Dominant selection criteria	Technical competence	Cultural adaptability; language skills	Technical competence; cross-cultural communication	Motivation and potential
Team vs. individuals	Teams and individuals	Individuals	Teams and individuals	Individuals
Rewards	Medium emphasis on extrinsic and intrinsic rewards	High emphasis on extrinsic rewards	High emphasis on intrinsic rewards	High emphasis on intrinsic rewards

Internal vs. external recruitment

An interesting finding by a recent study on expatriate selection is that there is a perceived shortage of international managers, primarily due to the growing resistance to international mobility (Scullion 1994). The most common reasons for assignment refusal, as set out in the Price Waterhouse (1995) survey on international assignments are shown in Table 9.3. Domestic and family concerns, disruption of children's education and dual-career problems are the reasons most frequently given for assignment refusal in 37 per cent, 30 per cent, and 26 per cent of companies respectively.

The shortage of international managers creates problems in selection. From an organization's viewpoint, the selection decision is ideally made in circumstances

Table 9.3 Barriers to international mobility

Factor	*Most frequently cited* %
Career risk	5.8
Dual-career problem	25.5
Children's education	29.8
Domestic/family concerns	36.9
Security risks	1.5
Cultural differences	2.3
Language	3.6

Source: Price Waterhouse 1996

where the organization has a large number of applicants seeking an international assignment. However, given the limitation in the pool of candidates from which to choose, selection processes differ greatly from an ideal situation. In fact, availability seems to be the critical variable in the acceptance of an international assignment (Brewster and Scullion 1997).

In order to respond to this shortage the company can introduce external recruitment to fill management positions abroad. In spite of this possibility, it is well documented that the majority of firms rely almost exclusively on internal recruitment for foreign management positions (Torbiörn 1982; Scullion 1994). This selection option can be found even in markets where there is plenty of skilled labour (Boyacigiller 1990). This led us to pose the following question: Why is there not a greater emphasis on external recruitment?

To respond to this question, it is necessary to take into account the strategic role of expatriates in the different subsidiaries. Implementor and globally integrated subsidiaries exploit existing knowledge in other units of the organization. Much of the knowledge which is transferred among units of an MNE firm is not only tacit but also specific (Penrose 1959; Bartlett and Ghoshal 1995). Specific and tacit knowledge are of an idiosyncratic nature, referring to the specific ways in which things are done and can only be acquired through observation and experience within the company (ie advanced technological expertise or specific marketing activity). Therefore (a) if the company's strategic advantage is usually found in the MNE's specific knowledge; (b) if this specific knowledge can only be acquired within the company; (c) if, because of its tacit nature, this specific knowledge can only be transferred by expatriates; then the basic recruitment source of expatriates will be the company itself and not the external labour market.

A reliance on internal employees is also justified if the strategic purpose of an assignment is co-ordination and control of operations. The co-ordination function of expatriates in globally integrated units requires the assignment of people with broad experience in the firm, including a wide array of contacts throughout the company (Black *et al.* 1992). The control function of expatriates in autonomous subsidiaries requires the assignment of trustworthy people to guarantee that the interests of headquarters are well represented in the subsidiary. From this point of view, it is also logical to look within the firm in order to fill the management position with an internal manager who has an established track record and proven loyalty to the company.

However, in the case of learning units, recruiting can be from the external labour market. External managers can be assigned to one unit from a country with special competences in a certain area. Later, they can be assigned to other units in order to implement what they have learned. Resorting to external recruitment is not only a way of responding to the shortage of international managers, but is also consistent with the view that points to this recruitment source as one of the main methods of bringing into the organization individuals who have new skills and abilities and different ways of approaching job tasks.

Team vs. individual assignments

The function of control of expatriates in autonomous subsidiaries is highly individual. Just one expatriate in a key post can assure that the interests of the headquarters are well represented in the subsidiary. This can also be said of expatriates in globally integrated subsidiaries who perform a co-ordination function. Similarly, assignments to learning units for management development purposes can be performed by a single individual.

Yet, when we analyse assignments for the transfer of knowledge which takes place in both implementors and globally integrated units we get a different picture. As noted earlier, knowledge can be individual or collective. If the knowledge to be transferred is implicit individual knowledge (for instance, the knowledge of a brilliant intuitive stockbroker), the transfer will only involve that individual. On the other hand, collective knowledge is the product of the co-ordinated efforts of many individual specialists who possess different but complementary knowledge (Grant 1996). If this knowledge cannot be transferred upwards because of its tacit nature, then the transfer of such complex organizational knowledge may involve the transfer of the whole team. For example, the launching of new products involves the co-ordinated action of many individual specialists (i.e. market researchers, brand managers, advertising executives, sales representatives). The manager responsible for the launch knows only a fraction of what his subordinates know. For this reason, when a company wants to transfer this new product development capability to other subsidiaries it has to transfer a team, not just an individual.

Technical qualifications vs. other selection criteria

One of the questions most studied in expatriate management is that of the criteria used to select international assignees. In the survey by Organization Resources Counselors (1997) technical and other professional qualifications were by far the most frequently cited criteria employed when selecting a person for a job overseas (see Table 9.4). This finding is consistent with other surveys on expatriate selection criteria (Mendenhall *et al.* 1987; Tung 1981, 1982; Björkman and Gertsen 1993).

Despite the emphasis on technical qualifications and domestic performance, there is abundant evidence that other factors also play a critical role in the success of international assignees. In a recent study on the relative importance of factors that contribute to the success of expatriates, as perceived by 338 international assignees, Arthur and Bennet (1995) classified them into five categories:

- job knowledge and motivation;
- relational skills;
- flexibility/adaptability;
- extra-cultural openness;
- family situation.

Table 9.4 Selection criteria (n = 528)

	Importance		
	First %	*Second* %	*Third* %
Prior international living experience or assignment	3	4	15
Job performance	27	51	12
Job level	7	18	38
Marital status	3	2	3
Familiarity with assignment country	2	3	9
Language ability	2	5	17
Skills or competences	65	18	8

Note:
In selecting employees for international assignment, companies ranked the following seven factors from most important (1) to least important (7). The percentage of companies ranking each factor as first, second, or third most important are shown above.

Source: Organization Resources Counselors 1996

The authors found that family situation (adaptability of spouse and family, stable marriage, willingness of spouse to live abroad) and flexibility/adaptability (tolerance of ambiguity, listening skills, ability to deal with stress) were perceived as the most important factors in the success of expatriates. An interesting question then becomes: Why does expatriate selection tend to focus on technical competence?

According to Tung (1981), the emphasis on technical competence is due to the fact that this is more easily identified than other factors such as cultural adaptability. Since technical competence is always an important element in any job, those making the selection prefer to play safe to minimize possible errors.

From a strategic perspective, the firm must first pay attention to defining the strategic role of the assignment and then to assessing the factors required to accomplish this role successfully. This approach provides us with a new reason for the emphasis on technical competence: the nature of certain international assignments. If the fundamental reason for using expatriates is to transfer the skills and knowledge that provide the company with a strategic advantage over competitors – a typical assignment of implementors and globally integrated units – it is logical that technical competence and domestic track record become the dominant selection criteria.

Yet if the strategic purpose of an international assignment is co-ordination – also a typical assignment in globally integrated units – then the candidate will have to possess or develop a wide array of contacts throughout the company. Although technical competence will also be relevant in performing this co-ordination role, the dominant selection criteria must be to possess good cross-cultural communication skills.

The success of autonomous subsidiaries depends more on the ability to adapt to local conditions than on the technical support received from headquarters.

Therefore, cultural adaptability and language skills should be the criteria emphasized, rather than technical competence, when selecting expatriates to perform a control function in an autonomous unit. Similarly, given that management development is the main reason for assigning expatriates to learning units, motivation for learning and potential for advancement as a manager will be the criteria to emphasize.

Extrinsic vs. intrinsic rewards

This choice refers to the type of incentive offered by the organization to accept an international assignment. Such incentives can be extrinsic or intrinsic. Extrinsic rewards involve types of tangible or monetary reward, while intrinsic rewards are intangible gains such as the opportunity for professional development, security or recognition.

A situational factor that determines the emphasis of one type of reward or another is repatriation (Adler and Ghadar 1990). In many organizations, employees find that their return to the country of origin after one or more assignments is accompanied by adaptation problems, loss of status and lack of recognition of the experience gained abroad. This problem is very obvious to the rest of the organization's employees and can influence a multinational firm's ability to recruit new employees for future assignments.

The repatriation problem is minimized if expatriates are assured that international experience will positively affect their professional development. However, this is not the normal practice as the purpose for providing personnel for international assignments seems more to cover immediate human resource needs than to create a career development strategy for future corporate directors (Mendenhall *et al.* 1987).

Taking into account the context specificity and the value of expertise acquired abroad, not all assignments generate the same repatriation problems, nor do they have the same impact on professional careers (see Figure 9.3). If the knowledge gained abroad cannot be applied once the assignment is concluded (e.g. because it is context specific), repatriation problems will arise. This would explain the results of several investigations (Howard 1974; Harvey 1982) which demonstrate that skills developed abroad by expatriates are barely exploited. On the other hand, if this knowledge is of benefit once the assignment is concluded, repatriation will be easier. Also, the company's long-term competitive advantage depends on constant updating of the knowledge on which it is based (Tallman and Fladmoe-Linquist 1994). Consequently, the value of knowledge acquired abroad will increase as it continues to accumulate with knowledge that already exists in the country of origin. If this value is high, it will have a positive impact on professional development. Otherwise, the impact will be more uncertain.

Figure 9.3 shows how repatriation problems and the impact on professional career assignments determine the type of reward offered by the organization.

Expatriates in autonomous units develop expertise that is totally heterogeneous with regard to that existing in any other unit. Therefore, these assignments result

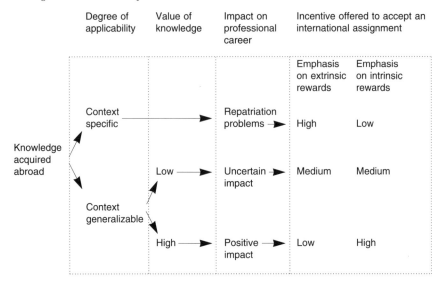

Figure 9.3 Knowledge acquired abroad, repatriation and type of reward

in more serious repatriation problems. In view of the uncertainty associated with repatriation, monetary incentives are strongly emphasized to attract human resources to the expatriation service (Adler and Ghadar 1990).

In the other three kinds of subsidiary, knowledge is shared between units, which facilitates repatriation. However, the value of the knowledge acquired abroad varies among subsidiaries. Thus, globally integrated units and learning subsidiaries contribute heavily to the generation of new expertise in the country of origin. Under these conditions, the incentives offered by the firm to accept international assignments could be less of a monetary type and related more to the intrinsic value involved in the opportunity to undertake a brilliant career within the organization. Thus, in strongly integrated companies such as Zara the condition for access to executive posts at headquarters is to have had at least one international assignment.

Finally, expatriates in implementor subsidiaries contribute very little to new know-how. An international assignment will therefore have a more indecisive impact on the professional career. As a result, the headquarters will also have to emphasize extrinsic rewards to motivate acceptance of the assignment.

Conclusion

Drawing on the theoretical notions of the resource-based view, in this chapter we have attempted to explain the strategic content of expatriate selection. Although there is still much empirical work to be done in this area of research, we believe that our analysis makes a number of important contributions. First, it helps us to clarify the linkage between expatriates and competitive advantage: if the primary source of sustainable competitive advantage is tacit and specific knowledge which is owned by people; if a firm's internationalization is based on the transfer to other markets of competitive advantages that it possesses in its domestic market and the acquisition of new knowledge; if the movement of tacit knowledge to other markets requires the movement of the people who possess it; then it is safe to say that international assignments of employees play a critical strategic role in a firm's internationalization.

The second contribution of our study points to areas of research that so far have received very limited attention. In particular, this study has found that international assignments may involve the transfer of teams, not just individual managers. This is consistent with the heavy emphasis of business literature on team-based structures, but conflicts with the prevailing 'individualistic' trend in the standard expatriation literature. Such a trend assumes that firms are hierarchical structures dominated by the superior knowledge of the senior management team. This conception can be questioned from two points of view. First, within a firm, different employees undertake different activities in the process of transforming inputs into outputs, and there is no reason to think a priori that top management's view is privileged (Spender, 1996). Second, to be imperfectly imitable is a requisite for a resource to be a source of sustainable competitive advantage. If knowledge is linked to an individual, competitor firms can imitate this advantage by hiring this individual. If the competitive advantage is a result of the integration of many co-operating individuals, it may not be apparent which personnel are responsible for it: in other words, there is causal ambiguity (Reed and DeFilippi 1990). This suggests that instead of focusing exclusively on individuals as the basic unit of analysis, a more comprehensive theory of international assignments must also embrace teams.

In addition to these contributions, our analysis also has implications for the international competitiveness of MNEs. It is well documented that the majority of MNEs fail to adopt a systematic and coherent approach to selection and that most assignments are short-term, problem-solving experiences (Brewster and Scullion 1997). Arguably, this ad hoc approach to staffing has performance costs. In accordance with the prevailing thinking in strategic human resource management, the integration of human resource practices and corporate strategy results in improved corporate performance (Lengnick-Hall and Lengnick-Hall 1988; Snell and Dean 1992). Therefore, it can be expected that empirical research will show that companies which select their expatriates in connection with the subsidiary's strategic objectives, as we have attempted to show in this work, will obtain better performance than those that operate in this area on an ad hoc basis.

Note

1   Grant (1995) does not speak of knowledge but capabilities. However, these are no more than the knowledge that the company possesses regarding the way to combine resources to perform a productive activity.

References

Adler, N.J. and Ghadar, F. (1990) 'Strategic human resource management: a global perspective', in R. Pieper (ed.), *Human Resource Management: An International Comparison*, New York: De Gruyter.

Amit, R. and Schoemaker, P.J. (1993) 'Strategic assets and organizational rent', *Strategic Manangement Journal* 14: 33–46.

Arthur, W. and Bennett, W. (1995) 'The international assignee: the relative importance of factors perceived to contribute to success', *Personnel Psychology* 48: 99–114.

Barney, L. (1991) 'Firm resources and sustained competitive advantage', *Journal of Management* 17: 99–120.

Bartlett, C.A. and Ghoshal, S. (1989) 'Managing across borders: new organizational responses', *Sloan Management Review* 10: 43–53.

—— (1995) *Transnational Management* 2nd edn, Boston: Irwin.

Björkman, I. and Gertsen, M. (1993) 'Selecting and training Scandinavian expatriates: determinants of corporate practice', *Scandinavian Journal of Management* 9(2) 145–64.

Black, J.S., Gregersen, H.B. and Mendenhall, M. (1992) *Global Assignments*, New York: Jossey Bass.

Boyacigiller, N. (1990) 'Role of expatriates in the management of interdependence, complexity, and risk of MNEs', *Journal of International Business Studies*, third quarter: 357–78.

Brewster, C. (1991) *The Management of Expatriates*, London: Kogan Page.

Brewster, C. and Scullion, H. (1997) 'A review and agenda for expatriate HRM', *Human Resource Manangement Journal* 7(3) 32–41.

Dierickx, I. and Cool, K. (1989) 'Asset stock accumulation and sustainability of competitive advantage', *Manangement Science* 35: 1504–11.

Edstrom, A. and Galbraith, J (1977) 'Transfer of managers as a coordination and control strategy in multinational organizations', *Administrative Science Quarterly* 22: 248–63.

Ghoshal, S. and Nohria, N. (1989) 'Internal differentiation within multinational corporations', *Strategic Management Journal* 10(4) 323–37.

Grant, R.M. (1995) *Contemporary Strategy Analysis*, Cambridge MA: Blackwell.

—— (1996) 'Toward a knowledge-based theory of the firm', *Strategic Management Journal* 17: 109–22.

Gupta, A.K. and Govindarajan, V. (1991) 'Knowledge flows and the structure of control within multinational corporations', *Academy of Management Review* 16(4) 768–92.

Harvey, M. (1982) 'The other side of foreign assignments: dealing with the repatriation dilemma', *Columbia Journal of World Business* 1: 53–9.

Howard, C.G. (1974) 'The returning overseas executive: cultural shock in reverse', *Human Resource Management* 13(2): 49–62.

Itami, H. (1987) *Mobilizing Invisible Assets*, Cambridge MA: Harvard University Press.

Kobrin, S.J. (1988) 'Expatriate reduction and strategic control in American multinational corporations', *Human Resource Management* 27(1) 63–75.

Lado, A.A. and Wilson, M.C. (1994) 'Human resource systems and sustained competitive advantage', *Academy of Management Review* 19: 699–727.

Lengnick-Hall, C.A. and Lengnick-Hall, M.L. (1988) 'Strategic human resources: a review of the literature and a proposed typology', *Academy of Management Review* 19: 699–727.

Lippman, S. and Rumelt, R.P. (1982) 'Uncertain imitability: an analysis of interfirm differences in profitability under competition', *Bell Journal of Economics* 13: 418–38.

Martínez, J.I. and Jarillo, J.C. (1991) 'The evolution of research on co-ordination mechanisms in multinational corporations', *Journal of International Business Studies* 20(3): 389–514.

Mendenhall, M.E., Dunbar, E. and Oddou, G.R. (1987) 'Expatriate selection, training and carreer pathing: a review and critique', *Human Resource Management* 26(3) 331–45.

Nohria, N. and Ghoshal, S. (1994) 'Differentiated fit and shared values: alternatives for managing headquarters–subsidiary relations', *Strategic Management Journal* 15: 491–502.

Nonaka, I. (1994) 'A dynamic theory of organizational knowledge creation', *Organization Science* 5: 14–37.

Organization Resources Counselors (1996) *Worldwide Survey of International Assignment Policies and Practices*, New York: Organization Resources Counselors, pp. 1–102.

Penrose, E.T. (1959) *The Theory of Growth of the Firm*, Oxford: Blackwell.

Peteraf, M.A. (1993), 'The cornerstones of competitive advantage. A resource-based view', *Strategic Management Journal* 14: 179–91.

Polanyi, M. (1966) *Personal Knowledge: Towards a Post-Critical Philosophy*, Chicago IL: University of Chicago Press.

Prahalad, C.K. and Hamell, G. (1990) 'The core competence of the corporation', *Harvard Business Review* 68(3): 79–91.

Price Waterhouse (1995) *International Assignments. European Policy and Practice*, London: Price Waterhouse.

Pucik, V. (1992) 'Globalization and human resource management', in V. Pucik *et al. Globalizing Management*, Chichester: Wiley.

Reed, R. and DeFilippi, R. (1990) 'Causal ambiguity, barriers to imitation, and sustainable competitive advantage', *Academy of Management Review* 15: 88–102.

Roth, K. and Morrison, A. J. (1992) 'Implementing global strategy: characteristics of global subsidiary mandates', *Journal of International Business Studies* 23: 715–35.

Scullion, H. (1994) 'Staffing policies and strategic control in British multinationals', *International Studies of Management and Organization* 24(3): 86–104.

Snell, S. and Dean, J. (1992) 'Integrating manufacturing and human resource management: conceptual model and empirical test', *Academy of Management Journals*: 179–191.

Spender, C. (1996) 'Making knowledge the basis of a dynamic theory of the firm', *Strategic Management Journal* 17: 45–62.

Tallman, S. and Fladmoe-Lindquist, K. (1994) 'A resource-based model of the multi-national firm', paper presented at the Strategic Management Society Conference, Paris, France.

Taylor, S., Beechler, S. and Napier, N. (1996) 'Toward an integrative model of strategic international human resource mangement', *Academy of Management Review* 21(4): 959–65.

Torbiörn, I. (1982) *Living Abroad: Personal Adjustment and Personnel Policy in Oversees Settings*, New York: Wiley.

Tung, R. (1981) 'Selection and training of personnel for overseas assignments', *Columbia Journal of World Business* 16(1) 68–78.

—— (1982) 'Selection and training procedures of US, European, and Japanese multi-nationals', *California Management Review* 25: 57-71.

Wernerfelt, B. (1984) 'A resource-based view of the firm', *Strategic Management Journal* 5: 171–80.

Wright, P. and McMahan, G. (1992) 'Theoretical perspectives for strategic human resource management', *Journal of Management* 18(2): 295–320.

Wright, P.M., McMahan, G.C. and McWillians, A. (1994) 'Human resources and sustained competitive advantage: a resource-based perspective', *International Journal of Human Resource Management* 5(2) 301–26.

10 International assignments across European borders

No problems?

Vesa Suutari and Chris Brewster

Introduction

Europe is changing. The integration of European societies through the European Union and the collapse of communism in Central and Eastern Europe (CEE) have increased interaction across European borders. More and more companies are doing business internationally, learning to deal with foreign markets and work-forces.

Increasing internationalization has been accompanied by a rise in the number of expatriates. Expatriates in international operations provide a number of clear benefits for their companies including:

- control of foreign operations;
- integration and co-ordination of subsidiary practices into company policies;
- transfer of organizational capabilities between units;
- effective communication between the foreign operation and the home country;
- development of internationally competent managers.

Partly because of the belief that it is often difficult to find sufficient numbers of high potential local staff and partly because of the perception that home country staff give the organization more control (Brewster 1991), a high proportion of international transfers involve sending HQ country staff to 'foreign' countries. This so-called ethnocentric approach – the use of people from the home country in key positions in foreign organizational units (Heenan and Perlmutter 1979: 18) – is still widely used among international companies as a basic human resource management strategy (Martínez and Jarillo 1991; Welch 1994; Mayrhofer and Brewster 1996).

The role of expatriates in the increasing internationalization of business, particularly within Europe, is now widely understood. This understanding has been accompanied by an upsurge in studies of the requirement for expatriates to adjust to their new situation (see among recent writings, Black and Stephens 1989; Bird and Dunbar 1991; Black *et al.* 1991; Brewster 1993).

The study of the adjustment process has developed as a reaction to the 'universalist' view of some writers and employing organizations. Lanier (1979) identified as typical the view that, for example, a good manager in one country will be a good manager in all countries, a point which has been made many times since. This assumption is widespread in organizations and accounts for the fact that most studies of selection criteria for expatriates find that the main focus is on current competence. There is substantial evidence in the literature that technical competence is seen as a crucial factor by MNEs (Ivancevich 1969; Hays 1971, 1974; Miller 1973; Howard 1974; Lanier 1979; Tung 1981, 1982; Zeira and Banai 1984, 1985), by the expatriates themselves (Gonzales and Neghandi 1967; Hays 1971; Harris 1973; Hautaluoma and Kaman 1975; Bardo and Bardo 1980; Hawes and Kealey 1981; Zeira and Banai 1984, 1985) and by host country nationals (Zeira and Banai 1985).

However, despite the importance of technical competence for expatriated employees, it is also clear from the literature that applying those skills in a different cultural environment is not problem free. On the contrary, much of the literature on expatriates takes almost as a given the impact of culture shock (identified by Oberg 1960; Gullahorn and Gullahorn 1963; Torbiörn 1982) and the requirement for the expatriate to adjust behaviour to what is expected by the local host culture. Thus, Black and Gregersen (1991) point out that 'generally . . . adjustment is conceptualised . . . as the degree of a person's psychological comfort with various aspects of a host country' (quoting Oberg 1960; Nicholson 1984; Black 1988). The process is necessarily an individual one (Brett *et al.* 1992), although, of course, family members who have also transferred will as individuals have similar experiences.

Adjustment has been described in terms of a U-curve theory (Gullahorn and Gullahorn 1963). Torbiörn (1982) was one of the first to apply this theory to expatriates. In his formulation, this predicts that expatriates arriving in the new country will have a short 'honeymoon' period where the excitement of the new country is the predominant feature. This is followed by a long 'culture shock' phase where disillusion with the new country settles in and morale declines. In a third 'adjustment' stage the expatriate learns to operate appropriately in the new environment. A fourth stage involves 'mastery'. More recently, U-curve theories have come under critical review (Black and Mendenhall 1990) and the theory has been found not to explain some European cases (Brewster 1991).

There is a further debate in the literature about the conceptual gap between expatriate adaptation and knowledge transfer (Brewster 1993): does the expatriate teach or learn? On the one hand expatriation can be seen as a means of teaching the organization in the host country how to behave as the overall organization requires; what Martínez and Jarillo (1991) refer to as one of the more subtle and informal control mechanisms of the international organization. On the other, as we have seen, there is the question of adjustment to the local environment. Adler (1972) referred to the possibility of seeing culture shock as a learning process (something to be undertaken enthusiastically) or as a psychological disease (something to be overcome). This choice may be more theoretical than real. The paradox is that the expatriates have to do both in order to be effective: to bring in ideas from HQ and to learn to operate in the new culture (Brewster 1993).

Much of the research on adjustment has focused on US expatriates, though some work has been undertaken in Europe (Janssens 1992; Brewster 1993; Kauppinen 1994). The usual assumption by MNEs, expatriates and the literature (Church 1982; Mendenhall and Oddou 1985) is that the greater the cultural distance, the more difficulty there will be for the expatriate to make the adjustment to the host culture. The main reason behind this is that the expatriate will simply not know, or even be able to identify, appropriate behaviours. This view has been challenged empirically: one study showed that the USA has most failures in joint ventures with Canada and Ireland, with cultural assumptions being a major point of stress (Franko 1971). Studies of US–Swedish interactions have shown that transfers between similar developed cultures can cause problems (Edstrom and Margolies 1986; Holmqvist 1989; Harris and Brewster 1995). It is clearly risky to make the assumption, reflected in the 'hardship supplements' paid to expatriates by many MNEs, that transfers within the developed world will automatically be easier.

In light of this background, it was decided to extend the work on expatriation by examining the adaptation issues faced by Finnish expatriates in Europe and to explore their understanding of the reasons for their problems, where any were identified. This research would thus concentrate on an area of the world where one effect of the European Union has been a substantial increase in expatriation, but where the research is less developed. By focusing on Finland it would constitute an important early contribution to the discussion of intra-Europe transfers for a country which has only recently (January 1995) joined the EU. This chapter focuses in the main on the adjustment of Finnish expatriates in other West European countries, but also presents some preliminary findings on the adjustment of Finnish expatriates in Eastern Europe.

Dimensions of adjustment

Attempts have been made to disaggregate the adjustment process into dimensions of adjustment: to the general cultural environment; to intercultural interaction; and to work and job responsibilities (Black 1988; Black *et al.* 1991). Black and his colleagues have also proposed more specific factors influencing adjustment.

In their model, the first factor, general cultural adjustment, has been divided into anticipatory adjustment and in-country adjustment. The elements of anticipatory adjustment include individual factors (i.e. training and previous experience) and selection mechanism and criteria. For in-country adjustment, two non-work elements were indicated: family–spouse adjustment and culture novelty (i.e. the cultural distance between home and host country). Elsewhere, social interaction has been proposed as an additional important factor in adjusting to the general cultural environment (e.g. Torbiörn 1982; Black and Gregersen 1991; Kauppinen 1994).

The second factor, organization culture, consisted of three subfactors: organization culture novelty, social support and logistical help. The first of these is closely related to cultural novelty and may be criticized as being a very broad factor. Kauppinen (1994) later suggested two additional factors influencing organizational adjustment: a need for the expatriate and preparations for repatriation (though the latter overlaps the anticipatory adjustment category of Black *et al.* 1991).

The third element in the model by Black *et al.* (1991), the job factor, includes role clarity, role discretion, role novelty and role conflict factors. In addition, the model represents three individual level factors influencing the adjustment: self-efficacy, relational skills, and perception skills. These earlier classifications were used as a starting point in the analysis of the research findings in the present study.

We note here, because it has relevance to the discussion of our findings, a proposed fourth category, emotional adjustment (Janssens 1992). 'An internationally-assigned manager has to adjust and respond to these different sources of change . . . newly assigned managers must find ways to adjust to the new cultural environment and this process may alter their values and beliefs' (Bird and Dunbar 1991: 6). Much of the work on expatriate preparation and training (for reviews see Black and Mendenhall 1990; Brewster and Pickard 1994) is built on the importance of this ability to understand and adjust. Much of the work on stress in this context (Cooper 1988) makes the same point.

European diversity: one continent, many cultures

Europe is the region of the globe with the largest number of well-established national cultures within a relatively small geographical base. Among West European countries there are many obvious differences although, as nominally Christian and democratic societies with market economies, there are also clear similarities from the point of view of expatriates and companies. To analyse Europe from the cultural point of view, we draw on the familiar contribution by Hofstede (1984), who identified four cultural dimensions or indices differentiating national cultures (i.e. power distance, masculinity, individualism and uncertainty avoidance). In this chapter we focus our brief summary of Hofstede's work by contrasting four West European countries (France, Germany, Britain and Sweden) and two East European countries (Russia and Estonia) in which our respondents were based with Finland, their home country.

According to Hofstede (1984), France, Germany and Britain can be described as countries of higher power distance than Finland. Sweden is similar to Finland. However, some other findings support the view that power distance could be even lower in Sweden than in Finland (Hoppe 1993). In line with these findings, French, German and British managers have been reported to be less active in allowing their subordinates to participate in decision-making or in giving them autonomy than their Nordic counterparts (see e.g. Brewster *et al.* 1993: 113; Myers *et al.* 1995; Suutari 1996b). The French, Germans and British were also found to stress masculine values more than the Finns and, in particular, the Swedes. In the organizational context this means, for example, that Swedes are very likely to take their subordinates' views and interests into account and stress the importance of human relations within organizations. Both Swedes and Finns have also been reported to be more active in informing their subordinates and encouraging co-operation and teamwork than their counterparts in Germany, France and Britain (Suutari 1996b). In line with higher levels of masculinity, Germans were reported to be very likely to emphasize efficiency and productivity and rewarding, giving recognition and criticizing their subordinates on the basis of their level of performance.

Hofstede (1984) found individualism to be higher in France, Britain and Sweden than in Finland, whereas Germany was very similar to Finland. The implication of this has been reported, for example, by Brewster *et al.* (1993: 55) who found that Swedish expatriates found British people to be very individualistic and disliked their selfishness. With regard to Hofstede's measure of uncertainty avoidance, the French were found to rank high and the Swedes low. Germany received similar scores to Finland in Hofstede's study, though some other studies seem to support the view that Germans might score even higher, with, for example, a high level of formalization in Germany (Laurent 1985; Suutari 1996b). Between the British and Finns, no clear difference seems to exist (Hoppe 1993; Hofstede 1984). We anticipated that all these differences would be relevant from the point of view of the Finnish expatriates in our sample.

A more diverse picture of Europe will be received if Central and East European countries are included. Studies of the specifics of CEE societies and organizations have increased during recent years. Post-communist societies and organizations have been described as having characteristics which differentiate them from their Western counterparts. Although each CEE country has its own history and culture, half a century of monolithic Soviet domination has meant that they also have much in common. For example, Nurmi and Üksvärav (1993) have stated with regard to Estonia that the fifty years of Soviet legacy have left their mark on the attitudes of Estonian people and the organizational cultures of Estonian companies. Still, it is also clear that there are differences between these ex-communistic countries. The Soviet domination was imposed on very distinct countries with varied cultural heritages; they responded differently to the communist regime and in important ways preserved their individuality. These differences can now have a more central influence on the values and behaviour of the people and will help to shape the extent of transformation.

Analysing Russia and Estonia, briefly, from the cultural point of view, they seem to have many similar characteristics. First, all ex-communist cultures have been described as having high power distance and thus managers have been very authoritative (see e.g. Bollinger 1994: 50; Puffer 1994; Suutari 1998). Second, uncertainty avoidance can be described as high. For example, Bollinger (1994: 51) reports that a group of Russian managers scored relatively high on this index. A high level of formalization and bureaucracy has also been frequently pointed out in both Russia and Estonia (Bollinger 1994; Garrison and Artemyev 1994; Nurmi and Üksvärav 1994: 66).

With regard to the masculinity index, the picture is more complex because it has been stated that the technical side of management has been stressed more than its human dimensions (e.g. Garrison and Artemyev 1994; Holt *et al.* 1994: 134; Kozminski 1993). It has also been pointed out that personal relationships are important in, for example, Russia and that masculine values like success, advancement and efficiency have not been primary goals among Russians (Smith 1990: 184). In line with this, Bollinger (1994: 52) reports that a group of Russian managers scored low on the masculinity scale. Individuality has been reported to be relatively low under communist rule because the key economic orientation was collectivism, which emphasized group solidarity and social equality (Kozminski 1993; Bollinger 1994: 51; Garrison and Artemyev 1994).

A transformation is taking place in these societies: the picture is changing. For example, Veiga *et al.* (1995) have reported that in Russia individualism is increasing and power distance decreasing. Similarly, other recent studies indicate that significant changes have already appeared, for example, in managerial behaviour and practices, although there is still a need for extensive transformation (Filatotchev *et al.* 1996: 99; Nurmi and Üksvärav 1993: 180; Veiga *et al.* 1995: 22). However, in Hofstede's phrase, cultures are, 'sticky': a more extensive cultural change will always take time.

Data collection

The sample of Finnish expatriates in Western Europe included 33 expatriates that had experience in the following European countries: France (12), Great Britain (8), Germany (7), Sweden (6). The expatriates represented three different companies all operating in the metal industry. It was seen as relevant that all companies operate in the same sector when this kind of relatively small sample was used. This, of course, should also be seen as a limitation when making generalizations. The contact addresses of expatriates were received from personnel managers within the companies and the expatriates were then contacted by telephone in order to arrange an interview. All expatriates were males except one female operating in Germany. The average age of the expatriates was 40.5 years. Most had technical (70 per cent) or business education (18 per cent) and worked in managerial positions (67 per cent). The functions of units in which they worked were production/maintenance (36 per cent), sales/marketing (18 per cent), general management (12 per cent), finance/accounting (12 per cent) or project management (12 per cent). Forty-two per cent of them had previous expatriate experience and the average length of an assignment was 3.1 years.

The data were collected by interviewing or by sending questionnaires to those who could not be interviewed, usually because they were still abroad. During interviews, expatriates were asked to talk freely about adaptation problems for themselves and their families when they started work in a new country and a new foreign organizational unit. When questionnaires were used, the same open question (i.e. 'what kind of problems have you or your family faced during the foreign assignment?') was presented in a written form and an open response phase was indicated. Thus, no prior categorization of problems of adaptation was formed. However, earlier categorizations proposed in the literature were used in the data analysis phase in order to classify the adaptation problems that the expatriates presented. Expatriates were also asked about the preparation and advice they would give to new expatriates based on their own experiences.

Because some preliminary observations on Finnish expatriates in Russia and Estonia are also presented, we also provide some sample characteristics of that study. At the time of writing, the experiences of 32 Finnish expatriates in Russia (15) and Estonia (17) have been gathered. This time all the interviews were carried out on the telephone, but otherwise the research methodology was the same as above. The expatriates' average age was 41 years and the majority of them (except six) were males. All the expatriates worked in managerial positions and 56 per cent of them were on their first international assignment. Most had technical (34 per cent) or business education (41 per cent). On average, their recent assignment had lasted 2 years and 10 months.

Research findings: problems of adaptation

We will use the three-dimensional model of in-country adjustment represented in the introduction to present the data. Thus, we will cover in turn:

- adjustment to interacting with host country nationals;
- adjustment to the general non-work environment;
- adjustment to the work.

In each case we show first the detailed responses from the West European context and then the preliminary observations from the East European.

In general, for Finnish expatriates the 'easiest' country, where there were least adjustment problems, was clearly Sweden. Very few problems were reported by expatriates there. Many of the expatriates came from the Swedish-speaking minority in Finland and thus could use their native language. In Britain the situation seemed to be fairly similar to Scandinavia, because most of the Finnish expatriates reported no problems: only two expatriates had experienced any major problems. In the other two West European countries, Germany and France, almost all the Finnish expatriates in these countries had adaptation problems. It should be emphasized that not all problems were judged to be serious, though in France and Germany some more severe problems were encountered.

The preliminary findings for the Eastern Europe context indicate that more adjustment problems have been faced by Finnish expatriates in that geographical area. The problems seem to arise in similar issues in both countries, although Russia seems to be a more difficult country for Finns than Estonia.

Adjusting to interaction with host country nationals

The expatriates were clear about the main reasons for their problems. The most commonly reported issue concerned problems related to social interaction with locals. These findings give support to the importance of social interaction as an adjustment dimension (Black and Gregersen 1991; Torbiörn 1982; Kauppinen 1994). Most frequently, expatriates reported problems related to inadequate language skills. An inability to speak the local language with proficiency is related to another problem experienced by many expatriates: that of establishing contacts with local people and, thus, getting integrated into the local community. Among these countries, this kind of problem was faced in Germany and France in particular. In Sweden, by contrast, despite the widespread image of a taciturn nation, the Finnish expatriates commented on the Swedes' very open and active communication style, which they said made it fairly easy for an expatriate to create contacts with locals.

In Russia and Estonia similar issues arise. Few Finns speak Russian and even fewer Russians speak Finnish. However, in Estonia the expatriates found they could manage with the Finnish language since many Estonians speak good or at least passable Finnish; thus the adjustment is to some extent easier. Still, several expatriates stressed their view that one should also learn the local language.

Adjusting to the general non-work environment

The second adjustment dimension outlined by Black *et al.* (1991) was 'general non-work environment'. In the present study, expatriates had met difficulties with simple practical arrangements. In France, particularly, some expatriates described the situation as 'a lot of bureaucratic procedures' and found that 'there was a lot of paper work with the system'. Several expatriates found it difficult to find and rent an apartment, open a bank account, get the telephone connected, and so on. These kinds of issues were also identified by Black *et al.* (1991) as influencing the adjustment process. However, they discuss them under a 'logistical help' category, focusing more on the role of the company to help expatriates with these problems. From the point of view of adjustment problems, 'practical arrangements' were seen as a critical problem for the expatriates in our study.

In the East European context these kinds of problems are even more common, perhaps unsurprisingly given the recent upheavals there. There were certainly many complaints about the problems caused by the high level of unnecessarily restrictive bureaucracy, particularly on the part of local authorities. In addition, the more mundane, if still important, problems were widespread. Due to the lower standard of living, the expatriates commonly faced problems in finding suitable accommodation and difficulties with the availability of basic requirements such as warm water, electricity and necessary services. On the other hand, many expatriates commented that the situation has already improved noticeably during their assignment, in Estonia in particular.

Once we start examining the specific non-work adjustment problems that expatriates faced, a key issue was seen by many to revolve around family–spouse adaptation. Several expatriates reported that the situation was significantly more difficult for their families than for themselves. This finding supports the importance of family–spouse adjustment which has been raised frequently by other commentators (Tung 1982; Harvey 1985; Black and Stephens 1989; Handler and Lane 1997). In the model by Black *et al.* (1991), family adjustment was identified as a factor influencing the success of the expatriate assignment. On the basis of the expatriates' reports in our research, this can be confirmed but it would seem that this factor is of major significance and perhaps needs to be assigned a category of its own.

The most commonly reported causes of adaptation problems for families/partners were again inadequate language skills and difficulties in creating contact with the locals. Here too, this kind of problem appeared more frequently for expatriates located in Germany and France than for those located in Britain and Sweden. One expatriate in Germany said the beginning of the assignment was 'a very unpleasant experience' for his wife. Another, in France, pointed out that his wife's communication problems made her very dependent upon him in everyday routines. Furthermore, wives often found it difficult or even impossible to get a job in the host country. In the context of families from a country like Finland where most woman have paid employment, they found it frustrating to be a 'housewife'. Not surprisingly, some expatriates whose children were of school age found their children had similar problems at the start of their schooling, again largely because they had no adequate language skills. However, these expatriates confirm others' experience that in most cases children are very good at adapting to the new situation in which they find themselves. Some of the expatriates also reported difficulties with the healthcare of their children because of different assumptions about such issues as the use of vaccines and medical instructions or dissatisfaction with the quality of the healthcare system.

With regard to the Finnish expatriates in Russia and Estonia, both the picture and the stresses were different. In the majority of cases the expatriates working in these two countries, which are close to Finland, had left their families at home. This created a different set of strains. However, in all cases where families had been taken to the host country non-work adjustment problems had appeared. These were generally the same problems as those which occurred in West Europe, but in addition, in these two countries and particularly in Russia security issues were causing extra stress for expatriates and their families.

Adjusting to the workplace

Adaptation in the workplace was the third major category. With regard to such adjustment problems, the model by Black *et al.* (1991) gives very little help in obtaining a more detailed picture of difficulties which are faced by expatriates. In examining the organization-related factors influencing adjustment, Black *et al.* noted three elements: organization culture novelty, company support and logistical help. Only the first of these describes the areas of adaptation problems in the workplace; the other two describe support practices through which companies can help expatriates with handling their problems. Thus, a further desegregation of adaptation problems related to work adjustment was seen as necessary in the present study. The research data show considerable adjustment problems related to this factor, giving support to the need for clearer disaggregation. We propose the following subcategories.

Leadership styles

In the present study one common experience concerned the difficulties caused by differences in leadership styles. Germans were reported to have a more authoritative decision-making style which did not allow subordinates to participate. The German style was described as 'manager focused', which one might expect on the basis of comparative studies (Hofstede 1984; Myers *et al.* 1995; Suutari 1996a, b). Because of this, expatriates had faced pressures to change to a more authoritative leadership style. In France too almost all Finnish expatriates reported problems concerning the French leadership style. Many expatriates said that it was difficult for them to get used to French authority and the belief that 'a boss is really a boss'; one had to get used to giving direct orders in order to get something finished. One expatriate said that he learned that he should have kept more 'distance' from his subordinates in order to sustain the required respect. All these adjustment problems give support to the high power distance in France (Hofstede 1984; Hoppe 1993; Myers *et al.* 1995; Suutari 1996b). Furthermore, supporting the picture of high masculinity in the French culture, one expatriate said, 'the French culture is tougher than the Finnish one' and thus stressed the need for a 'tougher' leadership style in France than in Finland.

Only a few of the expatriates in Britain and Sweden reported adaptation problems related to leadership styles. One expatriate in Britain stated that the British style was more 'direct order–direct control' than would be expected from a Finnish leader. Another said that in the UK the manager has to exercise control all the time to ensure that subordinates do what has been agreed. This kind of adjustment problem fits with the power distance differences between UK and Finland (Hofstede 1984). Sweden was perhaps a case of the opposite: one expatriate stated that he found it difficult to adapt to the culture because the Swedish decision-making style required significantly more participation of subordinates. Another stated that he had to change his way of behaving to a 'softer' style and had to increase the amount of team working. Thus, the low power distance and femininity of Swedish culture reported elsewhere reflects the experience of these expatriates (Hofstede 1984; Myers *et al.* 1995; Suutari 1996b).

In Eastern Europe, expatriates very commonly reported problems caused by differences in leadership styles. These were faced in two areas in particular. First, there was a frequent comment that one had to be extremely authoritative and give direct orders. Second, one had to supervise the work of employees continuously in order to ensure that the work was carried out adequately. A lack of self-initiative was found to be typical among local employees and work morale was reported to be low. These findings are in line with the writings on CEE organizations presented in the literature.

Organizational systems

Adaptation problems were commonly faced by expatriates with regard to differences in organizational systems across European countries. The most common issue reported by almost all Finnish expatriates in Germany was the high level of formality in German organizations. This finding is in line with other research regarding the characteristics of German organizations (Laurent 1985; Stewart *et al.* 1994: 193; Myers *et al.* 1995; Suutari 1996a, 1996b). Because of the expectation of high formality, it was reported by expatriates that 'everything' had to be put into written form, that strict norms had to be followed in organizations, and that the prescribed organizational hierarchy had to be strictly followed in decision-making. Co-operation between departments was found to be very formal. Additionally, the central role of German unions was reported as a problem by one expatriate. With regard to France, it was reported by some that one special characteristic of French organization was the clear hierarchy and 'bureaucracy' which was difficult to adjust to. One expatriate said, 'French organizations have a heavy structure'. These adjustment problems are exactly those that the literature indicated that Finns might expect to face in typical French organizations (Hofstede 1984; Laurent 1985; Suutari 1996b).

Some adaptation problems related to organizational systems were caused by differences in human resource management systems between countries. In particular, the characteristics required of managers had caused difficulties. In the case of one young expatriate in France, his age caused problems because older French subordinates did not approve of him as their manager. The result was that they did not follow his orders, afterwards arguing that they must have understood wrongly or, if they do as requested, everything happened very slowly. Similar comments regarding the respect for age in French organizations have been pointed out by Trompenaars (1993). The low speed of career advancement in France was supported by another Finnish expatriate who stated that, combined with a low level of job rotation, this caused employees' experience to be very limited. In the case of one expatriate manager in Germany, the fact that she was female caused problems. She felt that within the company in Germany 'a woman is like a second-class citizen' and that male colleagues were 'chauvinistic'. She believes that it was easier to convince the customers than colleagues inside the department. This finding supports the view of the masculinity of German culture (Hofstede 1984).

In Russia and Estonia, expatriates reported a very high level of formalization and bureaucracy. Expatriates stated, for example, that 'local employees require clearly defined tasks and rules'. Similar comments have been presented in the literature (Bollinger 1994; Garrison and Artemyev 1994). The expatriates felt that the interpretation of tasks was very different from the approach in the West.

For example, the tasks of the management group and the board were unclear to locals. The basic problem with human resources was reported to be a low work morale among local employees.

Communications

A third specific group of adaptation problems relating to adjustment to the work concerned communication. This was not just a language issue: other difficulties were found which related to the style and extent of communication. Some expatriates who had worked in Germany explained that they had difficulties creating an open atmosphere or getting clear answers to questions. This finding is similar to those reported, for example in comparative leadership studies by Suutari (1996a, b). The opposite appeared to be the case in Sweden where one expatriate complained that he had 'to discuss everything, all the time', while another argued that such openness made it easy to adapt to the local organization. Active communication in Sweden has been reported elsewhere (Lawrence and Spibey 1986; Brewster *et al.* 1993; Myers *et al.* 1995; Suutari 1996b). One expatriate who had worked in France said that he had had to learn to communicate more 'diplomatically' than he was used to. Another in Germany had learned that he should not call any of his subordinates by their first name because others took it as a form of 'favouritism'. Thus, high formality in Germany was also related to the communication style.

Problems related to communication were also faced in Russia and Estonia. Expatriates reported that local communication styles are not as open as in Finland. Hence it was not easy for expatriates to get the information they needed or to create critical discussion on existing problems. Similar comments have been presented elsewhere (Ivancevich *et al.* 1992; Kozminski 1993; Nurmi and Üksvärav 1993).

The job environment

A further specific area of work adjustment in which several expatriates had difficulties concerned adaptation to the job environment. Expatriates in every country frequently feel that the host location is inferior to the usually much bigger headquarters operation with which they are familiar. There was also evidence of a mild form of 'paranoia' – attributing negative motives to actions that they did not understand. Black *et al.* (1991) discussed four job-related factors that influence work adjustment: role clarity, role novelty, role conflict and role discretion. Several relevant comments related to these factors appeared in the present study. First, expatriates' reports about unclear work assignments in the subsidiary operation showed evidence of uncertainty about their role. Second, some expatriates reported a lack of professional experience in the way their job developed in the host country, thus giving support to role novelty as a useful factor in the understanding of adjustment problems. As an indication of the relevance of role conflict, it was reported more than once that the expatriate's own job was made more difficult because local supervisors and colleagues were inadequately informed about the expatriate. There was a feeling that local colleagues were suspicious of the expatriate's role in the organization and felt that they were being reported on to headquarters, Whether these feelings reflect reality is impossible to tell from our data, but the expatriates believed that these were significant issues. In general, the expatriates also reported that they had more scope to do their jobs in most host countries than they did at home: role discretion.

Some difficulties faced by expatriates were related to specific situations and organizations that might have occurred in Finland and were not 'expatriate' problems. Such issues included the negative attitude of an earlier owner, who worked as a director of the company but resigned after a couple of months; uncertainty among employees because of an extensive change process; the need to change a management team; and problems with the overall performance of a local unit.

Implications for expatriates

Expatriates in Western Europe were asked to advise new expatriates, based on their own experiences. The most frequently mentioned issues are noted in Table 10.1.

As can be seen from Table 10.1, the most commonly given advice related to getting integrated into the local community from the beginning. Many expatriates said that one should 'try as soon as possible to live like they do', 'experiment with local ways of living', 'change oneself, because one cannot change the local way of thinking' and 'behave according to local customs or go away'. Some of them also suggested that expatriates should avoid socializing only with other Finnish expatriates (the 'expatriate ghetto syndrome'). Such people tend to discuss only what they miss about Finland or wonder at the strange habits of local people.

Table 10.1 Expatriates' advice to new expatriates

	No. of comments
Try to integrate yourself in the local community as soon as possible	17
Ensure that your family is motivated and prepared for the time of the assignment	15
Obtain knowledge of the country and its culture and history before you go	14
Be positive and open-minded, not critical or suspicious	12
Learn the local language if possible beforehand	10
Clarify details of your job description so that you know what is expected of you	6
Clarify the details of your contract (issues like car and telephone benefit, education costs of children)	6
Visit the place beforehand	5
Discuss the situation with expatriates who have worked in the country	5
Make sure you have good professional skills for your new job	4

There is a real danger of assuming that home ways are the best: one expatriate said, 'I have seen many Finns stumble because of this'. According to another expatriate, one should be prepared to discover that people of larger countries are very patriotic and may not easily accept that they could learn something from Finnish people and organizations.

Our research replicates previous findings (Brewster 1991; Scullion 1991; Tung 1982) that the family is a source of potential difficulty for expatriates; hence the importance given to emphasizing that the family has to be motivated to move abroad. The expatriates pointed out that family relations should 'be in good order', because the expatriate assignment will cause extra stress on the marriage. Going abroad as a way of 'renewing' a family situation is almost bound to fail. Expatriates advised taking good care of the family and making sure that they learn the language so that they too can get into the local community. Two expatriates stated that the role of the family becomes much more central while abroad, linked to the problems of creating contacts with local people.

The third piece of advice noted in Table 10.1 is to prepare: get good knowledge of the country and its culture before departure. Expatriates who gave such advice emphasized the importance of receiving cultural training or at least reading about the culture. This kind of prior knowledge makes it much easier to understand the differences which will be met. The expatriates argued that it is much easier to influence issues when one knows and understands the local ways of thinking and acting. One of them stated that because technical issues are easier to deal with than cultural issues, the latter should take priority in preparation. Language training was given high priority. In general the expatriates believed that Finnish companies too often sent employees and their families abroad without any training at all. Most have survived, as one put it, only with the help of Finnish perseverance. New expatriates were also advised to talk to more experienced expatriates; to visit the country beforehand, over a longer period than just couple of days, in order to get a realistic view of what to expect.

Many expatriates also emphasized the importance of attitudes. They believed that expatriates should try to be positive and open-minded and not allow small problems in the beginning to depress them. Nor should they have too high expectations: it was necessary to be prepared for difficulties in the beginning.

In this respect our data replicates previous work. The 'universalist' assumptions of many employers help to account for the low levels of preparation for expatriate assignment typically found in the research. Studies in the 1970s found that among US MNEs only two-thirds provided any training at all (Baker and Ivancevich 1971). Less than 25 per cent provided any formal orientation training (Baker and Ivancevich 1971; Lanier 1979; Baliga and Baker 1985), though this may be improving (NFTC 1995). Other research shows around 40 per cent of American firms providing cultural orientation and two-thirds providing language training (Tung 1982: 66). European MNEs tend to do more (Tung 1982, Torbiörn 1983; Baliga and Baker 1985; Brewster 1991). It is clear that expatriates are significantly more enthusiastic about training programmes than their employers (Domsch and Lichtenberger 1991; Brewster and Pickard 1994).

For our sample of Finnish expatriates in Western Europe, the only prior training commonly received, mentioned by 12 expatriates, was in languages. In most cases this included only a two-week intensive training period which provided little more than the basics. The need for language training is clearly related to the host country: most expatriates that were going to France had participated in some kind of language training, but none of the expatriates going to Sweden had done so. Any other kind of preparation was scarce. Four expatriates had received some professional or technical training and four had visited the host organization beforehand. Two expatriates had participated in a two-day course on French business culture, but one did not find it very useful because it focused on the financial issues involved in starting a business in France. Three expatriates had received an internal training document which provided some basics about the French environment and business. Six of them had organized their own preparation, reading literature about the culture and history of their host country. Two had discussed the country with earlier expatriates who had worked there.

The picture was similar in Eastern Europe, although prior language training and a visit to the foreign unit were to some extent more common (almost half of the group had such preparation).

Other issues received less than seven mentions. Clarifying the job description was important so that expatriate, host organization and headquarters know what to expect of this foreign assignment. In the case of the employment contract, expatriates mentioned that one should, in addition to basic salary, negotiate issues like telephone and car benefits, substitution of wife's salary if she is not able to get a job, and the education costs of children. Thus, salary should take into account the cost of living which may be higher. The last advice on the list was to make sure that one has good professional skills for the new job because these make it easier to prove that one is needed in the organization. Other points mentioned, but not frequently enough to get on this list, included: collecting information about the company; being prepared to communicate more than one has been used to in Finland; being prepared to work longer days; thinking seriously about whether it is a good idea to leave at all, and being prepared to come back if it does not work out.

With regard to the adjustment of Finnish expatriates in Russia and Estonia, quite similar views seem to emerge. However, in the preliminary analysis of the data some clear differences also appeared. First, expatriates in Eastern Europe stressed the importance of being patient and having a high level of tolerance. It was suggested, for example, that new expatriates should 'try to be patient because everything takes so much time'. The expectations of Western companies were felt to be too optimistic and this had caused extra pressures for expatriates. Second, the importance of security issues appeared again. Expatriates commented, for example, that 'one should take care of the security issues as much as possible'. A third distinctive piece of advice for new expatriates suggested that Western expatriates should not behave as if they were the only ones who knew how things should be carried out. It was stated, for example, that 'many Western businessman do not honour local manners at all and insult local people' and that 'one should sell his ideas to local people – otherwise they will not adopt them effectively'.

Implications for international organizations

For international organizations, this study provides some useful guidance to enable them to ensure that their expatriates become adjusted in the most effective way. Pre-departure cultural training is comparatively inexpensive and is clearly seen as a requirement by experienced expatriates. So is language training, where appropriate, although this should start before departure and continue once in the host country. Our Finnish expatriates had not expected to face such clear differences between Finland and these nearby, relatively well-developed countries. They did not expect their adjustment to countries in the Western European context to be so problematic. With regard to Eastern Europe, the common experience was that the expatriates anticipated differences across countries, but in reality these were even more prominent than expected. With good prior preparation, such expectations could be made more realistic, which would make it somewhat easier for expatriates to adjust themselves from the beginning. There are also some important messages here about ensuring that both the expatriate and the host organization are clear about the role and tasks of the expatriate and the skills and knowledge that are being brought to the new assignment.

Implications for theory

This study has examined expatriate managers from Finland who are operating in other European countries. Focusing on transfers between developed countries is unusual (although see Brewster 1993 for another example) and raises questions about the applicability of the findings elsewhere. The evidence here shows that assumptions made by many MNEs about the ease of adaptation within continents may have to be re-examined. In this respect, the cultural differences literature is useful in identifying the contrasts that exist within a continent such as Europe. A more careful integration of the cultural differences literature and the expatriate adaptation literature is still needed.

This research has reinforced the importance of disaggregating the adaptation process (Black *et al.* 1991), but found that the categories used in previous research conflated important areas of adaptation that need to be separated out, thus risking the loss of important elements of the expatriate experience. In a continent such as Europe, at least, the categories of general cultural adjustment, inter-cultural adjustment, work and job adjustment and emotional adjustment are not discrete. There is a theoretical and practical overlap between emotional adjustment and the other categories and, certainly for the developed countries, the other areas identified by Black and his colleagues overlap too much. The value of the categorization in steering our understanding is manifest in the use we have made of the model here; but we have had to adapt the model and further research may reveal a need for further adaptation. We still need further research on the adaptation process, particularly between developed countries. At an early stage this research should focus on establishing and exploring more fully the antecedents of adaptation and developing clear and discrete categories for disaggregating the adaptation process.

References

Adler, N. (1972) 'Culture shock and the cross-cultural learning experience', in L.F. Luce and E.C. Smith (eds) *Towards Internationalisation*, Cambridge MA: Newbury House.

Baker, J. and Ivancevich, J. (1971) 'The assignment of American executives abroad: systematic, haphazard or chaotic?', *California Management Review* 13(3): 39–44.

Baliga, C. and Baker, J. (1985) 'Multinational corporate policies for expatriate managers', *Advanced Management Journal* 50(4): 31–8.

Bardo, J. W. and Bardo, D. J. (1980) 'Dimensions of adjustment for American settlers in Melbourne, Australia', *Multivariate Experimental Clinical Research* 5(1): 23–8.

Bird, A. and Dunbar, R. (1991) 'The adaptation and adjustment process of managers on international assignments', Stern Working Paper, New York University.

Black, J.S. (1988) 'Work role transitions: a study of American expatriate managers in Japan', *Journal of International Business Studies* 30(2): 119–34.

Black, J.S. and Gregersen, H.B. (1991) 'The other half of the picture: antecedents of spouse cross-cultural adjustment', *Journal of International Business Studies* 22(3): 461–77.

Black, J.S. and Stephens, G.K. (1989) 'The influence of the spouse on American expatriate adjustment in overseas assignments', *Journal of Management* 15(4): 529–44.

Black, J.S. and Mendenhall, M. (1990) 'Cross-cultural training effectiveness: a review and a theoretical framework for future research', *Academy of Management Review* 15(1): 113–36.

Black, J.S., Mendenhall, M. and Oddou, G. (1991) 'Toward a comprehensive model of international adjustment: an integration of multiple theoretical perspectives', *Academy of Management Review* 16(2): 291–317.

Bollinger, D. (1994) 'The four cornerstones and three pillars in the "House of Russia" management system', *Journal of Management Development* 13(2): 49–54.

Brett, J.M., Stroh, L.K. and Reilly, A.H. (1992) 'Job transfer' in C.L. Cooper and I.T. Robinson (eds) *International Review of Industrial and Organisational Psychology*, Chichester: Wiley.

Brewster, C. (1991) *The Management of Expatriates*, London: Kogan Page.

—— (1993) 'The paradox of adjustment: UK and Swedish expatriates in the UK and Sweden', *Human Resource Management Journal* 4(1): 49–62.

Brewster, C. and Pickard, J. (1994) 'Evaluating expatriate training', *International Studies of Management and Organisation* 24(3): 18–35.

Brewster, C., Lundmark, A. and Holden, L. (1993) *A Different Tack: An Analysis of British and Swedish Management Styles*, Lund: Studentlitteratur.

Church, A.T. (1982) 'Sojourner adjustment', *Psychological Bulletin* 91(3): 540–72.

Cooper, C. (1988) 'Executive stress around the world', *Multinational Employer* 5(9): 5–10.

Domsch, M. and Lichtenberger, B. (1991) 'Managing the global manager: pre-departure training and development for German expatriates in China and Brazil', *Journal of Management Development* 10(7): 41–52.

Edstrom, A. and Margolis, R. (1986) 'Swedish and American management styles: a cultural comparison', paper presented at the conference on Strategies and Leadership for Success, Princeton.

Filatotchev, I., Hoskinsson, R.E., Buck, T. and Wright, M. (1996) 'Corporate restructuring in Russian privatizations: implications for U.S. investors', *California Management Review* 38(2): 87–105.

Franko, L.G. (1971) *Joint Ventures Survival in Multinational Corporations*, New York: Praeger.

Garrison, T. and Artemyev, A. (1994) 'Managing people in Russia', in T. Garrison and D. Rees (eds) *Managing People across Europe*, Oxford: Butterworth-Heinemann.

Gonzales, R.F. and Neghandi, A.R. (1967) *The United States Executive: His Orientation and Career Patterns*, East Lansing: MSU Graduate School of Business Administration.

Gullahorn, J.T. and Gullahorn, J.E. (1963) 'An extension of the U-curve hypothesis', *Journal of Social Issues* 19(3): 33–47.

Handler, C.A. and Lane, I.M. (1997) 'Career planning and expatriate couples', *Human Resource Management Journal*, 7(3): 67–79.

Harris, J.C. (1973) 'A science of the South Pacific: analysis of the character structure of the Peace Corps volunteer', *American Psychologist* 28: 232–47.

Harris, H. and Brewster, C. (1995) 'Preparation for expatriation: evidence about current needs', paper presented at the 2nd European Workshop in International Staffing and Expatriate Management, Braga, Portugal, June.

Harvey, M.G. (1985) 'The executive family: an overlooked variable in international assignments', *Columbia Journal of World Business*, spring: 131–44.

Harzing, A.W. (1995) 'The persistent myth of expatriate failure rates', *International Journal of Human Resource Management* 6(2): 457–74.

Hautaluoma, J.E. and Kaman, V. (1975) 'Description of Peace Corps volunteers' experience in Afghanistan', *Topics in Culture Learning* 3: 79–96.

Hawes, F. and Kealey, D. (1981) 'An empirical study of Canadian technical assistance: adaptation and effectiveness on overseas assignment', *International Journal of Intercultural Relations* 5(3): 239–58.

Hays, R.D. (1971) 'Ascribed behavioural determinants of success–failure among US expatriate managers', *Journal of International Business Studies* 2(1): 40–46.

—— (1974) 'Expatriate selection: insuring success and avoiding failure', *Journal of International Business Studies* 5(1): 25–37.

Heenan, D.A. and Perlmutter H. (1979) *Multinational Organisation Development*, Reading MA: Addison-Wesley.

Hofstede, G. (1984) *Culture's Consequences: International Differences in Work-related Values*, Beverly Hills CA: Sage.

Holmqvist, H. (1989) 'Leadership and management style: an American–Swedish comparison', paper presented to the Ninth EFMD Corporate Members' Meeting: 'Managing Culture Clash. Conflict or Collaboration: The Business Imperative', March, EIA, Marseilles.

Holt, D.H., Ralston, D.A. and Terspstra, R.H. (1994) 'Constraints on capitalism in Russia: the managerial psyche, social infrastructure, and ideology', *California Management Review* 36(3): 124–41.

Hoppe, M.H. (1993) 'The effects of national culture on the theory and practice of managing R&D professionals abroad', *R&D Management* 23(4): 313–25.

Howard, C.G. (1974) 'The returning overseas executive: cultural shock in reverse', *Human Resource Management* 13(2): 49–62.

Ivancevich, J.M. (1969) 'Selection of American managers for overseas assignments', *Personnel Journal* 18(3): 189–200.

Ivancevich, J.M., DeFrank, R.S. and Gregory, P.R. (1992) 'The Soviet enterprise director: an important resource before and after the coup', *Academy of Management Executive* 6(1): 42–55.

Janssens, M. (1992) 'International job transfers: a comprehensive model of expatriate managers' cross-cultural adjustment', paper presented at the EIASM Conference on Industral Staffing and Mobility, Cranfield, September.

Kauppinen, M. (1994) 'Antecedents of expatriate adjustment: a study of Finnish managers in the United States', dissertation B-140, Helsinki School of Economics and Business Administration, Helsinki.

Kozminski, A.K. (1993) *Catching up? Organisational and Management Change in the Ex-Socialist Block*, New York: State University of New York Press.

Lanier, A. R. (1979) 'Selecting and preparing personnel for overseas transfers', *Personnel Journal* 58(3): 106–63.

Laurent, A. (1986) 'The cultural diversity of Western conceptions of management', in P. Joynt and M. Warner (eds) *Managing in Different Cultures*, Oslo: University Press.

Lawrence, P. and Spibey, T. (1986) *Management and Society in Sweden*, London: Routledge.

Martínez, J.I. and Jarillo, J.C. (1991) 'The evolution of research on coordination mechanisms in multinational corporations', *Journal of International Business Studies* 20(3): 489–514.

Mayrhofer, W. and Brewster, C. (1996) 'In praise of ethnocentricity: expatriate policies in European multinationals', *International Executive* 38(6): 33–47.

Mendenhall, M. and Oddou, G. (1985) 'The dimensions of expatriate acculturation: a review', *Academy of Management Review* 10(1): 39–487.

Miller, E.L. (1973) 'The international selection decision: a study of some dimensions of managerial behaviour in the selection decision process', *Academy of Management Journal* 16(2): 239–52.

Myers, A., Kakabadse, A., McMahon, T. and Spony, G. (1995) 'Top management styles in Europe', *European Business Journal* 7(1): 17–27.

Nicholson, N. (1984) 'A theory of work role transitions', *Administrative Science Quarterly* 29: 172–92.

Nicholson, N. and West, M.A. (1988) *Managerial Job Change: Men and Women in Transition*, Cambridge: Cambridge University Press.

Nurmi, R. and Üksvärav, R. (1993) 'How Estonian managers experienced the transformation to independence and market economy in 1990–1991', *Management International Review* 33: 171–81.

Oberg, K. (1960) 'Culture shock: adjustment to new cultural environments', Practical Anthropologist 7: 177–82.

Puffer, S.M. (1994) 'Understanding the bear: a portrait of Russian business leaders', *Academy of Management Executive* 8: 41–54.

Scullion, H. (1991) 'Why companies prefer to use expatriates', *Personnel Management*, November: 32–5.

—— (1992) 'Strategic recruitment and development of the "International Manager": some European considerations', *Human Resource Management Journal* 3(1): 57–69.

Smith, H. (1990) *The New Russians*, New York: Random House.

Stewart, R., Barsoux, J., Kieser, A., Ganter, H. and Walgenbach, P. (1994) *Managing in Britain and Germany*, New York: St. Martin's Press.

Suutari, V. (1996a) 'Leadership ideologies among European managers: a comparative survey in a multinational company', *Scandinavian Journal of Management* 12(4): 389–409.

—— (1996b) 'Variation in the leadership behaviour of Western European managers:

Finnish expatriates' experiences', *International Journal of Human Resource Management* 7(3): 677–707.

—— (1998) 'Leadership behaviour in Eastern Europe: Finnish expatriates' experiences in Russia and Estonia', *International Journal of Human Resource Management* (forthcoming).

Torbiörn, I. (1982) *Living Abroad: Personal Adjustment and Personnel Policy in the Overseas Setting*, New York: Wiley.

Trompenaars, F. (1993) *Riding the Waves of Culture*, London: The Economist Books.

Tung, R.L. (1981) 'Selection and training of personnel for overseas assignments', *Columbia Journal of World Business* 16(1): 68–78.

—— (1982) 'Selection and training procedures of US, European, and Japanese Multinationals', *California Management Review* 25: 57–71.

Veiga, J.N., Yanouzas, J.N. and Buchholz, A.K. (1995) 'Emerging cultural values in Russia: what will tomorrow bring?', *Business Horizons*, July–August: 20–27.

Welch, D. (1994) 'HRM implications of globalization', *Journal of General Management* 19(4): 52–68.

Zeira, Y. and Banai, M. (1984) 'Selection of expatriate managers in MNEs: the host-environment point of view', *International Studies of Management and Organisation* 15(1): 33–51.

—— (1985) 'Present and desired methods of selecting expatriate managers for international assignments', *Personnel Review* 13(3): 29–35.

11 Irish expatriates in Moscow

Exploratory evidence on aspects of adjustment[1]

Michael Morley, Christopher Burke and Geraldine Finn

Introduction

Recent years have shown a marked increase in the internationalization of business in areas such as international strategic alliances, foreign subsidiaries and overseas representative offices (Katz and Seifer 1996–7; Harvey 1996; Hiltrop and Janssens 1990). Arguably, according to Hippler (1996), the question nowadays from many companies is no longer whether or not to internationalize, but how to do so. For those already abroad, the critical issue is how to sustain their foreign operations. This is particularly true in Europe. The dismantling of trade barriers between the EU countries and the development of a free market system in Central and Eastern Europe have resulted in increased intra-regional trade and investment between EU countries and from non-EU countries (Hippler 1996; Brewster and Scullion 1997). The collapse of communism has attracted massive international investment to the area. Russia alone had attracted $4.5 billion in foreign capital by the middle of 1995, while up to 22,940 joint ventures operations had been registered in Poland by the end of 1995 (EIU 1995; Knight and Webb 1997; Montezemolo 1996). Investors are attracted by a huge, skilled and relatively inexpensive labour pool and geographic proximity to most countries in Western Europe (Dillon and Higgins 1994). Investment is likely to increase as the infrastructure of a market economy is put in place and the political and economic situation continue to improve. This growth in overseas business in Central and Eastern Europe has put increasing pressure on MNEs to develop a pool of dynamic, well-trained individuals who have the necessary technical and functional skills as well as the ability to manage effectively and succeed in a post-communist scenario. In this context, research demonstrates that there is a lower rate of expatriation among establishing companies, with most aiming to have as high a host country national presence as possible (Borg and Harzing 1995; Hippler 1996). According to Edkins (1995) the rationale for this may well be that 'an assignment to Central or Eastern Europe is likely to be more challenging than most . . . even one who has travelled to Central or Eastern European countries many times is likely to find living in the region a culture shock'. However, it is also worth noting that Irish and UK MNEs 'tend to rely more heavily on expatriates to run their foreign operations' (Scullion 1994).

Using a sample of Irish nationals (n = 30) working in Irish firms operating in Moscow, the aim of this chapter is to explore a number of factors which are thought to influence expatriate adjustment. The available literature on the expatriation process is reviewed. The theoretical base that underlies the factors which are thought to influence or inhibit expatriate adjustment are outlined. Job factors such as role discretion, role novelty, role conflict, role overload and role ambiguity are analysed, as are organizational variables such as pre-departure training, level of company support, organizational cultural novelty and subsidiary structure. Non-work variables relating to cultural novelty and family situation are also examined.

Expatriate failure and recall

Culture shock, differences in work-related norms, isolation, homesickness, differences in healthcare, housing, schooling, cuisine, language, customs, gender roles and the cost of living are just some of the elements that have contributed to making expatriate failure one of the most significant problems facing today's multinationals (Mendenhall *et al.* 1987). Other major issues identified in the expatriate literature include: inadequate selection criteria (Scullion 1991; Tung 1981; Harvey 1996); poor pre-departure training (Mendenhall and Oddou 1985; Scullion 1991; Philips 1993; Brewster and Pickard 1994; Brewster and Scullion 1997); poorly designed compensation packages (Toyne and Kuhne 1983; Hamill 1989). However, the most commonly identified cause of expatriate failure has been 'the expatriate's and/or his/her partner and family's inability to adjust to the new culture' (Torbiörn 1982; Hamill 1989; McEnery and Des Harnais 1990; Black *et al.* 1991; Scullion 1991; Harvey 1997).

Traditionally, expatriate failure has been defined as 'the number of staff who return home before the agreed end of the international assignment because of poor work performance and/or personal problems' (see Forster 1997). Although Tu and Sullivan (1994) argue that a definition of this nature hides low achievers, who for different reasons might not choose to terminate their assignment prematurely. It would appear that turnover rates, at least for US firms, commonly fall in the 20 per cent to 50 per cent range for expatriate transfers (Copeland and Griggs 1985; Black 1988; Hogan 1990; Harvey 1996). However, Tung (1982) notes that recall rates among US MNEs are two to three times above those of European MNEs. In her study, only 3 per cent of European MNEs had recall rates greater than 10 per cent of the expatriate transfers. The idea that European MNEs have lower recall rates than MNEs of other nationalities is reinforced by the findings of Brewster (1988), Hamill (1989) and Scullion (1991), who each found that the majority of European MNEs had failure rates of less than 5 per cent. A number of reasons have been advanced which might account for the difference between US and European MNEs. European firms seem to have developed more effective international human resource management policies (Hamill 1989; Scullion 1991) especially in relation to the provision of pre-departure training programmes (Brewster 1991, 1993; Brewster and Pickard

1994). Hamill (1989) and Scullion (1991) also suggest that European MNEs are more prepared to accept lower standards of performance than US firms before instigating action to recall their overseas employees.

The cost of failure and recall

Most international human resource managers agree that it is expensive to send expatriates abroad. Brewster (1988) estimates that it costs the company three times as much as it would to keep them at home. In general, expatriate managers receive their base salary, which is supplemented with relocation allowances, cost of living differential, travel expenses and education costs (Hiltrop and Janssens 1990; Harvey 1996). Dowling and Schuler (1990) argue that direct costs may be as high as three times the domestic salary plus the relocation expenses, while Ronen (1989) estimates the expenses incurred by an expatriate during the first year to be four times that person's yearly salary. If the expatriate fails, the cost increases substantially when one takes the implicit costs into account such as the potential loss of foreign suppliers, creditors and customers, and damaged company reputation. The expatriate may also suffer negative psychological consequences such as loss of self-esteem, low self-esteem among peers and a career set-back (Coyle and Shortland 1992; Punnett and Ricks 1992; Harvey 1996). Tung (1981: 68) notes that 'many of those who failed had good track records in the home office prior to assignment overseas'. In addition to these costs, the company will likely have to replace the failed expatriate which is often done, according to Hippler (1996: 7), 'in a rather ad hoc manner'. The replacement expatriate is often not subject to a well-structured selection process, may lack sufficient pre-departure preparation and, accordingly runs a higher that average risk of repeated failure (Hippler 1996).

The adjustment process

Adjustment has variously been described as 'the re-establishment of routines that provide valued outcomes and feelings of control that are predictable' (Brett 1980); or the 'process by which the individual (with his unique set of abilities and needs) acts, reacts and comes to terms with his environment (Dawis *et al.* 1964). Thus, adjustment can be said to occur when the individual adopts new behaviours which produce similar results to those used prior to the transfer. The degree to which the individual adjusts is influenced by two issues: the individuals' desire to maintain their own cultural identity and the extent to which they want to integrate with host nationals.

Berry *et al.* (1988) have outlined four different approaches to adjustment. *Assimilation* takes place when individuals wish to integrate with host nationals and have no desire to maintain their own culture. *Integration* occurs when individuals continues to have an interest in their own culture while also interacting with host nationals. Other individuals adopt a *separatist* mode of acculturation when they want to keep their cultural identity without any desire to integrate with host country nationals. *Marginalization* arises when there is no desire to identify with one's own culture or to mix with host nationals. Marginalization and separation do not lead to successful expatriate adjustment (DeCieri *et al.*,1991.)

The most common approach to successful expatriate adjustment is integration. Brett (1980) observes that in an attempt to integrate, expatriates may try a variety of approaches before establishing a new set of behavioural norms that will enable them to adapt to the new environment. Aptly labelled as 'sense-making' by Louis (1980), the objective is to allow individuals to develop a 'map' of their new environment.

Variables that influence expatriate adjustment

A review of the extant literature suggests that there are four main groups of variables which seem to affect the acculturation process: individual, job, organizational and non-work variables.

Individual characteristics

Many researchers claim that an individual who is chosen to work on an overseas assignment should possess certain personal characteristics: flexibility, a desire to adjust, tolerance of ambiguity, leadership qualities, interpersonal skills and self-confidence, cultural empathy, emotional stability (Hiltrop and Janssens 1990; Coyle and Shortland 1992; Brewster 1993; Collins 1995). An individual's desire to learn the host country language may also influence the adjustment process. Language ability allows the individual to communicate with host nationals and enables them to identify the subtle differences between cultures, thus making it easier for them to learn and adopt the necessary behaviours for the new culture (Smalley 1963; Tung 1987; McEnery and Des Harnais 1990; Dietrich 1995; Giershe 1995). Tung claims that:

> While knowledge of a host society's language will not always guarantee effective interaction and communication with local nationals, it does promote greater understanding of the subtleties and innuendoes of the culture and norms of the target country.
>
> (Tung 1995: 122)

Brein and David (1971) observe that expatriates who learn the language of their host country acquire what they term 'conversational currency', which allowes them to relate more easily to host country nationals. They are viewed less as foreigners by those around them and are more easily accepted into the business world as a result. Black and Mendenhall (1991) have argued that the increased interaction with host nationals leads to better adjustment. Host country nationals can be a source of information and modelled behaviours which the expatriate might copy and therefore develop appropriate behaviours for the host culture. The greater the exposure to host nationals, the easier it will be to learn the necessary behaviours.

Black and Gregerson (1991) claim that individuals who have previously worked overseas can use their previous adjustment experience to adapt more easily to the new environment. Black and Stephens (1989) found a positive relationship between previous international work experience and work adjustment, but not general adjustment. However, Torbiörn (1982) found that the length of time on the overseas assignment may not influence adjustment to the foreign environment.

Job variables

It has been suggested that five specific variables affect expatriate adjustment: role novelty, role clarity, role discretion, role conflict and role overload.

Role novelty

Role novelty reflects the degree of difference between the expatriates' previous position and their new one (Black 1988; Morley *et al.* 1997). If the new position is substantially different, the expatriate may experience greater feelings of uncertainty and unpredictability. These might make it more difficult to know which behaviours are appropriate for the new situation. Several researchers have claimed that culture has a large impact on all facets of the working environment. Large cultural differences between two countries could result in greater role novelty for the expatriate (Hofstede 1980; Trompenaars 1993; Hoecklin 1994). If the country is undergoing dramatic change, the expatriate may have to face new situations on a daily basis. This might make it difficult to establish an effective strategy which might put increasing pressure on the expatriate to perform successfully.

Role ambiguity

Role clarity refers to the extent to which expatriates know what duties they are expected to perform in the overseas assignment. If the role is ambiguous, the expatriates may find it difficult to choose the necessary behaviours, which may cause them to feel ineffective and frustrated (Black 1988). When working in a foreign environment an expatriate is often dependent on the host nationals for information about the new role and the general running of the organization. If the expatriate has not acquired the necessary language ability, this may result in valuable information being lost or taken up incorrectly. This could undermine the expatriates' relationships with the host nationals while also making them less effective in their new role. Feldman and Thomas (1992a) point out that certain cultures are less open to foreigners than others; thus they may not be willing to disclose the necessary information to the new expatriate. Zamet and Bovarnick (1986) found that this was especially true in communist countries.

Role discretion

Role discretion reflects the expatriates' authority to determine the parameters of the new position. Greater role discretion will enable the expatriate to use past actions that proved effective in a previous role. This should make adjustment easier as it reduces uncertainty and increases the expatriates' confidence in their ability to perform in the new environment.

Role conflict and overload

Role conflict takes place when expatriates receive conflicting information about what is expected of them in their new role. Role conflict may arise when the management style of the parent company is different to that of the subsidiary, which may result in feelings of uncertainty and confusion. Role overload also has a negative impact on expatriate adjustment. It occurs when excessive demands are placed upon the expatriate in the new position. Role overload may occur due to the parent company's lack of awareness of what the overseas position actually involves. This might reduce the expatriate's ability to perform the job satisfactorily, thus making adjustment more difficult.

Organizational variables

Empirical research indicates that certain organizational variables have a significant impact on the expatriates' ability to adjust: pre-departure training; company support; subsidiary structure (Macmillian 1991; DeCieri *et al.* 1991; Brewster and Pickard 1994).

Training

Once an expatriate has been chosen for an overseas position, researchers recommend that MNEs provide formal training for the expatriates and their families (Tung 1981; Mendenhall and Oddou 1985; Odenwald 1993; Brewster and Pickard 1994; Harris and Brewster 1996; Brewster 1997). Mendenhall and Oddou (1986) found a positive relationship between training and the expatriates ability to perform effectively in the foreign environment. Pre-departure training provides the individual with information about the new environment such as geography, housing, climate, educational facilities, cultural orientation and language training, if necessary (Tung 1981; Mendenhall and Oddou 1986). Several advantages of pre-departure training have been outlined. It helps to reduce the ill-effects of culture shock. It reduces the time necessary for expatriate adjustment. It results in more realistic expectations. These factors should help to reduce expatriate failure (Black and Mendenhall 1990).

However, despite the existence of a substantial body of literature and support among academic researchers for pre-departure training, research indicates that rather little training actually takes place. The majority of programmes offered lasted for just one day (Hogan 1990). Torbiörn (1982) found that more than 50 per cent of Swedish companies provided pre-departure training, as did approximately 50 per cent of European MNEs (Tung 1982).

MNE and subsidiary support

The greater the difference between the MNE and the host country corporate culture, the more difficult it will be for the expatriate to adjust to the new work environment (Aycan 1997; Morley *et al.* 1997). The greater the similarity between the systems and structures of the subsidiary and the parent company, the greater the likelihood that the expectations of expatriates (which will have been shaped by parent company experiences) will be accurate and met (Naumann 1992). Greater similarity should help to reduce the level of uncertainty, particularly in relation to the work environment. Macmillan (1991) noted that MNEs tend to apply isomorphism to subsidiaries as a control mechanism, whereas Johnson and Scholes (1993) believe that corporate culture is dependent on the national culture. They argue that the greater the cultural difference between the parent and host country, the more divergent the corporate cultures of the two work environments are likely to be. It has been argued that overseas environments are often more dynamic than the domestic market (Naumann 1992). Thus the expatriate may need to operate in a more decentralized flexible structure, while maintaining some similarity to the parent company (Macmillan 1991).

Level of company support

Research indicates that company support has an important impact on the expatriates' ability to adapt to the new environment (Hiltrop and Janssens 1990; Coyle and Shortland 1992; DeCieri *et al.* 1991; Brewster and Scullion 1997). If there is poor communication between the parent company and the overseas company, an information gap may develop which could result in the expatriate feeling isolated and frustrated. If expatriates fail to receive clear instructions about their new role, this often increases uncertainty and impedes their ability to adapt to the new role. Logistical support such as information on housing, education and travel should help to reduce this uncertainty, thus facilitating adjustment.

Non-work characteristics

Family situation

The inability of the spouse and children to adapt to the cultural environment is frequently cited as a common cause of expatriate failure (Harvey 1985; Coyle and Shortland 1992; Moore and Punnett 1994; Collins 1995; Jones 1997). However, Tung (1988) found that less than 40 per cent of the companies in her survey interviewed the spouse. If a spouse or family member is undergoing severe culture shock or experiencing difficulty in making the cross-cultural adjustment, the morale and performance of the expatriate may be adversely affected (Tung 1982; Harvey 1985; Torbiörn 1997). Children are also very resistant to moving due to educational and social disruption. Research has shown that the older and greater the number of children, the greater the likelihood of adjustment problems (Church 1982). It would appear that a positive family situation is likely to enhance the expatriates' cross-cultural adjustment and increase the chances of a successful assignment (Tung 1982; Brewster 1991; Punnett and Ricks 1992; Collins 1995).

Cultural novelty

As with organizational cultural novelty, the degree of cultural difference between the home and host country can have a significant influence on the expatriates' ability to adapt. If the host country culture is very different to the home culture, the expatriate may have to develop a complete set of new behaviours in order to 'make sense' of this new macro environment and to work successfully in the culture. The expatriate may find it difficult to perceive and learn these behaviours, thus increasing the period of time required for expatriate acculturation.

The methodology and sample

In terms of the actual number of Irish people living and working in Moscow, there seems to be some disagreement on the numbers. The *Irish Times* reports that the Irish expatriate population in Moscow expanded from 150 in 1991 to over 400 by June 1993 (*Irish Times*, 4 June, 1993). Laird (1994) maintains that official estimates such as these grossly understate the extent of the Irish presence.

Structured telephone interviews were held with 30 Irish expatriate employees working in Moscow between January and April 1994. This not only allowed for the completion of the questionnaire which forms the basis of this study, but also for the collection of some qualitative data on respondents' experiences. Respondents were selected at random from 13 Irish firms operating businesses in Moscow. As no directory of Irish firms in Moscow yet exists, businesses were simply identified through the national press. Table 11.1 profiles the organizations involved in the study.

Turning to the actual respondents, in contrast to the findings of other studies (Tung 1982; Black 1988; Black and Stephens 1989) where the majority of participants were usually married males, a surprisingly large number of respondents in this study were female (12), and single (24) (see Table 11.2.) Of the small number of respondents that were married, half had been accompanied by their partner/family on the assignment. Respondents ranged in age from 20 to 44 years with a mean age of 27. They worked in a variety of functional areas but were concentrated in the managerial, administrative and technical fields. Women were more likely to be concentrated in the areas of marketing and administration, whereas technical and managerial positions were exclusively

Table 11.1 Profile of Irish companies involved in the study

	Length of operation in Moscow	*Total no. of Russian employees*	*Irish staff*	*Business activity*
Company A	18 months	6	3	Architectural consultancy
Company B	2 years	82	9	Business services
Company C	3 years	20	5	Construction
Company D	14 months	8	4	Engineering services
Company E	18 months	1	1	Retail services
Company F	18 months	44	19	Catering
Company G	2 years	400	36	Retail
Company H	2 years	190	22	Sales
Company J	5 years	1,000	70	Sales
Company K	1 year	3	1	Construction
Company L	5 months	2	2	Contract cleaning
Company M	1 month	1	1	Sales

male domains. On average, respondents had been on assignments in Russia for 19 months. The majority had previous overseas work experience and had worked abroad in at least two different countries.

Individual Variables

Previous overseas experience

A total of 26 participants had previous overseas experience, primarily in the UK, USA and Australia. It is plausible to argue that previous exposure to 'Anglo cultures' (Hofstede 1980) does not assist significantly in the adjustment process. This study did not find evidence of a relationship between previous overseas experience and the ability to adjust to living in Moscow. It is quite likely that the behaviours required to adjust to Russian culture are highly divergent from those required in Anglo cultures. The learning which the individual had undergone may not be readily transferable to a culture as novel as this Slavic one. Indeed, Coll (1996), an Irish expatriate working in Poland, claims that while Poland is 'an agreeable place to work for 2 to 3 years', he finds several differences in the work culture between Ireland and Poland which are not prevalent among the Polish workforce, for example, the concept of initiative. Titles and positions are very important to the Poles, reflecting the different levels of power distance between the two countries. Such differences might affect the Irish expatriates' ability to adjust to the Polish environment. He also points out that the social life in Poland is quite different to Ireland and, on an experiential basis, cites cultural novelty/distance as a critical variable impacting on adjustment/non-adjustment.

Table 11.2 Respondents' profile

Male	18
Female	12
Single	24
Married	6
Age	
20–25	9
26–30	12
31–35	6
35–40	3
Length of assignment	
1–3 months	4
3–6 months	2
6–12 months	3
1 year +	5
Open ended	16
Length of service in Russia	
0–3 months	5
4–6 months	11
6–12 months	9
1–2 years	3
2 years +	2
Profession	
Accounting	1
Managerial	7
Technical	7
Administrative	10
Marketing	4
Other	1

Job factors

Role novelty

The majority of respondents indicated that they experienced a significant amount of novelty in their new position. While some of this novelty may certainly have been contingent upon the cultural environment in which the job was taking place, it is also possible that the high levels of novelty may have been a result of cross-functional moves within the organization. Naumann (1992) has noted that international assignments can result in greater task variety which may be a concept similar to role novelty. Task variety has been shown to have a positive effect on work satisfaction in domestic settings. A similar relationship may exist for international assignments. Feldman and Thomas (1992) have pointed out that one of the reasons employees choose to go on overseas assignments is because of the expanded work opportunities and greater discretion they are likely to experience.

Role ambiguity

Respondents were asked to what extent they agreed or disagreed with a set of statements regarding the clarity of their job. The results are summarized in Table 11.3.

The survey revealed that a significant proportion of respondents suffered from a considerable degree of ambiguity in their jobs. While they appeared to have a clear picture of what the purpose or goal of their job in Russia was, they were less likely to possess sufficient information to enable them to do it properly. Managerial employees were more likely to report higher levels of ambiguity than other categories of employees. This may be as a result of the nature of the work in which managers are involved. Due to the dynamic nature of international markets, expatriates often have less role clarity in their position (Naumann 1992). Zeira and Shenkar (1992) have suggested that higher level employees may be more susceptible to role ambiguity because they lack sufficient information regarding the different expectations of the various and diverse stakeholders in the organization. Technical/engineering work may be independent of the context in which it is carried out and there may be little contact with host nationals or other stakeholders in the organization for technical employees.

A surprisingly large number of respondents from all functional areas indicated that they felt dissatisfied with the quality of information and instructions received. In many cases the subsidiary operation was highly dependent upon the parent firm in Ireland. In the case of retail and construction ventures, all purchasing and design decisions were made in Ireland and work often could not get underway until information relating to these items was received by the Moscow operations. Qualitative comments by respondents indicated that the quality of telecommunications links hindered their ability to obtain the information they needed to adequately perform their job and resulted in considerable time lapses between the two operations. Among others, Parry (1990) and Boylan and Shortall (1992) have commented on Russia's poor telecommunications structure as a major obstacle to business development and expansion in the region.

Table 11.3 Role ambiguity

(N = 30)	1 SD (strongly disagree)	2 D (disagree)	3 NS (not sure)	4 A (agree)	5 SA (strongly agree)
Clear job goals	5	4	11	7	3
Know job responsibilities	2	3	3	15	7
Clear instructions	2	6	7	13	2
Insufficient information	1	7	7	8	7

Role discretion

Respondents were asked whether they had more discretion in their current assignment compared to their previous one. The majority of respondents (21) had considerably more discretion in their present assignments. Managerial employees were more likely to have discretion in their job. While the relationship between role discretion and work effectiveness has proven significant in other studies (e.g. Black 1988), the pattern of responses in this research did not point to any particular relationship. Arguably, working in Russia is significantly different from working in other countries and the knowledge and experience gained from other positions may not be of relevance to the new job in Moscow and may not be of use in helping the individual to adjust.

Role conflict

The balance of company and subsidiary needs, orders and contradictory demands were used to measure the extent to which individuals experienced conflict in their job. The results are summarized in Table 11.4.

The pattern of responses indicates that respondents believe there are considerable levels of conflict in their work situation. Zeira and Shenkar (1992) have suggested that conflict in international assignments may be a result of the need to meet the expectations of different interest groups in the company, including, for example, Irish employees, Russian employees and joint venture partners. For managerial employees, conflict was more likely to arise as a result of the organizational structure rather than particular aspects of their job. Managerial employees were obviously more likely to feel a need to balance both operations because of their positions as a link between the two organizations. Technical employees were more likely to feel conflict as a result of having more than one boss or experiencing contradictory demands.

Role overload

Again a majority of respondents felt that excessive demands were being made upon them at work and they had insufficient time to complete the tasks assigned to them. There were no significant differences among respondents across functional areas. Respondents did not indicate that the nature of the Russian environment contributed to these particular aspects of their job, although Naumann (1992) has suggested that the dynamism of foreign markets may result

Table 11.4 Role conflict

	SD	D	NS	A	SA
Balance company and subsidiary needs	4	7	3	5	7
Orders from more than one person	7	11	2	7	3
Contradictory demands	4	9	2	11	4

Table 11.5 Role overload

(N = 30)	SD	D	NS	A	SA
Excessive demands	2	7	5	12	4
Insufficient time	1	7	7	8	7

in reduced turnaround times on tasks leading to a feeling of insufficient time in order to complete projects. The significant levels of overload felt by respondents may be a result of poor job design. (see Table 11.5.)

Organizational variables

Pre-departure training

It was also hypothesized that pre-departure training would help to facilitate adjustment because it would reduce the uncertainty associated with the transition and would also facilitate the formation of accurate expectations. However, there seems to be a general lack of awareness of the importance of training in cross-cultural encounters on the part of Irish firms. Only two of the respondents indicated that they received formal training prior to their arrival in Moscow.

A number of respondents indicated that they had received what could be termed 'informal training', either in the form of discussions with returning expatriates or in talks with senior executives relating to the assignment. Where such informal training did occur, respondents indicated that they felt that discussions with returning expatriates were the most beneficial in terms of providing information and practical advice on living and working in Moscow.

Although firms were quite poor at providing training prior to their employees' arrival in Moscow, a significant number (24) did provide language training upon arrival. Predictably, those who reported higher levels of language ability also reported higher levels of interaction with host country nationals and a greater degree of comfort with aspects of Russian culture.

Level of company support

It was also hypothesized that the level of company support would be related to both greater cultural and work adjustment as it would remove many of the worries and uncertainty associated with the transfer. While a majority of respondents did receive company support (28), it was generally limited to the provision of free accommodation, domestic travel arrangements (such as the provision of drivers) as well as a generous number of return flights to Ireland each year.

Some respondents indicated dissatisfaction with the standard of accommodation provided, particularly in terms of hygiene. Several expressed dissatisfaction with the fact that the turnaround time between being offered the job and arriving in Moscow was extremely short and did not allow them adequate preparation time. Brewster (1991) has noted that this is a common feature of expatriate assignments. It emerged that Irish companies were least likely to provide support or gave significantly lower levels of support to those employees who had not been transferred from the parent company (i.e. those who had acquired their positions after their arrival in Moscow). Respondents indicated that this was a major source of discontent for those affected.

Organizational cultural novelty

It was also believed that the greater the degree of similarity between the Russian and Irish operations, the easier would be the transition for the expatriate. Respondents were asked to rate the degree to which they thought the two operations were similar.

However, this question was interpreted by many respondents as referring to their physical working environment, which is only one aspect of corporate culture. Qualitative comments by respondents indicated the quality of their working environment was much poorer than in Ireland and the majority suggested that this difficult working environment had made adjusting to the new work role more difficult. Tung (1986) and Parry (1990) have commented that the standard of office space in communist countries is significantly below that of Western countries.

Non-work characteristics

Family situation

As previously mentioned, a small minority of expatriate employees were married (6). Of these, only two had brought their spouse with them to Moscow. Both cases were quite unusual: one respondent was actually married to a Russian national; the second had a spouse who also worked for the same company and had been transferred to Moscow at the same time as the partner. Tung (1986) and Zamet and Bovarnick (1986) have noted that expatriates in other communist countries such as China are more likely to be single or unaccompanied by their family, because of the difficulties associated with living in these regions. This may also be the case as regards assignments in Moscow. Alternatively, personnel departments in Irish firms may be making a conscious decision to employ single people, given the difficulties associated with expatriate families. The small sample size (2) does not really allow an investigation of the effect of the family on Irish expatriate adjustment.

Culture novelty

Respondents were asked to rate on a scale of 1–5 the extent to which Irish and Russian attitudes to certain aspects of culture were similar. Items were adapted from questionnaires used by DeCieri *et al.* (1991) and Black (1988). The

Table 11.6 Similarity of Irish and Russian attitudes

	Not at all similar				Very similar
	1	2	3	4	5
Morals and values	4	9	16	1	0
Respect for other people	2	10	13	3	1
Time	11	9	8	2	0
Work attitudes	13	12	4	1	0

pattern of responses demonstrate that Irish and Russian cultural values are highly divergent, particularly in terms of work and time (see Table 11.6).

Discussion and conclusion

Despite the globalization trend, Brown (1994) maintains that many companies are reassessing their need for expatriates, and there is increasing evidence that candidates for expatriation are thinking longer and harder before accepting foreign assignments. From a research perspective, traditional approaches which emphasized the importance of cultural characteristics as predictors of expatriate failure or turnover failed adequately to assess the impact of job and organizational variables on expatriate satisfaction in international assignments. Firms can take a more active role in easing the adjustment of employees on overseas assignments. The following section outlines some of the strategies which could be pursued by Irish firms in Moscow in facilitating their employees' adjustment. This will not only benefit them by reducing the time proficiency of their employees but it may also limit the instance of expatriate failure.

Career issues

The majority of Irish expatriates appear to be on open ended assignments with no fixed finishing dates. Feldman and Thomas (1992) have pointed to the rather haphazard manner in which expatriate assignments are arranged. They suggest that assignments should be of a fixed term duration with definite repatriation career plans for the individual concerned. They argue that if individuals know that an assignment has a definite end, they are more likely to see it through to its conclusion. However, open-ended assignments would seem to increase the likelihood that expatriates could quit at any time. Furthermore, Solomon (1995) argues that repatriation is often overlooked as a career issue, instead of being seen as the final link in an integrated circular process: 'Often when they return home, expatriates face an organization that does not know what they have done for the past several years, does not know how to use their knowledge and does not care' (Solomon 1995: 29).

Training

Although Irish firms do not seem to place great emphasis on training, that is not to say that it is not of benefit. Empirical studies (Tung 1982) have demonstrated a positive relationship between training and adjustment. One of the Irish firms which does offer training to its expatriate staff is Aer Rianta. Prior to their departure, Aer Rianta employees undergo a week-long formal training course which offers practical advice on living and working in Moscow. Aspects of Russian history and culture are also covered and employees have the option of Russian language training prior to and after their arrival in Moscow. Fionnuala Gill, Training Director for the CIS, has noted that there has been a definite improvement in the satisfaction of Aer Rianta's expatriate workforce since the introduction of the course. Tung (1986) suggests that a cross-cultural training programme should contain four elements:

- area studies programmes providing the trainee with factual information about the country;
- language training;
- field experiences, short trips to the host country prior to the actual assignment;
- sensitivity training, making individuals more aware of cultural differences and their consequences.

The net effect of this approach would be to raise 'consciousness/awareness' (Tung 1995).

Job design

Predictably, the clearer the job, the easier it will be for the individual to adjust to the new work situation. One way of achieving greater clarity in overseas assignments would be through the use of more formal job descriptions (Black 1988). Another possible method is through the use of an overlap period, where an expatriate employee who is due to return remains on in his assignment to train the newcomer (Black and Gregerson 1991). Brewster (1991a) has also suggested that firms make use of 'shadowing', where an individual works on a project related to the host country prior to his transfer. Again this would help to reduce some of the uncertainty and ambiguity associated with the move.

Company support

Company support appears critical. Sappinen (1993) has argued that a company should try to recreate home country conditions as much as possible for expatriates on assignments. In this study respondents placed particular emphasis on the number of flights to Ireland they received as part of their compensation package. Many respondents felt they needed regular breaks from Russia to 'recharge themselves'.

Quality of working environment

In a domestic situation it is generally accepted that the quality of the working environment has a significant impact on performance. However, it is a fact that appears to be often overlooked in international assignments. Many respondents expressed concern at the poor state of their working environment. It has been pointed out that because of the risks associated with doing business in Russia many firms are adopting a 'wait and see' attitude before making any capital investment there.

Finally, by way of a caveat in the present study and as a possible direction for future research, it should be noted that adjustment occurs over time (Black 1988). This study was cross sectional and does not adequately address this issue. In order to get a more accurate picture of the influence of each of these variables one would have to design a longitudinal study programme.

Note

1 This chapter is an extended version of a paper 'The Irish in Moscow: a question of adjustment' which appeared in *Human Resource Management Journal*, 7(3), 1997.

References

Advanced Management Review (1985), autumn: 31–8.

Aycan, Z. (1997) 'Expatriate adjustment as a multifaceted phenomenon: individual and organizational level predictors', *International Human Resource Management Journal* 8(4): 402–14.

Berry, J., Kim, R. and Boshi, P. (1988) 'Psychological acculturation of immigrants', in Y. Kim and W. Gudykust (eds) *Cross Cultural Adaptation Current Approaches*, Beverley Hills: Sage.

Black, S. (1988) 'Work role transitions: a study of American expatriate managers in Japan', *Journal of International Business Studies* (19): 277–94.

——— (1992) 'Relationship of expatriate expectations with repatriation adjustment and job performance', *Human Relations* 45(2): 177–93.

Black, S. and Gregerson, H. (1991a) 'Antecedents to cross cultural adjustment for expatriates in Pacific Rim assignments', *Human Relations* 44(5): 497–515.

——— (1991b) 'When Yankee comes home: factors related to expatriate and spouse repatriation adjustment', *Journal of International Business Studies* 22: 671–94.

Black, S. and Mendenhall, M. (1990) 'Cross cultural training effectiveness: a review and theoretical framework for future research', *Academy of Management Review* 15(1): 113–36.

Black, S. and Mendenhall, M. (1991) 'The U-curve adjustment hypothesis revisited: a review and theoretical framework, *Journal of International Business Studies* 20(2): 255–47.

Black, S. and Stephens, G. (1989) 'The influence of the spouse on American expatriate adjustment and intent to stay in Pacific Rim overseas assignments', *Journal of Management* 15(4): 529–44.

Black, S., Mendenhall, N. and Oddou, G., (1991) 'Towards a comprehensive model of expatriate adjustment: the integration of multiple theoretical perspectives', *Academy of Management Review* 16(2): 291–317.

Borg, M. and Harzing, A. (1995) 'Composing an international staff', in A. Harzing and

J. Van Ruysseveldt (eds) *International Human Resource Management: An Integrated Approach*, London: Sage.

Boylan, J. and Shortall, P. (1992), 'Electronics markets in East and Central Europe', in J. Boylan and J. Waldron (eds) *Central and Eastern Europe in Transition, Proceedings of the Third Annual Conference of the College of Business*, University of Limerick, Limerick: University of Limerick Press.

Brein, M. and David, K. (1971) 'International communication and the adjustment of the sojourner', *Psychological Bulletin* 76: 73–8.

Brett, J. (1980) 'The effect of job transfer on employees and their families', in C. Cooper and R. Payne (eds.) *Current Concerns in Occupational Stress*, London: Pitman Press.

Brewster, C. (1988) 'Managing expatriates', *International Journal of Management* 9(2): 17–20.

—— (1991) *The Management of Expatriates*, London, Kogan Page,

—— (1993) 'The paradox of adjustment: UK and Swedish expatriates in Sweden and the UK', *Human Resource Management Journal* 4(1): 49–62.

Brewster, C. (1997) 'International human resource management: beyond expatriation', *Human Resource Management Journal* 7(3): 31–100.

Brewster, C. and Pickard, J. (1994) 'Evaluating expatriate training', *International Studies of Management and Organisation* 24(3): 18–35.

Brewster, C. and Scullion, H. (1997) 'Expatriate HRM: an agenda and a review', *Human Resource Management Journal* 7(3): 32–41.

Brown, M. (1994) 'The fading charms of foreign fields', *Management Today*, August: 48–51.

Chorafas, D. (1967) 'Developing the international executive', AMA Research Study no. 83, Washington, DC: American Management Association.

Church, A. (1982) 'Soujourner adjustment', *Psychological Bulletin* 91(3): 540–72.

C.I.S. Quarterly Report, Economic Intelligence Unit (1994) first quarter, London: Economist Intelligence Unit.

Coll, P. (1996) 'Members overseas, Poland', *Accountancy Ireland*, August.

Collins, Sinead (1995) *Expatriation: A Moving Experience*, Michael Smurfit Graduate School of Business, August.

Copeland, L. and Griggs, L. (1985) *Going International*, New York: Random House.

Coyle, W. and Shortland, S. (1992) *International Relocation*, Oxford: Butterworth-Heineman.

Darby, R. (1995) 'Developing the new Euro-manager', *European Business Review* 95(1): 13–16.

Dawis, R., England, G. and Lofquist, L. (1964) 'A theory of work adjustment', *Minnesota Studies in Vocational Rehabilitation* 15, Bulletin 38, Minnesota, January.

DeCieri, H., Dowling, P. and Taylor, K. (1991) 'The psychological impact of expatriate relocation on partners', *International Journal of Human Resource Management* 2(3): 377–415.

Dietrich, J. (1995) 'International service in your language', *Telcom Report International* 18(2): 1–12. http//www.jou.ufl.edu/siemens/articles/0295 diet.htm

Dillon, F. and Higgins, C. (1994) 'The Irish invasion', *Management*, April: 3–4.

Dowling, P. and Schuler, R. (1990) *International Dimensions of Human Resource Management*, Boston: PWS-Kent.

Economist Intelligence Unit (EIU) (1995) *Country Report, Russia*, 3rd quarter.

Edkins, M. (1995) 'Making the move from West to East', *People Management*, 29 June.

Feldman, D. and Thomas, D. (1992a) 'Career management issues facing expatriates', *Journal of International Business Studies* 23: 271–3.

—— (1992b) 'Life as an expatriate in Saudi Arabia during the Persian Gulf crisis', *Organisational Dynamics* 20(2): 37–48.

Forster, N. (1997) 'The persistent myth of high expatriate failure rates: a reappraisal', *International Journal of Human Resource Management* 3(4): 414–34.

Giershe, R. (1995) 'Business people and foreign language learning', *Language Learning Journal* 11: 17–27.

Hamill, J. (1989) 'Expatriate policies in British multinationals', *Journal of General Management* 14(4): 18–34.

Handler, C. and Lane, C. (1997) 'Career planning and expatriate couples', *Human Resource Management Journal* 7(3): 53–67.

Harvey, M. (1985) 'The executive family: an overlooked variable in international assignments', *Columbia Journal of World Business* 20(1): 84–91.

—— (1996) 'The selection of managers for foreign assignments: a planning perspective', *Columbia Journal of World Business* 31: 102–18.

—— (1997) 'Dual-career expatriates: expectations, adjustment and satisfaction with international relocation', *Journal of International Business Studies*, third quarter: 627–58.

Hiltrop, J. and Janssens, M. (1990) 'Expatriation: challenges and recommendations', *European Management Journal* 8(1): 19–27.

Hippler, T. (1996) 'Relocation support for expatriates on international assignments: an analysis of the human resource management issues involved and how these are addressed by German companies assigning German executives to their subsidiaries in the Republic of Ireland', Fachhochschule Ostfriesland, Emden, December.

Hoecklin, L. (1994) *Managing Cultural Differences*, Harlow: Addison-Wesley Longman.

Hofstede, G. (1980) *Culture's Consequences: International Differences in Work-Related Values*, Beverly Hills: Sage.

Hogan, G. (1990) 'The key to expatriate success', *Training and Development Journal*, January.

Jones, B. (1997) 'Getting ahead in Switzerland', *Management Review* 86(6): 58–61.

Kabanoff, B. (1980) 'Work and non-work: a review of models, methods and findings', *Psychological Bulletin* 88(1): 71–103.

Katz, J. and Seifer, D. (1996–97) 'It's a different world out there', *Human Resource Planning* 19(3): 32–34.

Knight, K.G. and Webb, D. (1997) 'Investing in Poland and the Czech Republic: the experience so far', *European Management Journal* 15(3): 326–33.

Laird, L. (1994) 'Irish Expatriates in Moscow', *Europe: Magazine of the European Community*, April: 14.

Louis, M. (1980) 'Surprise and sense making: what newcomers experience in entering unfamiliar organisational settings', *Administrative Science Quarterly* 25: 226–47.

McEnery, J. and Des Harnais, G. (1990) 'Culture shock', *Training and Development Journal*, April: 43–8.

Macmillan, C. (1991) 'Foreign direct investment flows to Eastern Europe and their implications for developing countries', *Journal of International Studies* 20(2): 130–47.

Mendenhall, M. and Oddou, G. (1985) 'The dimensions of expatriate acculturation: a review', *Academy of Management Review* 10(1): 39–47.

—— (1986) 'Acculturation profiles of expatriate managers: implications for cross cultural training programs, *Columbia Journal of World Business* 21(4): 34–67.

Mendenhall, M., Dunbar, E. and Oddou, G. (1987) 'Expatriate selection, training and career-pathing: a review and critique', *Human Resource Management* 26: 331–45.

Morley, M., Burke, C. and Finn, G. (1997) 'The Irish in Moscow: a question of adjustment', *Human Resource Management Journal* 7(3): 53–67.

Montezemolo, G. (1996) 'Greater Europe: moving the goalposts', *Business Europe* 20 November.

Moore, S. and Punnett, J. (1994) 'Expatriates and their spouses: a pilot study in the Limerick region and directions for future research', *Irish Business and Administration Research* 15: 178–84.

Naumann, E. (1992) 'A conceptual model of expatriate turnover', *Journal of International Business Studies*, 3rd quarter: 449–531.

Odenwald, S. (1993) 'A guide for global training', *Training and Development*, July: 22–32.

Parry, T. (1990) 'Wild east pioneers', *International Management*, November: 32–4.

Philips, N. (1993) 'Cross cultural training', *Journal of European Industrial Training* 17(2): 1–11.

Punnett, B.J. and Ricks, D. A. (1992) *International Business* Boston: PWS-Kent.

Ronen, S. (1989) 'Training the international assignee', in I. Goldstein and associates (eds) *Training and Development in Organisations*, San Francisco: Jossey-Bass.

Sappinen, J. (1993) 'Expatriate adjustment on foreign assignment', *European Business Review* 93(5): 3–12.

Scullion, H. (1991) 'Why companies prefer to use expatriates', *Personnel Management*, November: 20–1.

—— (1994) 'Creating international managers: recruitment and development issues', in P. Kirkbride (ed.) *Human Resource Management in Europe: Perspectives for the 1990s*, London: Routledge.

Smalley, W. (1963) 'Language shock, culture shock and the shock of self discovery', *Practical Anthropology* 10: 15–27.

Solomon, C. (1995) 'Repatriation, up, down, or out?', *Personnel Journal* 74(1): 28–30.

Torbiörn, I. (1997) 'Staffing for international operations', *Human Resource Management Journal* 7(3): 32–42.

—— (1982) *Living Abroad: Personal Adjustment and Personnel Policies in the Overseas Setting*, New York: Wiley.

Toyne, B. and Kuhne, R. (1983) 'The management of the international executive compensation and benefits process', *Journal of International Business Studies* 14(3): 578–90.

Trompenaars, Fons (1993) *Riding the Waves of Culture*, London: Nicholas Brealey.

Tu, H. and Sullivan, S. (1994) 'Preparing yourself for an international assignment', *Business Horizons* 37(1): 67–70.

Tung, R. (1981) 'Selecting and training of personnel for overseas assignments', *Columbia Journal of World Business* 16(): 68–78.

—— (1982) 'Selection and training procedures of US, European and Japanese Multinationals, *California Management Review* 25(1): 57–71.

—— (1986) 'Corporate executives and their families in China: the need for cross-cultural understanding in business', *Columbia Journal of World Business* 21(1): 60–72.

—— (1987) 'Expatriate assignments: enhancing success and minimizing failure', *Academy of Management Executive* 1(2): 117–26.

—— (1995) 'Strategic human resource challenge: managing diversity', *International Journal of Human Resource Management* 6(3): 482–93.

Zamet, J. and Bovarnick, M. (1986) 'Employee relations in multinational companies in China', *Columbia Journal of World Business* 21: 50–65.

Zeira, Y. and Shenker, O. (1992) 'Role conflict and role ambiguity of chief executive officers in international joint ventures', *Journal of International Business Studies* 21(1): 55–75.

12 An integrative framework for pre-departure preparation

Hilary Harris and Chris Brewster

Existing research into expatriate preparation

The growth of international business at a time when most international organizations are under increasing cost pressures has led these organizations to take a sharp look at their policies for expatriates. As discussed in Chapter 1, there is some evidence from the USA that multinational enterprises (MNEs) have reacted by trying to cut the number of expatriates that they employ (Kobrin 1988). Although there are some occasionally quite spectacular cases of this happening for European MNEs, it is likely that the overall number of expatriates from these organizations will continue to grow (Brewster 1993). The latest evidence from the USA seems to show another resurgence in the use of expatriates by US MNEs (Windham International and NFTC 1997).

In these changed circumstances, international organizations have responded by trying to find alternatives to expatriation, such as relying more heavily on locally recruited staff, short-term transfers, more frequent international travel, international commuting or even teleconferencing. Most commonly, however, international organizations have attempted to increase the cost-effectiveness of their expatriates. A key element in this has been a growth in attention to appropriate preparation for the assignment.

Attention to preparation is linked to research into international adjustment which indicates that it includes at least three dimensions: adjustment to the overseas workplace, adjustment to interacting with host nationals and adjustment to the general overseas environment (Black *et al.* 1991). These authors identify from the literature various individual level skills which need to be developed in order to cope with international assignments; skills which include self-efficacy, relational and perceptual skills. A fourth factor, emotional adjustment (Janssens 1992), has also been suggested. 'An internationally-assigned manager has to adjust and respond to these different sources of change. Newly assigned managers must find ways to adjust to the new cultural environment and this process may alter their values and beliefs' (Bird and Dunbar 1991: 6). Much of the work on expatriate preparation and training (for reviews see Black and Mendenhall 1990; Brewster and Pickard 1994) is built on the importance of this ability to understand and adjust. However, it has also been pointed out that this is a complex process. The expatriate has at the same time both to adjust to the environment and maintain the distinguishing characteristics that they are intended to bring in to the host country (Brewster 1993). Therefore, preparation itself becomes a complex process.

International companies undertaking training and development programmes for expatriates face significant problems.

> However imperfect training may be as a substitute for actual foreign living experience, it is valuable if it can reduce the often painful and agonising experience of transferring into another culture and avoid the great damage that culture shock and cultural misunderstanding can do to a firm's operating relationship.
>
> (Robock and Simmonds 1983: 562)

Two problems make training and development for international assignments more complex than for domestic assignments. First, the expatriate not only has to adjust to a new job and a new role, but also to a new culture (Mendenhall and Oddou 1985). Second, since the stress associated with a foreign assignment falls on all family members (Harris and Moran 1979; Harvey 1985) the issue of training programmes for the spouse and family need to be addressed. US MNEs tend to use pre-departure training programmes less frequently than European and Japanese firms (Torbiörn 1982; Tung 1982; Brewster 1991). There is evidence that expatriates are very positive about the value of training programmes (Brewster and Pickard 1994). Other forms of preparation – briefings, shadowing, look–see visits – are more frequent than formal training programmes (Brewster 1991; Scullion 1993) and may be more cost-effective.

Cross-cultural training has long been advocated as a means of facilitating effective cross-cultural interactions (Brislin 1986), yet in practice most firms do not use cross-cultural training (Black 1988; Black and Mendenhall 1990). The main reason appears to be that top management just does not believe that training is necessary or effective (Mendenhall and Oddou 1985; Dowling and Schuler 1991). Models of training and development for expatriate managers, developed over the last decade, consider the task, the individual and the environment before deciding the depth of training required (Tung 1981; Rahim 1983). Tung's (1981) framework for selecting cross-cultural training methods identified two main dimensions that should be used: the degree of interaction required in the host culture and the similarity between the expatriate's home culture and the host culture. Mendenhall and Oddou (1986) developed this framework to include the degree of integration and level of rigour required and translated this into the needed duration of time for each type of training programme. This framework consisted of three levels:

- information-giving approaches (e.g. factual briefing and awareness training);
- affective approaches (e.g. culture assimilator training, critical incidents and role plays);

- immersion approaches (e.g. assessment centres, field experience, and simulations).

However, Mendenhall *et al.* (1995) point out that this model does not specify how the level of rigour is determined and refers only to cross-cultural training. They observe that the Tung (1981) and Mendenhall and Oddou (1985) models do not specify a theoretical basis and therefore do not substantiate why they are useful and valid.

A more recent framework by Black and Mendenhall (1989) is based on social learning theory. They develop a decision-tree model which logically links and integrates the variables of culture novelty, required degree of interaction with host nationals, job novelty and training rigour. Black and Mendenhall (1989) argue that this model can be adapted for expatriate spouses and children with a rewording of job novelty to role novelty, thus allowing an evaluation of the rigour of the training programme for those accompanying expatriates to be determined. Black and Mendenhall's framework acknowledges the need for job-related training content in terms of job demands, constraints and choices. At the highest level of rigour identified, the training content should also include economic, political, historical and religious topics. None of the other levels specify the need for training in the general business environment.

Mendenhall *et al.* (1995) make the point that while these models are well known among academics, to date few human resource directors use them when selecting and designing cross-cultural training programmes for their companies. They argue that training programme design and selection in the global context of human resource management is still done informally, with little regard to findings in the research literature

The overall purpose of Mendenhall and Oddou's (1985) review of expatriate acculturation was to determine the key dimensions involved in the expatriate adjustment process and to examine their implications for the selection and training of expatriates. Studies by Tung (1981), Mendenhall and Oddou (1986), Black (1988), Ronen (1989) and Black and Porter (1991) bring together the dimensions of expatriate success, identifying five categories of attributes of success:

- job factors;
- relational dimensions;
- motivational state;
- family situation;
- language skills.

The link between preparation, adjustment and performance is crucial but tenuous, in part due to difficulties in determining the criteria by which to measure expatriate performance (Brewster 1991). Clearly the three major variables affecting performance are the personality characteristics of the individual, the environment (culture), and the job requirements (Schuler *et al.* 1991). The first issue can be addressed through recruitment and selection and the other two through preparation.

The requirement and opportunities for preparation will vary considerably. Some basic issues, such as the job that the person is going to, the country involved and whether the family is going as well, have a significant impact on the need for preparation and the kind of preparation that is necessary (Brewster 1995). Similarly, the evidence that about half of the European MNEs in one study (Brewster 1991) generally managed to give their expatriates less than two months between the decision to expatriate and departure means that the time available for preparation was very limited – particularly in view of the pressures of completing current work, making family, home and other arrangements and organizing the move itself. A later survey of Finnish expatriates (Suutari and Brewster 1998) found that they had much more time – three and a half months on average. Instructively, this later survey found a clear statistical correlation between those expatriates who had a short time to make the move and those who were dissatisfied with their preparation

Alternatives to training

Preparation is not the same as training. Indeed, it may be that some of the alternatives are more expedient and more cost-effective (Brewster 1991). They include a variety of different approaches.

Informal briefings

Studies have found that two-thirds of European organizations use informal briefings for expatriates. Arguably, the chance to meet and discuss the host country with people who know it well, perhaps other employees of the company from there or who have just returned, is among the cheapest and best forms of preparation. If the whole family is involved this can be particularly useful. These briefings can be arranged easily, fit in with the hectic schedules of the 'soon to move', and can provide the sort of information and even contacts not available elsewhere. Many expatriates make their own arrangements of this sort. Properly managed they can be even more valuable. It is easy for the putative expatriate to meet with one or two people who have limited knowledge and miss some important aspects of living and working in the host country, or to meet with individuals who may have an unwarrantedly prejudiced and jaundiced view of the country – or an impossibly romantic one. Careful selection of the briefers, so that they provide a rounded and comprehensive view, makes the process more effective

Look–see visits

Some companies provide look–see visits. The costs here are obviously higher, particularly if, as one might hope, the family was included. However, the pay-off can be substantial. Increasing numbers of the larger MNEs seem to be using this approach (two-thirds in a recent survey of Finnish MNEs, Suutari and Brewster 1998). It is obviously a very good way for the expatriate or the family to prepare. They arrive in the country knowing something about it; having some, however limited, experience of living there; knowing the work environment; and having made contacts both at work and in the community which can be activated when they make the transfer. Some MNEs have found that they need to be carefully managed. They are to a degree unreal. The expatriates and their families will meet important people and be on their best behaviour; they will stay in the best hotels and eat at the best restaurants – their image of the country may take a hard knock when they arrive 'for real'.

Overlaps

Handovers from one expatriate to another are common and in some organizations are extended to ensure an overlap, particularly for managers. This has the significant advantages of allowing one to brief the other, to introduce them to key clients, government officers and so on and to 'show them the ropes' in the working environment. However, such overlaps are expensive, difficult to organize and can lead the local staff to be unclear about who is actually in charge.

Shadowing

In some cases, particularly where the expatriates have been working in head office, it is possible for them to 'shadow' the country concerned – being responsible for the reports, communications with and results of the country concerned. The effect is that they may well visit the country, meet with members of the staff there when they visit HQ and get a good feel for the country's issues, concerns and performance, at least as far as the MNE is concerned.

The need for training

Most of the discussion of preparation naturally turns to the issue of training for the new position, and it is on this topic that we now focus our attention.

As already noted, it has been suggested that there are three key variables involved in the decision as to whether to provide training and the relative degree of rigour required in each case:

- job novelty, meaning the degree to which a new job is different from the current one;
- degree of interaction with host nationals;
- culture novelty, meaning the degree of difference between the home country and host country in terms of value systems, behavioural norms and so on (Mendenhall *et al.* 1995).

The same authors argue that differing degrees of cross-cultural training will need to be provided depending on the extent to which each of these variables is present in the expatriate assignment.

Previous work on preparation and training for expatriation has shown, as the most significant finding, that such preparation is far from widespread. Studies in the 1970s found that among US MNEs only two-thirds provided any training at all (Baker and Ivancevich 1971) and less than 25 per cent provided any formal orientation training (Baker and Ivancevich 1971; Lannier 1979; Baliga and Baker 1985). Other research shows around 40 per cent of American firms providing cultural orientation and two-thirds providing language training (Tung 1982: 66). European MNEs tend to do more (Torbiörn 1982; Tung 1982; Baliga and Baker 1985; Brewster 1991).

The belief that expatriates could be effective without preparation for their assignment is built upon the assumption of 'universalism': a technician or even manager who has proved to be successful in one environment will be successful in any other (Lannier 1979; Mendenhall and Oddou 1985). Research into selection criteria for international assignments shows a split between theory and practice, with the theory stressing the need for interpersonal skills and the practice stressing technical competence. In surveys asking for general views on what makes effective international managers, the criteria mentioned as being critical differ from those reported as being used in practice.

Phillips (1993) suggests that there is little or no difference between the personal qualities required for success in managing domestic or international business, but successful development of international business demands a higher level of skills and qualities than for managing in a domestic market. This is because managers working overseas will be involved in a wider range of activities, roles and respon-sibilities than those required in the home market. Likewise, Trompenaars (1993) suggests that the international manager has many characteristics of the effective manager operating in a less complex environment. The international manager, however, needs additional skills to reconcile the cultural problems created by the international environment. Possessing an awareness of the difficulties is not enough in this situation.

This confusion may in some ways be related to the fact that the majority of the studies are not specific in defining the type of expatriate such criteria relate to (Tung 1982). Equally there is little consideration as to whether criteria will vary according to country, host country role and number of expatriates employed (Torbiörn 1982; Björkman and Gersten 1990; Tung 1982). However, Forster (1996) notes that the many different criteria presented in the literature tend to fall into three broad categories: technical competence at work; personality traits/attributes; interpersonal social skills and personal and family situations.

In Brewster's (1991) review of the literature relating to selection criteria, he argues that successive authors have adapted previous categorizations of criteria, or developed new ones, so comparability between studies is limited. He notes that many of the American studies use the *Business International* list of fifteen categories of skills for the international manager:

Experience, adaptability and flexibility, technical knowledge of the business, competence, ability and past performance, managerial talent, language skills, potential, interest in overseas work, appreciation of new management and sensitivity, proper education, initiative and creativity, independence, good ability to communicate, maturity and emotional stability.

(*Business International* 1970)

A number of researchers have added to the list. For example, Hays (1974) emphasized the importance of 'relational abilities' and the 'family situation'. Zeira and Banai (1985) introduced country of origin and 'appearance (dress and looks)', the latter also discussed more recently by Stone (1991) as an unwritten but critical selection factor for women expatriates.

Ashridge Management Research Centre's study of international managers (not necessarily expatriate managers) revealed clear agreement among respondents of attributes which appear desirable, whatever the company's strategy. These include strategic awareness, adaptability in new situations, sensitivity to different cultures, ability to work in international teams, language skills and understanding of international marketing (Barham and Devine 1991). The list is significant in that four out of the top six characteristics identified represent 'soft' skills, underlining the human relations aspect of international management and an ability to handle unfamiliar situations.

Several authors have attempted to produce more discrete, wider categories. Rehfuss (1982), for example, identifies five groups: 'relational' or interpersonal abilities: 'cultural empathy' (including motivation, language, maturity and an 'x' factor, operationally defined as the ability to live abroad); technical skill; domestic performance; and spouse/family. Torbiörn (1982) identifies eight criteria: adaptability; language; motivation; level of education; social manners; family adaptability; medical status; status of the job.

Mendenhall and Oddou (1985) identify three sets of individual cross-cultural skills as follows:

1   Self-efficacy skills – including reinforcement substitution, stress reduction and technical competence.
2   Relational skills – including relationship development, willingness to communicate and language.
3   Perceptual skills – including understanding why host nationals behave and think in the way they do and making correct inferences as to the motives behind these behaviours.

A key observation from this literature is the emphasis on interpersonal and cross-cultural skills as determinants of success for international assignments. The stress on 'soft skills' reflects a more general departure from reliance on traditional 'hard' skills for successful management.

Given the emphasis on interpersonal skills in management theory, it is somewhat surprising to find evidence of the continuing adoption of more traditional criteria for selection of expatriates in research into current practices of MNEs.

Brewster's (1988) survey of international personnel executives from European multinational corporations identified the following top criteria used to select expatriates: 'technical expertise; language; family support; potential; knowing company systems; experience; marital status; medical status; independence and motivation'.

The prominence of technical skills in selection criteria in practice has traditionally been reported by researchers (Ivancevich 1969; Hays 1971, 1974; Miller 1973; Howard 1974; Lannier 1979; Tung 1981, 1982; Zeira and Banai 1984, 1985; Brewster 1988), by the expatriates themselves (Gonzales and Neghandi 1967; Hays 1971; Harris 1973; Hautaluoma and Kaman 1975; Bardo and Bardo 1980; Hawes and Kealey 1981; Zeira and Banai 1984, 1985) and by host country nationals (Zeira and Banai 1985). Research evidence therefore supports the 'universalist' stance.

Based on the assumption that it is mainly technical competence rather than the ability to operate differently in different environments that determines the success of an expatriate assignment, we developed our first proposition:

Proposition One: Expatriates will share the organizational assumption that technical and managerial skills are universal; that individuals who have exhibited these skills in one country will, therefore, have a minimal need for training when they transfer to another country.

The business training requirement

Whatever the importance of technical competence for expatriate employees, much of the literature suggests that applying those skills in a different cultural environment is not problem free. On the contrary, much of the literature on expatriates takes almost as a given the impact of culture shock (identified by Oberg 1960; Gullahorn and Gullahorn 1963; Torbiörn 1982) and the problems that expatriates face in operating in countries other than their own.

Numerous training programmes have been developed to help expatriates operate more quickly and more effectively in the new country. Many of these have been drawn up by experienced expatriates who have moved into management development, training roles or consultancies or colleges. In many cases their experience as expatriates will have been gained at a time when the pressures on cost reduction and performance were much lower. As a result the progammes are usually strong on what might be termed the cultural hygiene factors – ensuring, usually anecdotally, that the potential expatriate does not make immediate embarrassing or insensitive cultural mistakes and that they can handle the issues raised by living in the country. They are rarely focused on resolving business problems. These programmes tend to take as models the picture of middle-aged, confident, male professionals moving from a developed Christian country to a less developed area with noticeably different religions and social customs such as Africa or the Middle East (Pickard and Brewster 1992).

The world of the expatriate is changing rapidly in at least two significant areas. First, there are important changes in host location. It is necessary, here, to disaggregate the expatriate population. It may well be that in recent years there has been a substantial growth in expatriation from the First World/North to the Third World/South among aid and charity workers and people working for international intergovernmental organizations. Even here, the pressures for performance are increasing: the new United Nations Task Group on efficiency within the organization is a clear, but by no means the only, example.

However, among the international profit-oriented organizations the movement has been away from the Third World towards the First World. This reflects an increased unwillingness on the part of Third World governments to keep renewing work permits and a recognition by MNEs that there are many talented people in most countries able to do the work they require. Often, because they are close to the local market and permanent, they do it better and much more cheaply. It also reflects, of course, the changing focus of trade. Companies such as Cable and Wireless, which were traditionally based in the old British Empire (or latterly Commonwealth), have moved into alliances and markets in North America, Japan and, of course, in Europe. For many of these traditional MNEs the growth in recent years has been as much about the developed world as the underdeveloped. The establishment of the European Union and other trading blocs has given an undoubted fillip to these activities. Furthermore, the EU, for example, has opened up and facilitated international activity for an extensive range of organizations which had not until recently imagined that they could operate outside their own country. There are now large numbers of organizations which in the last few years have established their first or second operation in another European country with their first few international employees. A significant feature of these changes is that there are now fewer organizations operating as a kind of quasi-colonial government monopoly in a poor country. There are more and more MNEs operating in intensely competitive and pressured markets with substantial demands for adequate (or better) performance from every single business unit.

Equally, the changes to which we have already alluded in the demographic profile and educational make-up of expatriates will affect traditional patterns of expatriation and will create demands for a clearer focus on the assignment as part of career progression and a means of developing broader senior management capabilities. There will be a more explicit attempt by the expatriate to ensure rapid job success. It is in the light of these changes that we developed a second possible approach to expatriate training, which we outline as our second proposition:

Proposition Two: Expatriates in the 1990s will be concerned to receive training and preparation that is focused on operating in the business environment.

Methodology

In order to explore these issues we developed and piloted a questionnaire. The format consisted of an initial section asking for demographic information; a second section which asked about practical knowledge requirements; a third section related to business arrangements; a fourth section covering worries and concerns about the move; and a final section examining social and family issues.

Items covered under the practical knowledge section included: language; immigration procedures; general bureaucracy; hygiene; personal finance; children's education; shopping; climate.

Items in the social and family section included: social customs; political and economic background; basic history of the country; underlying ethnic or religious divides; local social dress code; relationships with host nationals on a day-to-day basis; socializing with host nationals; how host nationals view expatriates; finding children's activities; dealing with security concerns; support from the expatriate community.

Under the business relationships section items included: local business law; dealing with local partners; relations with host nationals at work; local business practice; local contacts for guidance; structure of financial markets.

The appropriate population was clearly expatriates who were currently on assignment, so that they had experience and were able to answer the question-naire with this rather than prognosis or hindsight in mind.

The questionnaires were distributed in 1994 through a magazine circulating to expatriates. The nature of this method meant that although we were sure that the survey was getting to a wide range of current expatriates, we have no information about how many received copies or the demographic composition of the original sample. It is not possible therefore to give statistical details of response rates. Comparisons of the demographic profile of respondents with other surveys of expatriates indicate that the sample is not obviously unrepresentative.

In the event, 205 usable pairs of responses were obtained by the cut-off date. The respondents completed the questionnaire and a considerable number added extensive comments. Examples of these are included in the chapter.

Of respondents, 51 per cent were based in the Middle East; 20 per cent in Western Europe; 12 per cent in the Far East; 5 per cent in Africa; 3 per cent in North America and the Caribbean; 3 per cent in Eastern Europe and the rest were distributed between South America, Australia and New Zealand and the Pacific Islands.

Of the population, 75 per cent were employed by commercial companies, with the remainder being government, charity or aid workers, or self-employed.

Approximately 70 per cent of respondents were accompanied by their partner on their assignment; 12 per cent had partners at home and 18 per cent were single.

The occupational breakdown of survey respondents showed that most fell within the managerial sector (24 per cent senior management and 30 per cent other management) with another 39 per cent being made up of specialists. The only other occupational classification noted was administrative (6 per cent).

Findings

Our findings refuted the assumption of *Proposition One* that the universalism of technical and management skills would lead to a minimum need for training. Despite the predominance of managers and specialists in the survey sample, the overall level of pre-departure knowledge among survey respondents across all categories showed that 46 per cent said they had little or no knowledge in terms of practical items; 54 per cent had little or no knowledge relating to social and family items; and 70 per cent indicated that they had little or no knowledge in the area of business relationships.

The expatriates' views of what they should have received in terms of preparation were rather different. On average, approximately 34 per cent felt they needed more information relating to practical items; 41 per cent needed more information relating to social and family items; 54 per cent required more information concerning business relationships. (See Table 12.1.)

Comments from respondents highlighted the desire for more pre-departure training in all areas:

> *Japan*: Wish I'd known more. Social relations here are very delicate and people need to be well briefed in them.

> *UAE*: Although there is a lot of information available, it is often a question of you don't know what you need to know. More understanding of culture, especially culture shock, . . . which is difficult to be prepared for.

> *Kuwait*: Although information received is sufficient in amount, it wasn't in its depth or how it may affect you.

> *Switzerland*: Just realised how lousy my company briefing was!

Both quantitative and qualitative data from the survey therefore suggest that expatriates want more training in all three areas of the survey, namely general practical knowledge, cultural knowledge and local business knowledge. This was the case even for technical expatriates. Their views match the findings from other research that there is a positive relationship between training and adjustment and performance (Black and Mendenhall 1990).

The survey data (see Table 12.1) verified *Proposition Two* which assumed the need for a more tailored approach to preparation in the business environment.

Seventy per cent of senior managers and 85 per cent of other managers across the board had little or no knowledge of local business law. Although it may be argued that this was not a particular need for the job, over 60 per cent of senior managers and nearly 70 per cent of other managers reported a need for more knowledge in this area. An equally high level of need was identified in the area of local business practice, with 70 per cent of all respondents indicating they had little or no knowledge and only 34 per cent receiving any company briefing; 57 per cent wanted more information in this area. This item was seen to be especially critical for respondents in Eastern Europe:

Table 12.1 Knowledge level before leaving home country

	None	Little	Average	Good	Further information required
Practical					
Language	52	26	6	15	40
Immigration procedures	20	33	28	19	34
Other bureaucracy	42	27	18	13	43
Hygiene: e.g. drinking water, washing vegetables, etc.	9	23	30	37	22
Personal finance/local banking	27	28	24	21	44
Cost of living	17	28	33	22	39
Medical problems: what medicines to take, etc.	17	18	35	30	30
Medical facilities: what will be available	18	25	29	29	34
Transport: e.g. can you rely on taxi or bus; is a 2nd car essential?	17	20	31	32	28
Accommodation: did you know what choice was available?	22	25	21	33	44
What to take with you	8	30	31	32	36
Safety related 'do's and dont's'	18	22	34	26	27
Children's education	28	20	26	27	37
Shopping	20	31	27	23	27
Climate	3	13	28	55	12
Business relationships					
Local business law	54	28	14	4	58
Dealing with local partners	44	29	17	10	50
Relations with host nationals at work	25	37	21	17	53
Local business practice	34	36	21	10	55
Business etiquette	25	33	25	17	44
Local contacts for guidance	38	32	19	10	54
Structure of financial markets	42	32	15	12	51
Social and family					
Social customs	9	47	26	17	46
Political and economic background	6	31	43	20	43
Basic history of country	8	32	37	23	39
Underlying ethnic or religious divides	11	36	36	17	44
Local social dress code	10	23	38	30	27
Relationships with host nationals on a day-to-day basis	18	32	28	22	44
Socializing with host nationals	24	31	26	19	47
How host nationals view expatriates	29	31	24	16	54
Education for children	32	18	33	17	39
Finding children's activities	40	30	21	9	48
How to deal with local security concerns	28	32	26	14	44
Support from expatriate community	31	38	21	10	48

Czech Republic: New office, many aspects (legal and social and business) were in total flux in 1990. It was pioneering work.

Discussion

Much work on expatriate preparation and training (for reviews see Black and Mendenhall 1990: Brewster and Pickard 1994) is built on the importance of an ability to understand and adjust. Much of the work on stress in this context (Cooper 1988) makes the same point.

The 'universalist' assumptions of many employers help to account for the low levels of preparation for expatriate assignment typically found in the research. However, the evidence here reflects the fact, discovered in other research (Domsch and Lichtenberger 1991; Brewster and Pickard 1994; Suutari and Brewster 1998), that expatriates themselves are significantly more enthusiastic about training programmes than their employers.

The findings also demonstrate a need to tailor preparation for expatriation to the specific job function. Jobs requiring a great deal of interface with local nationals, either within the organization or outside it, will necessitate greater cultural interpersonal skills than others which remain fairly protected from the local environment. In our survey, respondents appeared to reflect this concern, with 68 per cent of senior managers stating that training in the complexities of socio-cultural norms when socializing with host nationals is a critical need, as compared to just under 50 per cent of middle managers. The more senior level may indicate a greater need to attend to external relations.

Our survey data provide tentative evidence that there is a need for training in all three areas of practical knowledge, social and family concerns and business related knowledge. Existing frameworks for expatriate preparation have focused on dimensions of adjustment in expatriate assignments (Black *et al.* 1991) and have identified variables relating to the degree of difference in the job and host country culture and the amount of interaction required with host nationals. Attempts have then been made to relate combinations of variables to different training scenarios in terms of rigour, duration, approach and content (Tung 1981; Mendenhall and Oddou 1986; Black and Mendenhall 1989).

From our review of the literature and analysis of current trends in expatriate preparation we have observed a gap in existing approaches in terms of a lack of consideration of the dynamics in the external environment and a focus on issues which are relevant, directly, to the work context. Such influences include the nature of the international operation, size of home country organization, host country location, objective of assignment, nature of job, level of organizational support; together with individual variables in terms of the expatriate profile and partner considerations. A significant influence is that of the local business culture. (See Figure 12.1.)

In view of this we have developed a framework of expatriate preparation which allows for a broader perspective to be taken in the analysis of preparation needs (Figure 12.1). This framework suggests that organizations take into account

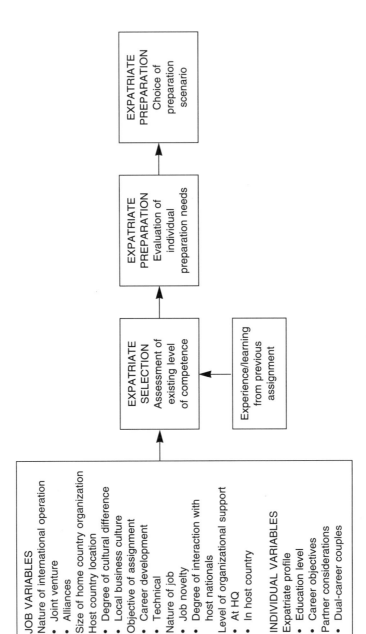

Figure 12.1 Harris–Brewster framework for expatriate preparation, 1995

JOB VARIABLES
Nature of international operation
- Joint venture
- Alliances
Size of home country organization
Host country location
- Degree of cultural difference
- Local business culture
Objective of assignment
- Career development
- Technical
Nature of job
- Job novelty
- Degree of interaction with
  host nationals
Level of organizational support
- At HQ
- In host country

INDIVIDUAL VARIABLES
Expatriate profile
- Education level
- Career objectives
Partner considerations
- Dual-career couples

**EXPATRIATE
SELECTION**
Assessment of
existing level
of competence

Experience/learning
from previous
assignment

**EXPATRIATE
PREPARATION**
Evaluation of
individual
preparation needs

**EXPATRIATE
PREPARATION**
Choice of
preparation
scenario

both the job and individual variables and use this information conjointly during the selection process in order to make a full assessment of the individual's current level of competence in the areas of international adjustment. Various methods can be used in this respect, but it is outside the scope of this chapter to itemize them. We would also suggest that organizations attempt to ascertain the level of learning obtained from previous assignments. Leading on from this assessment, an evaluation of preparation needs can be developed for the expatriate and partner/family and a suitable preparation scenario produced.

Clearly more research is needed, especially to refine further this framework to include specific preparation scenarios. However, already our research shows that training needs are changing, necessitating a more tailored approach.

Expatriates are among the most expensive people that an organization employs and are usually in crucial positions. There is a clear need for more and better preparation in order to ensure that they are able to be as effective as possible, as quickly as possible. Within the overall framework of the total costs of an assignment the expense of such preparation is small. Cost-effective management of expatriates would involve making this investment.

References

Baker, J. and Ivancevich, J. (1971) 'The assignment of American executives abroad: systematic, haphazard or chaotic?', *California Management Review* 13(3): 39–44.

Baliga, C. and Baker, J. (1985) 'Multinational corporate policies for expatriate managers', *Advanced Management Journal* 50(4): 31–8.

Bardo, J.W. and Bardo, D.J. (1980) 'Dimensions of adjustment for American settlers in Melbourne, Australia', *Multivariate Experimental Clinical Research* 5(1): 23–8.

Barham, K. and Devine, M. (1991) *The Quest for the International Manager: A Survey of Global Human Resource Strategies*, London: Economist Intelligence Unit.

Bird, A. and Dunbar, R. (1991) 'The adaptation and adjustment process of managers on international assignments', Stern Working Paper, New York University.

Björkman, I. and Gertson, M. (1990) 'Corporate expatriation: an analysis of firms and country-specific differences in Scandinavia', unpublished paper.

Black, J.S. (1988) 'Work role transitions: a study of American expatriate managers in Japan', *Journal of International Business Studies* 30(2): 119–34.

Black, J.S. and Gregersen, H.B. (1991a) 'When Yankee comes home: factors related to expatriate and spouse repatriation adjustment', *Journal of International Business Studies*, 4th qtr: 671–94.

Black, J.S. and Gregersen H.B. (1991b) 'The other half of the picture: antecedents of spouse cross-cultural adjustment', *Journal of International Business Studies* 22(3): 461–77.

Black, J.S. and Mendenhall, M. (1989) 'A practical but theory-based framework for selecting cross-cultural training methods', *Human Resource Management* 28: 511–39.

Black, J.S. and Mendenhall, M. (1990) 'Cross-cultural training effectiveness: a review and a theoretical framework for future research', *Academy of Management Review* 15(1): 113–36.

Black, J.S. and Porter, L.W. (1991) 'Managerial behaviours and job performance: a successful manager in Los Angeles may not suceed in Hong Kong', *Journal of International Business Studies* 34(1): 99–113.

Black, J.S. and Stephens, G.K. (1989) 'The influence of the spouse on American expatriate adjustment in overseas assignments', *Journal of Management* 15(4): 529–44.

Black, J.S., Mendenhall, M. and Oddou, G. (1991) 'Toward a comprehensive model of internatioinal adjustment: an integration of multiple theoretical perspectives', *Academy of Management Review* 16(2): 291–317.

Brewster, C. (1988) 'Managing expatriates', *International Journal of Manpower* 9(2): 17–20.

—— (1991) *The Management of Expatriates*, London: Kogan Page.

—— (1993) 'The paradox of adjustment: UK and Swedish expatriates in Sweden and the UK', *Human Resource Management Journal* 4(1): 49–62.

—— (1995) 'Effective expatriate training', in J. Selmer (ed.) *Expatriate Management: New Ideas for International Business* Westport CT: Quorum Books.

Brewster, C. and Pickard, J. (1994) 'Evaluating expatriate training', *International Studies of Management and Organisation* 24(3): 18–35.

Brislin, R.W. (1986) 'The wording and translation of research instruments', in W.J. Lonner and J.W. Berry *Field Methods in Cross-cultural Research*, Beverly Hills: Sage: 137–64.

Cooper, C. (1988) 'Executive stress around the world', *Multinational Employer* 5(9): 5–10.

Domsch, M. and Lichtenberger, B. (1991) 'Managing the global manager: pre-departure training and development for German expatriates in China and Brazil', *Journal of Management Development* 10(7): 41–52.

Dowling, P. and Schuler, R. (1991) *International Dimensions of Human Resource Management*, Boston: PWS-Kent.

Forster, N. (1996) *A Report on the Management of Expatriates in 36 UK Companies 1994–1996*, Cardiff: Cardiff Business School.

Gonzales, R.F. and Neghandi, A.R. (1967) *The United States Executive: His Orientation and Career Patterns*, East Lansing: MSU Graduate School of Business Administration.

Gullahorn, J.T. and Gullahorn, J.E. (1963) 'An extension of the U-curve hypothesis', *Journal of Social Science* 19(3): 33–47.

Harris, J.C. (1973) 'A science of the South Pacific: analysis of the character structure of the Peace Corps volunteer', *American Psychologist* 28: 232–47.

Harris, P.R. and Moran, R.T. (1979) *Managing Cultural Differences*, 2nd edn, Houston: Gulf.

Harvey, M.G. (1985) 'The executive family: an overlooked variable in international assignments', *Columbia Journal of World Business*, spring: 131–44.

Hautaluoma, J.E. and Kaman, V. (1975) 'Description of Peace Corps volunteers' experience in Afghanistan', *Topics in Culture Learning* 3: 79–96.

Hawes, F. and Kealey, D. (1981) 'An empirical study of Canadian technical assistance: adaptation and effectiveness on overseas assignment', *International Journal of Intercultural Relations* 5(3): 239–58.

Hays, R.D.(1971) 'Ascribed behavioural determinants of success–failure among US expatriate managers', *Journal of International Business Studies* 2(1): 40–46.

—— (1974) 'Expatriate selection: insuring success and avoiding failure', *Journal of International Business Studies* 5(1): 25–37.

Howard, C.G. (1974) 'The returning overseas executive: cultural shock in reverse', *Human Resource Management* 13(2): 22–6.

Industrial Democracy in Europe (IDE) Research Group (1981) 'Industrial democracy in Europe: differences and similarities across countries and hierarchies', *Organisation Studies* 2(2): 113–30.

Ivancevich, J.M. (1969) 'Selection of American managers for overseas assignments', *Personnel Journal* 18(3): 189–200.

Janssens, M. (1992) 'International job transfers: a comprehensive model of expatriate managers' cross-cultural adjustment', paper presented to EIASM Conference on Industrial Staffing and Mobility, Cranfield, September.

Kobrin, S. (1988) 'Expatriate reduction and strategic control in American multinational corporations', *Human Resource Management* 27(1): 63–7.

Lannier, A.R. (1979) 'Selecting and preparing personnel for overseas transfers', *Personnel Journal* 58(3): 106–63.

Mendenhall, M. and Oddou, G. (1985) 'The dimensions of expatriate acculturation: a review', *Academy of Management Review* 10(1): 39–487.

—— (1986) 'Acculturation profiles of expatriate managers: implications for cross-cultural training programs', *Columbia Journal of Business*, winter: 73–9.

Mendenhall, M., Punnett, B.J. and Ricks, D. (1995) *Global Management*, Cambridge MA: Blackwell.

Miller, E.L. (1973) 'The international selection decision: a study of some dimensions of managerial behaviour in the selection decision process', *Academy of Management Journal* 16(2): 239–52.

Oberg, K. (1960) 'Culture shock: adjustment to new cultural environments', *Practical Anthropologist* 7: 177–82.

Philips, N. (1993) 'Cross-cultural training', *Journal of European Industrial Training* 17(2).

Pickard, J. and Brewster, C. (1992) 'Evaluation of expatriate training', Farnham Castle: Centre for International Briefing.

Rahim, A. (1983) 'A model for developing key expatriate executives', *Personnel Journal* 62(4): 312–17.

Rehfuss, J. (1982) 'Management development and the selection of overseas executives', *Personnel Administrator* 27(7): 35–43.

Robock, S. H. and Simmonds, K. (1983) *International Business and Multinational Enterprises*, Homewood IL: Irwin.

Ronen, S. (1989) 'Training the international assignee', in I. Goldstein (ed.) *Training and Career Development*, San Francisco: Jossey-Bass.

Schuler, R.S., Fulkerson, J.R. and Dowling, P. J. (1991) 'Strategic performance measurement and management in multinational corporations', *Human Resource Management* 30: 365–92.

Scullion, H. (1993) 'Creating international managers: recruitment and development issues' in P. Kirkbride (ed.) *Human Resource Management in Europe*, London: Routledge.

Stone, R.J. (1991) 'Expatriate selection and failure', *Human Resource Planning* 14(1): 9–18.

Suutari, V. and Brewster, C. (1998) 'The adaptation of expatriates in Europe: evidence from Finnish companies', *Personnel Review* 27(): 89–103.

Torbiörn, I. (1982) *Living Abroad: Personal Adjustment and Personnel Policy in the Overseas Setting*, New York: Wiley.

Trompenaars, F. (1993) *Riding the Waves of Culture*, London: The Economist Books.

Tung, R.L. (1981) 'Selection and training of personnel for overseas assignments', *Columbia Journal of World Business* 16(1): 68–78.

—— (1982) 'Selection and training procedures of US, European and Japanese Multinationals, *California Management Review* 25: 57–71.

Windham International and the National Foreign Trade Council (1997) *Global Relocation Trends 1996 Survey Report*, New York: Windham International.

Zeira, Y. and Banai, M. (1984) 'Selection of expatriate managers in MNEs: the host-environment point of view', *International Studies of Management and Organisation* 15(1): 33–51.

—— (1985) 'Present and desired methods of selecting expatriate managers for international assignments', *Personnel Review* 13(3): 29–35.

13 Repatriation and career systems

Finnish public and private sector repatriates in their career lines

Tuomo Peltonen

Introduction

Within management of international staff, issues related to selection, training and expatriate adjustment have received plenty of attention in international HRM research (Mendenhall *et al.* 1987; Sparrow and Hiltrop 1994). The repatriation phenomenon, however, is still largely left empirically unexplored or is approached from such a variety of perspectives (e.g. Adler 1981; Harvey 1989; Black 1992) that no coherent research programme can be established. As a result, our understanding of what is happening in repatriation, what factors are behind it and how they operate is very limited. The need to increase theoretical and empirical understanding of repatriation is further multiplied by the immediate re-entry problems with which the HR function is coping (e.g. Hamill 1989).

It is now acknowledged that repatriation from an international assignment often poses greater adjustment difficulties than the initial expatriate transition (Black and Gregersen 1991; Black 1992). Theoretically, previous research has explained the problems encountered by repatriates as an indication of a malfunctioning career and HR system (Harvey 1989; Oddou and Mendenhall 1991). Repatriates are received by their home organizations not as learners but as strangers (Adler 1981), manifesting an ethnocentric, xenophobic corporate culture (Adler and Ghadar 1990). Repatriates feel that their competence boost is not valued or utilized in their home unit tasks. This is irrational, given the multinational firms' urge to develop a management and organization culture capable of balancing local relativism and global homogenization (Evans 1992; Peltonen 1993; Kamoche 1997). The repatriate career outcomes, which tend to downplay international experience, are thus seen as manifestations of the actual values and norms of the firm (Welch 1994). These contradict the official rhetoric and thus lead to frustration and turnover as investing in international experience does not bring about the expected raise in status.

An understanding of the organizational logic behind repatriate career outcomes would be helpful for HR and line managers in their design of international HR strategies and staffing policies which are more sensitive to the structure and culture of the organizations in which international careers evolve. To advance this, a wider view of the structures underlying re-entry phenomenon is needed to inform empirical research. First, to grasp fully the career culture at work in an international firm, it is appropriate to assume that current systems are rational enough in themselves, rather than to juxtapose in advance 'rational' global logic with 'malfunctioning' ethnocentric logic. Researching, for example, the actual preferences which are employed in selection and promotion situations (Pfeffer 1989) or manifested in the orientation of strategic managers (Gunz 1989) gives a more grounded view on what traits and dispositions are valued in the firm.

Second, though the way a career culture values international experience often becomes explicit first when repatriate career rewards are allocated, the career logic structures paths and opportunities from the time an individual enters an organization or occupation (Kanter 1977; Rosenbaum 1984). The real but latent status differences of a cohort may not be visible until central posts come to be filled. From the research viewpoint it is misleading to focus solely on status changes during the expatriate–repatriate transition because by that time career paths are already to a large extent differentiated and the rankings of each individual informally set (Peltonen 1997). Longitudinal constructions of processes and career trajectories could shed more light on how repatriate outcomes evolve in and through gradual socialization and division of careerists in organizational practices.

Informed by these insights from the contemporary career theory, this chapter reports two studies of Finnish repatriates in their career systems and career lines. The chapter first introduces the data and method of analysis of the two sub-studies. It then presents the findings from both studies separately and summarizes the main findings. This is followed by a concluding section.

The two studies: data and method

Study 1 A survey of Finnish International Development repatriates

This study was a survey of Finnish professionals with an academic degree. The sample group consisted of expatriates who had worked on projects organized or financed by the Finnish International Development Agency. The target group included expatriates who had worked abroad for at least six months. Also, their repatriation had taken place at least one year but not more than six years prior to the time of research. The questionnaire included questions relating to the respondents' background, the work history prior to expatriation, the time spent abroad and the return. The initial analysis concentrated on the impact on careers of an international development assignment and factors related to the career impact. Career impact was classified as being either positive, neutral or negative. Next, an analysis of factors such as the motivation to seek the assignment, educational background, the type of expatriate position held as well as the perceived learning impact of expatriate experience and their connection to the career impact, was carried out. The analysis thus sought to construct career paths and career orientations retrospectively from the answers which respondents had given regarding their work history. The method used in constructing the structural logic of careers was a grounded theory approach to quantitative data, in which theoretical propositions on causal mechanisms are heuristically generated from the data (Glaser and Strauss 1967: Ch. 8). Analysis did not seek to test any pre-existing set of hypotheses, but to generate new insights on career logic producing repatriate outcomes. Because the aim was to generate theoretical propositions, tests of significance were not used to verify the connections. The study is reported in detail in Peltonen (1991) and its theoretical findings are developed in Peltonen (1997).

Study 2 A study of career culture in two Finnish firms

To develop the initial propositions of the first study further, another study was conducted. It employed organization level and individual level qualitative data from two MNCs as well as secondary quantitative data from Finnish white-collar labour market structures to produce a richer description of how internal labour market career logic operates in practice. The study was made in a Finnish subsidiary organization of ABB (Asea Brown Boveri) and at Inc,[1] a major Finnish-based international company. ABB is a conglomerate in electrical engineering with over 200,000 employees worldwide. Inc operates in business areas related to electrical engineering with over 20,000 employees in more than 30 countries.

The career system properties were analysed using secondary data on Finnish business culture, engineering profession and managerial labour markets as well as interviews with HR managers in the case study organizations. Data on individual expatriates were obtained by interviewing the sojourners in their foreign locations. In ABB, expatriates were working in a sister unit of a Finnish organization. Here four engineers were interviewed. Two of them were assigned to manage a technology transfer project and two were involved in systems sales. At Inc interviews with four people, one senior manager, two middle managers and one product engineer, were included.

Expatriates in the interviews outlined their work history, career orientations, motivations and views on expatriation and gave their insights on repatriation and career future. These interviews were part of a larger study on career forms in corporations. For this chapter the expatriate material was analysed from two perspectives. First of interest were the objective careers, the work history from corporate recruitment through expatriation to the repatriation position. The aim of the analysis was to reveal patterns of rising and declining careers and thus to shed light on the structures and logic behind career advancement. To extend the career description to repatriation outcomes, the expatriates' objective career was followed after the field work to see to what kinds of positions they were then holding. ABB expatriates' location was checked four years after the interview, Inc expatriates one year after the interview session. This further research gave information on whether the person was still employed by the same firm, whether he had repatriated or not, what formal position he held and in what functional area he worked at that time. Although the repatriate check on Inc expatriates was done after a shorter period of time than the ABB expatriates, their careers were already in the process of differentiating. Two of them were continuing their careers in core tasks in Finland, while two others were continuing volatile expatriate careers in the subsidiary.

Second, the meanings attributed to career path and self during the expatriate period were subject to analysis. Following Barley's (1989: 55–7) notion that career narratives and scripts are differentiated according to the ranking status of the actor, a textual analysis of how narratives and interpretations of career varied already during the expatriate period was undertaken.

Empirical findings on career lines and norms

Study 1

The survey indicated re-entry career outcomes similar to those observed in other studies (Table 13.1). Of the sample, 27 per cent reported a positive career impact, 63 per cent indicated that career level was the same, while for 10 per cent the expatriate assignment resulted in a demotion as compared to pre-expatriation status.

Elsewhere, Forster (1994) reports that of a UK sample, 21 per cent enjoyed repatriate promotion, while 30 per cent felt they were demoted upon return. Oddou and Mendenhall's (1991) study found that 29 per cent of the sample had a positive impact on career and 20 per cent felt repatriation was a demotion. Furthermore, Derr and Oddou (1991) report that in their study, 23 per cent were promoted, with 18 per cent suffering from downward career mobility.

From the career system point of view, the sample studied in this survey was not homogeneous. Expatriate career cycles included in the study contained both internal assignments within a corporation and external professional transfers from one domestic employer to another. Internal assignments in the case of Finnish International Development are mainly technology transfer projects, implemented by engineering firms. External assignments take place when the person is a professional moving in a freelance type of career with the aim of gaining competence for management of international relations and international development, mainly in Finnish or international governmental organizations.

Table 13.1 Career impact of the International Development expatriate experience among Finnish repatriates

Career impact of the assignment	%
Positive	27
Neutral	63
Negative	10
Total	100
N	165

These two career fields may embody different career logics. To investigate this, the sample was divided into two categories according to the type of repatriation transfer: either back to the pre-expatriate employer or to an organization different from the pre-expatriate workplace. Note that the focus here is on the career impact from pre-expatriate to repatriate position. As the domestic career system posits continuities through picking up pre-expatriate stigmas upon re-entry, the links between expatriate and repatriate positions are of lesser importance (Peltonen 1997).

When classified into two career system categories, repatriate career outcomes are distributed in different ways in each category (Table 13.2). Those within internal transfer type experience less positive or negative changes compared to the pre-expatriate position. Instead, most (76 per cent) indicate that expatriate experience had no notable impact in either direction. External labour market repatriates, in contrast, had more variance in career impact: 44 per cent indicated promotions, while 17 per cent had received a less prestigious position.

This suggests that career stakes get higher when the re-entry takes place in an external professional career system. The chance of getting ahead is higher, but so is the possibility of ending up in an inferior career position. This observation further supports the view that there are two career systems in operation in the sample.

Within each career system, evidence for particular dependencies and mechanisms of career mobility was found. Within the internal re-entry, those with positive career impact had an instrumental approach to expatriation. They mentioned gaining merit for international tasks most often as the motivation for expatriation, whereas for the others this category was fourth or sixth in the list of factors behind the decision to accept the expatriate post. They also perceived that they were well prepared for the assignment: 74 per cent said that their competence was sufficient for the expatriate tasks, while in the other groups 39 per cent and 57 per cent thought they were very well prepared professionally for the tasks.

To some extent, the climbers in the internal career system category seem to have pre-rationalized the impact of the expatriate experience on their

Table 13.2 Career impact of the International Development expatriate experience by transfer type

Career impact of the assignment	Type of transfer	
	Internal %	*External* %
Positive	18	44
Neutral	76	39
Negative	6	17
Total	100	100
N	111	54

development. Those with a steady or downward career trend, in turn, were initially more motivated by the international environment (most and second most frequently mentioned) and the stimulus it might bring (third most and most frequently mentioned), but did not link this to instrumental career planning. Also, those reporting a negative career impact indicated that most changes in attitudes and skills were not directly linked to professional competence. They were four times more likely to indicate these cross-cultural experiences than professional changes, whereas in other career impact groups professional and non-professional learning impacts were mentioned in equal numbers. Over half of those demoted also worked in managerial tasks as compared to the 18 per cent and 33 per cent in other career impact groups.

It could be reasoned from these findings that the career system underlying the expatriate–repatriate transitions favours an instrumental and opportunistic career style and neglects the merits of those with an open attitude towards cross-cultural learning opportunities. As Rosenbaum's (1984) study on corporate career systems suggests, showing signs of career success is crucial for being thought of as high potential. As an organization scans a cohort for high potentials, it draws attention to signals of ability instead of objective competence criteria. Central in the search for signals is the perceived potential to receive managerial tasks in the future. This is often read from the impressions of being an upwardly mobile person and moving fast to esteemed positions (Whitley *et al.* 1981). Once identified, high potentials are then moved to a track where they are being trained and assessed as managerial candidates, that is, where their signalled potential becomes anchored in definitions and biased assessment criteria naturalizes them as bearers of specific abilities. Those not chosen for the core high potential cohort are often labelled as having less potential, and in their subsequent career they are constantly assessed as to their 'inherent' low potential skills (see Goffman 1961). In this way novel experiences indicating potential for managerial tasks do not get registered among less central employees

Table 13.3 Internal transfer repatriates: typical characteristics in each career impact group

Career impact group	Typical characteristics in the group
Positive impact	• Instrumental orientation towards the international experience as a career step • Pre-rationalized the expatriate period as smooth and as one without difficulties
Neutral impact	• Getting change from routine work an important motivation for expatriation • Had no plans for international work period prior to expatriation
Negative impact	• Have experienced more non-professional changes as a result of the expatriate period • Occupied responsible, managerial tasks during the expatriate period

because such abstract and strategic skills do not fit the prescribed profile of an individual labelled as a low potential.

The tournament career logic is also capable of explaining why so many responses in the survey indicated international development assignments as having a neutral career impact. This categorization is probably the result of the considerable length of time over which career rankings reveal themselves. Most of the repatriates had not as yet experienced clear evidence of succeeding or failing to gain an aspired-for post by the time of the second survey.

For those who repatriated in external labour market career systems, different mechanisms were found to be at work. In this category, the positive career impact group consisted of younger and better educated persons as compared to the two other groups: 57 per cent were under 40 years of age, while in other groups the share of this age group was 11 per cent and 45 per cent. Of the career advancers, 10 per cent had a doctoral degree, while none in other groups had one. Of those belonging to the positive career impact group 76 per cent had a master's degree: in the other groups 29 per cent and 56 per cent. Advancers were also most likely to have started planning an international development assignment while still in higher education. This timing was chosen twice as many times as other stages of occupational life among the career advancer group. Responses from the other groups revealed an equal split between the education period and later occupational stages to indicate the start of conscious plans for international development assignments. Of those reporting a positive career impact, 45 per cent had had more than one international assignment: 43 per cent of respondents reporting a neutral career impact had had more than one expatriate experience whereas of those reporting a negative career impact only 22 per cent had had several several international assignments. Additionally, of those reporting a positive career impact, only 10 per cent had a technical education, most being medical, agricultural or social experts (these three fields totalling 71 per cent). In the other groups these three educational backgrounds amounted to 24 per cent and 44 per cent. Those with negative career impact were strikingly older than the rest: 44 per cent per cent were over 50 years of age as compared to 10 per cent and 15 per cent in other groups. Of those demoted, 78 per cent were also on their first expatriate assignment. (See Table 13.4.)

These findings suggest that career values in this system are somewhat different from those found in the internal labour market career system. The research suggests that commitment to the substantial issues of international development and practical experience are valued. Critical success factors also included the fact that advancers had been planning international career steps for a long time and often had a non-technical education in fields close to the activities of FINNIDA development projects.

The career system behind these tendencies and values is close to what Kanter (1989) describes as the professional career logic. In a professional career structure, rewards and status are dependent on reputation and social networks. As these are developed from early educational experiences onwards and nurtured thereafter, opportunism and high-speed style are not necessarily suitable career

Table 13.4 External transfer repatriates: typical characteristics in each career impact group

Career impact group	Typical characteristics in the group
Positive impact	• Highly educated in the specific area of expertise • Has specialized in the field closely linked to International Development activities • Committed from early on to an international career • Possesses international experience
Neutral impact	• Possesses international experience • Works directly for UN or other International Development agency or association
Negative impact	• In average older than the repatriates in other groups • Had been out on an expatriate assignment only once

strategies. Instead, long and patient commitment to the body of knowledge and professional practice as well as to occupational networks are the main assets in getting ahead.

Furthermore, as in this case, professional networks are basically international from the outset. Cross-national transfers are not necessarily movements across systems or to margins of a system, rather, they are most of all encounters with actors of importance at the moment of expatriation and also well beyond that into the future. Therefore the system favours professionally oriented expatriates for whom expatriation–repatriation is an integral element in the expansion of knowledge and contacts. A succession of international assignments expands the network coverage and can assist the individual in becoming central to the organization. These careerists are also logically relatively young, because this way the network capital is useful in forthcoming challenges in international work. Those with negative career impact have, from the professional career logic's viewpoint, little chance of creating credibility as recognized professionals within the occupational community. They are not in the business of gaining reputation and social capital, but have either drifted to such tasks or are motivated by the extrinsic rewards of expatriate life. Consequently, in this system they are not provided upon re-entry with such opportunities as the committed international development professionals.

Summary of the results from Study 1

The survey evidence gave support to the idea that repatriate career outcomes have an underlying structural logic. The findings also showed that there are different kinds of career systems and that each system embodies specific norms and arrangements for allocating individuals into central and marginal careerists. The subsequent study sheds some additional light on how repatriate careers are structured in the corporate context. It also illustrates some of the complexities created by organizational and professional career systems overlapping each other.

Study 2 Engineer dominance in expatriate and managerial labour markets

The first observation drawn from the group of expatriates studied in the two firms is that the sample is engineer dominated. Furthermore, top management in both of the case study firms was dominated by engineers. This domination by one occupational group raises several queries concerning career paths. Why is it that only engineers have access to esteemed posts and the expatriate labour market? How does the engineer-manager career unfold in firms?

'Engineering' of industrial management is noted and some explanations of the maintenance of the elite position of this group through career and socialization are provided in studies of Finnish business culture. As Lilja and Tainio (1996) have noted, an engineering background is the prerequisite for access into prestigious career lines in industrial firms in Finland (see also Lilja, Räsänen and Tainio 1992). Historically, the professional status of engineers is a product of Finnish nation-building between the World Wars. Engineers were raised by the state into a position of technologist leaders of industry (Särkikoski 1993). Today the normal career pattern of a university engineer is well institutionalized and one of its functions is to supply into firms new technological specialists who are also capable of handling managerial issues (Lilja and Tainio 1996: 178). The success of this strategy is reflected in the composition of top management: 42 of Finland's 77 exchange-listed companies are led by engineers (Vesikansa 1998).

Seen from the career development standpoint, an engineering background is a prerequisite for career paths to the top in industrial firms in Finland. As an expatriate post is nowadays taken as a key developmental experience for the future managerial cadre, it is logical that the engineering system reserves the international assignment post primarily for its own members. Yet the engineering community has its own internal divisions. In the Finnish educational system, an academic engineering degree can be obtained both at master and at bachelor level. BSc engineers graduate from technical colleges, MSc engineers from universities of technology.[2] College engineers very seldom proceed to general management. Frequently they start in peripheral sales and marketing functions in firms. Though these non-technological duties may take them quickly into tasks resembling a high-potential career, this is not an indication of a prestigious career line. College engineers often stay in sales and marketing tasks and are subject to transfers, demotion and, subsequently, turnover.

University engineers start their work life in projects (Lilja and Tainio 1996: 164). Their career advances very subtly, often in successive R&D assignments. Little by little university engineers assume more responsibility in the project teams. This apprenticeship time in technology driven projects also involves socialization into the tactics of the engineering elite. The move from engineering into management may then take place rather dramatically as university engineers are promoted from seemingly operative tasks to assume general responsibility.

Differentiated repatriation outcomes in the sample

The repatriate career outcomes in the small sample of individual expatriates seemed to take two shapes: those with continuity and promotion and those in which the individuals experienced difficulties in linking international experience to career opportunities and were therefore likely to leave. A closer look revealed that this division was connected to the educational background and related career paths. Of the whole sample, three university engineers out of four returned within a year after the interview and are all continuing to work in the same organization and in tasks related to their previous experience. For all three the repatriate position was higher in the hierarchy than their pre-expatriate post. One university engineer did not have a degree in electric engineering but in mechanical engineering. He had not started his career in domestic R&D or production technology tasks but had worked abroad for several years in technical sales and international operations. He had also changed employer during this time. After a year he still worked in the foreign office. Of three college engineers, two had returned within a couple of years but both had left the firm after repatriation and were now working elsewhere. The third was continuing his assignment abroad. This suggests that repatriation outcomes are differentiated along the college engineer–university engineer divide. The university engineer with a 'deviant' specialization in mechanics and an international sales-oriented work history had a career pattern closest to college engineers. This was also the probable reason for him to suffer from the limited opportunities and the delay of repatriation.

The analysis of objective and subjective careers shows that university and college engineers were embedded in different patterns and that they interpreted their expatriate task in a dissimilar fashion.

Career lines leading to repatriation

College engineers had started in international tasks. Three of them were especially recruited to handle international sales and marketing. For all four this career line had brought about, during their early careers, a change of employer in search of suitable vacancies in semi-external corporate labour markets. The four university engineers, in contrast, had all started their careers in technical duties, often after company-based thesis work. Their career path had continued steadily ever since, involving internal moves within the corporation.

The college engineer group had been out on assignment before: three out of four had previous expatriate experiences. These were mostly in the field of marketing and coordination of international activities. Two had been abroad for several years and could be seen as career expatriates. The university engineer group also included two individuals with more than one expatriate period. However, these multi-sojourners had been involved in operative technology transfer duties and had normally returned to continue a 'domestic' career. Thus they were not career expatriates in the same way as several of the college engineers.

This evidence could be taken as an indicator of two main career lines among engineers in Finnish corporations. Following Kanter (1977), career lines are here understood as prestructured career paths that lead from entry gates into distinct status positions. The university engineer line starts with an apprenticeship in R&D and production and leads to centrality and potentially to general or technology management. The college engineer career begins with a formal recruitment into technical sales and develops mostly within marketing; in operative or middle management.

Expatriation is included in both career lines. University engineers often pass during international assignments from operative to managerial tasks. College engineers, in contrast, are abroad as a logical outcome of their international marketing career and continue similar tasks upon re-entry. Taking two career lines and the location of sojourner post into account, the repatriation outcomes observed in the sample become understandable. University engineers move ahead into centrality and higher status as they go through the expatriate transitions, while college engineers become trapped into a group of less central 'internationalists', whose advancement has already peaked in international assignments. Hence emerges the positive career impact of university engineers and the negative career impact of college engineers.

Interpretations of career goals during the expatriate period

The different status of university and college engineers leading to varying repatriation effects is probably already evident during the expatriate period. As Barley (1989) has noted, the ranking status of actors is often reflected in their accounts of personal career trajectory. The cultural and discursive resources used by the group of Finnish expatriates presented above, as well as the narrative strategies of university and college engineers, are analysed in depth elsewhere (Peltonen 1998a, b). This chapter will not go into such detailed textual analysis, but draws out findings related to differences in the way engineers set their goals and aspiration levels for their careers.

College engineers saw as their initial career motivation an interest in international business, especially marketing. Many emphasized their conscious choice to acquire international experience and competence and later to find a work environment where they could pursue this orientation.

The university engineer included in the marginal group said: 'I wanted to have a job that suits my character . . . Since I was at the university, certain internationalism has fascinated me. There is some indefinable attraction in being abroad.'

A college engineer recounts: 'My career wishes were: international work in a technical environment; that was a pretty natural career choice. I spent a couple of student summers in Europe, travelled a lot, and so on . . . Only the few international firms in Finland attracted me when I graduated.'

Within the international career 'anchor', an expatriate post seems to stand for the ultimate goal for career advancement. Being an expatriate is in many ways treated in accounts as the intensification of all the challenges and requirements which an international business life can pose. Therefore to cope with expatriate life is to reach for the career peak. This was illustrated in comments which emphasized the hard work of cultural adjustment and learning and the shallowness of other expatriates' attitudes towards these issues.

For example, a college engineer contrasts the ideal cosmopolitanism he is pursuing and the brutal Finnish attitude to internationalism in a sarcastic manner:

> For me the most important thing is that life works. I can say to my family that in two hours we'll move to another country, and they will say 'a-ha' and start packing.
>
>   I would like the people in Finland to remember that the globe does not circle around Finland . . . When you are abroad you cannot go and say to a foreigner that I am smarter than you because we have more demanding matriculation examinations in Finland than you have here.

College engineers, with longer exposure to expatriate life, construct their career project as one of becoming a truly global player in business. This created some ambivalence as they all faced, sooner or later, a return to Finland. This meant in their narrative a move away from pursuing the individual career project of 'internationalism' (Peltonen 1998b). Re-entry was, in their accounts, a compromise in development but also, to ease the image of an unfinished global project, a move towards new goals.

University engineers spoke less about internationalism as their career motivation. In their stories, technology and practical competence figured more often. Many emphasized adolescent experiences with technological hobbies and linked these traits to career choices. Accounts of pre-expatriate work history centred around the engineering world, with occasional struggles to come to terms with team management and business logic. Expatriation is seen as an abrupt change and is narrated as an extrinsic offer rather than a voluntary choice.

An engineer who had worked in product development comments on his expatriate transition as follows: 'To answer how I ended up being an expatriate: I have got into here; there is no personal plan behind the move.'

As far as expatriation's role in career goals is concerned, university engineers interpreted the international experience as one, albeit special, experience among others on their way to management. As sojourners, university engineers were putting all their competence into use in coping with the complexity of their situation. Simultaneously, however, they believed they were transforming themselves through this coping into more perceptive generalists.

All the experience accumulated in previous phases of life is put into use as in expatriate settings stretching and sacrificing as a champion is required in the face of organizational problems. For example an engineer says: 'I left for abroad as a technical specialist and I have acted as one, but that aside, as one looks how this firm works . . . I have the habit that I cannot keep my mouth shut . . . Quite a lot

I have been compelled – and have had the chance – to talk about whether the things could be made with less bureaucracy and better . . . '

Along with this stretching, the transformation into a more generalist identity occurs in stories seeing the expatriate post as involving potential for reflection on and distancing of one's past. As a result, both personal self-identity and organizational relations appear now in stories for engineers from a more comprehensive perspective. This superior perception is noted, for example, in the following comment: 'This [expatriation] opens one's view and stands for a moment to take some breath. I hope that when I go back I would be capable of seeing better what to develop in our organization.'

To conclude, college engineers saw expatriate positions as the goal of their career development. University engineers, in contrast, saw themselves moving in a trajectory which leads through a sojourner experience into more substantial challenges in Finnish management.

College engineers' career goals were thus lower than university engineers. As Barley (1989: 55–7) suggests, lower status employees are provided with a script which sets their aspiration level lower. In this way social order is maintained, despite the stratification of employees and managers into hierarchically differentiated positions.

The lower status of college engineers is visible in the way they signify their work history and career future. The dependence of repatriation outcomes on career systems and organizational structuring occurring throughout the transitions is hereby further supported.

Summary of the results from Study 2

Study 2 explicated the process of career and repatriate outcomes in Finnish electrical engineering business. We noted first that engineers dominate the prestigious career lines in Finnish industrial firms. This culture was also illustrated in the composition of the expatriate staff in two case firms, which included almost solely engineer-educated specialists and managers. Moreover, within the engineering community, university engineers occupy the central position and reach the highest ranks in corporations. College engineers, in contrast, are relegated to a less central career line. In a university engineer career line, expatriation equals an upward career swing as operative tasks are often changed into managerial duties. College engineers' careers, in contrast, lead to marginality by first taking them into international tasks and later bringing about a repatriate career plateau. This hierarchical setting that separates university and college engineers was also to be observed in the way engineers narrated their career from the expatriate location. University engineers set their career goals higher than college engineers. University engineers saw expatriate posts as a springboard for more challenging posts whereas college engineers held internationalism as their career goal and interpreted expatriate life as the culmination of the project of personal development.

Conclusions

This chapter set out to understand the logic behind the repatriation career outcomes in Finnish public and private sector contexts. This enterprise was informed by a number of theoretical insights. First, assuming that repatriation career experience is only the tip of the iceberg in processes structuring paths and the terrain of careers, the chapter focused on empirically examining the systems in which career structuring occurs. Common to all career systems are norms which identify what dispositions are valued and a differentiation of individuals into those closer to the ideals and centrality of each organization and those further away from the core (Schein 1971). Being relegated to marginal positions causes at certain points disappointments and constraints on work opportunities, whereas centrality is associated with an increasing access to rewards and prestigious posts. However, in the temporal unfolding of individual careers these positions are often latent and may even temporarily contradict the formal status occupied by central and marginal employees. As repatriation is frequently associated in theory and practice with unexpected or irrational career moves, it was reasoned in the chapter that what were previously latent rankings in work history are often during the re-entry actualized into a more permanent division into central and less central individuals. For example, in Study 2, the college engineers, despite being internationally competent and having occupied visible positions, could not access higher level posts upon re-entry.

Second, the career outcomes faced in the repatriation are related to patterned career paths. Career paths are structured so that certain types of career lines lead to higher ranks while others do not. Some career lines do not even reach the expatriate level. This is probably true for most women, as Harris indicates in Chapter 14 of this volume. Some lines enjoy the expatriate transfer but do not proceed to higher ranks upon repatriation. Finally, the most central employees move through international assignments into prestigious posts.

Third, career systems channelling people into career lines leading to centrality and marginality are not universal. Rather, they vary from country to country and industry to industry, and are not homogeneous even within an organization (Barley 1989; Derr and Laurent 1989; Evans *et al.* 1989; Kanter 1989). In Study 1, this was illustrated in two rather different logics according to which repatriate career rewards were allocated. Internal labour market systems valued high-flyer styles, external labour market systems valued professional commitment and network capital. Both studies showed how occupational groups are often organized into career systems, with their own norms and institutional arrangements for professional and managerial career paths (Grey 1984; Van Maanen and Barley 1984). In the case of Finnish engineering careers, the occupational system installs its norms and logic into the organizational practices and power structure.

The variance of career systems at work in repatriate decisions implies that it is a matter of empirical research to find out the career lines and norms behind the repatriate stratification and to explore the institutional conditioning of the local career system in operation: whether there are many systems at work and whether they operate separately or in concordance. Apart from purely descriptive studies, an HR policy view is obviously interested in the rejection of international learning and cosmopolitanism as a credit in career systems. As the Finnish evidence shows, corporate career systems seem to reward instrumental attitude towards expatriate career development rather than a learning commitment. Also, if a careerist is on a central career line, expatriation becomes necessarily a mere formal merit or credential. In the professional international development career system international learning was valued more and building cross-cultural capabilities and network capital comprised a key feature in central career lines. This implies that unless the actual 'business' of the organization is related to international relations and cultural interaction, career culture has difficulties in rewarding expatriate learning and international exposure. More research is, of course, needed on other career contexts to verify this inference. Anyway, even though corporate career systems may have difficulties in truly valuing cultural and societal learning, there is always the possibility of change, either intended or unintended, in the culture of career.

Notes

1 To protect the anonymity guaranteed, a pseudonym is used to refer to this company.
2 College engineers gain a BSc degree after three years of full-time study.

References

Adler, N.J. (1981) 'Re-entry: managing cross-cultural transitions', *Group and Organization Studies* 6(3): 341–56.

Adler, N. and Ghadar, F. (1990) 'International strategy from the perspective of people and culture: the North American context', in A. Rugman (ed.) *Research in Global Strategic Management*, vol. 1. Greenwood CT: JAI Press.

Barley, S. (1989) 'Careers, identities and institutions', in M. Arthur, D. Hall and B. Lawrence (eds) *Handbook of Career Theory*, Cambridge: Cambridge University Press.

Black, J. (1992) 'Coming home: the relationship of expatriate expectations with repatriation adjustment and job performance', *Human Relations* 45: 177–92.

Black, J. and Gregersen, H. (1991) 'When Yankees come home: factors related to expatriate and spouse repatriation adjustment', *Journal of International Business Studies* 22: 671–94.

Derr, C.B. and Laurent, A. (1989) 'The external and internal career: a theoretical and cross-cultural perspective', in M. Arthur, D. Hall and B. Lawrence (eds) *Handbook of Career Theory*, Cambridge: Cambridge University Press.

Derr, C.B and Oddou, G. (1991) 'Are US multinationals adequately preparing future American leaders for global competition?', *International Journal of Human Resource Management* 2(2): 227–44.

Evans, P. (1992) 'Management development as glue technology', *Human Resource Planning* 25(1): 85–106.

Evans, P. Lank, E. and Farquhar, A. (1989) 'Managing human resources in the international firm: lessons from the practice', in P. Evans, Y. Doz and A. Laurent (eds) *Human Resource Management in International Firms*, London: Macmillan.

Forster, N. (1994) 'The forgotten employees'? The experiences of expatriate staff returning to the UK', *International Journal of Human Resource Management* 5: 405–25.

Glaser, B. and Strauss, A. (1967) *The Discovery of Grounded Theory*, New York: Aldine.

Goffman, E. (1961) 'The moral career of the mental patient', in E. Goffman *Asylums. Essays on the Social Situation of Mental Patients and Other Inmates*, New York: Doubleday Anchor.

Grey, C. (1994) 'Career as a project of the self and labour process discipline', *Sociology* 28(2): 479–97.

Gunz, H. (1989) *Careers and Corporate Cultures: Managerial Mobility in Large Corporations*, Oxford: Blackwell.

Hamill, J. (1989) 'Expatriate policies in British multinationals', *Journal of General Management* 14: 18–33.

Harvey, M.C. (1982) 'The other side of foreign assignments: dealing with the repatriation dilemma', *Columbia Journal of World Business* 2: 53–9.

—— (1989) 'Repatriation of corporate executives: an empirical study', *Columbia Journal of World Business* 20: 131–44.

Kamoche, K. (1997) 'Knowledge creation and learning in international HRM', *The International Journal of Human Resource Management* 8(3): 213–25.

Kanter, R.M. (1977) *Men and Women of the Corporation*, New York: Basic Books.

—— (1989) 'Careers and the wealth of the nations: a macro-perspective on structure and implications of career forms', in M. Arthur, D. Hall and B. Lawrence (eds) *Handbook of Career Theory*, Cambridge: Cambridge University Press.

Lilja, K. and Tainio, R. (1996) 'The nature of the typical Finnish firm', in R. Whitley and P.H. Kristensen (eds) *The Changing European Firm*, London: Routledge.

Lilja, L., Räsänen, R. and Tainio, R. (1992) 'The forest sector business recipe in Finland and its domination of the national business system', in R. Whitely (ed.) *European Business Systems*, London: Sage.

Mendenhall, M., Dunbar, E. and Oddou, G. (1987) 'Expatriate selection, training and career-pathing: a review and critique', *Human Resource Management* 26: 331–45.

Oddou, G. and Mendenhall, M. (1991) 'Succession planning for the 21st century: how well are we grooming our future business leaders?', *Business Horizons*, 34: 26–34.

Peltonen, T. (1991) *Ammattilaisten kehitysyhteistyökokemukset ja niiden vaikutus urakehitykseen* (Professionals' international development assignment and its impact on career), MSc thesis, Department of Management, Helsinki School of Economics and Business Administration, Finland.

—— (1993) 'Managerial career patterns in transnational corporations: an organizational capability approach', *European Management Journal* 11: 248–57.

—— (1997) 'Facing the rankings from the past: a tournament perspective on repatriate career mobility', *International Journal of Human Resource Management* 8(1): 106–23.

—— (1998a) 'Narrative construction of expatriate experience and career cycle: discursive patterns in Finnish stories of international career', *International Journal of Human Resource Management* (forthcoming).

—— (1998b) 'Managing becoming internationalized: narration of biography as performance of developmental subjectivity and strategies of normalization among Finnish expatriate engineers', a revised version of the paper presented at the 2nd international Conference on Organizational Discourse, University of London, 24–5 July 1996.

Pfeffer, J. (1989) 'A political perspective on careers: interests, networks and environments', in M. Arthur, D. Hall and B. Lawrence (eds) *Handbook of Career Theory*, Cambridge: Cambridge University Press.

Rosenbaum, J. (1984) *Career Mobility in Corporate Hierarchy*, New York: Academic.

Särkikoski, T. (1993) 'Teorian ja Käytännö Välissä: Tikniikan Professionalistumine. Suomessa' (In between theory and practice: the professionalization of technology in Finland) in E. Konttinen (ed.) *Ammattikunnat, Yhteiskunta jo Valtio: Suomalaisten Professioiden Kehityskuvia* (Occupations, society and the state: on the development of Finnish professions), publication of the Department of Sociology, no. 55, Jyväskylä, University of Jyväskylä.

Schein, E. (1971) 'The individual, the organization and the career: a conceptual scheme', *Journal of Applied Behavioral Science* 7: 401–26.

Sparrow, P. and Hiltrop, J.-M. (1994) *European Human Resource Management in Transition*, Hemel Hempstead: Prentice Hall.

Van Maanen, J. and Barley, S. (1984) 'Occupational communities: culture and control in organizations', in B. Staw and L. Cummings (eds) *Research in Organizational Behavior*, vol. 6, Greenwich CT: JAI Press.

Welch, D. (1994) 'Determinants of international human resource management approaches and activities: a suggested framework', *Journal of Management Studies* 31: 139–64.

Vesikansa, J. (1998) 'Teekkarin haaareista kuoritutuu superpomo', *Talous-Sanomat* 7(2): 15–16.

Whitley, R., Allen, T. and Marceau, J. (1981) *Masters of Business? Business Schools and Business School Graduates in Britain and France*, London: Tavistock.

14 Women in international management

Why are they not selected?

Hilary Harris

Introduction

One of the few facts about women in international management is that there are
very few of them. Statistics show that women make up between 2 per cent and
15 per cent of the total international management population (Adler 1984a;
Brewster 1991; Reynolds and Bennett 1991; ECA 1994; Harris 1996). The
paucity of women in international management has been attributed primarily to
factors external to the home country organization: women's own lack of interest;
dual-career couple constraints; host country managers' and clients' prejudice.
This chapter provides evidence that the real cause for concern may lie within
organizations' own selection systems for international assignments, which result
in few women being picked to take up a position abroad.

A business justification

As we have seen in Chapter 1, key trends in the business environment suggest
that in the future, the ability of women to progress to senior management
positions in major organizations is likely to be influenced by the extent to which
they have been able to gain international experience. The need to operate effectively on an international level has resulted in an increasing use of international
management assignments as an integral part of career development for potential
senior managers (Feldman and Thomas 1992; Forster 1992; Scullion 1994).

Precluding women from taking international assignments, as the statistics
suggest, is particularly puzzling if one considers that women now comprise 26
per cent of junior and middle managers in the UK (*Labour Force Survey* 1989). It
is from these positions that most international managers are picked: either as
management development exercises for young, high-potential candidates (Adler
1986–7; Dowling *et al.* 1994; Scullion 1994; Mendenhall *et al.* 1995); or to give
promising middle managers broader experience to equip them for senior
management positions. Linked to this is evidence of the minimal participation
of women at board level, with a figure of approximately 0.5 per cent women
executive directors and 3 per cent women non-executive directors reported for
1995 among FT-SE 100 companies in the UK (Conyon and Mallin 1996). Again

this reflects the absence of diversity and the failure to make full use of organizations' human resource assets. The minimal participation rate of women in international assignments may therefore have long-term career implications.

Organizational acceptance of the existing reliance on male appointments to international management roles must be questioned on a number of counts. First, from a purely economic viewpoint, assumptions that the existing system is satisfactory must be measured against US-based evidence of high rates of expatriate failure and the substantial costs entailed in such a situation (Mendenhall and Oddou 1985; Mendenhall *et al.* 1987). Second, changing socio-cultural norms suggest that fewer men will be willing to take up international assignments as a result of dual-career couple and balance of life considerations (Cooper and Makin 1985; Brett and Reilly 1990; Forster 1990; Scullion 1994). Third, demographic changes in the workforce support the need to widen the pool from which potential international managers are selected. Within the UK, women now make up just under 45 per cent of the total labour force (*Labour Force Survey* 1995), with this figure expected to rise to approximately 50 per cent by the end of the decade. Limiting international experience to only half the workforce implies that organizations are not maximizing the effectiveness of their human resources. Fourth, the emphasis on interpersonal, intuitive and co-operative skills for effective international management has been argued to be more suited to a woman's style of management (Marshall 1984; Vinnicombe 1987; Rosener 1990; Sharma 1990). Finally, the legislative framework in Europe calls for equal opportunities within the workplace.

A theoretical gap

Despite the paucity of women in international management, little previous research has been carried out. Of the research which has been done, the most significant relates to the North American context and deals primarily with empirical evidence. As yet, the area does not have a well-developed theoretical foundation.

The paucity of women in international management is mainly perceived to be a result of individual factors: women's lack of interest; family constraints; foreign managers' and clients' prejudice. Adler (1984b, c) undertook several pieces of research to test the veracity of three 'myths' which, although widely held by both men and women, had never been tested for accuracy:

1   Women do not want to be international managers.
2   Companies refuse to send women abroad.
3   Foreigners' prejudice against women renders them ineffective, even when women are interested in international assignments and are successful in being sent.

Women are not interested

Adler (1984b) addressed the first myth by carrying out research among 1,129 graduating MBA students in Canada, the USA and Europe. The results of the research showed that new women graduates expressed as much interest in international assignments as their male counterparts, but both groups were aware that barriers exist for women in this sphere. The causal attribution for such barriers differed between male and females, with males more likely to feel the problem was caused by women themselves, whereas women attributed barriers to company policies (Adler 1984b, 1986; Dawson *et al.* 1987). The differing causal attributions are worrying if related to research on the process of attribution. Colwill (1984) observes that male managers will often attribute the success of women to luck, while the success of men is attributed to hard work. In this case, the fact that male MBA students feel that there is something inherently problematic in being a woman implies that it will be more difficult for women to prove themselves as acceptable for international management positions. For women, the barriers are not seen to be so intransigent in that a change in company policy could improve their chances of success.

Companies refuse to send women abroad

The veracity of the second myth was addressed by Adler (1984c) through a survey of international personnel managers from 60 Canadian and American corporations. In general, the findings appeared to confirm that companies refuse, or at best are very reluctant, to send women abroad. The survey responses from the international personnel managers revealed that the major perceived barriers to women moving into expatriate positions were: foreigners' prejudice (72.7 per cent) and dual-career marriages (69.1 per cent). In addition, more than half of the managers (53.8 per cent) saw their own company's reluctance to select women as a major barrier. This reluctance was attributed to: a) traditional male chauvinism; (b) recognition of the higher risk involved in sending an unproven quantity; (c) lack of suitably qualified or experienced women.

Foreigners' prejudice

The findings outlined above subsume the third myth, that foreigners' prejudice against women renders them ineffective, even when they are interested in international assignments and are successful in being sent. The survey responses would suggest that organizational decision-makers view foreigners' prejudice as a very strong barrier. In addition, this view was echoed by 83 per cent of the MBA population surveyed by Adler (1984b). However, a different picture is presented by Adler (1987) in her study of female expatriate managers who were or had been on assignments in the Pacific Rim area. From the women's perspective the fact that they were foreigners was more salient than the fact that they were female. Adler argued therefore that in this context the primary descriptor is 'foreign', and the best predictor of success is that of other North Americans in the country. Adler also argues that a woman who is a foreigner (*gaijin*) is not expected to act like the locals. Therefore the rules governing behaviour of local women, which limit their access to management and managerial responsibility, do not apply to foreign women. The difference between this perspective and that of home country organizational managers is explained by Adler (1984a) as being a result of organizations' lack of experience in assigning women expatriates. They predict female expatriates' success, or the lack thereof, based on the role and treatment of local women within the particular foreign culture. Her research among women expatriates, however, questions the validity of such an assumption.

Despite the fairly small sample size and the acknowledged problems of definition of expatriate success, it is argued that Adler's (1987) study is significant as an indicator that the reality of sending women to cultures where the traditional role of women is not equated with management may be very different to existing assumptions. It is acknowledged, however, that there is a need for further research to explore more fully the nature of host country nationals' acceptance of women in international management positions. In this respect it is important to note that the question of host country cultural prejudices as a major barrier to women's employment in expatriate positions appears to have been debated only from the point of view of women going to traditionally male-dominated cultures. Little research has been carried out on the types of barriers facing, for instance, British women expatriates working in North America or Europe, or female expatriates from Pacific Rim countries working in Australia or North America, where the literature would argue there should be less problems of acceptance for female managers/professionals.

Dual-career couples

While Adler did not specifically address the issue of dual-career couples, research into work–family conflict suggests that organizations' perceptions that dual-career couple restrictions are more problematic for women may in part result from prevailing socio-cultural norms which identify the dominant gender role profile of women as homemakers (Lewis and Cooper 1988; Sandqvist 1992). From this perspective, it is argued that women will experience greater stress than men when faced with work-related pressures, particularly those which include mobility requirements. This arises because of the degree of incompatibility between role pressures from work and family domains, given the assumption that the male partner is more likely to have a 'competing' job (better) job (Rapoport and Rapoport 1971; Gupta and Jenkins 1985; Sekaran 1986; Wiersma 1994).

The traditional profile of the expatriate manager has been male, married and accompanied on the assignment by his family. This profile is now changing, with the US Dept of Labor predicting that, by 1995, 81 per cent of all marriages will be dual-career partnerships (Reynolds and Bennett 1991). Such dynamics imply that fewer employees will be willing to relocate, either domestically or internationally, without assistance for their spouses.

While there appears to be a willingness to look for solutions to the dual-career issue for male employees, companies still tend to use dual-career problems as a reason for not selecting potential female expatriates (Adler 1984a). This behaviour is essentially illogical if an assumption is made that dual-career couples fall into a pattern of 'superordinate partners' (Powell 1988), who value both work and family activities and set the goal of achieving satisfaction in both domains for both partners. In this respect, potential male expatriates will experience as many constraints as females.

This argument is supported by research into changes in socio-cultural norms concerning gender roles and a resulting shift in men's attitudes towards work and family. *The Organization Man* (Whyte 1956) portrayed an individual who was willing to devote his life to working up the company hierarchy while his wife looked after the home and children. Traditional expatriate appointments closely mirrored this belief in company loyalty, with the expectation that the family unit (namely wife and children) would accompany the employee on all assignments. Indeed many companies use them as (unpaid) hostesses, children's nurses, etc. It is argued that male managers' willingness to accept such traditional expatriation policies is being influenced by changing attitudes to work commitment. Recent research has suggested that male managers may be becoming less 'psychologically immersed' in their work and are therefore less prepared to make sacrifices which might harm their domestic lifestyles (Scase and Goffee 1989; Forster 1992).

It is argued, therefore, that the issues surrounding dual-career couples and broader constraints as a result of family obligations will remain a significant part of the decision of whether or not to send an employee on an international assignment. However, this will not be limited solely to women, as research has shown that men are facing more and more problems relating to the balance between work and family life. This section has suggested that work–family constraints are not the sole responsibility of the individual employee, but require a large degree of organizational support. Without this support, both women and men are less likely to be able to overcome the personal and domestic complexities of international transfers.

The role of home country selection processes

The role of organizational processes in the home country as determinants of women's participation rates has received little attention. The literature on expatriate management provides no evidence to show that women actually fail while on assignment. This leaves a gap in the research to explain why women are not selected in the first place. Is it because of any inherent weaknesses in organization selection processes which may permit the use of individual bias amongst selectors?

Despite the fact that in the last ten to fifteen years there has been so much research carried out on discrimination in selection in both the UK and USA, there is no previous research on the impact of selection processes on women's participation rates in international management. The selection literature addresses the issue of 'fit' from both a sociological and social psychological perspective. From a sociological perspective, selection is seen as a social process to be used by those in power within the organization as a means of determining the continuing form of the organization by recruiting and promoting only those individuals who most closely conform to organizational norms (Alimo Metcalfe 1993, 1995; Rubin 1997; Townley 1989). Individuals would therefore be judged more on the basis of their acceptability than their suitability (Jewson and Mason 1986). Social psychological studies explore the role of individual values in perpetuating discrimination in selection through the use of schemas and stereotyping (e.g. Heilman 1983; Futoran and Wyer 1986). Such studies suggest that individual selectors will develop schemas of 'ideal' jobholders and will use them as a yardstick against which all prospective candidates are measured during the process of selection. They also suggest that the less distinct the information concerning the vacancy and/or the candidate, the more likely selectors are to use schemas and stereotypes.

A major limitation of many of the social psychological studies into discrimination in selection and assessment is the laboratory-based nature of the experiments, which makes it difficult to assess the extent to which these practices would actually occur within the workplace. In contrast, sociological studies are mainly field based and therefore present a more realistic picture of actual organization practices, though they find it hard to capture psychological concepts such as the use of schemas or stereotypes.

Given the emphasis on 'fit' as a key determinant of selection decisions in both the sociological and social psychological literature, the 'gender blindness' of research into expatriate management represents a significant gap for any study trying to assess the role of selection systems for international assignments on women's representation rates. Previous research has argued that occupations where there is a predominance of one gender over the other can lead to gender-typed job-holder schema in the minds of selectors (Perry *et al.* 1994). The gender of expatriates is, however, rarely acknowledged as a significant factor in the literature on expatriate selection. Descriptive and prescriptive studies of the features of expatriation therefore tend to perpetuate the profile of an expatriate manager as being male and married with a trailing spouse. Discussions of appropriate selection, preparation and repatriation systems subsequently tend to reflect both a lack of appreciation of gender-related needs and a reluctance to acknowledge the possibility of alternatives to the prevailing model.

The 'gender blindness' of the majority of research into expatriate management is reflected in feminist discussions concerning the patriarchal nature of organizations. They argue that the organizational population has traditionally been predominantly male and that therefore the holders of organizational power, in terms of shaping structures and beliefs, have been almost exclusively male. The need to acknowledge this perspective is seen to be critical to the development of a theoretical framework analysing female international management selection, as gender-role assumptions have been seen to be important components of decisions about 'fit' (Webb 1991; Alimo-Metcalfe 1993, 1995; Rubin 1997).

Typology of international manager selection systems

A preliminary conceptual model of the impact of home country organizational selection processes on women's representation in international management can be drawn up from the key themes and debates emerging from the literature.

It has been argued that increased formalization of selection processes will make concealment of discrimination more difficult and allow for more effective monitoring by senior management and external bodies (Jenkins 1982). The term 'scientific selection' has been coined to denote the objective selection of candidates for jobs on the basis of 'scientifically' derived criteria (Hollway 1991; Alimo-Metcalfe 1993, 1995). Intuitively, one would argue that organizations which espouse equal opportunities and have formal HR systems for initial selection and internal career development purposes should see proportionate numbers of women progressing to middle and senior manager ranks in line with the initial intake numbers.

It is clear, however, from research into women in management, that this does not happen. Within the broader based women in management literature, reasons have been attributed both to women not wishing to progress to senior management positions, for a variety of reasons, and to a questioning of the extent to which formal systems can assure gender-neutral objectivity. Within the context of women in international management, possible reasons for the non-functioning of the model have been identified as: lack of interest on the part of the women themselves; prejudice from host country nationals; dual-career couple constraints. The first two reasons have been largely refuted by Adler (1984a, b, 1987), while it has been shown that dual-career couple obstacles are likely to be as problematic for the male candidate pool as they are for the female candidate pool for international assignments.

What then contributes to unequal outcomes in international manager selection? Is it because organizational selectors' individual preferences, which may not be in line with equal opportunity oriented organizational criteria, are allowed to influence selection decisions? If so, how is this rendered possible by the nature of the organizational selection processes?

Previous research in this area has identified problems with the use of the 'rational–liberal' model of equal opportunities which attempts to reduce bias through advocating gender-neutral or 'same' treatment (Adler 1986–7; Meehan and Sevenhuijsen 1991; Bock and James 1992). This has been translated within organizations into the use of formalized organizational practices in the areas of selection and assessment in which criteria and procedures are rendered more explicit.

Alimo-Metcalfe (1993) demonstrates the problems involved in ensuring that such processes are neutral and objective in her summary of potential sources of gender bias in assessment of potential. She identifies problems at three stages: the identification of criteria or dimensions on which assessments are based; the techniques or predictors chosen as methods of assessment; and the judgement or assessment by people using the data collected. In relation to the initial identification of criteria, Alimo-Metcalfe points to feminist research into the use of patriarchal power to devalue women within organizations, as a result of men's dominant position within society. Models of career progression might therefore reflect the male pattern of continuous employment, high workload which frequently overlaps into family life, chronological career timetables, and the need to be highly mobile. At the stage of assessing candidates, she notes the role of the selector's stereotype of the 'ideal' candidate as being potentially detrimental to women applying for 'out-of-role' jobs. Finally, problems are seen in relation to male assessors' views of whether women are suitable and acceptable in management positions. Alimo-Metcalfe does not discuss the likelihood of women assessors sharing the same views about women's suitability–acceptability, although Powell (1993) suggests that women who have made it to senior management positions may well share the same socialization as men and might perceive other women as less suitable–acceptable.

In defining suitability and acceptability as different components of selection decisions, the ability to remain objective in assessing appropriate personality and/or behavioural traits is seriously questioned. An emphasis on acceptability, defined in Jewson and Mason's (1986) typology of modes of discrimination in recruitment as particularism, calls into the foreground the importance of unquantifiable judgements in assessing the extent to which a person can be judged to fit into an organization without causing problems. It is argued that in the broad spectrum of international assignments currently being carried out by individuals from UK-based organizations, there are greater possibilities for women to be seen as less acceptable rather than less suitable.

Within a selection context where the nature of the vacancies reflect a male-typed bias, there appears to be even more need for selection systems to ensure that potential 'prejudice' on the part of selectors is constrained by a process which forces them continually to question their assumptions about women's suitability and, critically, their acceptability in international management positions. The nature of such a system is also more likely to engender debate about the extent to which criteria for selection follow equal opportunity principles. Within such a system, individual preferences of selectors should be more consistent and coherent as a result of the constant discussion and debate in which the likelihood of equal opportunity issues being raised is increased. However, research into selection systems for international assignments points to a preponderance of systems where primarily subjective knowledge of an individual determines who is seen to 'fit in' best with existing organizational norms may flourish (Brewster 1991; Scullion 1994).

These arguments support the need to examine how different organizational selection processes for international management assignments constrain or encourage the use of individual preferences among organizational selectors and how these affect the numbers of women in international management. A typology of international manager selection systems is used to assess their different implications on the numbers of women selected.

The typology is developed from the general literature on formalization of selection procedures and from the literature relating to expatriate management selection practice, which identify four possible variations of selection systems in the field of international management.

The first two variations relate to the nature of selection procedures. The expatriate management literature identifies the use of both 'open' and 'closed' selection procedures in organizations. An 'open' system is one in which all vacancies are advertised, anyone with appropriate qualifications and experience may apply and candidates are interviewed with greater or lesser degrees of formalized testing. Selection decisions are taken by consensus among selectors. In contrast, a 'closed' system is one in which selectors at corporate headquarters choose or nominate to line managers 'suitable' candidates. In this situation, there may be only one manager involved in the selection process at head office. The candidate is only informed once agreement about acceptability has been reached between head office personnel and the line manager. The selection interview in this process consists of a negotiation about the terms and conditions of the assignment.

The second two variations of the selection process relate to the existence of formal and informal systems operating at organizational level. As has been discussed before, substantial evidence exists of the mediating effects on the formal organizational systems of informal mechanisms, leading to unintended outcomes with respect to stated organizational policy. It is argued that these four categories combine together to provide a typology of selection processes which will exercise different influences on outcomes, in terms of the representation of women in international management. (See Figure 14.1.)

A *closed–informal* system is seen to be the worst situation for equality of opportunity in this area. Within this scenario, individual preferences of selectors, which may be more or less unclear, will be allowed to determine who is seen to be acceptable due to the lack of influence of formal systems, the lack of open debate about criteria and the lack of accountability engendered by the fact that employees are unaware that the process is happening. Under this typology, it is argued that the individual preferences of selectors may be inconsistent and incoherent and will probably not include equal opportunity considerations.

An *open–informal* system is also seen to provide few opportunities for women to enter international management positions. Although employees have access to vacancies, decisions as to who should be selected are usually arranged between relevant managers on the basis of personal recommendation and reputation. Although candidates may be put forward for interview, the selection decision is made before any formal interview takes place. In this scenario, the tendency for managers to select 'clones' of existing managers may well reduce the possibility of women being considered for positions. This type of system will see formal selection criteria agreed. However, the extent to which these and the match of candidates are debated and discussed may be limited. This will lead to decreases in consistency and coherent thinking concerning the key characteristics of effective international managers, less attention to formal criteria and less opportunity to bring in equal opportunity considerations.

	Formal	Informal
Open	• Clearly defined criteria • Clearly defined measures • Training for selectors • Open advertising of vacancy (internal/external) • Panel discussions	• Less-defined criteria • Less-defined measures • Limited training for selectors • No panel discussions • Open advertising of vacancy • Recommendations
Closed	• Clearly defined criteria • Clearly defined measures • Training for selectors • Panel discussions • Nominations only (networking/reputation)	• Selectors' individual preferences determine criteria and measures • No panel discussions • Nominations only (networking /reputation)

Figure 14.1 Typology of international manager selection systems

A *closed–formal* system involves selectors assessing candidates against formal criteria and discussing candidates' match with them. However, the lack of personal contact with the candidate and the fact that the field of potential applicants is determined by the selectors with the attendant risk of omission of suitable candidates may allow individual preferences of selectors to be reflected in the nominating process. Under this system the numbers of women entering international management is likely to be lower, given the influence of networking and reputation inherent in the process.

An *open–formal* system is seen to be the most likely to produce greater numbers of women entering international management positions because employees will have access to the selection process and selectors will have to interview them. The necessity for selectors to assess candidates against formalized criteria and to determine the best 'fit' through continual comparison of their own assessments against other selectors' assessments will constrain the use of individual preferences and ensure a questioning of assumptions. This will be reflected in more consistency in evaluations and greater clarity in thinking in relation to the critical components of effective international management. This type of system is also likely to produce a close match between individual selectors' schemas and formal selection criteria, including equal opportunity principles. The objectivity of this type of system will be enhanced by the use of psychometric and other tests.

Methodology

In order to investigate the appropriateness of the typology in organizational contexts a two-stage research process was carried out.

The first stage consisted of carrying out in-depth interviews with international human resource directors at nine UK-based international organizations. All the organizations shared the following points in common: leaders in the field;

household names; largest in the area; wide range of expatriate positions; world-wide spread of expatriate posts including tough Third World countries. The majority of the organizations espoused equal opportunities. The interviews explored in depth the nature of international management selection processes and the context of international management assignments within each organization. As a result of these discussions, three organizations were picked for case study research. These organizations (Amstar, Brymay and Cirus) fell at the closed, middle and open ends of the *Open–Closed* continuum as defined in the typology discussed above. At this stage of the research, it was not possible to define the nature of international manager selection processes further in terms of the degree to which these systems were *formal* or *informal*.

The methodology employed for the second stage of the research consisted of a case study approach. Information about international manager selection processes was collected from two sources; the first through semi-structured interviews with HR personnel and key selectors within the individual organizations; the second via an examination of organizational literature in the form of policies and administration forms. A critical part of the research was seen to be the identification of personally held beliefs about the characteristics of effective international managers. To try to ensure an unbiased summary of the characteristics of effective international managers (both from the researcher's part and that of the individual selectors), Repertory Grid technique was chosen as integral to the case study design. This consisted of asking individual selectors to compare and contrast up to nine international managers whom they knew personally, split into categories of highly effective, moderately effective and not effective. As far as possible, women international managers were included in the sample.[1]

The results from the Repertory Grid interviews yielded a set of 'constructs', or statements concerning effective/non-effective international manager behaviour which were further analysed using the Grid Analysis Package (GAP) developed by Slater (1972). An explanation of how to interpret the results from this package is available from Smith (1986). In order to be able to see if there was any inherent gender bias in the constructs used by the selectors, they were compared to the 92-item inventory designed by Schein (1973, 1975). Schein designed the inventory to use in two studies to test for a relationship between sex-role stereotypes and the perceived personal characteristics for middle managers. The results from both the studies and further replications of the studies (Brenner *et al.* 1989; Schein *et al.* 1989; Schein and Mueller 1992; Schein *et al.* 1996) confirmed Schein's original hypothesis that successful middle managers were perceived to possess those characteristics, attitudes and temperament more commonly ascribed to men in general than to women in general.

Research findings

This detailed exploration of the nature of the international manager selection process within the three organizations allowed them to be plotted onto the typology of international management selection systems. Amstar was placed in the *closed–informal* quadrant, Cirus was placed in the *open–formal* quadrant, while Brymay fell across the quadrants on the typology, with different systems being used for different appointments. The description of the system was seen to fall almost equally between the *open* and *closed* quadrant, but in terms of degree of formality it was argued that it fell more into the *informal* quadrant. This positioning was seen to indicate a very hybrid system in which there were real tensions between espoused formal policy and current organizational practice.

The degree to which differences in selection processes resulted in the posited outcomes with respect to the use of selectors' individual preferences in selection decision-making was explored via the Repertory Grid analyses. This analysis is presented in two stages. The first addresses the extent to which the type of selection process resulted in the posited outcomes with respect to clarity and consistency of thinking in relation to effective international managers and the degree to which the constructs derived from the Repertory Grid interviews with selectors matched formal company criteria. The second stage addressed the potential for gender bias with respect to the way women international managers were viewed within the Repertory Grid responses and in respect of the degree to which the constructs used were masculine or feminine typed.

Degree of clarity, consistency and link with formal criteria

For the first stage, three key analyses were used. These were: the extent to which the grids depicted a clarity of thinking in relation to the characteristics of effective international managers; the degree of consistency both within and across individual selectors' grids within each organization; the degree to which the individual grids reflected formal selection criteria within the organization.

Clarity of thinking

The constructs emanating from the Repertory Grid analyses indicated that there was a large degree of difference in terms of sophistication of thinking about characteristics of international managers among the selectors at Amstar, the only construct which is used consistently being mobile. The focus of the grids with respect to determinants of effective performance appears to be based more on determinants of effective domestic performance.

In contrast, selectors in Cirus were seen to be clearer in their thinking about the characteristics of effective international managers. In discussion with staff at head office, the constructs which were seen to be specifically related to the needs of working in an overseas environment were: linguist; effective communicator with regional groupings; good relations between field and head office; good emissaries; understands responsibilities towards local environment and agencies; values different approaches to work in cross-cultural respect; culturally sensitive; strong interpersonal skills; secure with feedback inter-organization and more flexible/adaptable.

The analysis of clarity of thinking in relation to characteristics of effective international managers in Brymay revealed more of an emphasis on specific international skills than was the case in Amstar, but a more limited scope of constructs than with Cirus. The constructs could be grouped around the themes of: confidence based on experience overseas; manages interface between centre and field; more internationalist and cultural empathy. Most of the selectors, however, still rated effective business management capabilities as the most important distinguishing factor between good and bad international managers.

Consistency

Consistency within grids was evaluated by a qualitative examination of the number of times a particular construct was used more than once in relation to the three sorts of effectiveness of international manager. Degree of consistency of thinking across individual selectors' grids was done by a qualitative analysis of the constructs identified as most distinctive to the selector, to see to what extent the constructs arising were replicated across grids at an organizational level.

Analyses within Amstar indicated a lack of consistency both within and across grids. There were wide variations in the constructs used to describe effective international managers by the same selector and comparisons across grids revealed no areas of commonality in terms of the constructs used to describe effective international managers.

In contrast, the results from Cirus showed a high degree of consistency within grids, with the majority of selectors using a common set of criteria to describe the effective managers. The degree of consistency across grids was also seen to be quite high, with four common themes emerging: consultative management style; team management skills; linguistic/communication skills and professional management skills.

In the case of Brymay, the degree of consistency of thinking within individual selectors' grids reflected a mixed picture. Two of the grids showed little or no consistency in criteria related to effective international managers, while the other four showed slightly more consistency. Consistency of thinking across grids was limited. Only two common themes were detected in more than one grid: high energy and business sense.

Match with formal criteria

In terms of linkage with formal criteria, the results were in line with the general propositions from the typology. Amstar's *closed–informal* international management selection system meant that it was not possible to identify formal criteria for the majority of selection cases. However, a key component of selection is the potential rating of the individual which is assessed as a result partly of the annual performance and development reviews. This is supported by the focus on determinants of effective domestic management behaviours revealed by the constructs elicited from selectors within Amstar. An assessment of the degree of coherence between individual selectors' constructs and formal assessment criteria contained within the annual performance and development review revealed very little correlation with the formal system in relation to competences, but a greater degree of agreement in relation to appraisal qualities. In three out of the four grids, more than half of the formal competences listed in the annual review of performance were not seen to be linked to the constructs relating to effective management behaviour, from either an international or domestic perspective. More linkages could be detected between the grid constructs and the appraisal qualities, with all but one of the grids containing constructs which could be subsumed into the formal list of appraisal qualities. Three main qualities were seen to be important in all grids: achievement motivation; capacity to motivate and helicopter vision.

Cirus demonstrated a high degree of coherence with formal selection criteria. The analysis of the link of constructs to the formal criteria included in the person specification for field director/programme manager positions showed that by far the majority of constructs fitted within the official list of selection criteria. The linkage was seen to be extremely strong in relation to consultative, team management skills, with less priority ascribed to the very specific international aptitudes such as awareness of the cultural, social and political environment.

An analysis of the extent to which the constructs reflected formal criteria within Brymay was difficult to assess due to the variance in usage of any formal job specifications. The emphasis on business performance could be seen to relate to the way in which performance was measured in Brymay, where performance against key result areas (KRAs) was the main method of determining good or bad performance. The grid from the head office personnel manager showed more agreement of constructs with formal criteria set out on the official interview assessment form used in country manager selection, although this is hardly surprising given that the manager was involved with the creation of the form.

Gender implications of the Repertory Grid analyses

These findings provide support for the propositions developed in the Typology of International Management Selection Systems. It was argued that an *open–formal* system would engender greater clarity and consistency in thinking about international managers and a greater link with formal criteria. In contrast, a *closed–informal* system would result in incoherent and inconsistent thinking about international managers, with little linkage to formal criteria. A *closed–formal* system was argued to result in similar outcomes to the *open–formal* system in terms of clarity and consistency and linkage with formal criteria. However, an *open–formal* system would decrease clarity and consistency and linkage with formal criteria.

A key element of the posited outcomes in terms of their effect on the numbers of women entering international management positions was the extent to which the four types of system allowed for equal opportunity considerations to be part of the selection process. In this respect, it was posited that both the *open–formal* and the *closed–formal* system would ensure the inclusion of equal opportunity considerations throughout the selection process, whereas in the *open–informal* and to a greater extent, in the *closed–informal* typology, there would be less necessity to bring in equal opportunity considerations.

The extent to which equal opportunity considerations could be seen to be working was tested in two ways. The first was the extent to which male and female international managers were seen to be similar within the grids. This was assessed by an analysis of the number of women mentioned, the degree of clarity of thinking about them and whether this was different to thinking about the male managers. The second consisted of an analysis of the extent of gender typing inherent in the constructs provided from the grids against the descriptive statements in Schein's Descriptive Index (SDI).

Thinking about women international managers

The results for Amstar show that, for the four females identified in each grid, none of the grids saw the female managers as being distinctive. Effective and non-effective female international managers were described in very limited ways, usually with only one construct being highlighted, such as aggressive. The successful male international manager, however, was seen in broader general management terms.

For Cirus, the results were different. Four out of the six selectors were able to identify three female international managers. The female managers identified were also seen in very similar ways to their male counterparts. The determining factor in terms of thinking relating to managers was the performance rating of the individual (i.e. whether the manager was seen as highly effective, moderately effective or not effective).

The results for Brymay were more similar to Amstar. Only one selector out of six could name more than one female international manager and one selector could not think of any female international managers to use within the grid. Of the female managers chosen, two of the selectors' thinking about the female managers identified was less distinct than for the other male managers. In the other three grids, the women appeared to be viewed in very similar ways to the male managers, the main differentiation being their performance rating as with the selectors in Cirus.

SDI results

The results from the SDI analysis indicate that a more subtle form of gender bias may be in existence. Within Amstar, the SDI results for all the grids displayed a masculine-typed bias, while in Brymay the results were more equally split between masculine-typed bias and neutral constructs. Only Cirus displayed a tendency towards neutral–feminine-typed constructs.

Discussion

These results support the argument that a more *open–formal* system creates more requirements for the discussion and debate of equal opportunity issues which thus become integral to organizational discussions of 'fit'. Results from Cirus indicate that the selectors have clear views of the women international managers included on the grids and are therefore less likely to be picking clones of male managers when selecting. None of the grids show any negative thinking about the managers being female. The position of the managers on the grid is determined exclusively by their indicators of performance. In addition, the SDI analysis of the constructs elicited through the grid interviews show a tendency towards a *neutral–feminine* gender typing, thus suggesting that equal opportunity considerations are used by selectors in the decision-making process.

In contrast, a *closed–informal* system does not force selectors to question their assumptions, which in the area of international management selection will be influenced by the profile of existing expatriates and the nature of expatriate assignments in terms of the type of jobs and locations, as well as organizational values concerning appropriate traits and behaviours. Results from Amstar support this argument. The majority of selectors were not clear in their thinking about the female managers included in the cognitive maps. Although the female managers were positioned on the cognitive maps in relation to their performance ratings, in general they were positioned closer to the centre of the maps, which indicates that they were seen to be less distinctive than the male managers. In addition, the SDI analysis for Amstar displayed a masculine-typed bias.

The picture at Brymay again provided tentative, but limited support for the posited relationship between *closed–formal* and *open–informal* systems and the number of women entering international management positions. The number of women selected for inclusion on the grids and their general lack of distinctiveness for the selectors reflected the situation in Amstar, where thinking about women managers was generally less clear than in Cirus. It was argued that this situation would give rise to cloning of existing male international managers. The SDI results for Brymay, however, show a more equal split between masculine and neutral-typed constructs, which might again reflect the positioning of Brymay at the centre of the Typology of International Management Selection Systems.

It is argued that the difference in the numbers of women in international management positions within the three case study organizations – Amstar, Brymay and Cirus (with Amstar having less than 5 per cent representation; Brymay having a representation of 25 per cent and Cirus having a representation of 45 per cent) – support the arguments derived from the Typology of International Management Selection Systems as presented in this chapter.

In conclusion, the study presents data to support a closer focus on the role of international management selection processes as a determinant of the numbers of women entering international management positions. It is acknowledged, however, that the nature of such a focused research study does not and should not preclude other influences on women's participation rates. In this respect, work–family issues are seen to constitute serious barriers. It was not possible to incorporate such issues into the current study, but I am aware that in the 'real world' all these factors intermingle in many different permutations and cannot readily be disentangled.

Note

1 (For an explanation of the method and applications of Repertory Grid see Bannister and Fransella (1986), Stewart *et al.* (1981)).

References

Adler, N. (1984a). 'Women in international management: where are they?', *California Management Review* 26(4): 78–89.
—— (1984b). 'Women do not want international careers: and other myths about international management', *Organizational Dynamics* 13(2): 66–79.
—— (1984c). 'Expecting international success: female managers overseas', *Columbia Journal of World Business* 19(3): 79–85.
—— (1986) 'Do MBAs want international careers?', *International Journal of Intercultural Relations* 10(3): 277–300.
—— (1987) 'Pacific Basin managers: a *Gaijin*, not a woman', *Human Resource Management* 26(2): 169–192.
—— (1986-7) 'Women in management worldwide', *International Studies of Management and Organisation* 16: 3–32.
Alimo-Metcalfe, B. (1993) 'Women in management: organizational socialization and assessment practices that prevent career advancement', *International Journal of Selection and Assessment* 1(2): 68–83.
—— (1995) 'An investigation of female and male constructs of leadership and empowerment', *Women in Management Review* 10(2): 3–8.
Bannister, D. and Fransella, F. (1986) *Inquiring Man: The Psychology of Personal Constructs*, London: Croom Helm.
Bock, G. and James, S. (eds) (1992) *Beyond Equality and Difference: Citizenship, Feminist Politics, Female Subjectivity*, London: Routledge.
Brenner, O., Tomkiewicz, J. and Schein, V. (1989) 'The relationship between sex role stereotypes and requisite management characteristics revisited', *Academy of Management Journal* 32: 662–9.
Brett, J.M. and Reilly, A.H. (1990) *The Effect of Job Transfer on Employees and their Families*, Washington, DC: Employee Relocation Council.
Brewster, C. (1991) *The Management of Expatriates*, London: Kogan Page.
Colwill, N. (1984) 'Lucky Lucy and able Adam: to what do you attribute your success?', *Business Horizons* 44(1): 93–4.
Conyon, M.J. and Mallin, C.M. (1996) *Women in the Boardroom: Evidence from Large UK Companies*, Warwick: Warwick University.
Cooper, C. and Makin, P. (1985) 'The mobile managerial family', *Journal of Management Development* 4(3): 56–66.
Dawson, G., Ladenburg, E. and Moran, R. (1987) 'Women in international management', in D. Clutterbuck and Devine, A. (eds) *Businesswomen Present and Future*, London: Macmillan.

Dowling, P., Schuler, R. and Welch, D. (1994) *International Dimensions of Human Resource Management*, 2nd edn, Belmont CA: Wadsworth.

Employment Conditions Abroad (1994) *Managing Mobility*, London: ECA International.

Feldman, D.C. and Thomas, D.C. (1992) 'Career management issues facing expatriates', *Journal of International Business Studies* 23(2): 271–94.

Forster, N. (1990) 'A practical guide to the management of job changes and relocation', *Personnel Review* 19(4): 26–35.

—— (1992) 'International managers and mobile families: the professional and personal dynamics of trans-national career pathing and job mobility in the 1990s', *International Journal of Human Resource Management* 3(3): 605–623.

Futoran, G.C. and Wyer, R.S. (1986) 'The effects of traits and gender stereotypes on occupational suitability judgements and the recall of judgement-relevant information', *Journal of Experimental Social Psychology* 22: 475–503.

Gupta, N. and Jenkins, G. (1985) 'Dual-career couples: stress, stressors, strains and strategies', in T. Beehr and R. Bhagat (eds) *Human Stress and Cognition in Organisations: An Integrated Perspective*, New York: Wiley.

Harris, H. (1996) 'Women in international management: new UK-based evidence', paper presented at the Fifth Conference on International Human Resource Management, San Diego, June.

Heilman, M. (1983) 'Sex bias in work settings: the lack of fit model', *Research in Organisational Behaviour* 5: 269–98.

Hollway, W. (1991) *Work Psychology and Organizational Behaviour: Managing the Individual at Work*, London: Sage.

Jenkins, R. (1982) *Managers, Recruitment Procedures and Black Workers*, Working Papers on Ethnic Relations, no.18, London: SSRC Research Unit on Ethnic Relations.

Jewson, N. and Mason, D. (1986) 'Modes of discrimination in the recruitment process: formalisation, fairness and efficiency', *Sociology* 20(1): 43–63.

Labour Force Survey (1989) London: HMSO.

—— (1995) London: HMSO.

Lewis, S. and Cooper, G. (1988) 'Stress in dual earner families', in B. Gutek, A. Stromberg and L. Larwood (eds) *Women and Work: An Annual Review*, vol. 3, Newbury Park CA: Sage.

Marshall, J. (1984) *Women Managers: Travellers in a Male World*, Chichester: Wiley.

Meehan, E. and Sevenhuijsen, S. (eds) (1991) *Equality Politics and Gender*, London: Sage.

Mendenhall, M. and Oddou, G. (1985) 'The dimensions of expatriate acculturation: a review', *Academy of Management Review* 10: 39–47.

Mendenhall, M., Dunbar, E. and Oddou, C. (1987) 'Expatriate selection, training and career pathing – a review and critique', *Human Resource Management* 26(3): 331–45.

Mendenhall, M., Punnett, B.J. and Ricks, D. (1995) *Global Management*, Cambridge MA: Blackwell.

Perry, E.L., Davis-Blake, A. and Kulik, C. (1994) 'Explaining gender-based selection decisions: a synthesis of contextual and cognitive approaches', *Academy of Management Review* 19(4): 786–820.

Powell, G.N. (1988) *Women and Men in Management*, Newbury Park CA: Sage.

Rapoport, R. and Rapoport, R.N. (1971) *Dual Career Families*, London: Penguin.

Reynolds, C. and Bennett, R. (1991), 'The career couple challenge', *Personnel Journal* March: 46–8.

Rosener, J. (1990) 'Ways women lead', *Harvard Business Review* 68(6): 119–25.

Rubin, J. (1997) 'Gender, equality and the culture of organisational assessment', *Gender, Work and Organisation*, special issue.

Sandqvist, K. (1992) 'Sweden's sex-role scheme and commitment to gender equality', in S. Lewis, D. Izraeli and H. Hootsman (eds) *Dual Earner Families: International Perspectives*, London: Sage.

Scase, R. and Goffee, R. (1989) 'Women in management: towards a research agenda', in *Third Annual Meeting of British Academy of Management.*

Schein, V.E. (1973) 'The relationship between sex role stereotypes and requisite management characteristics', *Journal of Applied Psychology* 57: 95–100.

—— (1975) 'Relationships between sex role stereotypes and requisite management characteristics among female managers', *Journal of Applied Psychology* 60(3): 340–44.

Schein, V.E. and Mueller, R. (1992) 'Sex role stereotypes and requisite management characteristics: a cross cultural look', *Journal of Organizational Behavior* 13(5): 439–47.

Schein, V.E., Mueller, R. and Jacobson, C. (1989) 'The relationship between sex role stereotypes and requisite management characteristics among college students', *Sex Roles* 20: 103–10.

Schein, V.E., Mueller, R., Lituchy, T. and Liu, J. (1996) 'Think manager–think male: a global phenomenon?', *Journal of Organizational Behavior* 17(1): 33–41.

Scullion, H. (1994) 'Staffing policies and strategic control in British multinationals', *International Studies of Management and Organization* 24(3): 86–104.

Sekaran, U. (1986) *Dual-Career Families: Contemporary Organizational and Counseling Issues*, San Francisco: Jossey-Bass.

Sharma, S. (1990) 'Psychology of women in management: a distinct feminine leadership', *Equal Opportunities International* 9(2): 13–18.

Slater, P. (1972) *Notes on Ingrid and Grid Analysis Package*, Manchester: University of Manchester Regional Computing Centre.

Smith, J.M. (1986) 'An introduction to repertory grids – part two: interpretation of results', *Graduate Management Research*, autumn: 4–24

Stewart, V., Stewart, A. and Fonda, N. (1981) *Business Applications of Repertory Grid*, Maidenhead: McGraw-Hill.

Townley, B. (1989) 'Selection and appraisal: reconstituting "social relations"?' in J. Storey (ed.) *New Perspectives on Human Resource Management*, London: Routledge.

Vinnicombe, S. (1987), 'What exactly are the differences in male and female working styles?', *Women in Management Review* 3(1): 13–21.

Webb, J. (1991) 'The gender relations of assessment', in J. Firth-Cozens and M. West (eds) *Women at Work: Psychological and Organizational Perspectives*, Milton Keynes: Open University Press.

Whyte, W.H. (1956) *The Organization Man*, New York: Simon and Schuster.

Wiersma, U. (1994) 'A taxonomy of behavioral strategies for coping with work–home conflict', *Human Relations* 47(2): 211–21.

Part IV

New research
perspectives on IHRM

15 Qualitative research strategies in international HRM

Christine Mattl

Introduction

This chapter deals with methodological issues in international HRM research exemplified by an ongoing research project by an academic research team based in Vienna.[1] The objective of our project is to investigate the differences and similarities in co-operation patterns of work groups in different cultures and countries. From a methodological point of view we chose the qualitative approach as a promising basis for cross-cultural research. Qualitative research means that the emphasis lies on processes and meanings. It emphasizes the socially constructed nature of reality, the relationship between the researcher and what is studied and the situational constraints that shape inquiry (Denzin and Lincoln 1994: 12).

The subject matter of our project is that international organizations are faced with the problem of providing people from differing cultural contexts with a working framework that enables successful co-operation. On the basis of original research our intention is to extend the knowledge of the internal and external relationships of work groups in various cultural contexts. As co-operation processes play a central role in teams we focus on processes centred on co-operation in and between groups with teams understood as social systems which define themselves in relation to their organizational and social surroundings.

Critical points for cross-cultural research

When undertaking cross-cultural research, the following issues are seen to be critical for cross-cultural comparison.

Researcher's culture as anchor point?

A critical point in cross-cultural research is the researcher's biases and cultural background. Reading books on cross-cultural issues could give the impression that the authors stand 'beyond (their own) culture' (Hall 1976). They write as if they were free of culture and could generate dimensions or standards from an objective point of view, neglecting that they act and write under the influence of the culture in which they live or were brought up in. Usually the anchor point is not outside the cultures of this world but to be found within the culture of the respective researcher. From the anchor point of the researcher's culture, valuations are made, and the descriptions of such dimensions or standards are not value-free. How can we take the researcher's personal and cultural background into account?

Conceptualization of culture

Culture is a construct that, depending on the discipline and school of thinking, has been defined hundreds of times already (see the classic collection of definitions from Kroeber and Kluckhohn 1952). In trying to find a way through the jungle of definitions, a distinction made by Karmasin and Karmasin (1997) may be helpful. They see two ways of conceptualizing culture:

1   Culture is described as 'material' culture. Rules are not described, but content, values and norms are analysed and used to make distinctions between cultures. This can lead to a definition of cultures as 'good' and 'bad' by values being present or absent. If it is on a descriptive basis only, it can lead to an extreme form of relativism, where every culture is unique in itself and no common bases for comparison can be found.
2   Culture is used as a processual, interactive term. Cultural distinctions derive from different ways of organizing society and culture is defined by rules and systems of rules. Here the aim is to find dimensions (systems of rules, structures) that allow us to describe cultures in a way that makes them comparable.

When talking about cross-cultural research in an organizational setting, there are also different layers of culture to be taken into account, each with specific rules, but one influencing the other:

*   national culture (cross-cultural research as comparison of different national cultures; mono-cultural/intercultural work groups as groups with members from one/different national cultures);
*   regional culture;
*   organizational culture (in multinationals: do they favour ethnocentric, polycentric or geocentric politics?);
*   professional culture;
*   (work) group culture;
*   diverse subcultures.

The crucial question is how and when is conceptualizing carried out in the research process and which layers of culture is the researcher interested in.

Language of the interviewers, interviewees and the transcript

When asking questions cross-culturally the selection of the language is an enormous problem. Should the language of the researchers be used? Even under the conditions that the research subjects may be fluent, there are different ways of saying things. If the research subjects' language is chosen and it is not the researcher's language, the same problems arise. When using an interpreter, there will be more than one layer of meanings, biases and interpretations. Even when the researcher knows both languages perfectly well, there are many problems in comparing them linguistically (Fontana and Frey 1994: 366). Therefore the question is: Which language should be used for the interviews?

Specific response behaviour

In cross-cultural research the interviewer–respondent interaction and the response behaviour also acquire new dimensions. Brislin *et al.* (1973: 68) identified the following biases: 'rudeness bias'; 'I-can-answer-any-question bias'; 'courtesy bias'; 'sucker bias' (meaning that in some cultures it is acceptable to fool strangers); 'reticent–loquacious bias'; 'social desirability bias'; 'status difference bias'; 'individual–group opinion bias'. All are said to be found in different forms in different cultures and to influence the interviewees' behaviour towards the interviewer. How can the researcher take these response behaviour patterns into account?

Analysis and the art of interpretation of cultural clues

There is a certain danger in that cross-cultural research is looking for clues that provide hints for certain cultural characteristics. When data such as observations or findings such as beliefs and values are decontextualized, culture is decimated to its artefacts and the structures of the underlying meanings cannot be reconstructed. An example could be the 'earlier ethnographers [who] were effective in romanticizing and making vivid the situation of the fieldworker and in demonstrating how exotic customs made sense in their own contexts' (Marcus and Fischer 1986: 48). An example would be Malinowski, one of the forefathers of modern ethnography, who lived in the Western Pacific in the 1920s: 'Malinowski [who] invites readers to imagine him, a white man unwilling to retreat to the company of other white men, drinking, reading, lonely and ultimately enjoying the company of "savagery". His portraits are painted entirely of Them (the Other), introducing "order" into the "chaos" of their lives' (Fine 1994: 79). Here the other culture is seen looking down upon or trying to 'help' the people from the other culture.

The result can be a jigsaw lacking a table on which to assemble it (decontextualized) or the wrong (too small, too large) table (because it is the researcher's context). How can we put the cultural clues into the right context?

Presentation and feedback

The research process is not finished with the stage of analysis. Even after the first phase of writing and presenting the findings to other scientists, there is something substantial lacking. The usual way of presenting the findings as the final result to the participants–research subjects, if they do present them at all, seems quite ironic, as they are supposed to be the experts of their own point of view. They see that the researchers take their results as final and are not interested in feedback or in any information which could disturb their perception or generated model. How can we take advantage of the participants' point of view?

Research strategies considering these problems

The qualitative way to deal with most of these critical points is led by the following crucial principles for qualitative research: openess, communicativity, contextuality and theoretical sampling:

1   *Openness*: this principle demands that the theoretical structuring of the subject matter has to be postponed until it has emerged from the participants, the research subjects (Hoffmann-Riem 1980: 343). Openness is required in the focus of the research's guiding questions, the research design, the selection of the participants, the research subjects, the research situation, the methods used and finally towards possible alternative interpretations in data analysis.

2   *Communicativity*: this means that researchers can retrieve data/information that is structured by meaning only if they establish everyday communication with their research subjects and respect the research subject's system of communication rules (Hoffmann-Riem 1980: 347). Communication should also be included in the interpretation process, or example, in the form of conversation analysis.

3   *Contextuality*: communication and action can only be understood when their context is taken into account.

4   *Theoretical sampling*: the qualitative research process has to be done step by step, integrating new data and findings, also in the selection of participants and cases. The two main strategies for the selection of new cases for comparison are minimizing differences or maximizing differences (Glaser and Strauss 1967: 45ff.).

Researcher as a multicultural subject

The question is: How can we take the researcher's personal and cultural background into account? The researcher is not supposed to neglect her or his background. The researcher as a 'bricoleur understands that research is an interactive process shaped by his or her personal history, biography, gender, social class, race and ethnicity, and those of the people in the setting' (Denzin and Lincoln 1994: 3). It is important to reflect these conditions as well as all presumptions, theoretical knowledge on the subject matter, and so on.

Our way of making these influences as transparent as possible was to create an interdisciplinary research team. To help with the process of recognizing personal biases, our method was to have a junior doing interviews with the other team members, concluded by a presentation of the findings of the interviews (e.g. holding a workshop and having each researcher write an autobiography). Such information on the researchers would also be of value for readers or students.

Contextuality instead of a priori conceptualization

How and when is conceptualization carried out in the research process and in which layers of culture is the researcher interested? Our way of working on the conceptualization of culture is determined by two of the principles of qualitative research: openness and contextuality. Here, openness means that instead of allowing the research subjects to fill our concept of culture with content (life, colours), the researchers try to understand what kinds of rules they see/make, their dimensions, frames, the glasses through which they perceive 'reality'. By theoretical sampling of cases/groups of traders in different countries, we seek to learn the role that culture plays in the co-operation of traders. When comparing various groups of traders to get insights into how they co-operate as professionals within their groups and towards the organization or their surroundings, we can discover the influence of culture on their actions. Analysing case by case within its specific context, we can identify specific rules that play a role. Moving from the most similar to the most different case allows us to reconstruct a system of the underlying meanings to the rules and to recognize the rules that lead to the establishment of new rules.

To make it easier to separate the different layers of culture, we are doing this research among traders (same professional culture) in one organization which, it is supposed, has more or less the same organizational culture when an ethnocentric strategy is applied. This assumption is discussed later in the text. If we take subcultures within these professional groups in one organizational culture into account, a national culture should emerge.

Selecting an adequate language

Which language should be used for the interviews? We have not yet found an optimum way to handle this issue. We suppose that one can only try to come as close as possible to ideal cross-cultural communication. Perhaps the ideal researcher should be able to speak as many languages as possible and let the interviewee choose the language. What we did in the Prague study was to conduct the interviews in English as it is the traders' professional language. Most of the terms that characterize their specific language are English words, sometimes adapted into the respective language. The computer programs they use are in English and they mostly have to speak English on the phone to their brokers. Of course this does not give any guarantee, that they are articulate, for example, on the subject of the relation between work and private life. Ideally, to minimize risks, there should be a 'cultural expert' who is a native researcher on each site to support our data collection and provide us with culture-specific information. The 'cultural expert' should also help in the translation and interpretation of documents. Moreover, when analysing and interpreting the English transcripts we are also trying to involve a linguist in the English language.

Communicativity and experts

How can the researcher take response behaviour patterns into account? We worked with narrative interviews in the qualitative tradition of conducting them as closely as possible to natural, everyday conversation. We tried to create an atmosphere of trust and rapport by explaining what our research project is about, what we want from the interviewees and what we are going to do with the resulting information. An important fact is to guarantee anonymity. Creating an everyday conversational atmosphere rather than that of an interview should prevent some of the biases mentioned previously from arising. For the remainder, the native cultural experts add their knowledge about such biases, if any. This procedure should help these biases to be considered; not only are the transcripts of the interviews to be analysed, but also the context in which the interaction took place is noted and taken into account.

Making use of triangulation

Our answer to the question of how we can put the cultural clues into the right context is the reconstruction of the context as thoroughly as possible. One way to come close to it is triangulation (Janesick 1994: 214). The use of multiple (not just three) methods reflects an attempt to secure an in-depth understanding of the phenomenon in question. There are different forms of triangulation that we followed in our study:

1   *Data triangulation*: we use data from the following sources in the study: documents such as brochures, open letters, internal newsletters or papers; field notes (minutes from observation with assumptions and ideas written directly after the field work); transcripts of interviews, photographs from the site (the dealing room and the traders during office hours).
2   *Investigator and interdisciplinary triangulation*: the team consists of seven researchers from four different disciplines. Some of us go into the field and some do not. All participate in the analysis stage. Cultural experts take part in data collection and analyses. The feedback from the participant, can also be seen as additional to the evaluation by other researchers.
3   *Theory triangulation*: for the interpretation of a single set of data we use different methods of analyses. The content analysis as well as the sequential analyses are explained later.

Presentation and feedback on work in progress

How can we take advantage of the participants' point of view? We believe that taking the resulting model back to the participants is a good modality. The presentation of preliminary findings and discussion with the participants ensures feedback. Informants will often be able to confirm the accuracy and validity of the study and may even offer additional stories to confirm the model further. However, sometimes the results reveal findings that are implicit to the setting. Then, even the participants may not be aware of the findings and must themselves verify the results (Morse 1994: 230).

It should be taken into account that the presentation has to be done at an early stage of the research because the participants might present unforeseen comments which may make it necessary to change or adapt the model. When presenting research results in organizations, one must be conscious of factors such as power and hierarchy. The results presented must be abstract enough that no personal opinion can be identified.

The composition of the discussion group has an important impact on the behavioural patterns shown by the participants. For example, some of the younger traders, who had previously been extraordinarily locquatious in informal situations, did not participate in the discussion at all.

This procedure also assures that saturation, another principle in qualitative research, is respected. In qualitative research the investigator continues the research until repetition of the data from multiple sources is obtained. This provides concurring and confirming data and ensures saturation (Morse 1994: 230).

Presentation of the research project

A cross-cultural qualitative comparison on co-operation in work groups

The research team is interested in two topics. On the working level the question is: How is co-operation in work groups organized in different cultures/countries? The second question was formulated on a methodological level: What are the consequences of different research methods for generating knowledge in cross-cultural research?

So far we have undertaken two empirical studies: the pilot study in Vienna and the Prague study that is still in progress. We have also planned to do studies in five more countries.

The five initiators and the two junior researchers come from four disciplines (organizational behaviour, marketing, sociology and economics). Although all of them are Austrian, they are teaching and working at universities in four different countries (Austria, Germany, France, USA) and are therefore able to bring in various perspectives.

Warm-up period

Researchers own biases and ideologies

> Qualitative researchers accept the fact that research is ideologically driven. There is no value-free or bias-free design. The qualitative researcher identifies his or her own biases early on and articulates the ideology or conceptual frame for the study. By identifying one's biases one can see easily where the questions that guide the study are crafted. This is a big difference among paradigms.
>
> (Janesick 1994: 212)

In our case we had to deal with the researchers' identification of their own biases and ideologies as well as with clarifying the expectations in team research (Punch 1994: 87).

For both purposes the junior researcher carried out open interviews on the other five members of the research team. This instrument was used to help them think aloud about their biases and expectations, as well as to integrate the junior assistant into an already existing research group. It also helped the junior to practice 'becoming the research instrument' (Janesick 1994: 212). 'Becoming the research instrument' means that the researcher must have the ability to observe behaviour and must sharpen the skills necessary for observation and face-to-face interview.

Formulating the questions guiding the study

The question we formulated on a working level is: How is co-operation in work groups organized in different cultures/countries? Associated with this question are issues concerning the external factors (cultural, organizational and profession specific) and internal factors affecting the means of operation of work groups as well as their interplay. We are also interested in the identification and analysis of culturally specific factors for the regulation of action, the dynamics of the internal organization of heterogeneous environmental relations (how do different work groups handle different environments), and the logic of action.

Selection of a site and participants

After a series of research team meetings where the above mentioned topics were discussed and developed, we went in search of a site and participants for the field-work.

The site was supposed to be a company operating in various countries of the world that pursues an ethnocentric (Perlmutter and Heenan 1979) strategy. Our idea was that it would be easier to see from a cross-cultural comparison how national culture makes itself apparent when the organizational culture is supposed to be ('more or less') the same. Further, the participants of the study should be members of work groups.

It proved to be rather problematic[2] to find a company that is capable of and willing to accommodate a qualitative intra-company, cross-cultural study where narrative interviews and participant observation as well as documentary analysis will be used.

Selection of appropriate research strategies and timeline for the study

A timeline for the study has to be made in the warming-up stage and goes hand in hand with the selection of appropriate research strategies. For the pilot project (the Vienna study) we considered six months to be appropriate for making the contacts and appointments for interviews and participant observation; two phases of collecting the data in the company; transcribing the interviews and observation minutes; analysing the data within the team; the writing process; making a brochure for the company presenting the findings and considering the feedback.

For the other six countries where we planned to do our research, we planned three months for each country, while analysing the data should be started right after the first country was finished and carried out in parallel with data collection in other countries. For the interpretation of the data the whole team would be reunited with the knowledge from different disciplines flowing in. After each country a meta-seminar on theoretical and comparative aspects with the whole research team was planned. The interpretation of the data was projected to be finished six months after the last country study. We assumed three months for the comparative study plus a further three months for the final report.

The Vienna study

Entry into the field

The first study took place in Vienna, in the foreign exchange and money dealing department of an Austrian bank, consisting of approximately eighty traders and two managers. We arranged an initial meeting with the manager who had given us access, his deputy, and four members of the research team. We presented the research project, explaining the data collection phase as well as the instruments and proposed a presentation and discussion of the findings afterwards. The managers nominated a young employee as contact person for the organization and the junior researcher was named contact person for the team.

As entering the setting for the first time is said to be the most difficult part of an entire project (Morse 1994: 228) this will be described in detail. (See Figure 15.1.)

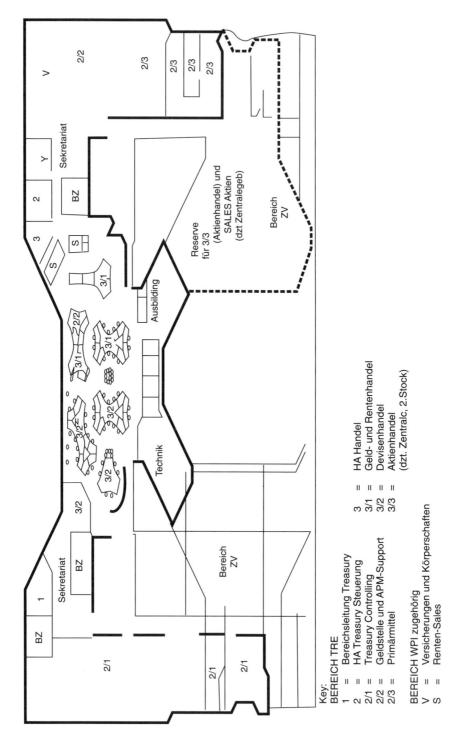

Key:
BEREICH TRE
1   =   Bereichsleitung Treasury
2   =   HA Treasury Steuerung
2/1 =   Treasury Controlling
2/2 =   Geldstelle und APM-Support
2/3 =   Primärmittel

3   =   HA Handel
3/1 =   Geld- und Rentenhandel
3/2 =   Devisenhandel
3/3 =   Aktienhandel
        (dzt. Zentrale, 2.Stock)

BEREICH WPI zugehörig
V   =   Versicherungen und Körperschaften
S   =   Renten-Sales

Figure 15.1 Map of the traders' office as an example of field material

Observation

When we entered the field on a Monday morning we (two female junior researchers) were introduced to a meeting of the group managers, where the study was explained. Most named their employees for interview, while two offered to give interviews and one invited me to join his group for the participant observations. Thus I ended up spending an entire day with eight traders at one out of eight large oddly shaped tables with three screens in front of me, a giant telephone and four brokers shouting prices down four hotlines.

The observation we practised is also known as 'complete observer' (Atkinson and Hammersley 1994: 248), which means that the researchers were known to be researchers by all those being studied and were complete outsiders. In a more general view, any observation is participant, the researcher being part of the social context that is studied. Usually, the first observation in an unknown field is rather unstructured. Researchers try to get a feeling for the scene and the actors and help themselves, for example, by trying to draw a plan. Orientation became easier once we had a map of the room (Figure 15.1) with the oddly shaped tables, their occupants, and the names of the groups sitting there. We learned that all traders sitting at one table together are considered to be a work group or team. We were then able to concentrate on communication structures and patterns, the very specific language, the way of addressing each other and specific jokes, as well as reactions to superiors' decisions or material culture such as the decoration of tables. Each of us took minutes whereby the time, observed actions and particular expressions of the participants were noted.

Narrative interviews

As an interview technique we used an adapted form of the Schütze 'narrative interview' (Schütze 1977). Its main characteristics are that trust and rapport must be established (at the latest) during the interview. The interviewer poses the interviewee a very general question which allows for a broad spectrum of response and elaboration on her or his part. The opening question is of great importance (and took interviewees up to 45 minutes to answer it). During the interview the researcher is open to any topic that the interviewee brings up. The interviewer tries to talk as little as possible, asking questions only to generate more (story) telling about subjects which the interviewee has already mentioned in context. At the very end the interviewer may ask for subjects that the interviewee has not mentioned already (which is an alteration to Schütze's technique).

All interviews are recorded on tape and afterwards transcribed very thoroughly, with length of pauses and disturbances also noted.

Analysing the data

There was no coding scheme generated before the interviews had been transcribed. As we were interested in the themes that matter for our participants/

interviewees within the context of their work and co-operation with their colleagues, we carried out a content analysis. Themes, issues and recurring motifs within are isolated and interpreted (Denzin and Lincoln 1994: 358). For selected passages a sequential analysis was conducted. This means that from a small passage (4–8 lines of text) one unit of meaning after the other is analysed by means of questions such as: 'what is the information', 'which function could this statement have for the interviewee', 'which latent moments could lie behind the surface', and so on. A research group needs up to four hours to analyse such a passage (Oevermann *et al.* 1979; Froschauer and Lueger 1992).

Place of theory in the study

The researchers' theoretical backgrounds were brought in explicitly as soon as the interpretation phase was concluded. When the writing process started, Bourdieu's field theory (Bourdieu 1983, 1985) was brought in by one member of the team and was found useful in bringing additional insight to the understanding of some important issues. It was attempted to make implicit theories (i.e. those 'in the researchers' heads') that influenced interpretations as transparent as possible.

Findings

As preliminary results from the Vienna study, the following issues were found to be important for understanding how co-operation works in the trader groups in Vienna:

- formal organization of the group;
- hierarchy, structure of the group, control of work;
- characteristics of the job;
- specific communication patterns and styles, co-operation as defined by the management and the groups;
- co-operation in competitive conditions;
- how relationships remain dynamic in the field, career patterns and conditions of promotion;
- stabilization of relationships within the work groups;
- mechanisms of integration, mobility and exclusion, the connection between work and private life.

The report by Hofbauer *et al.* (1997) on the Vienna study contains description and analysis of the listed issues. We also generated a model of how co-operation works within and between the work groups in Vienna. From the qualitative point of view it is then important not to transfer the model simply to the next research field (in our case the Prague study) but first to try to understand and reconstruct the communications and actions in its unique context without the 'glasses' (the presumptions) of a model generated from the Vienna study.

From the Prague study we would like to present one issue on the methodological side. Regarding the aspect of different layers of culture, we learned that, in this case, professional culture is stronger than organizational culture. Whereas the bank as a whole has a rather traditional, conservative and respectable image in Austria as well as in the Czech Republic, the interesting difference is, that this reputation and image applies to the foreign exchange and money dealing department in Vienna but not for the same department in Prague. This can be illustrated in various ways:

In the Vienna department it is not politically correct to refer to the activity of trading as 'gambling' or 'making money for the bank', whereas in Prague this is quite usual, even for the head of the department.

The traders in Prague work within a highly competitive field, where moves from one bank to another occur very frequently and the time they stay with one bank is much shorter than in Vienna. Traders do consider their work group as a team but in contrast often do not care which bank they are actually making money for as long as the department they are working in has an excellent reputation within the professional field.

The traders in the Vienna department are committed to the bank as it promises security (no hire and fire policy) even if the average income of traders in other Vienna-based banks is higher. The traders' income in the Prague department is more dependent on performance, as high as other banks in Prague and many times higher than the income of other employees of the bank or the average of the Czech population.

Here the layers of professional and national culture overlay in part or entirely. The next step we have to analyse thoroughly is the interplay between the 'globalized' culture of foreign exchange traders all over the world and the ongoing transformation processes in Czech society. Again native experts will be invited to join the research team.

Summary

This contribution has described a project in progress where the research team works within the qualitative, interpretive approach. We believe that applying qualitative research strategies can help to solve some critical methodological issues in cross-cultural HRM research.

We have concluded our analysis of the data collected in Vienna by means of observation, interviews, examination of written materials and feedback and have generated a model of co-operation. We are now studying trader work groups at the Prague office of the bank using the same methodology. By this means we shall, on the one hand, gain comparative data and, on the other, be able to evaluate the research design once again before conducting the projected studies in five more countries.

Notes

1 Author's note: I would like to thank my research team members and teachers: Johanna Hofbauer, Hartmut H. Holzmüller, Monika Kindl, Manfred Lueger, Wolfgang Mayrhofer and Andreas Novy for the opportunity to work with and learn from them.
2 A German research team that wanted to accompany multicultural project teams had to change the design after trying hard to find a partner for a long time. They conclude that nowadays companies do not engage in long-lasting partnerships with researchers for projects which do not promise to improve efficiency immediately or have positive effects on competitive advantages (Zeutschel 1996: 12).

References

Atkinson, Paul and Hammersley, Martyn (1994) 'Ethnography and participant observation', in Norman K. Denzin and Yvonna S. Lincoln (eds) *Handbook of Qualitative Research*, London: Sage, pp. 248–62.

Brislin, R.W. and Lonner, W.J. and Thorndike, R.M. (1973) *Cross-Cultural Research Methods*, New York: Wiley.

Bourdieu, Pierre (1983) 'Ökonomisches Kapital, kulturelles Kapital, soziales Kapital', in R. Krekel (ed.) *Soziale Ungleichheiten. Soziale Welt*, Göttingen: Sonderband, pp. 183–98.

—— (1985) *Sozialer Raum und Klassen' Leçon sur la leçon*, Frankfurt am Main: Vorlesungen.

Denzin, Norman K. and Lincoln, Yvonna S. (1994a) 'Introduction', in Norman K. Denzin and Yvonna S. Lincoln (eds) *Handbook of Qualitative Research*, London: Sage, pp. 1–19.

—— (1994b) 'Methods of collecting and analysing empirical materials', in Norman K. Denzin and Yvonna S. Lincoln (eds) *Handbook of Qualitative Research*, London: Sage, pp. 353–361.

Fine, Michell (1994) 'Working the hyphens: reinventing self and other in qualitative research', in Norman K. Denzin and Yvonna S. Lincoln (eds) *Handbook of Qualitative Research*, London: Sage, pp. 70–83.

Fontana, Andrea and Frey, James H. (1994) 'Interviewing: the art of science', in Norman K. Denzin and Yvonna S. Lincoln (eds) *Handbook of Qualitative Research*, London: Sage, pp. 361–77.

Froschauer, Ulrike and Lueger, Manfred (1992) *Das qualitative Interview zur Analyse sozialer Systeme*, Vienna: Wiener Universitätsverlag.

Glaser, Barney G. and Strauss, Anselm L. (1967) *The Discovery of Grounded Theory: Strategies for Qualitative Research*, New York: Aldine de Gruyter.

Hall, E.T. (1976) *Beyond Culture*, New York: Anchor.

Hofbauer, J., Holzmüller, H.H., Kindl, M., Lueger, M., Mattl, C., Mayrhofer, W., Wolfgang-Novy, A. (1997) 'Arbeitsgruppen im Devisenhandel. Eine qualitative Fallstudie zur Kooperation in einer österreichischen Bank', in *Dresdner Beiträge zur Betriebswirtschaftslehre 7/97*, Dresden.

Hoffmann-Riem, Christa (1980) 'Die Sozialforschung einer interpretativenn Soziologie', Kölner Zeitschrift für Soziologie und Sozialpsychologie 2: 339–72.

Janesick, V.J. (1994) 'The dance of qualitative research design: metaphor, methodolatry and meaning', in Norman K. Denzin and Yvonna S. Lincoln (eds) *Handbook of Qualitative Research*, London: Sage, pp. 209–20.

Karmasin, Helene and Karmasin, Matthias (1997) *Cultural Theory. Ein neuer Ansatz für Kommunikation, Marketing und Management*, Vienna: Linde.

Kroeber, A.L. and Kluckhohn, C. (1952) 'Culture: a critical review of concepts and definitions', Harvard University Peabody Museum of American Archeology and Ethnology Papers no. 47/1, Cambridge MA.

Marcus, George E. and Fischer, Michael M.J. (1986) *Anthropology as Cultural Critique. An Experimental Moment in the Human Sciences*, Chicago: University of Chicago Press.

Morse, Janice M. (1994) 'Designing funded qualitative research', in Norman K. Denzin and Yvonna S. Lincoln (eds) *Handbook of Qualitative Research*, London: Sage, pp. 220–36.

Oevermann, Ulrich, Allert, Tilman, Konau, Elisabeth and Krambeck, Jürgen (1979) 'Die Methodologie einer "objektiven Hermeneutik" und ihre allgemeine forschungslogische Bedeutung in den Sozialwissenschaften', in Hans-Georg Soeffner (eds) *Interpretative Verfahren in den Sozial- und Textwissenschaften*, Stuttgart: Metzler, pp. 352–434.

Perlmutter, Howard V. and Heenan, David A. (1979) *Multinational Organization Development*, Reading MA: Addison-Wesley.

Punch, Maurice (1994) 'Politics and ethics in qualitative research', in Norman K. Denzin and Yvonna S. Lincoln (eds) *Handbook of Qualitative Research*, London: Sage, pp. 83–99.

Schütze, Fritz (1977) 'Arbeitsberichte und Forschungsmaterialien: Die Technik des narrativen Interviews in Interaktionsfeldstudien. Dargestellt an einem Projekt zur Erforschung kommunaler Machtstrukuturen', Bielefeld: Universität Bielefeld Fakultät Soziologie.

Zeutschel, Ulrich (1996) 'Erster Zwischenbericht des Forschungsprojects "Interkulturell Synergie in Arbeitsgruppen", April 1995 bis Juli 1996', Universität Regensburg, Institut für Psychologie, unpublished.

Index